D0914989

The Children's Book of
FAMOUS
LIVES

The Children's Book of

FAMOUS LIVES

Galley Press

THE PEOPLE IN THIS BOOK

5

6

Alexander's blood was up, and he leapt from the wall,
alone, into the town

8

Alexander the Great

CONQUEROR OF KINGS

Aubrey de Selincourt

I

THE little kingdom of Macedon, a wild and mountainous region lying to the north of Greece and inhabited by fierce men who loved fighting, was, in the fourth century before Christ, ruled by King Philip the conqueror of Greece, and his barbaric wife Olympias. Stories were told that Olympias was a witch; she would be seen, people said, fondling snakes which she allowed to twist themselves about her arms and neck; and when her son Alexander was born she gave it out that the room, where she lay in bed, was filled with the flicker and glare of lightning, terrifying her attendants and showing to the people of Macedon that Alexander was, in some miraculous way, not the son of his mortal father the King, but of Zeus himself, the King of the Gods.

So much for stories—it was clear enough, however, with or without a miracle, that the son of such parents would be no ordinary boy.

It was in June of the year 356 B.C. that Alexander was born, in the town of Pella, the Macedonian capital.

As soon as he was old enough to learn, the best teachers in Greece were brought to Pella to instruct him, and he took to his books like a duck to water. He learned to live hard. His body grew as tough as his brain was quick, and he passionately loved all out-door sports, hunting, shooting with the bow and javelin, riding and running.

All women loved the young prince, for he was beautiful as well as brilliant and brave. His skin was as fair as a girl's, flushed with the quick blood underneath it; his fair hair thick and curling. When he sat, his head hung a little to one side, as if he were dreaming; but any man who met his eyes full, soon knew that he could keep from Alexander no secrets. Olympias the Queen worshipped her son; he was her pride; and through him she longed to satisfy her ambition to rule the world.

II

When the prince was sixteen, a man came from Thessaly to King Philip with a splendid black horse, which he offered to sell at a high price. The horse had a fleck of white, shaped like the head of an ox, upon its neck, and was named Bucephalus —'Oxhead'.

"Let my men ride him, to show me his paces," said the King. But the first who mounted was immediately thrown. The second fared no better. A third came forward and grasped the reins; but Bucephalus plunged and reared so wildly that the man could not even get upon his back.

The King looked at the man from Thessaly and smiled. "So you ask all that money for a horse no one can ride?" he said. "Take him away."

But Alexander could not bear to see the noble creature go. He pressed through the crowd to where Bucephalus stood, foam in his nostrils, his great flanks quivering with rage. He gently laid his hand upon the bridle, turned Bucephalus to face the sun, and then, dropping his cloak on the ground, lightly leapt upon his back. With a touch of the hand and a quiet word he calmed the horse's fury, and rode away from the crowd of on-lookers, slowly at first, then faster, then at full gallop, until he finally returned to where the King stood watching. Bucephalus's dark and shining flanks still quivered, but no longer with rage. He had acknowledged his master.

There were tears in Philip's eyes as he looked at his son: "When you are a man," he said, "you must have a kingdom greater than Macedon, for Macedon will not hold you."

III

Four years passed. They were troubled years, and all was not well in the palace at Pella; there were mutterings against the King, and one night he was murdered in his bed. No one knew who had done the deed, but there were dark whisperings that the Queen herself had hired the murderer. At least she did not grieve that her husband was gone; she had her son, and to him she looked to see her hopes fulfilled.

Alexander was now a king. He was twenty years old, scarcely more than a boy. In his court the fierce Macedonian nobles quarrelled and intrigued for power; north of the kingdom wild and warlike tribes were threatening invasion, and southward, throughout conquered Greece, the spirit of revolt was abroad. But Alexander did not flinch from his task. He had seen the bright eyes of danger, and already loved them; he had read in Homer of the old Greek heroes who fought at Troy, and he would show the world that the old heroism was not yet dead. He would make Macedon a kingdom fit to hold him.

At the head of his army he swept through rebellious Greece. The ancient city of Thebes was razed to the ground—all but the house where the poet Pindar had lived more than a hundred years before. To Alexander that house was sacred, like all things which the spirit of Greece, with its passion and poetry and wisdom, had meant to the world in her great days now gone. It was already his purpose to carry that spirit to the ends of the earth and to make it live again throughout Asia and the unknown lands of the East; he already dreamed of a world united and at peace, but to make the dream come true there must first be war. The nations must be taught to submit, and made, like Bucephalus, to acknowledge their master.

Swiftly Alexander's plan unfolded. Across the narrow Aegean Sea lay the empire of Persia, the enemy of Greece ever since, 150 years before, King Xerxes had invaded her with an army of a million men. Darius now sat upon the Persian throne, and Darius must be humbled.

Alexander's strokes were like lightning. His little army, perfectly trained—infantry battalions armed with enormous pikes, twenty feet long and pointed with steel, gallant cavalry regiments and picked troops with the proud name of Companions of the King—was across the Dardanelles before Darius knew it had started, and at the first encounter scattered the Persians like leaves before a gale, Alexander himself on Bucephalus's back fighting where the work was hottest. Again on the plain of Issus, where the Persians were herded like sheep into a pen between the mountains and the sea, Alexander triumphed. Darius fled, leaving his wife and daughters as prisoners in

Alexander's hands. Alexander, who had no quarrel with women, treated them courteously. The defeated King offered half Asia to the conqueror and his daughter in marriage as the price of peace.

"My lord," said Parmenio, the most experienced of the Macedonian generals, "if I were Alexander, I should accept such terms."

"And I," Alexander replied, "should accept them, if I were Parmenio."

Haughtily he refused Darius's offer. "If I wish to marry your daughter," he wrote, "I shall do so without your leave; and your whole kingdom is already mine for the taking." The port of Tyre next fell to him; then the fortress of Gaza; then all Egypt without a blow. The Persian navy was paralysed. Darius, in his palace at Susa, knew that if what was left of his empire was to be saved, he must muster new courage and new men to meet the conqueror in another battle by land. The time would come, and all too soon.

IV

Meanwhile in Egypt, that ancient land whose priests still thought of the Greeks as children and where the palaces and pyramids were old before Greece was born or thought of, Alexander paused to dream. Often his mother had told him of her queer fancy that he was the son of Zeus, and now that fancy came back upon his mind. Egypt was a strange land, a haunted land, so old, so wise, her history stretching back thousands of years into the darkness and the desert sand; and out of that ancient darkness a voice seemed to whisper that his mother's tale was true. Alexander was young, and young men have strange dreams.

Suddenly, to the astonishment of his officers, he announced that he intended to cross the desert, with a small company of troops, to Siwa, where from time immemorial there had been an oracle of Zeus—the temple standing in a little oasis surrounded by the sands which once, men said, had swallowed a Persian army ten thousand strong. The journey was made. The young king entered the temple alone, and all knew that his purpose was to ask the god if he was indeed his son. When

12

he returned to his waiting officers, his face was flushed, his eyes shining.

"Is it well with you, my lord?" they asked.

"It is very well," Alexander replied. And never again did he speak a word of what had passed in the temple.

Back in Asia, Alexander turned eastward, bent upon the final destruction of Darius and his Persians. He caught them near the upper reaches of the Tigris, at the village of Gaugamela. As before, the issue of the battle was never in doubt. Darius again made his escape, but this time only to be murdered by a traitor from his own people.

V

Alexander was now acknowledged as the Great King of the Persian empire. The fabulous treasure of Susa and Persepolis, of Babylon and Ecbatana, was his; his power was absolute; life and death for millions of men were in his hands. For most Greeks the Persians were a barbarous race, only to be despised when they were not feared; but Alexander liked them, and found much in their way of life to admire. Many of their great nobles he allowed to remain as governors of provinces, and he himself, when the fancy took him, used to wear Persian dress at court on occasions of ceremony. His own Macedonian officers resented this, and they were still more angry when he allowed the Persians at court, when they came into his presence, to fall flat on their faces at his feet, as they had always done before in sign of reverence to their Kings. Cleitus, one of the two friends whom Alexander most loved, was amongst those who feared what such things might lead to and one night at supper he boldly spoke his mind. The King and many Greeks and Persians of the highest rank were present, and all had been drinking far into the night.

"Let the Persians do as they please," Cleitus cried. "But when we are home in Macedon again—what then? Will the King demand that we bow down to him like oriental slaves?"

The King was himself hot with drinking. He bit his lip in anger, but made no reply.

"Is not the King a man, like the rest of us?" Cleitus went on. "Does he think himself a god?"

Alexander started to his feet, his eyes alight with fury. Those

13

next him laid restraining hands upon him, fearful of what might come. But Cleitus was reckless too.

"What?" he cried. "Did I not with my own hands save him from death when the enemy horsemen were pressing him hard on the banks of Granicus? Did not *my* shield save him? And is he now a god?"

Alexander shook himself free, and seizing a spear which was leaning against the wall of the banqueting room drove it through Cleitus's heart.

Alexander's remorse was as bitter as his rage. For three days he neither ate nor slept. "Call me no longer my lord the King," he said; "call me the man who murdered his friend."

VI

But there was work to do. Alexander was a thousand miles from home. For three years now his soldiers had marched and fought and conquered with him; Persia, the hereditary enemy of Greece, was humbled, and to the troops, at any rate, their purpose seemed to have been achieved. They would dearly have liked to go home, to spend their pay and plunder and brag to the stay-at-homes of their deeds. But it was not yet to be—for Alexander had only begun. A new desire was rising in him, a desire not of conquest only but of discovery. Brought up in all the learning of the Greeks, the most inquisitive of men, to whom no facts about this strange and wonderful world ever came amiss, Alexander found a thousand things which he now longed to know. He had read in legends of the One-Eyed Arimaspians and of the Griffins who guard the gold—*were* they only legends? He had heard tales of mountains in the East, compared with which the hills of Macedon were molehills, and of rivers beyond the Indian Caucasus greater than the Danube or the Nile. Now he would seek these things; he would find them or perish in the attempt. He would march with his men through unknown countries—Bactria, Sogdiana, Areia, the Chorasmian wastes, names strange to Greek ears, lands where Greek feet had never yet trod—and on, if he could, across the mountains to the fabulous Indian cities, whose princes in jewelled turbans rode to war on elephants. Youth is the time for adventure; Alexander was young; his heart stirred and his forehead flushed as he dreamed of what he would do.

Once more the order to march was given. The troops obeyed. Some murmured; some thought of their little farmsteads in Macedon, a thousand miles away, or of the familiar Grecian sea; but the King's word was law, and go they must.

The army made its way eastward through the heart of Asia. Alexander still rode Bucephalus, though the horse was old now and had been wounded in battle. He was stolen once, when the army was encamped near a village, and Alexander threatened to raze every house to the ground unless he was found and brought back to him. The threat took effect. The old horse was to have a few more years of life, and when he died his master built a town on the bank of the Indus and named it Bucephala in his memory.

Through deserts, through populous country, across great rivers the army marched, often fighting its way, until it came to the mighty barrier of the Hindu Kush mountains. There was a legend amongst the Greeks that the god Dionysus had crossed those mountains in some dim and forgotten age; and now Alexander was to follow his steps. The mountains were crossed, and Alexander feasted his eyes upon the valleys and rivers of India. The way forward was now utterly unknown; but Alexander did not care; his desire was to press on, always to the east, if need be to the end of the world.

The Indians were hard fighters; many times they tried to oppose the army of strange men who had come from so incredibly far away, but Alexander, as ever, was invincible. Porus, the greatest of the Indian chieftains, met him in desperate battle with 300 elephants and innumerable fighting men, but was forced to yield. After the battle he came to the conqueror's tent to make his submission. He was a brave man and had fought bravely, and Alexander knew it.

"How," Alexander asked, "do you wish me to treat you?"

"Treat me," Porus answered, "like a King."

It was a proud answer. Alexander gave him back his kingdom, and won his friendship for ever.

VII

Alexander still pressed on, eager to cross the greatest of all Indian rivers, the Ganges. He had no maps and he believed that the eastern shores of India were the last land in the world, bounded by the ocean. Suddenly, however, his soldiers refused to go any further. In a passion of disappointment and rage, "If you have suffered," he cried, "I, too, have suffered no less. I have marched with you and fought with you—no part of my body is without the scar of a wound. I have endured hunger and cold and weariness with you; I have slept on the ground as you have slept; I have watched through the night that you might sleep in safety—— Will you leave me now, in an enemy's country, like runaways and traitors? Go then, and tell them in Macedon that you have abandoned your King."

The men loved their King. But, though deeply moved by his reproaches, they would not alter their decision. They had had enough, and Alexander was forced to turn back. For the first time in his life he had been beaten—and by his own troops.

Nevertheless, many adventures yet remained. India was by no means conquered. Alexander's little army was surrounded by hostile tribes, and it had to fight its way back as it had fought its way forward. Still determined to press his explorations, Alexander chose to return by way of the southern coast. He followed the course of the Indus southward to the sea, and himself took ship in the great tidal estuary and sailed out into the Indian ocean. He laid the foundations of a town at the head of the delta, to serve as a centre for Eastern trade as the Egyptian Alexandria, the greatest of his cities, served, and still serves today, as a port for the West.

The soldiers, indeed, after these years of campaigning were sick of fighting, but Alexander himself was not. For him the clash of battle still had its old lure. He was growing ever more reckless of his own life, and at the town of Multan he came within an inch of losing it. Multan stood on a hill and was defended by a high earthen parapet and a wall. Ladders were brought to scale the parapet, but the shower of missiles from above made it difficult to approach. Impatiently Alexander sprang forward, and, under cover of his shield, climbed one of the ladders. Three of his officers, Peucestas, Leonnatus and Abreas, followed. They reached the wall and flung down the Indians who defended it. The Macedonian troops, seeing their King and his three companions alone on the wall, dashed for the ladders and began to climb; but the ladders broke under the weight.

Very well. The Saxons should charge them in two columns also, he himself leading the one against the kings while his young brother, Alfred, took on the earls. But first, as a devout Christian, he would go back to his tent and hear Mass. The Danes could wait another half-hour. They would not run away . . . but they would not do anything else.

Alfred, standing at the head of his men, glancing every few moments from the enemy in front to the Saxon camp behind him, wondered if his brother had made a mistake. He wished Ethelred would come.

Neither of them had had much experience of fighting the Danes—they had to go on what they had learnt from others. Years ago, in their father's reign and their elder brother's, the Danes had made raids into Wessex, but ever since then they had been fully occupied conquering and digesting the other English kingdoms north of the Thames. Wessex had shown herself the hardest nut to crack, and they had left her to the end.

If Wessex fell to them now, it was the end of Saxon England. Alfred saw that as plain as the raven banners fluttering against the winter sunrise, plain as the thorn-tree lifting its gnarled branches above the frost-nipped turf. It was the end of Christianity in the island, the end of all he understood by culture and civilization. And he had a clear, shining picture of all those things, a vision which had never left him since his father had taken him, as a small boy, to live for a year in Rome.

If only Ethelred would come! But no kingly figure moved along the pale chalky trackway which ribboned back along the hill-top towards the royal tent.

The tension was terrible. So was the responsibility. Alfred knew what it meant if the Danes got their charge in first. The attacker had the physical advantage—the sheer impetus of his rush—and the psychological advantage too. The Danes could often afford to miss those advantages, but the Saxons could not, especially with the memory of their defeat a few days ago. No, they needed the whipped-up enthusiasm of the charge. If they just stood still in their ranks, coldly waiting for the enemy, the battle might be lost before it started.

The King was on his knees before the improvised altar in his tent . . . and the Danes—there was no shadow of doubt about it now—were on the move.

21

Strident war-horns, hoarse as ravens, rang through the thin upland air. In mail-shirts twinkling like fish-scales, brandishing their heavy-pommelled swords or the fearsome battle-axes they had developed from the lumber-axes they were used to in the Scandinavian forests, the Danes were advancing to the attack.

Alfred glanced back once more. No sign of his brother. Young though he was, he must take charge of the situation. He nodded to his thanes, and gave an order. Closing their ranks, so that each man's shield overlapped the rim of his neighbour's, the men of his column began to move. After a moment's hesitation the King's column started to advance parallel with his own —but without the King. Yelling their war-cries, gathering speed with every step as their excitement gripped them, the twin-columned armies plunged down to meet each other in the dip between the hills.

They crashed, head-on, close by the leafless thorn-tree. The shield-wall buckled with the force of the impact. Bearded faces, distorted with hatred, glared at each other through the twirling, flashing melée of sword and axe and spear. There was a snarling almost as of animals—a sobbing breathlessness—thuds, the clang and grate of metal, the sharp scream of human agony.

In the midst was Alfred, fighting (as his friend, Bishop Asser, wrote afterwards) 'like a wild boar'.

He had made the right decision. The Danes broke and ran. One of their two kings, five of their noblest earls, and many of their best warriors, lay dead on the trampled turf. The Saxons harried them along the ridge all through that January day. No one ever again believed that the heathen from the North were invincible.

II

That was 871—later called 'the year of battles', because there were several more, with varying results, before a treaty was made and the Danes retired into the Midlands.

It was also the year in which Alfred became King of Wessex, and thereby ancestor of every royal house in England down to the present day.

His brother died in the May following the winter victory at Ashdown. It was small wonder that men spoke of a curse on Alfred's family. One after another his three elder brothers had

In the midst of the battle was Alfred,
fighting like a wild boar

reigned for a brief year or two, until death had plucked each in turn. Alfred himself—though he had proved his strength and valour on the battlefield—had a mysterious complaint which brought him spells of cruel pain, followed by fits of depression. It was whispered that he had been bewitched. No one could feel confident that he would live any longer than his brothers had done.

However, he was the last hope of Wessex, even as Wessex was the last hope of Saxon England. Ethelred had left sons, true, but they were only children. They were no more fit to defend the country than Alfred's own babies were—for, young though he was, Alfred already had a family. He had been only nineteen when he married Ealswith, a princess of Mercia, that Midland kingdom now overrun by the Danes.

The crown did not automatically go to the last king's son. It was for the Witan, the council of senior Churchmen and thanes, to decide. They offered the crown to the young hero of Ashdown, and he accepted 'with the full consent of all the inhabitants of the kingdom'.

III

After the Danes withdrew at the end of that year, he had four years of peace in which to reorganize his country. Wessex covered all southern England except Cornwall. There were a few little towns such as Winchester and Canterbury (but London was not included); mainly, though, the Saxons were farmers, scattered over the countryside and very thinly at that —probably the whole population of Wessex was only a few hundred thousand. In earlier days there had been fine monasteries, centres of education and craftsmanship. Of late, however, the monks had grown slack. Civilization had been declining, in some ways, even before the Danes appeared in their hordes to burn and plunder what was left.

Alfred, remembering all he had seen in Rome as a boy, saw that his life's work must be to hold back the Danes, to restore the one-time standards of Saxon civilization, and to lead his people forward to fresh heights. Could he do it?

Not if the Danes had their way. Alfred had scarcely begun to piece together his broken country when he had to take up the sword again. The enemy swept across Wessex, right to the

24

Channel coast. There was a year or more of hard fighting and marching, of burning villages and neglected fields. Then—as it seemed by the hand of God Himself—the Danish fleet ran into a storm off the Dorset coast. A hundred and twenty long ships rolled over in the waves, spilling the helpless mail-burdened warriors to their doom. The rest of the invaders made peace and retired hastily into the Midlands.

IV

Wessex seemed safer that Christmas than it had been for a long time. Alfred and his family kept the twelve-day festival at their royal manor of Chippenham in Wiltshire. And, while the Christians feasted and sang and told stories round their blazing fires, the Danes plotted revenge.

It was their King Guthrum who had led the recent invasion into Wessex. He was now at Gloucester, his shattered forces made up with fresh bands from other parts of England and from Scandinavia. Another Danish host was spending the winter in South Wales. It was arranged that they should cross the Bristol Channel and land in North Devon, while Guthrum struck at Chippenham and marched on to the English Channel, cutting Wessex in half.

At first all went splendidly for the Danes. The surprise attack on Chippenham took place on Twelfth Night—that last glorious burst of Christmas celebration when the Saxons were least prepared to defend themselves. The blow fell without warning. Alfred had no time to do what he would normally have done—send out messengers to the aldermen of each shire, telling them to turn out every able-bodied fighting man. All he could do, for the moment, was to escape with a small band of followers, the thanes of his court and his household troops. Even so, he did not give himself up to blind flight. He was thinking all the while of how he could best hamper the Danes and win time to rally Wessex for a counter-stroke.

V

Sedgemoor was the answer. Here in Somerset, bounded by hill-ranges and the sea, was a vast tract of fenland, a bewildering maze of swamp and mere and wooded islet. There was one island especially, named Athelney, covered with a jungle of

25

alders and a rich haunt of deer and other game. Alfred made it his headquarters. Log-huts were built and provisions were smuggled in by boat from the loyal Saxons in the neighbouring villages.

Not only was Athelney a safe hiding-place, it was ideally placed for Alfred to watch and harry Guthrum. If Guthrum tried to turn westwards through the Vale of Taunton Deane, to join his allies in Devon, Alfred could cut his road. On the other hand, if Guthrum kept to his original plan of striking southwards to Hampshire and the English Channel, he would be leaving a dangerous enemy on his flank. The Danish King realized this as well as Alfred. Though he did not know Alfred's exact whereabouts he had plenty of painful evidence that Alfred was still very much alive, because of the guerrilla raids that were continually being made upon his forces. Not knowing what to do for the best, he did nothing. He stayed in Wiltshire for the rest of the winter, making himself as comfortable as he could at Chippenham.

At Easter wonderful news came from the west to hearten Alfred and his followers: the Danish invaders of Devon had been wiped out in a great battle, their king was a prisoner, his famous Raven standard was a trophy of war. There was now only Guthrum to fight. The nut-crackers, which were to have finally cracked the stubborn Wessex nut, had themselves been broken down one side by the thanes of Devon.

Now was the time to rouse the people. As the earth stirred and quickened after the winter, so did Wessex come to life. Alfred's messengers rode hither and thither with the summons —down the long green road of the Fosse Way, over the ancient tracks that were older than the Romans, sometimes speeding across Salisbury Plain, sometimes plodding doggedly over the Quantock ridges or the crumpled masses of Exmoor. The *fyrd* —the great levy of the people—was to turn out, each man armed and under his local leader. They were to meet in Selwood Forest, at the high point where three shires joined and there was a well-known landmark called Egbert's Stone.

It was little more than four months since Guthrum had struck his surprise blow at Chippenham. Only part of that time had been spent on Athelney. The famous anecdotes of Alfred, the cake-burning and the disguised visit to Guthrum's camp—truth or legend, who can be sure?—belong to this very short period of his life. By the middle of May he was at Egbert's Stone, commanding his army again, a king 'restored to life after many tribulations'.

Once more, as at Ashdown in the beginning, he met his enemies on the open chalk downs, though this time it was in Wiltshire at Ethandun, which is probably the modern Edington. And this time there was no hesitation. Alfred was no longer the younger brother, the untried boy, but an experienced general and a well-loved king. 'England's darling', they called him, and 'shepherd of the English'. When he gave the order to advance, the Saxons went forward confident of victory.

It was a hard fight they fought at Ethandun, only one day's march from Egbert's Stone. But it was the Danes who broke and ran, as they had done at Ashdown years before, fleeing for the shelter of their stockade at Chippenham. Alfred harried them without a pause and besieged them there. After a fortnight Guthrum surrendered and accepted Christian baptism, with Alfred himself as godfather. Under his new name of Athelstan the Dane finally settled down (after only one lapse) and for the rest of his life he troubled Wessex no more.

But this did not mean that Alfred could relax his watch. There were plenty of other wolves threatening his flock, and like any shepherd he had to take precautions against them. There were other Danish war-bands wandering over England, whose chiefs cared nothing for Guthrum's oath of peace. There was the chance, too, that some fresh wave of invaders would come buzzing like hornets out of Scandinavia, steering their long ships up the river-mouths or into the western coves.

VI

Alfred's greatness lay in his ability to do many things at once —to defend his country and, behind defences, to build up its civilization. His day's work was mapped out by candles: having no other kind of clock, he invented a horn lantern to make sure that each candle would burn for the same length of time, unaffected by draughts. Even as he washed his hands before dinner he would be discussing public business, perhaps giving a decision on some point of law.

Three things he did for the defence of the kingdom. He

designed and commissioned 60-oar galleys, twice as long as the so-called 'long' ships of the Danes. He brought in men from Holland to help in the building and sailing of these new vessels, the first true navy England ever had. Secondly, he established forts at key-points, usually on rivers, to prevent the Danes sailing inland as their habit was: there were about 25 of these forts or 'boroughs', many of which grew by degrees into towns, like Oxford. Finally, he divided the *fyrd* so that men were not liable all the time for 'call-up'. They took turns, so that if danger threatened half took up their arms and the other half stayed at home to carry on the everyday work.

VII

Fine soldier though Alfred was, his heart was elsewhere—in religion and law, education and art and literature. His own schooling had been sketchy, and he did not find that learning came easily. But he persevered, knowing that without learning his people could not progress.

At his court he gathered all the scholars he could persuade to settle with him. There were Welshmen, Mercians, a Scot, a Frenchman, a German . . . Because they were men of learning they could all talk together in Latin, but Alfred knew very well that Latin would never mean anything to the mass of his people. So he had translations made—often finding time to make the translations himself—so that ordinary men, if they could read at all, could have large parts of the Bible available to them, as well as books on history, geography and other subjects. Always he had the English reader in mind, and if necessary the text was adapted to make the meaning clearer. So that the Englishman might read the history of his own country, Alfred started the famous record which we now call the *Anglo-Saxon Chronicle*.

One of his dearest ambitions was to see "all the freeborn youth of England set to learning until they can well read English writing". A school was set up at Court, and his own children did their lessons with the sons of his thanes and aldermen and other officials. Truth to tell, many of the fathers would have made a poor showing beside their children. Alfred was sympathetic, he knew only too well that they had not enjoyed the same chances, what with a lifetime of Danish raids and the general decay of Saxon education—but he was prepared

28

to study, and so should they, if they expected to hold a top place in his government. Altogether nearly half of his small revenue was spent on the encouragement of learning.

Like the bygone Romans he admired, Alfred knew that 'law' must go with 'order' in a peaceful civilization. There had been precious little respect for law during that century—a sword in your hand and a stout bolt on the door, men reckoned, were better than a library of law-books. Much of the law, anyhow, had never been written down. It was a question of custom, varying from place to place even among the Saxons.

Alfred consulted the older men who were wise in the law, who remembered what had been agreed on such and such an occasion, and what was usually considered fair. Alfred collected all the information and set it out as plainly as possible, so that people should know where they stood. There was nothing hard and fast about his system—he was a shepherd, not a drover. When in doubt, men must decide disputes in a commonsense way and a Christian spirit. Rough and ready his methods might be, but they were so much better than the anarchy which had been developing that the people gratefully saluted him as 'lawgiver'.

VIII

Alfred died in 901. He was just over fifty, not old by modern reckoning, but for an ailing man, who had had to face the perils of hand-to-hand battle and the hardships of guerrilla warfare as well as the health hazards of the ninth century with its lack of scientific knowledge, he had lived a long life and a full one.

Full it had certainly been. In spite of everything he had enjoyed his share of happiness. A good wife, children and grandchildren, friends and fighting comrades, books, sport, music, conversation. . . . More than all personal pleasures, though, he had known the joy of work worth doing. A few lines of his own writing are the best summary of his life:

"*So long as I have lived I have striven to live worthily. To the men who come after me I wish to leave a remembrance in good works.*"

That remembrance is still fresh, after more than a thousand years.

29

Robert Baden-Powell

CHIEF SCOUT OF THE WORLD

Arthur Catherall

I

SHOTS and shouts, then a sudden pinky glow which grew rapidly into the flickering light of flames leaping among the native houses in the east side of Mafeking. From the look-out tower on top of his headquarters Baden-Powell watched and waited. An orderly hurried up.

"There's a strong force of Boers creeping up on the west side of the town, sir."

Colonel R. S. S. Baden-Powell nodded and watched the glow of the fires to the east. Another messenger arrived, panting and white-faced.

"Colonel Hore and a lot of the men have been captured, sir. The Boers are everywhere among the native houses."

"Thank you." The defender of Mafeking nodded and smiled and the messenger hurried down to ground level, somehow not quite so upset as he had been a few moments before.

The night was alive now with the sound of shots and shouts. The previous day, May 11, the Boers had pounded Mafeking with every piece of artillery they had, and even their mighty seige gun, Long Tom, had kept at it throwing shells into the battered, dusty streets of the little veldt town. For 200 days Colonel R. S. S. Baden-Powell had kept a force of 9000 Boers at bay. Now at long last, the enemy were in the town. B-P suddenly made a decision. He withdrew practically every man from the west side where he knew a large force of Boers was drawing nearer. Flinging his whole strength into the east side he gave orders for the enemy to be split up, and beaten in small groups. Within a few minutes the tide had turned, the attackers were beaten, and even their leader, energetic Sarel Eloff, was made prisoner.

30

The large force to the west of the town, under General Snyman, did not rush into Mafeking at the crucial moment. Had they done so the town would have fallen. B-P smashed Eloff's daring raid, then repulsed the older Snyman. It was the last opportunity the Boers were to have, for a few days later Mafeking was relieved.

II

It was not cowardice which had made Snyman hesitate to press home an attack. The Boers were not cowards. Snyman hesitated because he feared some booby-trap. He thought Eloff had got into Mafeking too easily; and there were good reasons for Snyman's suspicions and wariness. Throughout that long and weary siege Colonel R. S. S. Baden-Powell had out-thought and out-manœuvred the superior forces against him.

When war was finally declared on October 11, the Boer forces, with plenty of guns, surrounded the town, certain of victory. B-P's artillery consisted of four 7-pounder guns, a 1-pounder Hotchkiss gun and one 2-inch Nordenfeldts. A pitiable armament to defend a town of even such a small size as Mafeking. Cronjé was in command of the Boers, and after bombarding Mafeking on October 16 he sent in a surrender demand to avoid further bloodshed.

The reply was typical of B-P. He rejected the demand to surrender and added: "So far the only blood that has been shed is that of a chicken."

With only a handful of regular soldiers, a few police, and a volunteer force of local inhabitants, B-P knew he must show them that they could hit back at the Boer, and make him hesitate to use his superior forces. So, with a crudely armoured train he attacked an advancing enemy column coming in to reinforce Cronjé, and had his first success. The Boers remembered that armoured train.

Later, having two wagon-loads of dynamite which he felt must be got rid of, in case an enemy shell should explode them, he had them driven out of town by an unattached engine. At the top of a long slope the engine gave the trucks a good push, then chuff-chuffed back to Mafeking. The Boers did not wait to be attacked this time, they opened fire on the wagons which blew up.

Day after day as the siege wore on B-P was busy thinking up new tricks to keep the powerful enemy from over-running his defences. He got one of his men to make a searchlight from an acetylene lamp and a biscuit tin. This was mounted on a trolley and pushed round the perimeter of the town at night. The 'searchlight' would flash its beam for a minute or so from one point, then the light would be extinguished. The trolley would be hustled along a few hundred yards, the light lit again, and a 'second' searchlight would probe the Boer lines. By the time this had gone on for a few nights the enemy were convinced that in the event of a night attack they would be shown up at once by a battery of searchlights.

Seeing the Boers erecting barbed wire defences B-P decided he must have some, too; but there was no barbed wire in Mafeking. Nevertheless the defences went up. Men were sent out to drive in stakes at regular intervals while other men pretended to fix barbed wire. B-P knew the party would be under scrutiny from the Boers, and he had drilled his men to move 'across the wire' time after time . . . lifting their legs carefully as if to avoid catching them in a wire entanglement which did not exist. It was a game of make-believe which played no small part in keeping the enemy from making night attacks.

During the first month or so of the siege there were many native spies among the 8000 Africans living in Mafeking, and B-P was certain that some of these men slipped out to the Boer lines to sell information from time to time. With this in mind a hut was set aside for secret work, and a man spent much time in there, with a guard to see that he was not disturbed. Then one day natives were called upon to carry out of the hut a great number of boxes. They were warned not to drop any of them as a disastrous explosion might follow.

The boxes were buried along the front of the defences . . . the first minefields of modern warfare. Wires were then laid connecting the buried boxes to a central point in the town. It was all very secret. Then B-P called in the officer who had been helping him.

"Major Panzera, I want notices posted throughout the town, in English and Dutch, warning everyone of the danger of allowing children or cattle to stray out where we have been

32

Baden-Powell sent out men to drive in stakes at regular
intervals while other men pretended to fix barbed wire

working. If they wander out there they do so at their own risk. Make that very clear."

"Yes, sir."

"Oh, one other thing, Major. Tomorrow I want everyone to keep clear of the east front from noon until two p.m. We are going to see if the minefield is in working order." There was a twinkle in B-P's eyes, and the suspicion of a grin on Major Panzera's lips as he nodded, saluted, then went off to see the orders carried through.

Next day B-P and Major Panzera went out of a town strangely quiet to the land beyond the eastern defences. The sun winked here and there from the lens of field glasses directed on them from the Boer lines. News had probably gone over of what was going to happen.

Bending down B-P and his assistant placed a stick of fused dynamite in an ant-bear hole, lit the fuse, then retired as quickly and unobtrusively as possible.

There was a tremendous roar, a great column of brown smoke and yellow dust, and a minute or so later a man pedalled off as hard as he could. The news would soon be out of this devilish minefield. Yet every box so carefully buried, and connected by wires to a spot in the centre of the town, was filled with nothing more deadly than sand.

There is a saying that you cannot make bricks without straw, yet B-P withstood a siege for 217 days against 9000 well-armed Boers with the minimum of men and material. Only once did there seem to be a chance of defeat for him— when Sarel Eloff burst into the town. But the cautious Snyman as we have seen failed or feared to press home his advantage. His chance was lost and, with Eloff made prisoner, Snyman a few days later was driven away by an advancing relief force.

It is doubtful if any man has used bluff so effectively and for so long; but there was something else beside bluff which enabled this man who was to give Boy Scouts and Girl Guides to the world, to hold out. That 'something' he had within him— the spirit of adventure, and the knowledge of what good scouting can accomplish.

Many and many a time it must have appeared to the Boers that the British possessed second sight. Things they were doing, preparing, hoping to do. were countered so successfully that it

34

was obvious the enemy was warned in advance. The 'spy' in many instances was B-P himself. At night, doing his rounds of the forts, he would slip off through the defences and worm his way close to the Boer lines; good ears and good eyes told him much. Not for nothing had Major Frederick Burnham called him Hawk Eye, or the warriors of the Matabele, 'Impeesa', the Wolf-that-never-sleeps.

Somehow he inspired men, women and children, white and coloured, to have confidence they could beat their besiegers; somehow they stood by him even though 20,000 shells were poured into the little town. Of his force of about 1500 some 326 were killed, wounded, or were missing, but 213 days after the declaration of war they still beat off a night attack, and made Mafeking safe.

III

What sort of a man was this B-P, before Mafeking, and after Mafeking?

Born on February 22 in 1857 at Paddington, London, he was one of a family of ten children. His father died when B-P was only three years of age. Robert Stephenson Smythe Baden-Powell's Christian names are interesting, for he got the Robert Stephenson from his godfather of that same name, the man who built bridges, railways, and was the son of George Stephenson who built the 'Rocket'. The name 'Smythe' came from Admiral (Mediterranean) Smythe, a great cartographer who claimed descent from John Smith, noted Elizabethan adventurer and colonizer of Virginia. The Admiral was B-P's uncle.

From Rose Hill School, Tunbridge Wells, B-P gained a scholarship to Charterhouse school. When he first went to Charterhouse the school was in London, but later moved to Godalming, Surrey. It was in the woods surrounding the new school (strictly out of bounds to the boys) that young B-P learned how to stalk, how to light an almost smokeless fire, how to trap, skin and cook a rabbit. Often, he recounts, he stalked the very masters who were on the prowl looking for bounds-breakers.

Those were the days which were to help him later when he was scouting for the army in India, Ashanti, Matebele land, and finally in the no-man's land outside the defences of Mafeking.

In school he was not an outstanding scholar. One of his end-of-term reports say of him: ". . . mathematics—has to all intents given up the study; French—could do well, but has become very lazy and often sleeps in school."

Notwithstanding such reports he gained second place in an open examination for the Army and was commissioned straight into the 13th Hussars. With this regiment he served in India, Afghanistan and South Africa.

Once he was fortunate not to get into trouble. The regiment was at Kokoran, awaiting orders, and to while away one of the evenings a concert was arranged. The officers were seated at the front, and the show was on when there was a slight disturbance at the back of the hall. A few moments later an agitated orderly whispered to the Commanding Officer, Colonel Baker Russell:

"Sir, a visiting general has arrived. He is at the back of the hall."

The colonel hastily looked at himself to make sure he was smart enough to meet a visiting general. His other officers rose, and a minute or so later Colonel Baker Russell was leading the visitor towards the front of the hall.

"Would you like to sit here, sir?" Colonel Russell suggested. "We're . . . er . . . in the middle of a little light entertainment. Gets very boring for the men out here."

"Of course, of course," the visiting general agreed. "Very good idea. Look, Colonel, I think I could do a turn myself. A song. What do you say?"

"You, sir?" Colonel Baker Russell was dumbfounded. He had never heard of a visiting general going on to a platform to sing. Before he could collect himself his visitor snapped: "And why not, pray? Don't you think I can sing?"

"Oh, no, sir . . . I mean, yes, I'm sure you could . . . can, sing," the colonel spluttered. "If you . . . this way, sir."

He showed the general round the back and up the steps to the platform. Dead silence reigned in the hall. Not one soldier there had ever seen a singing general.

A few moments later they were listening to a song from the latest Gilbert and Sullivan opera: *The Pirates of Penzance*. Then, and not till then, did the assembled officers and men realize that their visitor was Baden-Powell. Luckily for him

36

his Colonel was an exceptional man and enjoyed the joke as much as anyone.

IV

B-P proved then that he could disguise himself well enough to take in men with whom he was working from day to day; men who thought they knew him very well indeed. This ability to use disguises was more than useful later on when he was serving as Intelligence Officer for the Mediterranean. On holiday he spent time collecting information of military interest. In Dalmatia, known today as Yugoslavia, he posed as a butterfly collector. When his drawings of various butterflies were inspected by the police not one of them suspected that the markings on the butterfly wings were of forts and gun emplacements.

To study the Turkish defences of the Dardanelles he persuaded the Scots skipper of a small cargo steamer to anchor close enough to the forts for him to sketch them at his ease while pretending to fish from one of the ship's small boats. The angry military officials who came off to discover why the ship was anchored so close to the forts were met with a smile and a headshake, while from the engine-room came a clatter and banging as the men below pretended to be hard at work making some repairs to the machinery.

In Austria, posing as an artist, he was able to watch military manoeuvres and even follow the troop movements with the aid of maps actually belonging to Austrian officers. After going up to a party to ask their advice about sketches he was making for a proposed picture entitled: 'Dawn among the Mountains', the Austrian officers were so impressed by his obvious skill as an artist they invited him to breakfast with them, and he remained as their guest for the day.

From these and other experiences with the army he collected material for a little book he proposed to write under the title of *Aids to Scouting*. It was to be a military textbook, and it was published during the time of the siege of Mafeking.

V

When he finally returned to Britain after the war in Africa ended, and he had successfully organized the South African

37

Constabulary, he discovered that throughout the length and breadth of the land boys and girls, were wearing little button-hole pictures of him, in his broad-brimmed 'scout' hat. He was the hero of the hour, and people connected with the training of boys were beginning to use his military textbook *Aids to Scouting* for peace-time work.

He began to get hundreds of letters from young men and leaders of boys, asking for advice. It made him think about his corps of boys who had served him so well in Mafeking. These cyclists and runners had never shirked a job. They had made him see that if a boy were given responsibility, he became a bigger and a better boy.

In 1907 B-P took a number of boys, some rich, some poor, to camp on Brownsea Island, Poole Harbour, Dorset. Though he did not realize it then, it was to be something that millions of boys and girls, and later men and women, would look back on as the beginning of the Scout movement. At that camp B-P tried out some of his ideas, and later in the year got busy re-writing his *Aids to Scouting*. This time it was to have a title familiar to millions of boys throughout the world—*Scouting for Boys.*

It came out early in 1908 in fortnightly parts, and before B-P realized what was happening the Boy Scout movement had started. Patrols and troops were formed throughout the land, and girls with a love for adventure were insisting that there must be Girl Scouts.

The growth was so quick that in 1910 King Edward VII sent for B-P and suggested that he could do a far better job for his country if he resigned from the army and gave the whole of his time to organizing the Boy Scout movement.

It must have been a hard decision to take, to renounce his army career, for there was the prospect of a Field Marshal's baton ahead of him if he remained a soldier. Fortunately for the boys and girls of the world, and for the world itself, B-P decided that his King was right.

For nearly thirty years after that he gave to the Scout movement, and in a lesser degree the Girl Guide movement, the same restless energy he had shown as a soldier.

In a few years' time the boys of the movement made him Chief Scout of the world at one of the big jamborees when, as they rushed in towards him they all—black, white, brown, red and yellow—yelled: "Chief . . . chief . . . chief!"

Honours were showered on him. At the Coming-of-age Jamboree held at Birkenhead in 1929, Hungary conferred on him the First Class Order of Merit. Czechoslovakia honoured him, as did Greece. King George V honoured him, and B-P became Lord Baden-Powell of Gilwell. In all twenty-eight foreign powers conferred Orders and Decorations on him. He received Honorary Degrees from six Universities, and was made a Freeman of eleven cities and boroughs.

If any man did that it was B-P. In the early 1980s census figures showed that there was a total membership of over 16,000,000 Scouts, Wolf Cubs, Girl Guides and Brownies in more than 150 countries. They were all pledged, among other things, 'To do at least one good turn each day'. If they did that then B-P, if he was responsible for nothing else, ensured that some 16,000,000 little acts of kindness are being done throughout the world every day of every week of every year.

Hailed as a hero after the Boer War, this great man retired to Nyeri in Kenya in 1938 suffering from ill health, and passed quietly away at the age of eighty-three on January 8, 1941. On his simple headstone in the graveyard at Nyeri are the words: 'Robert Baden-Powell, Chief Scout of the World.' There is a Scout badge on one side, a Guide badge on the other.

B-P left these two wonderful movements to a world fraught with trouble and suspicion. He will be remembered long as the Chief Scout, but history may yet re-name him 'The Peacemaker'.

Ludwig van Beethoven

STORMY GENIUS OF MUSIC

Helen Henschel

I

BEETHOVEN is a gigantic figure in music, and needs space to do him justice and bring him to life. But I will try to present him in brief, because if you take any interest in music at all, or are studying any branch of it, you must certainly know about Beethoven.

Elsewhere in this book you can read about Mozart. If I had to compare *him* to anything in Nature, I would think of him as a beautiful smiling sunny landscape; there would be grey skies too—and rain, and cloud, but always in the end, a shining rainbow.

Beethoven, on the other hand, conjures up a picture of almost indescribable grandeur and vastness: tremendous craggy mountains and snow-capped peaks rising as far as the eye can see. Often, great storms arise—wind-driven clouds and angry seas. But, too, there are valleys full of singing-birds and flowers—so beautiful and so peaceful that all the storms and stresses are forgotten.

There is one thing that Beethoven and Mozart had in common: they were both born into musical families. Beethoven's grandfather, also called Ludwig, was born in Belgium in 1712. He became a fine singer, and was soon called by the Elector of Cologne to be Court musician in Bonn. He stayed in the Elector's service for 42 years, and ended by being *Kapellmeister*, or chief, of the Court musicians. One of his sons, Johann, became the father of 'our' Beethoven. He too was a Court musician, but probably only kept his position through his father's influence, for we know that he was a pretty good-for-nothing sort of man.

40

So much for Beethoven's immediate forebears, now let us get to Beethoven himself.

II

He was born in Bonn, in the Rhineland, on December 16, 1770, the second son of Johann. His mother was called Maria Magdalena Kewerich, and was a daughter of the head cook in the palace of Ehrenbreitstein; we don't know a very great deal about her, except that she was clever and strong-minded and that her son Ludwig loved her very dearly and was very unhappy when she died. (In 1787, when Ludwig was only seventeen.) But even then he had already had to take a great deal of family responsibility because of his father's drunken habits and general unreliability; so—again like Mozart—he didn't have a very happy childhood.

All the same, his father, who gave him daily lessons on the violin and was often extremely rough and discouraging to him in the process, was very proud of him. He once said, "My son Ludwig, who is my only consolation, progresses in music and composition at such a rate that he astonishes everybody. My Ludwig, I perceive, will in time become a great man in the world." How right he was!

It is nice to know that Beethoven and his brothers took great care of their father, and tried not to let people see when he had taken a little too much to drink. The family life was quite reasonably peaceful, but it is said that Maria van Beethoven, the mother, was hardly ever heard to laugh.

Beethoven was never the child prodigy that Mozart was, but, when he was thirteen, his first teacher, C. G. Neefe, wrote: "Louis van Beethoven is of most promising talent. He plays the clavier very skilfully—reads at sight very well, and plays chiefly the *Well-tempered Clavichord* of Sebastian Bach."

In later years Beethoven told his fellow musician, Carl Czerny (a famous pianist and teacher; you may be working at his exercises at this moment) that his musical education had been very bad. "But I had a talent for music," he added. Czerny said it was touching to hear the earnest tone in which Beethoven said this, as if no one had ever noticed it, for by that time he was very famous. But *really* great people are never conceited.

Well, Beethoven's musical education may in some ways have

41

been 'very bad', but it is certain that he learnt much of musical practice from a very early age. His teacher, Neefe, took him when he was only thirteen, as his assistant harpsichordist in the electoral orchestra in Bonn. This position also involved some conducting, and occasional violin-playing as well.

When he was seventeen, he managed to get to Vienna, the greatest musical city in the world, and the goal of every aspiring musician. There he met Mozart, who was much impressed with his extemporization. (This is the gift of being able to compose while playing; it is sometimes called 'improvising'.) While Beethoven was playing, Mozart called out to friends in the next room: "Watch this chap; some day or another he'll make a noise in the world." Later he gave him a few lessons. Unfortunately Beethoven had to hurry home after only a few months because of the illness of his mother, who died in July, 1787. Apart from the great sorrow it brought him, poor young Beethoven was now left to cope as best he could with his very difficult family.

At the same time he was fortunate in getting to know some of the aristocratic families who were the great patrons of music in those days. First there were the von Breunings, people of much culture and refinement. Madame von Breuning, who was a widow, had a great influence on the young man, cultivating in him a taste for literature which helped very much in the development of his character. The troubles and difficulties of his early life were producing an increasing roughness and a sort of protective arrogance in his manners, but below the surface he grew into a man of deep religious feeling and humble spirit. His outward gruffness and uncouth ways, however, never seemed to prevent people of all classes from finding him fascinating.

Another of Beethoven's aristocratic friends was Count Waldstein, whose name Beethoven has immortalized in one of his greatest piano sonatas.

In 1792, the Elector sent Beethoven back to Vienna to study composition; first with the great composer Haydn and later with a celebrated musical theorist named Albrechtsberger. The latter will go down in history as a classical example of musical pedantry—not a very enviable reputation. Beethoven worked with him at musical theory with great conscientiousness, even though at times he could not resist expressing his own opinions with the characteristic strength and freedom which had grown upon him more and more as his gigantic musical spirit developed. It is extraordinary to think that Albrechtsberger felt nothing but contempt for, his marvellous pupil; he once remarked, "He has never learnt anything, and will never do anything in a decent style."

Altogether, Beethoven had to suffer more and more from the jealousy of his fellow musicians, who could only see in him a rather uncouth figure, careless in his dress and speaking with an uncultured accent. This did not worry Beethoven at all, especially as the truly cultivated and distinguished musical amateurs in Vienna were coming to appreciate more and more the greatness of both his music and his character, and they accepted him as their equal in every way.

It is an interesting point that these great Viennese families— von Breuning, Lichnowsky, Lobkowicz, Waldstein—were the same who had befriended Haydn and Mozart, but had made servants of them. Whereas they treated Beethoven as one of themselves—I think by the sheer force of his belief in his own genius. He felt, and rightly, that such genius was a much greater thing than riches and titles, and so he compelled the bearers of these titles to accept him at his own valuation.

When he was twenty-four, Prince and Princess Lichnowsky even took him to live with them in their palace, and treated him as their own son. But after two years Beethoven found it irksome, and from 1796 on he lived in lodgings by himself. Lodgings which he was perpetually changing; he has been called 'an inveterate mover'. Indeed, he was sometimes paying rent for three or four apartments at the same time. In justice to his landlords it must be confessed that he was doubtless an extremely tiresome tenant.

From his earliest days in Vienna Beethoven worked constantly at composition, but it was some time before he became known as a composer. However, from the time his *Opus 1* (three trios for pianoforte, violin and 'cello) was published in 1795, he began to make plenty of money by his compositions. But he was, like so many artists, over-generous and extravagant, so he never became as rich as he might have been; quite the contrary.

Before these days, it had been as a player that he first came into prominence; he used often to play to friends at Prince Lichnowsky's, but it was not till 1795 that he played his own *Piano Concerto in C* at a public concert. From then on, his reputation began to grow, both as player and composer, and in 1796 he played in Berlin, before the king, with great success. It was not till Beethoven was thirty that he produced his *First Symphony*—the first of nine, developing from the Mozartian charm and lightness of No. 1, right up to the monumental *Ninth*, one of the greatest of all his works. This last is known as the *Choral Symphony*, because it brings in a setting of Schiller's 'Ode to Joy', for chorus and soloists—an unusual development of a symphony.

It is not really possible to describe Beethoven's symphonies in words, but you can best get to know them by listening to records, or better still, 'live' performances. In this way you can follow the development of Beethoven's genius with the greatest clarity, and you will find it most fascinating.

III

All the time that this gigantic musical spirit was growing, however, Beethoven was grappling with a dreadful misfortune. When he was about twenty-eight, he realized that he was beginning to grow deaf.

For years he tried to keep it a secret; for what could be worse for a musician than deafness? None of the doctors he consulted could help him, and at last he could bear his secret no longer; in 1801 he wrote to his friend Wegeler, with splendid courage: "I will seize Fate by the throat; most assuredly it shall not get me wholly down—oh, it is so beautiful to live a thousandfold!" A year later he wrote his brothers a long letter now known as the Heiligenstadt Testament. In it he sums up the tragedy of his life as it then seemed to him; some day you must read it for yourselves, for in spite of its terrible unhappiness it is one of the great human documents of all time.

By 1814 he had to give up playing in public. By 1816 he had to use an ear-trumpet, and soon after that he could no longer take part in conversation, and had to carry a note-book and pencil so that people could write what they wanted to say to him.

Some may wonder how anyone as deaf as Beethoven could continue to compose any music at all, let alone some of the greatest of his career. The explanation, of course, is that, since Beethoven was not born deaf, he could hear *in his head* the music he created just as you can run over in your mind a familiar tune without yourself uttering—or hearing—a sound.

There was another great sorrow in Beethoven's life. His brother Caspar had died in 1815, leaving a son, Karl, whom he left to Beethoven's care. Beethoven was devoted to the boy, but he turned out a most unlovely character, who repaid all his uncle's fatherly love and care with the utmost callousness and ingratitude. Is it not amazing that with such constant personal worry and unhappiness as well as his deafness, Beethoven continued to create one sublime work after another?

The fact remains that he did, even after he had become completely deaf. After the first performance of the *Ninth Symphony* (in 1824, three years before his death), the audience in Vienna was reduced to tears because Beethoven, who had been standing in the orchestra with his back to the audience in order to indicate the tempos to the conductor, had to be turned round by one of the solo singers so that he might *see* the applause which he could not hear.

IV

In music, Beethoven may be said to have been the first great revolutionary. In a most interesting study of Beethoven by an American writer named Schauffler, he is presented as a liberator. "Delivering the music of his day," says Schauffler, "from the ignominious role of the hanger-on of the fashionable world; he made it a universal thing—a bringing to life of the utmost range of the human mind and spirit—all its height and depth. . . . He set personality free in music."

Schauffler then elaborates: "Beethoven was elementally original. Whenever the spirit moved him he could squeeze blood out of bricks, make rubies of the blood, and platinum of the residue, and organize these products into miracles of design that would put any great painter to shame. He could find laughter, beauty and wonder in his own blaze of ridiculous fury over the loss of a penny"—which refers to a piano piece

45

written after he had tried in vain to recapture a penny he had dropped and which went rolling along the gutter.

"He could make a tone-poem out of the peep of a small bird which was all but inaudible to his deaf ears." (Beethoven reproduces the song of many birds in his *Sixth Symphony*, often called 'the *Pastoral*'.)

"The reason why the musical embodiment of Beethoven's emotions was more original than that of his predecessors was that he thought more deeply than they, and his music represented that deeper thought."

Finally Schauffler sums up thus: "Beethoven found the art of music narrowed to the pastime of a special class of society. He made it broadly human. He left it superhuman."

The storms and tragedies of Beethoven's life were, fortunately, tempered by happier moments. Although he never married, he was constantly falling in love, and these love-affairs certainly brought him some joy while they lasted. He proposed to several of his lady-loves, including one who was only fifteen. But although they were doubtless flattered, they would none of them risk marrying him; in which they were surely wise, for in spite of Beethoven's capacity for love and devotion, his violent and erratic temperament would have made him an impossible husband.

After Beethoven's death, a letter addressed to 'The Immortal Beloved' was found among his papers. Nobody has ever been able to prove for certain which of his many 'beloveds' this one was. It is not even known whether the lady ever received it. But there is no doubt that whoever she was, she must have inspired some of Beethoven's most romantic music.

Speaking very broadly, Beethoven was not among the greatest of song-writers. His songs were not always 'comfortable' to sing, and in his great choral works—particularly the *Ninth Symphony*—he has no consideration at all for his sopranos, whom he requires to sing in their very topmost register for pages on end; this meant that he thought of human voices as pure instruments rather than as part of human beings, and points clearly to the fact that his genius was, as a rule, instrumental rather than vocal.

The two great works which prove the exception to this rule, however, are his opera, *Fidelio*, and the *Mass in D*. In both

46

The musical embodiment of Beethoven's emotions was
more original because he thought more deeply

47

these works we get voices and orchestra in perfect and glorious relationship. The *Mass* was Beethoven's last work but one on the grand scale. The very last was the *Ninth Symphony*, which was finished in 1823. After this he wrote only string quartets and smaller works—smaller in scope, but no less great. He contemplated more symphonies—his note-books are full of sketches for such works—but they were not destined to be completed.

Here I would offer you a personal word on the matter of listening to music; listen with your mind as well as your ears. Do not take it for granted that every single thing a great composer writes is necessarily beautiful, or even particularly interesting. There are, for example, quite a number of little piano pieces by Beethoven which I myself always find rather dull. Should you feel the same way, do not be afraid to say so. But don't say: "Oh, I hate BEETHOVEN!" because of this. Learn to use your own discrimination—to make up your own mind. If you happen to dislike a piece called *Für Elise*, for instance, wait until you hear the overtures and the symphonies!

V

In the winter of 1826, Beethoven went to stay with a brother who had a small country estate not far from Vienna. An account of his daily life there was given by a friend called Michael Krenn; it is so characteristic of him that I will quote a bit of it here, but you can read it all in the article on Beethoven in Grove's *Dictionary of Music and Musicians.*

"At half-past five he was up and at his table, beating time with his hands and feet, singing, humming and writing. At half-past seven was the family breakfast, and directly after it he hurried out of doors, and would saunter about the fields, calling out, waving his hands, going now very slowly and now very fast, and then suddenly standing still and writing in a kind of pocket-book. At half-past twelve he came in to dinner, and after dinner he went to his own room till three or so, and in the fields again till about sunset, for later than that he might not go out. At half-past seven was supper, and then he went to his room and wrote till ten, and so to bed."

But Beethoven could not endure this life for long, so he

started to return to Vienna on December 2, 1826. Unfor--
tunately there was only an open carriage for him to travel in,
and his health by this time being very bad, he became very ill
with inflammation of the lungs as soon as he got back to
Vienna. He was ill for a long time, as he had often been before,
but it was not until March 1827 that his friends began to realize
that this time he might not recover. He grew gradually worse,
and when he foresaw that the end was not far off, we are told
that he said to his friends, with characteristic grim humour:
"*Plaudite, amici, commedia finita est.*" ("Applaud, friends; the
comedy is finished.")

On the evening of March 26, a sudden storm arose, and in
the midst of its thunder and lightning, Beethoven died.

He was given a tremendous funeral, and all over the world,
people gathered together to pay tribute to his greatness.

To me, Beethoven is perfectly embodied in these lines by
Dryden; and I would like to leave them with you:

> "*From harmony, from heavenly harmony,*
> *This universal frame began;*
> *From harmony to harmony*
> *Through all the compass of the notes it ran,*
> *The diapason closing full in Man.*"

Robert the Bruce

RIGHT ARM OF THE SCOTS

Eileen Bigland

I

I N the poor hut which served him as lodging on the island of Rachrin off the Irish coast, a tall, bearded man lay on a bed of straw staring blankly at the rafters above his head. Despite his unkempt appearance there was an indefinable air of nobility about him, yet few would have recognized the famous Robert the Bruce, King of Scotland, in this gaunt figure clad in tattered garments. For the fortunes of Bruce were at their lowest ebb, and he who had been crowned so proudly at the Abbey of Scone but a year or two earlier was now an exile with a price upon his head.

And the tragedy of it all was, he reflected gloomily, that his own headstrong nature and wild temper had led him to this pass. Perhaps he had better give up all thought of regaining his kingdom and go off to fight for the Crusaders in Palestine—but just then his eye was caught by the antics of a spider trying to swing itself by its thread from one rafter to another. Six times it failed in the attempt, and as he watched Bruce remembered that he had fought six unsuccessful battles against the English. "So," he whispered to himself, "as I have no means of knowing what is best, I will be guided by this spider. If the insect will make another venture, and be successful, I will venture a seventh time to try my fortune in Scotland. But if the spider shall fail, I will go to the wars abroad."

To his surprise the spider *did* succeed at its seventh attempt and in his excitement Bruce leapt to his feet. Come what might, he would return to Scotland!

But all through the rough crossing to the Isle of Arran he kept brooding on memories he would have given much to forget. He remembered his carefree boyhood as Earl of Carrick

50

and the fervour with which, as a mere lad, he had followed the standard of the great Governor and Protector, Sir William Wallace, who had defied the might of Edward I of England and engaged his armies at the Battle of Falkirk in 1288. True, this encounter had led to an overwhelming English victory. Edward had flooded Scotland with troops, taken possession of her castles, subdued her nobles, and seven years later captured and executed Wallace, displaying the four quarters of his body on spits on London Bridge as a warning to all traitors. But how much braver Wallace had been than men like Bruce, who had weakly given in and fought for the English against his fellow Scots.

II

Wallace had been a true patriot, a fact not appreciated by Bruce until the day when, after a skirmish with the Scots, he had sat down to eat with the English nobles never noticing that his hands were still spattered with blood. "Faugh!" said one. "Look at that Scotsman eating his own blood!" In horror Bruce gazed at his hands—and against his brain beat the words of Wallace at his Westminster trial: "I could not be a traitor to Edward, for I was never his subject." There and then Bruce had gone to a nearby church and prayed God's forgiveness for his grievous sin, swearing to atone for it by delivering Scotland from her enemies; and from that hour he left the English army and devoted all his energies to rallying the Scottish nobles around him.

All might have been well but for his ungovernable temper. At that time Scotland had no king, and while Edward wished to set a puppet monarch on the throne, the Scots were determined it should go either to Bruce or to the Red Comyn, Sir John Comyn of Badenoch. In an effort to persuade his rival to support him, Bruce arranged a meeting with the Red Comyn in the Church of the Minorities in Dumfries. High words passed between the two and Bruce, forgetful of his surroundings, drew his dagger and stabbed Comyn at the very steps of the High Altar. He then rushed from the church, shouting to his followers, Lindesay and Kirkpatrick: "I doubt I have slain the Red Comyn!" Kirkpatrick whirled on his master. "Dae ye leave such a matter in doubt? I'll mak' siccar!" and so saying he and Lindsay entered the church and slew the sorely wounded man.

Bruce was crowned king in 1306, but as if in punishment ill-fortune continued to dog him, and after several defeats at the hands of the English he was obliged to flee with his wife, her ladies and a few loyal followers to the Highlands. Here, surrounded by enemies, they led a wretched, wandering existence but Bruce—who was a remarkable scholar for those days—strove always to keep up the spirits of the others by reading to them aloud. Finally, however, he was so hard-pressed that he had to leave his Queen with the Countess of Buchan at Kildrummie Castle in Aberdeenshire, under the care of his brother Nigel, while he himself fled to the lonely island of Rachrin. There, but a week or so back, he had received the dire news that the English had seized the castle, killed Nigel, and imprisoned the Queen and her ladies in the harshest possible manner.

So Bruce landed on Arran in no enviable state of mind, but the first woman he met on the shore told him that a body of armed men, who had lately killed the Governor of Brodick Castle and his garrison, were now hunting in the nearby woods. Bruce seized his horn, and the call he blew upon it was recognized by Lord James of Douglas, leader of the band and his greatest friend. Overjoyed, Lord James and his men greeted their King, and it was arranged that while Douglas should return to the mainland in disguise to rally the Scots, Bruce should remain in Arran until a follower named Cuthbert should light a bonfire on Turnberry Head, opposite the island. This was to signify that a sufficient force had been raised.

One night the fire blazed up. Bruce and his loyal men made haste to cross to the mainland but were greeted only by the shivering Cuthbert who told them the fire had been lit by somebody else. The Earl of Percy was ranging through the county of Carrick with 300 men and had so terrified the people that they refused to rebel against the English. To Bruce this seemed a death-knell to all his hopes, but his brother Edward begged him to remain on the spot. News of his arrival spread like wildfire and his people flocked to join him. First secretly, then more boldly, he sent his forces to attack the English, and in a very short time Earl Percy was obliged to quit the county.

This success was quickly followed by others, but Bruce was now wiser and less hot-headed than he had been in youth. It was one thing to rid Carrick of the enemy: it was quite another to regain possession of all the great Scottish fortresses up and down the country which were held by the English soldiery. Moreover, several of his own kinsmen, jealous of his growing power, had determined to put him to death, so, while he despatched Douglas and other nobles on many forays, he himself remained in hiding among the hills and glens he knew so well. This meant that he was often without guards and one day a relation, who had been offered a huge bribe to kill the King, saw him setting out unaccompanied save by a small page. Flanked by his two stalwart sons this man marched forward and made an obsequious speech about loyalty. The honeyed words made Bruce suspicious. Without more ado he snatched his page's bow and arrow, told the boy to stand back, and took aim. The arrow hit the man in the eye and he fell dead, but now the angry sons advanced upon the King, whirling their battle-axes. Fortunately one of them tripped over a tussock of grass, thus giving Bruce an opportunity to draw the great sword he always carried, and within a moment or two he had slain both his enemies. "You see," he told his page, "these three might have lived their lives as gallant men could they but have withstood their own greed."

III

After this episode Bruce retreated into Galloway. Here too, however, there were traitors, and on one occasion 200 or 300 of them set out to track him with bloodhounds. This time Bruce had 60 soldiers with him, but knowing they were weary he bade them lie down to sleep near a fast-flowing river while he and two henchmen stood guard over the only ford. Suddenly he heard the beat of horses' hooves and the baying of hounds. Shouting to his men to go back and rouse the others, he took up his position high up on the farther bank of the river. Since the enemy could only pass the ford singly Bruce was able to account for five or six of them before his own soldiers came running up and put the rest to flight.

Once again Bruce ordered his followers to disperse and he

and his foster-brother moved on alone, unaware that a noble-man named John of Lorne was also tracking him with a blood-hound. Five of Lorne's men caught up with them and these they managed to kill with a desperate effort—but they could still hear the cry of the dog in pursuit. Being near a river the King said: "Let us wade down this stream for a great way, and so this unhappy hound will lose the scent." The icy, swift-running water numbed their feet, but somehow they staggered on and at last thought it safe to land on the far side and lie down in a wood to rest. Not that their worries were over, for so soon as they resumed their way they met three rough-looking men who said they were seeking Robert the Bruce. "Come with me," answered Bruce, "and I will conduct you to the Scottish King." As he spoke he saw a crafty expression steal across their faces and realized at once that this was another trap. There was nothing for it but to travel forward with the men, and when they reached a tumbledown cottage the ruffians produced a hunk of mutton which they proceeded to broil. The meal made them all sleepy, but Bruce took care to move a considerable distance from the strangers before he lay down to rest. His foster-brother fell into an exhausted slumber, but the King only dozed fitfully, and presently he heard the ominous clink of swords. Leaping to his feet he advanced on the three, his own sword drawn. Alas, he was too late to prevent them from killing his foster-brother, but he avenged that good man's death by slaying all three villains.

Bruce had told his followers to meet him again at a distant farmhouse, and when he reached it the sturdy old Scotswoman who owned it told him all travellers were welcome there for the sake of one. "And who is that?" he asked. "Our rightful King, Robert the Bruce," she answered proudly, "who is lawful lord of this country; and though he is now pursued and hunted after with hounds and horns, I hope to live to see him King over all Scotland."

IV

Her wish came true sooner than any had dared to hope, for it was at her farmhouse that Bruce was rejoined by Lord James of Douglas, who reported many successes. Edward I, "Hammer of the Scots", had died in 1307 and been succeeded by

Edward II, a man lacking his father's sagacity, and the Scots now found their task of recapturing strongholds much easier. During the next few years Bruce and his men stormed one after another of the great Scottish castles, and the King who had been so lately a fugitive proved himself more than a match for the English ruler.

Edinburgh Castle was retaken by Sir Thomas Randolph and 30 soldiers who climbed the precipitous rock and surprised the garrison asleep and unarmed. Linlithgow was seized thanks to the ruse of a farmer named Binnock, who delivered cartloads of hay to the Castle each week. Eight fully-armed men hid under the hay in the leading cart and as this entered the gate under the raised portcullis Binnock ran the porter through with his sword, shouting out a signal: "Call all, call all!" which brought the main body of the Scots at a run. Roxburgh was recaptured by Lord James by means of another ruse. It was the Shrovetide holiday, and while the English garrison made merry an officer's wife was sitting on the battlements rocking her baby to sleep. Vaguely she saw some hunched black shapes approaching the moat, but a soldier told her they were merely straying cattle. So the woman went on singing to her child:

> *"Hush ye, hush ye, little pet ye,*
> *Hush ye, do not fret ye,*
> *The Black Douglas shall not get ye . . ."*

At that moment a hand in an iron glove fell on her shoulder and a voice said grimly: "Don't be too sure of that." It was Lord James himself and the black shapes had been his men wrapped in black cloaks!

V

When Edward II received the news that only Stirling Castle remained in English hands and feared it could not stand out much longer he raised a huge army of 100,000 men and marched into Scotland. Bruce, at the Scottish mustering place in the Torwood, managed to rally only 30,000 to his standard. But here his tremendous gift of strategy showed itself. On a hillside south of Stirling, he planted the Scottish standard in the big stone socket known as the Borestane

55

(which stands there to this day). Flanked on one side by a morass and on the other by a ravine, the open space in front through which he could be attacked was just over a quarter of a mile wide. This ground he had honeycombed with pits over which were placed turves and brushwood. Then he sat back and waited. On Sunday, June 22, 1314, the English army were reported at Falkirk, and the next morning they came in sight, their numbers being so great that it seemed as if the whole plain was covered with waving banners and shining mail.

As the vast force wheeled to the left to face the Scots Bruce noticed a body of cavalry, 800 strong, cantering off to the east. He guessed they were going to relieve Stirling Castle and said gravely to his nephew Randolph Moray, "See yonder, Randolph, a rose of thy chaplet has fallen." Mortified by the reproof—for it had been his duty to keep the English out of the town—Moray dashed off to intercept the invaders. A violent hand-to-hand encounter took place and eventually the English horse broke and fled.

This incident was followed by another even more significant one. Among the English knights was an exceedingly brave knight, Sir Henry de Bohun, who rode boldly forward and scanned the Scottish ranks. He was only a bow-shot away when he recognized Bruce by the crown set upon his helmeted head. Without hesitation he urged his horse to a gallop, his intention being to engage the King in single combat. But Bruce was ready. Standing up in his stirrups he swung his battle-axe and brought it down on de Bohun's head with such force that it crashed through his helmet and practically split his head in two.

That night both armies lay on their arms, and at dawn on Tuesday, June 24, the venerable Abbot of Inchaffray moved among the Scots to bless them and give strength to their cause. Bruce arranged his troops. He stayed behind the Borestane at the head of the reserve. On the hillside in front his brother Edward commanded a division on the right, Randolph Moray a division in the centre, and Lord James of Douglas with Walter Stewart (the King's future son-in-law) a division on the left. Then the English trumpets sounded, and squadron after squadron of mailed horsemen began to advance while a flight of the dreaded cloth-yard arrows rose into the air—those same

56

Standing up in his stirrups Bruce swung his battle-axe
and brought it down on de Bohun's head

57

arrows which had played havoc among the Scots at Falkirk twenty-five years before. At once Bruce sent Sir Robert Keith, marischal of his army, to drive the archers from the field.

Five hundred Scottish horse managed this feat, but now the English cavalry came on like a wall of steel. Nothing could have stopped them had their mounts not stumbled into the cunningly hidden pits which Bruce had dug for them. Those following plunged on top of the heaving mass of men and horses, and when succeeding squadrons tried to make a detour they found themselves bogged down in the morass. The men who got through were faced by a hedge of 12-foot spears and, while they fought madly to break these down, the Scottish archers poured in a shower of arrows against which no mail was proof.

From his point of vantage behind the Borestane Bruce watched the terrific battle. Above the clash of steel on steel, the shrieks of the wounded horses, the groans of the stricken men, there rose the thunderous battle-cries of the great Scottish houses as their vassals charged against some threatening body of the enemy. In the distance, beyond the Bannock Burn, he could see the figure of Edward II, with the English standard floating above his head and a crowd of mailed nobles around him. Every now and again one of these would set off at the gallop to rally the troops for a fresh attack, but as column after column came on each faltered before the long Scottish lances or the menace of the sweeping Lochaber bill-hooks. At last the English men-at-arms, awed by the mounds of dead before them, began to hesitate. At once the cry went up from the Scots: "On them! On them! They fail!" and even as the sound echoed across the hillside so there appeared over the brow of the Gillies Hill behind Bruce what seemed, to the exhausted English, to be a fresh Scottish army. In reality it was only the host of 15,000 camp followers who had been ordered to the rear by their King. Determined at least to see the battle, they had mounted their blankets on tent-poles and marched over the hill. But the mere sight of them was enough. The English began to withdraw, Bruce swept down the hill with his reserves, and the whole enemy force fled in disorder while Sir Aylmer Vallance put his hand on King Edward's bridle rein and led him from the field.

That night the English King with 500 horse—all that was

left of his fine cavalry—was fleeing to Dunbar with Lord James in hot pursuit. Behind them they left 30,000 dead and all their baggage. For the first time in many weary years Scotland was a free nation again.

VI

For the next fourteen years Bruce governed his country wisely and well, and under his firm guidance Scotland became a vastly different place from the wild, quarrelsome land she had been when he first came to the throne. But when he was fifty-three years old the King fell very sick and retired to the Castle of Cardross on the Clyde Estuary. According to legend his disease was the dreaded leprosy, but it seems more likely, in the light of our present day knowledge, to have been some complaint due to all the hardships he had suffered in youth. Unable to ride his war-horse any longer he contented himself by sailing down the estuary to the sea and back, but in the following year he sent for his old and trusted friend, Lord James of Douglas.

He was about to die, he said, and as he would not be able to carry out the intention he still had of going on Crusade as an expiation for the murder of the Red Comyn and other sins he had committed long ago, would his dearest friend carry his heart to the Holy Land?

Robert the Bruce died on June 7, 1329, and before his body was buried in Dunfermline Abbey, Douglas had the heart cut out and encased in a silver casket which he wore about his neck on a string of silk and gold. Then he set out for the Crusades, but on the way was persuaded to help the Spanish King drive out the Moors who were threatening his country. Here, in battle, Douglas was surrounded by the enemy. Tearing the casket from his neck he spoke to it as he would have spoken to his beloved King. "Pass first in fight, as thou wast wont to do," he cried, "and Douglas will follow thee, or die!" With these words he flung the casket among his foes and dashed after it, being killed just as he reached it.

When his followers sorrowfully returned to Scotland they brought the heart of Bruce with them and it now lies beneath the High Altar of Melrose Abbey.

Julius Caesar

BUILDER OF AN EMPIRE

Captain W. E. Johns

I

A MAN whose name and fame have lost nothing in the march of centuries, and will hold their place for as long as history is written, was the Roman known to us as Julius Caesar: or, to give him his full name Caius Julius Caesar. To us he is of particular interest, for it was he who led the Roman legions to the shores of Britain, although that invasion was only one of his many campaigns.

What is of greater importance is that the surname Caesar was to acquire a regal significance. Such was its renown that it was to become the title of the first twelve Roman emperors. Nor did it end here. The title Czar, Shah and Kaiser all derive from that same illustrious name, which is thought by some to have an association, in the early days of the family, with an elephant, that word having the same meaning as the name in the Punic language.

Do not make the mistake of supposing Julius Caesar to be nothing more than an historical figure. Such men not only shape the world in which they live. The things they do and say reach far into the future. They lay the foundations upon which our modern world is built.

The boy who was to become that rare combination of statesman, military genius, orator and man of letters, was born on July 12, in the year 100 B.C. (Some say 102 B.C.) He was the only son of Caius Julius, a member of one of the oldest families of Rome, and his wife, Aurelia. And since parents are important we must take a quick look at them.

Julius's father was rich, but he was simple and severe in his habits, and in politics never held a higher office than Praetor.

60

He suffered the curious fate of dropping dead one morning as he was putting on his shoes. Julius adored his mother, who appears to have been a strict, stately lady, with ideas which today would probably be called old-fashioned. She lived with Julius until the day of her death, moving into his house on his marriage.

Young Julius began his career early, leaving his father at the age of fifteen to hold, a year later, the office of Priest of Jupiter. We have a picture of him at this time, a tall, slight, handsome youth, with dark, piercing eyes, a sallow complexion, large nose, full lips, but with features refined and intellectual. He was particular about his appearance, bathing frequently and attending carefully to his hair. He arranged his dress with studied negligence, having a way of fastening his girdle to catch the eye. He remained particular about his appearance to the end of his life, in later years putting a broad purple stripe on his fringed toga. He shaved carefully, and was upset when his hair started falling out, leaving him bald in front.

Even at an early age he was in constant danger from enemies who perceived in his ambition a threat to their own advancement. He preserved his life by changing his lodgings every day, thus revealing an ability to take care of himself. It was necessary, for from this time until his assassination on March 15, 44 B.C., he was never entirely free from peril, either on the battlefield or at the daggers of jealous rivals at home.

II

To understand the career of this remarkable man we must now glance at the conditions into which he was born.

The Romans, having the faculty of government to a degree hitherto unknown and inspired by a passion for freedom, had become the most powerful military nation on earth. From Rome the legions had marched to the limits of the known world, carrying all before them. (Britain was not yet known; it was left to Julius Caesar to discover it.) Brave, highly trained and disciplined, every man was a skilled workman, an engineer or mechanic, able to turn his hand to anything. The Roman legions were invincible. Everywhere nations were enslaved and forced to pay tribute. But these conquests were not all bloodshed. The Romans took with them a culture. They raised magnificent public buildings. They built fine roads from one side of Europe to the other and performed feats of civil engineering that even today make us open our eyes. Julius Caesar built a bridge across the Rhine in a week. He built a fleet in a month, enough ships to carry an army.

What sort of men were these Romans? We may find the answer in their way of life. Their gods were the Virtues—or, let us say, they turned the Virtues into gods. They built temples to Truth, Modesty and Concord. Remember, this was a hundred years before the birth of Christ. Their creed, briefly, was this: Do not live for yourself alone, for, if you do, you will come to nothing. Be brave, be just, be pure, be true in word and deed. Care not for enjoyment, care not for your life, care only for what is right. So your Maker has ordered. Disobey at your peril.

That religion, if we may so call it, had made the Rome of Julius Caesar a mighty power, wise in politics and irresistible in war.

It may not be out of place to mention here that what today we call a soldier's Oath of Allegiance was known to the Roman as the *Sacramentum*. By this he swore never to desert his Standard, never to turn his back to the enemy and never to abandon his leader. From this came the word Sacrament as we use it today, the early Christians taking a similar oath, pledging themselves to be faithful soldiers and servants of Christ.

III

Young Julius had not intended to be a professional soldier, although he served a short apprenticeship as one. He had decided to be a barrister, a profession then, as today, wherein eloquence in a court of law could win or lose a case. But the fates willed otherwise.

Julius's first tutor had been Antonius Gnipho, an educated Gaul from Northern Italy. He now decided to go to the island of Rhodes where there was an academy wherein were taught the speech and gestures so important to an orator. On his way he met with an adventure that gives us a good indication of his character. He was captured by pirates.

At this time, although Roman galleys patrolled the seas,

pirates had become a menace. Greeks, Syrians, Egyptians, Africans, Spaniards and Gauls, trained to the sea from childhood, saw in the rich ships taking goods to Rome an easy road to wealth. The ship on which Julius was travelling fell into their hands and he was taken to the island now called Fermaco. A ransom was levied, but Julius astonished his captors by telling them that the sum named was not enough. He was worth more—a sum equal to about £10,000. The size of the sum, he said, was not really important, as one day he would come back and hang the lot of them. He remained a prisoner for 38 days.

Servants were sent to the nearest Roman station to fetch the money. While awaiting their return Julius joined the pirates in their games and sports, telling them occasionally that they were a lot of cut-throats and what their fate would be when he was released.

The ransom was brought and paid, and Julius was put ashore on the mainland near Miletus. He at once collected ships, returned to the island where he had been been held prisoner, and falling upon the pirates while they were sharing their plunder, seized them and carried them away for trial. They were sentenced to be crucified. Julius interceded, protesting at the severity of the sentence, whereupon they were strangled before being stretched on their crosses. Julius resumed his interrupted journey to Rhodes where he studied for two years.

IV

It is not possible in a survey of this length to recount all that Julius Caesar did in peace and war in an era of great events. In the Senate he was a great administrator, holding one high office after the other until he became dictator and virtual ruler of the Republic. According to a contemporary author he could employ at the same time his ears to listen, his eyes to read, his hand to write and his mind to dictate. He introduced many reforms—according to his critics not always good ones. With him power was a devouring passion, and this is illustrated by two stories told of him. Once, looking at a small village, he remarked to a friend that he would rather be the head of such a village than second in command in Rome. On another occasion it is said of him that while reading the life of Alexander the Great he burst into tears of chagrin because he could never achieve such greatness as the famous Macedonian leader.

Perhaps in Julius Caesar's military prowess lies his greatest claim to fame. At the age of twenty-one he had won the Civic Crown, equivalent to the Victoria Cross, for saving the life of a soldier at the battle of Myetelene. It was reckoned that in ten years of campaigning he conquered 300 nations, took 800 towns, and defeated 3,000,000 men, 1,000,000 of which fell on the field of battle. He carried another 1,000,000 prisoners into slavery. But also, it must be said, he invited many of his prisoners to join his service and later raised them to high positions.

The modern soldier, provided with mechanical transport, must consider with amazement the thousands of miles he marched, conquering new lands and settling insurrections in the old. From the north of Europe to the south, from Spain direct to Asia Minor and then on to Egypt he fought his way, sharing the discomforts of his men, eating the same coarse food, sleeping on the floor of his chariot.

A fearless horseman, he would sometimes demonstrate the firmness of his seat by riding at full gallop with his hands clasped behind his head. In Gaul he trained and rode a fierce horse which no other man in the army dare mount. In a battle he would expose himself in the thickest of the fighting, cheering his men on, bare-headed so that they could see his face. Once he grabbed a standard bearer who was turning away, telling him coldly that he had mistaken the direction of the enemy. He never lost his nerve, his head or his tremendous confidence. Always he carried himself with a graceful air of supremacy.

He could be shrewd, too. Before the battle of Phaesalia, in which he finally defeated his great rival Pompey, hearing that Pompey's cavalry consisted mostly of young aristocrats, he told his men not to strike at the horses but at the faces of the men, who would cover them to prevent disfigurement. And so it turned out.

In the civil war with Pompey, Pharnaces, King of Pontus, refused to join sides, whereupon Caesar marched against him and defeated him in one day. This was the occasion when he made his pithy remark, "*Veni, Vidi, Vici*," meaning "I came, I saw, I conquered."

V

But the event of greatest importance to us was Caesar's invasion and conquest of Britain, if for no other reason than, curious though it may seem, it is as a result of that, through despatches sent back to Rome, that we know as much about the Ancient Britons as we do.

It happened in 55 B.C., when Caesar was Governor of Gaul, now called France. He had driven out invading Germans, but the Gauls were receiving help from an unknown country across the sea to which some of them had fled. From Calais Caesar could see the white cliffs of Dover, but of Britain and the character of its inhabitants he knew nothing. To cross over and explore promised an adventure not to be declined.

At the beginning of August the weather was fine. The Gauls were quiet. Caesar ordered his ships to gather at Boulogne, enough to carry two legions—say, 10,000 men. On a calm evening they set sail and by morning were off Dover, to find the cliffs lined with painted warriors. The invaders hesitated to land, so Caesar sailed along the coast as far as Deal or Walmer, followed on shore by the natives.

Caesar took his ships in close and ordered the archers to clear a passage. Arrows showered upon the defenders. It was then that the officer of the 10th Legion, carrying the Eagle, leapt into the sea shouting to his comrades to follow if they wished to save their Standard. The Britons waded out to meet them and for a time the Romans could make no headway. But the odds were too great and at length the legionaries secured a foothold. The Britons fled. The ships were brought to anchor and the Romans made camp.

All went well until the fourth day, when a full moon brought along a high tide. For this the Romans, having no experience of such things, had made no provision, and the galleys had a rough time. Some were driven ashore and smashed; others parted their cables and drifted out to sea. For once Caesar was worried. He had no means of building another fleet and he had made no preparations to winter in Britain. The troops had travelled light, without tents or baggage. However, Caesar

Then the officer of the 10th Legion carrying the Eagle
leapt into the sea, shouting to his comrades to follow

rose to the occasion. The ships that had been damaged beyond repair were broken up to make the others seaworthy and the invaders returned to Gaul. Thus ended the first invasion. Caesar had now to travel fast to Eastern Europe to quell an uprising there.

But by the following April he was back, preparing to go to Britain and stay there. He built 600 transports and 28 armed galleys. At sunset on July 20 the fleet set sail, carrying five legions. By noon the following day they were at Deal, and this time there was no opposition. The Britons, dismayed by the size of the Armada, had fled to the interior. Caesar advanced as far as St. Albans. With the approach of winter he returned again to Rome, taking with him a number of prisoners. He could find no other spoil. But he knew now what lay beyond the Channel. At home, no conquest brought him greater fame than this.

VI

It is not to be imagined that Julius Caesar was without faults. No man is. He could be ruthless in war and unscrupulous where his civil ambition was concerned. As a young man he was without principle, squandering borrowed money, running into debt, and, later in life, spending public money recklessly. It is a point in his favour that he never denied this. He was not a hypocrite. He never pretended to be virtuous.

In war he was responsible for wholesale massacres, but that was how war was fought in those days. Atrocities that appear horrible to us now were accepted as a matter of course two thousand years ago. One should always read history in the light of the customs of the day.

The brutal murder of the brave Vercingetorex, defender of Gaul, must always be a black mark on Caesar's record. This noble man had surrendered himself to save his people from further bloodshed. After holding him prisoner for six years Caesar caused him to be put to death for no other reason than to provide a spectacle at a Triumph exalting his own prowess.

Yet this man who could be so cruel, so callous, had an emotional side. When he was told that his great rival in the civil war, Pompey, had been murdered in Egypt, and he was shown his signet ring to prove it, he sat down and cried.

Caesar's personal courage was never challenged even by his enemies. Certainly no leader was more dearly loved by his men. Where there was danger, there was Caesar. If there was a dangerous river to cross he was the first to jump in and swim to the other side.

Why, then, was he murdered? He was thought by some to have become too great. He was getting too much praise. Lesser men were envious, feeling they should have a share of it. Their excuse for killing him was that Rome was a republic, a democracy, and it was put about that Caesar intended to make himself king. He was saluted like one in the streets. He was offered the crown but declined it. His enemies said this was an act put on to give Caesar a chance to silence the gossip. That may have been so. Had Caesar wished to be king there was nothing to prevent it. He was without any real rival. The country was tranquil.

In a few days Caesar would be going to Parthia, when he would be out of reach of those who plotted against him. For them it was now or never. We must now pass on quickly to the last day of this supreme adventurer in the manner made familiar by Shakespeare's famous play which bears his name.

Every great man has his enemies, for in the baseness of human nature there are men who hate those who succeed. Julius Caesar had his. He was well aware of it. But because he was indifferent to death he chose to ignore them. Some of the conspirators were men he had pardoned. They hated him because it was in his power to do that. There was hardly one of them who had not received some favour from him. There was one man, however, he thought he could trust. Brutus. Yet Brutus was one of the first to strike.

The assassination was easy. Caesar would take no precautions. On the eve of the murder, March 14, there had been signs and portents. A great storm had raged. A comet had appeared in the sky. An uneasy atmosphere of suspicion and uncertainty hung over the city. Calphurnia, Caesar's wife, begged her husband not to go to the Senate. Friends tried to warn him, for such a plot could not be kept secret. He laughed them aside.

Caesar rose to go. As he crossed the hall his statue fell and shivered to pieces. As he made his way, on foot and without an escort (his usual practice) to the Senate where the conspirators were waiting, a man thrust a note into his hand, begging him to read it then. It divulged the plot and listed the conspirators. Caesar did not look at it. Had he done so the history of the world might have been different. Thus do the fates of empires hang upon a thread.

At eleven o'clock, March 15, when Caesar entered the Senate and took his seat, the conspirators were ready, their daggers under their togas. They closed in on him. Caesar stood up, reading his fate in their eyes. Cassius stabbed him in the throat. Caesar looked around, and seeing a ring of daggers pointing at him drew his gown over his face, dignified to the end. The daggers struck and he fell. The assassins fled, leaving the bleeding corpse of their victim lying where it had fallen at the foot of the statue of his old enemy, Pompey.

How Mark Antony, Caesar's friend, followed them and slew them, is another story.

Sir Winston Churchill

THE FIGHTING STATESMAN

Eric Williams

I

"PRISONER of War! That is the least unfortunate kind of prisoner to be, but it is nevertheless a melancholy state. You are in the power of your enemy. You owe your life to his humanity, and your daily bread to his compassion. You must obey his orders, go where he tells you, stay where you are bid, await his pleasure, possess your soul in patience. Meanwhile the war is going on, great events are in progress, fine opportunities for action and adventure are slipping away. Also the days are very long. Hours crawl like paralytic centipedes. Nothing amuses you. Reading is difficult; writing impossible. Life is one long boredom from dawn till slumber."

Thus wrote Sir Winston Churchill of the time when he was captured and held prisoner by the Boers in the South African War.

His list of things regretted makes a rounded description of the character of the man who wrote it—proud, courageous, energetic, with a zest for the struggle and a fine dramatic sense of history in the making. A man of action rather than a philosopher.

But the opportunity for adventure and action in great events was soon to be his again. Never a man to sit down and wait until the tide should turn in his favour, he had not long been a prisoner before making up his mind to escape.

The treatment of a prisoner of war is laid down by well-defined rules in international law. He must be taken away from the scene of battle as soon as practicable and housed, fed and cared for under the same conditions as his captors. He is entitled to try to escape, but there are agreed penalties if he is caught again.

Under the same law a war correspondent is classed as a non-combatant and is entitled to somewhat better treatment than a soldier. He is in fact sometimes returned to his own side in exchange for a non-combatant held by them.

A non-combatant however is on no account allowed to take part in the fighting. Should he do so he is liable to be placed before a firing squad if caught by the other side.

At the time of his capture Winston Churchill was a non-combatant, acting as war correspondent for the *Morning Post*. His behaviour before capture had given him, as we shall see, cause for apprehension. A drumhead court martial and a firing squad were not beyond the realms of possibility, and he had some anxious moments before it was decided that he would be treated as a prisoner of war and sent with his fellow-captives to the State Model Schools in Pretoria, which had been converted into a prison camp.

Once there he began to plan an organized mutiny of the prisoners, in which the guards would be overpowered and disarmed. But that was only to be the first step. Nearby was another prison camp in which there were nearly 2000 British soldiers. The scope of Winston Churchill's plan was not only his own liberty but the liberation of every other British prisoner, and the eventual capture of Pretoria itself—the enemy's capital city.

Perhaps it is just as well that the plan was not carried out. Although the rules of war protect the prisoner they also place him under certain obligations, and it is against the law for a prisoner to arm himself once he has been made captive.

Winston Churchill's second, less ambitious but more practical plan, was to scale the 10-foot high corrugated iron fence which surrounded the prison camp. Together with two fellow-prisoners he carefully watched the sentries who patrolled the inside of the fence, and noticed that sometimes—but never for more than a few minutes at a time—these guards were all unable to see the top of a certain stretch of fence. That part of the fence could be reached in a few strides by anyone hidden in a building conveniently near. The fact that the guards were armed with rifles and revolvers was a risk that must be taken.

Anxiously the three prisoners waited for a suitable night. Then, after lying hidden for some time, Winston seized his

71

moment, ran silently to the fence, hauled himself to the top and dropped down into the unknown blackness of the outside world.

There he waited impatiently for his two companions, but as soon as he had made his getaway the sentries had become suspicious. The other two were unable to make the climb and he was left alone on the far side of the fence.

He had £75 in his pocket and four slabs of chocolate, but the compass and maps—which would have been more useful —were with his companions in the prison.

II

Although he was free, it was nearly 300 miles to the nearest British post in Delagoa Bay. The town was picketed, and the country beyond its borders was patrolled. The trains were searched and the line guarded. He could not speak a word of Afrikaans or Kaffir. For the moment he was safely hidden in the shadow of the fence, but as soon as he began to walk he would be in the light of the street lamps and open to suspicion. Like many an escaper before and since he stayed where he was and thought it over.

He must get as quickly as possible away from Pretoria, and he must do this without human contact. By morning his absence would be known and his description sent out. Without a compass and maps walking would be out of the question. The obvious answer was to jump a train.

Keeping a rough plan of the city in his mind's eye, and taking his direction from the stars, he stepped boldly out into the lighted street and found his way to the railway. He walked along the track until he found a suitable place to settle down and wait for the next goods train going in his direction.

Suddenly he heard a whistle and an approaching rattle in the distance. Then the great yellow headlights of the engine flashed into view. Springing from his position by the side of the track he hurled himself at the train and managed to grab some sort of handhold on an open truck. Soon he was safely hidden among some empty coal-sacks.

So far so good, but he had no idea where the train was going. However, it was taking him away from the prison camp and that was the main thing. He fell asleep.

72

When he awoke it was nearly dawn and he decided that he would be wise to leave the train before daylight, lie-up hidden during the day, and jump another train after it was dark. Climbing over the side of the truck he balanced himself on the couplings, took a firm hold with his right hand, pushed hard with his left—and jumped.

He hit the gravel of the permanent way with his feet, took two gigantic jarring strides, turned head-over-heels and landed in a ditch at the side of the track. At first he thought he had broken every bone in his body but was relieved, on examination, to find himself without serious damage. He walked in the growing daylight to a small pool of water where he slaked his thirst and drank, as he thought, sufficient for the day. He then hid himself in a small grove of trees to pass the time until darkness fell again.

As the sun came up it grew very hot in the grove of trees but he was frightened to go in search of water. From his hiding-place he could see a Kaffir kraal and the figures of natives going about their business between the huts or in the fields. Once during the day a white man came with a gun and shot some birds in the wood where he was hiding, but he was not seen. His only other companion was an enormous vulture who watched him with a greedy eye, making ominous gurgling noises.

When at last darkness fell he came out of his hiding-place and took up a position by the railway line. Here he waited for several hours, but no trains came. Giving up in disgust he decided to walk, resolved to cover ten or fifteen miles before daylight.

Progress was slow and difficult. Every bridge on or over the line was guarded by armed men, and he was forced to make long detours across-country to avoid them.

During one of these deviations he saw fires burning in the darkness, and thinking that they marked a Kaffir kraal, he decided to go there and ask for help from the natives. Many Kaffirs were known to be pro-British, and perhaps he could get some food and possibly a pony to take him to the British lines.

As he approached he saw that this was no native village. The fires were burning in the furnace of a coal-mine. The

73

wheel which worked the winding-gear of the shaft was plainly visible against the early morning sky.

There was no time to turn back. Soon it would be morning and to be caught by daylight on the open plain would be as good as giving himself up. He must get into hiding as quickly as possible.

He hesitated for a moment only. Several British mining engineers had been allowed by the Boers to remain and continue to work their mines. Something told him that this was such a place—that he would get help here. Risking everything in one gesture he stepped up to the house and banged on the door.

"*Wie is daar?*"

His heart sank. The words were in Afrikaans.

"I want help, I've had an accident."

The man who unbolted the door and examined him by the light of a lantern now spoke in English. "I'd like to know a little more about this accident."

"I think," Winston replied, "I had better tell you the truth."

"I think you had," was the dry reply.

By an amazing stroke of luck the escaping prisoner had knocked at the door of John Howard, manager of the Transvaal Collieries. It was the only house within 20 miles that was British-owned. John Howard took him in, fed him and hid him down the mine until arrangements could be made to get him safely away.

III

No one, not even the Right Honourable Sir Winston Churchill, Knight of the Garter, Privy Councillor, Order of Merit, Companion of Honour, Fellow of the Royal Society, Member of Parliament, could now say exactly what passed through his mind in those dark hours he spent hidden in the coal-mine, fearful all the time that the Boers would find him, nervous now that his fate was in someone else's hands. For us perhaps it is a convenient moment to summarize his life until that time.

Winston Leonard Spencer Churchill was born on November 30, 1874, in Blenheim Palace, the ancestral seat of his grandfather the Duke of Marlborough. A red-haired, snub-nosed child, he spent his early years in Dublin where his father, Lord Randolph Churchill was secretary to the Duke, who had been appointed Lord-Lieutenant of Ireland.

Winston's earliest memories were of the gardens and shrubberies of the Little Lodge in Phoenix Park, of Mrs. Everest his nurse, and of his mother, upright and slim on a large horse or radiant in a ball-gown "shining like the evening star".

At the age of seven he was sent to a private school and then to Harrow where he remained until he entered Sandhurst. From his earliest days he had a deeply rooted objection to learning Latin and in consequence remained for three years under the same English master who gave him a thorough grounding in that difficult language. It is probably this teacher we have to thank for the magnificent prose which was later to do so much to inspire the British nation in time of war.

Winston Churchill entered Sandhurst in 1893. The threat of Latin was left behind and he began to learn things for which he could see the use—practical things which were directly related to the life he was to live. Now that he could see the purpose and the goal, his inheritance began to reveal itself. He passed out of Sandhurst eighth in a list of a hundred and fifty, and in the spring of 1895 he was gazetted to the 4th Hussars.

The closing years of the 19th century did not hold much promise for the ambitious soldier. Britain was at peace and as far as the young Hussar could see promotion would be slow. He applied for and obtained permission to go to Cuba where a revolution was in progress. The scheme was to attend as an official observer and so gain experience of war. To help pay his expenses he contracted with the *Daily Graphic* to act as their correspondent.

Returning to England from Cuba, where he had been under fire and become one of the very few junior officers to sport a campaign ribbon—the Spanish Order of Military Merit (1st class), he rejoined his regiment which was on its way to India.

In Bombay harbour, eager to be the first ashore, he hired a small boat and, reaching up to grasp an iron ring set in the side of the quay, he dislocated his shoulder as the boat fell on the rough sea. The injury was not serious, but it left a weakness which was to last throughout his life. It did not prevent him however from playing polo, the main occupation of the peace-time Army in India. The long afternoons when it was too hot for exercise he spent in reading. He began with Gibbon's *Decline and Fall of the Roman Empire*, worked through Macaulay's *History of England*, then his *Essays*; and so laid the foundation stones of his own later biographical and historical writings. Like so many great men Winston Churchill was a 'late developer' and in the long Indian afternoons, at the age of twenty-two, he began to make up for the learning he had refused at school.

IV

He had not been in India very long when trouble started on the North-West Frontier, where the fierce Pathans waged an intermittent war against the British. Keen as always to be in the fight, Second-Lieutenant Churchill applied for an attachment to the Bengal Lancers and with them saw action in the wild rocky blazing passes and narrow gorges of the Afghan border.

Back in Bangalore with his own regiment, Winston Churchill wrote an account of the fighting on the border. This book, *The Malakand Field Force*, gained him instant recognition as a writer.

His book finished, the young subaltern looked round him for more action. In the Sudan there was trouble with the Dervishes. An Expeditionary Force was going out under Sir Herbert, later Lord Kitchener. Winston determined to go there too.

He pulled wires and used every influence he could, and in the end he secured for himself an appointment to the 21st Lancers. Off he set in high spirits, picking up an assignment from the *Morning Post* on his way. This paper had agreed to pay him £15 per column for any despatches he might care to send them from the front line.

At Omdurman the young subaltern rode with the 21st Lancers in the last full-scale cavalry charge in modern history. Seeing the horses and riders fall to the bullets of the riflemen, he came to the conclusion that the day of cavalry as a weapon of war was over. It was at his instigation, in the First World War, that the tank was developed as an offensive weapon.

Once the Dervishes were defeated, Winston Churchill, now

more interested in journalism than in soldiering, decided to leave the army and stand for Parliament. A novel which he had written while in India had been accepted by a publisher and there was a book to be written on the recent war. His future as a writer and politician seemed more exciting, and promised to be more rewarding, than that of a soldier in a peacetime army.

The new candidate fought a by-election at Oldham, but failed to win the seat. He also finished the two volumes of *The River War*, his account of the war in the Sudan. Before this could be published the Boer War broke out, and the cavalry officer-turned-journalist dashed off to South Africa eager to be in the thick of the fighting.

Landing at Durban and hearing that Ladysmith had been besieged by the Boers, he hurried on to Eastcourt, the nearest British post to the beleaguered garrison. From there he sent despatches to his paper and accompanied military recon-naissance parties in an inadequately-armoured train known as Wilson's Deathtrap, which they drove up and down the line as near as they dared to the Boer positions.

On November 15 the armoured train containing detachments of the Dublin Fusiliers and the Durban Light Infantry, accom-panied by War Correspondent Winston Churchill, was am-bushed and derailed.

The Boers had set up artillery on the heights each side of a cutting, and under the fire of these guns and the rifles of the supporting troops the crew of the train fought for their lives.

The engine, which was in the centre, was unharmed, but the three trucks in the rear had been thrown across the track, making retreat impossible.

While the main body of soldiers held the Boers at bay the 'non-combatant-journalist' set about organizing a breakdown gang to clear the line. The engine was uncoupled and used as a battering ram. Inch by inch the obstructing trucks were barged and dragged out of the way until at last the line was clear. The engine was then loaded to overflowing with wounded and driven back to safety. Winston Churchill with the remnants of the troops who made up the reconnaissance party was taken prisoner.

While the soldiers held the Boers at bay, Winston Churchill
set about organizing a breakdown gang to clear the line

V

And here he was, huddled in this dark coal-mine in South Africa. An escaped prisoner of war, yet not a prisoner of war. A civilian in fact who had fought against the enemy. He was not at all sure that if caught again he would be treated with the same leniency.

The next three days passed slowly, in darkness, with only rats for company. There were natives working in the mine and he was frightened of discovery, but no one came into the section where he was. On the fourth day he was taken to the surface and hidden behind some packing-cases in John Howard's office. The hunt was slackening off.

In his new hiding-place there was light enough to read by, and the fugitive settled down to a volume of Stevenson's *Kidnapped*. He was reading that exciting incident when David Balfour and Alan Breck are escaping in the glens, following their every move with a very personal interest, when he was startled by the sound of rifle fire. His immediate thought was that the Boers had arrived, that John Howard and his handful of Englishmen were defending the house, or worse, were facing a firing squad. His first instinct was to dash out and discover for himself, to help or at least die with them. But he had been told to stay where he was, and he forced himself to remain in hiding. Presently he heard laughter and voices speaking Afrikaans, and he gathered that all was well. Later John Howard told him that a Boer Field Cornet had called on a routine inspection. To keep the man from searching too closely Howard had challenged him to a shooting match at bottles, had deliberately lost, and the Cornet had departed rejoicing.

That night Winston was smuggled on to a train and, hidden among some bales of wool, was carried eastward through the Transvaal into neutral Portuguese territory. There he put himself in the hands of the British Consul.

VI

Although his escape from the Boers had made Winston Churchill famous and set his feet firmly on the rungs of a political career, the excitement of the escape had left him with a desire to be in the Army again. He obtained a commission in the South African Light Horse, known as "The Cockyolly-birds" because of the plume of feathers worn at the side of their wide-brimmed hats. With them he fought through the rest of the South African War and only when peace was assured did he return to England to enter Parliament.

The rest of Winston Churchill's public life is part of England's history. First Lord of the Admiralty in the 1914–18 War, and Commander-in-Chief in the Second World War, his record of service to the nation has spanned six reigns. He became a Member of Parliament in the reign of Queen Victoria, he was a Minister under both her son Edward VII and her grandson, George V. Under her great-grandson George VI he led his country to victory in the Second World War, and under her great-great-granddaughter Elizabeth II he served as Prime Minister until his retirement in 1955.

But the end of the Boer War had not meant the last of fighting for Winston Churchill. He left political office to serve in the trenches in the First World War, and remained in London throughout the worst of the attacks by Nazi bombers in the Second. It was only by a direct order from the King that he was prevented from crossing with the troops to liberate France on D-Day, June 6, 1944. He was now far too valuable a man to risk in battle.

Of Sir Winston Churchill's statesmanship and service to the free world there is no doubt, and as an historian and biographer his fame is built on sure foundations. He is also a painter of no mean achievement. His pictures have been hung in the Royal Academy and are valued by private collectors.

Above all, it is as an inspiration to the British nation that he will be remembered. It was his fighting spirit that rallied the people of Britain in their direst need, and to him we owe perhaps more than we owe to any other man.

When he died in 1965 at the age of 90 the whole world mourned his passing and he was given a state funeral. He is buried at Bladon Churchyard, Oxfordshire, near his birthplace at Blenheim Palace.

Christopher Columbus

DISCOVERER OF A NEW WORLD

Kenneth Hopkins

I

I N the year 1492, a man might stand on any of the capes of Europe's western seaboard, looking out over leagues of tossing grey water towards the sunset and be in utter and complete ignorance of what lay beyond that barren horizon. Only rarely had any ship set her prow to the westward, where lay the island of Madeira, and (further still) the remote Azores. Beyond these, what? No man knew.

The world then was a compact set of countries bordering the North Sea and the Mediterranean—France, Italy, Spain, Turkey and Greece, Germany, Britain, and a few more. Beyond these familiar lands lay the great empires of the East, China, India, Persia; and the half-fabulous nations beyond the Nile, in unknown Africa. Men had learned that the earth was round, but no man had yet made a journey from east to west, or west to east, in a great circle to prove it. Their maps carried huge blanks, the question-marks of geography. And many countries that had no existence outside of the imagination were described and marked. An adventurer in those days had indeed a whole world before him waiting to be found.

In the middle of October, 1492, three small ships were nosing their way westward across the Atlantic: the *Santa Maria*, of 100 tons and with a crew of 52 under the Admiral of the Ocean, Christopher Columbus: and two caravels each carrying 18 men—88 men whose voyage was to add a vast continent to the maps and give a new frontier to the civilized world. Never was a commander despatched on so great an enterprise with so mean a set of companions, for the men were terrified as the hills of home fell away below the horizon behind them, and the empty ocean opened before. They expected never to see

D
81

their friends again, and one or two of them even feared that now they would sail over the edge of the world and fall into boundless space. Only Columbus stood with his eager face turned to the west, where honour and fortune lay, and never looked behind.

This Columbus was a Genoese sea-captain, now in the service of Spain. In this year, 1492, he was a man of about forty, an experienced seaman who had voyaged to the far-distant land of Thule, under the midnight sun: probably this was the country we call Iceland. His father had been a wool-comber, but the lad had never settled to follow this unexciting trade and from the age of fourteen he had been at sea, where his adventures had included, besides storms and the expected hazards of the sea, a running fight with pirates off Cape St. Vincent in which he was lucky to escape.

But although he followed the sea like any other sailor, Christopher Columbus was a very different person from the usual rough sea-captain of his time. He had made a special study of geography and astronomy, and had corresponded with learned men on these subjects. He was convinced that if the world was round it should be possible to steer west from Europe and come at last to Cathay—China, as we should say. The Venetian traveller, Marco Polo, had gone eastwards overland to China, and there he had seen the blue waters of the Pacific ocean lapping the sun-warmed shore. Columbus was convinced that those same waters, cold now and grey, washed the rocky coasts of Spain. If this were so, the gold and silks and spices of the east could be brought over in swiftly-sailing ships, instead of by the long overland routes that took a merchant and his caravan two or three years. in constant danger from robbers, famine and disease.

After his earlier voyages Columbus had settled for a time in Portugal, where he had married a Portuguese lady, and em- ployed himself in drawing maps. Portugal then was an enlightened centre of scientific curiosity, and only a few years earlier her famous explorers under the inspiration of Prince Henry the Navigator had begun to open up the sea-route round Africa. The Genoese captain decided that here, surely, would be the people to encourage the great plan that had been forming in his mind, to make westward for Cathay.

This project Columbus may first have put to his countrymen at Genoa, we are not sure; if he did, they laughed at him, as men often laugh at a new and bold idea. So Columbus came to the Court of Portugal, where a new king was reigning. This King John listened to all the Captain had to say, and made fair promises, and then treacherously sent off a ship of his own, in secret, to make the perilous journey and win the great prize. But the King of Portugal's ship returned after a few weeks, for her men had feared to launch into the unknown western ocean. When Columbus heard of this he departed from Portugal into Spain: some say because he was disgusted with the King's treachery, others say he went secretly only in order to avoid paying his debts! Whatever the reason, Portugal lost the opportunity to win a mighty empire.

II

Time moved slowly in those days, and it was two years before Columbus made any further progress with his enterprise. During those years he was the guest of the Count of Medina Celi, who encouraged him for a while with promises to fit out an expedition; and then, finding the cost much too great, wrote on his behalf to the Queen of Spain. Queen Isabella sent for Columbus, and for the next eighteen months he was kept about the Court with discussions and half-promises, but nothing definite. He was learning not to put his trust in Princes, but without finding any other patron powerful enough to equip an expedition. Then, in despair, he re-opened negotiations with the King of Portugal, and after four years he returned to Lisbon. There was more talk—always talk, talk and nothing done. Columbus sent his brother Bartholomew to England to ask aid of King Henry VII, and thence to France, but without success.

And now at last Columbus made one final effort to persuade the Spanish monarch to finance him. King Ferdinand was engaged in a war and had little time for visionaries with their demands for ships and men, but the Queen at last wrung from him a reluctant consent, and articles of agreement were drawn up under which Columbus undertook to discover unknown lands and annex them for the crown of Spain; and the King appointed him viceroy and governor-general over all such lands, with the title of Admiral; and Columbus should have for him-self one-tenth of all pearls, precious stones, gold, silver, spices and merchandise produced by his discoveries. Columbus also undertook to pay one-eighth of the cost of the expedition.

Things now went quickly forward. At the little port of Palos de Moguer, looking south-west towards the undiscovered coasts of Brazil, the new Admiral began supervising the gathering of his ships and men. The town at that time owed tribute to the King, and it was commanded to pay this by providing and fitting out two caravels—big, open boats with lateen (that is, triangular) sails, such as are commonly seen in the eastern Mediterranean. In addition, a third, larger vessel was to be fitted for Columbus as flagship. The Admiral's orders were clear and precise as they were read publicly in the church of St. George the morning after Columbus arrived, and at first the townsfolk hastened to put them into practice. But then the nature of Columbus's enterprise was revealed to them, and they began to murmur and to draw back. "We shall never see our ships or our sons again," they cried.

But there were two brothers in the town, ship owners and men of influence, named Martin and Yanez Pinzon, both skilled sea-captains, and they engaged to go with Columbus and com-mand the two vessels under him. This shamed the townspeople, and at last the ships were equipped and the crews assembled, although only after a good deal of obstruction from one of the wealthiest men in the town, whose ship, the *Pinta*, had been requisitioned for the little fleet.

By the beginning of August, 1492, the ships were ready: the *Santa Maria*, which had been built specially for Columbus, as his flagship; the *Pinta*, commanded by Martin Pinzon; and the *Nina*, commanded by Yanez Pinzon. On Friday, August 3, 'half an hour before sunrise' (as Columbus tells us) the three ships stood away from Palos, and steered for the Canary Islands, the last land (with the Azores) fronting the unknown.

III

That triumphant voyage began gloomily enough, and its final success undoubtedly was due to the resolution of one man alone, the Admiral of the Ocean. The men were afraid, and they looked for disaster in every wave and every cloud as the last land disappeared behind them. After a few days they saw the broken mast of a big ship drifting in the water, weed-covered and rotten: "That is what happens to ships that enter these unknown seas," they cried. Then the *Pinta*'s rudder came adrift and the seamen said, "Surely now we must turn back!" but her captain made a skilful repair and the fleet sailed on. Columbus began to keep two records of the distance travelled, one the true distance and one, apparently much shorter, to deceive the men; for their fears increased with every league they advanced. When they met an adverse wind they cried, "We shall never reach land!" and when the favourable trade winds drove them forward they cried, "We shall never be able to return!" And then, after seven weeks at sea they began to meet flights of birds—land birds. The men began to rejoice, and everyone strained his eyes, seeking land. For the King had promised a great reward to the first man to sight the shores of Cathay.

Cathay: for Columbus and the King were both certain that this was the land to which the fleet would come; so certain that the King had written, and Columbus carried, letters to the Grand Khan, or Emperor, of the empire of the East.

The birds passed; the empty ocean stretched before them.

And now ugly murmurs arose among the crew, that Columbus was sailing to death. They could never return, the men told one another, but they must sail on for ever in a barren waste of waters until their provisions failed, and the ships were engulfed in some storm, or rotted away. And the Admiral reasoned with them, and told them to be of good heart, for their voyage would prosper yet and bring them glory and riches. Then, when the crews were at their lowest ebb of spirits, there came the cry, "Land ho!" and a long, purple ridge of hills was seen rising from the western sea, so that Columbus and all his men fell on their knees and offered thanks to God. But as they sailed on the land receded, and began to break up before them: it was a bank of clouds!

By October 1, they had travelled 707 leagues, that is, more than 2000 miles; but Columbus had told the crew it was less than 600 leagues. A few days later the men again saw land, and again it vanished before them as they approached. Then the men became openly mutinous, and it is said that they had

85

Christopher Columbus believed he had reached
a southern shore of Cathay

begun to plot to turn the ships about and sail for home, having deposed their commander; but now at last they found something none could dispute—the branch of a tree, with berries on it, newly broken and floating in the water. There were many birds now, flying about the ships; and then one of the seamen picked up a carved staff floating alongside—a staff strangely carved, in a manner unknown to them. They were coming not only to land, but to men . . . That night, the Admiral saw a light a great way off, brightly shining.

On Friday morning, October 12, Christopher Columbus and his men made their landfall, coming up to the level shores of a long, low island covered with forest to the water's edge. As the ships stood in, a crowd of people came running on to the beach, calling and gesticulating. They were brown-skinned and naked, and they lifted their hands in astonishment at the tall, white-sailed ships, riding in like swans from the sunrise.

The ships entered a sheltered bay, and cast anchor. Columbus ordered the boats to be manned, and dressed himself in his robes of scarlet, and carried in his hand the embroidered standard of Spain; the other captains also entered their boats carrying banners, and the company rowed ashore, whereupon the natives ran into the woods and hid. Then Columbus, with his captains and officers about him, stood on a little rise above the beach and gave thanks for their safe landfall after so long at sea. He then drew his sword, and set up the royal standards, and took possession of the land in the name of his King, naming it San Salvador.

Slowly, shyly, the natives came down to the shore again, and stood looking at these white-faced, bearded men in bright clothes and shining armour; and the Spaniards looked with equal wonder on the bare brown bodies of these dwellers in the western islands. They called them 'Indians', for Columbus believed he had reached a southern shore of Cathay, and at that time the general name 'India' was used for all the Asian lands. From this first mistake we have still the name, West Indies, for the islands off the mainland of central America. "The islanders were friendly and gentle," we are told by the American historian, Washington Irving. "Their only arms were lances, hardened at the end by fire, or pointed with a flint, or the teeth or bone of a fish. There was no iron to be seen, nor did they appear acquainted with its properties; for, when a drawn sword was presented to them, they unguardedly took it by the edge."

The explorers distributed beads and bells and other trifles among the natives and tried to make it understood that they came in peace and friendship, and the natives offered parrots and cotton and gold—but the gold they appeared to possess only in small quantities, so that Columbus concluded that in this island the precious metal was rare, and he asked by signs where greater quantities of it might be found. The natives pointed to the southward, and said that there lay a land with a great king who dined off plates and vessels of solid gold. This news convinced Columbus that the ships had reached the outskirts of Cathay, for Marco Polo had written that off the shore lay many small islands, subject to the Grand Khan.

IV

When the ships had taken in fruits and water, they sailed on, and island after island rose out of the sea in their path, for they were now among the great string of islands we call the Bahamas, like a necklace flung across the entrance to the Caribbean Sea. Columbus wrote in his journal as the men filled their casks with clear water from a large island which is now called Exuma: "Here are large lakes and the groves of them are marvellous, and here and in all the island every thing is green as in April in Andalusia. The singing of the birds is such, that it seems as if one would never desire to depart hence. There are flocks of parrots which obscure the sun, and other birds, large and small, of so many kinds all different from ours, that it is wonderful; and beside, there are trees of a thousand species, each having its particular fruit and all of marvellous flavour, so that I am in greatest trouble in the world not to know them, for I am very certain that they are each of great value. I shall bring home some of them as specimens, and also some of the herbs."

A very few days' cruising, however, convinced Columbus that these islands were not close to the mainland of Cathay, and he determined to press on, ever westwards. The men were satisfied with what they had already accomplished, and wished now to return in triumph to Spain, but the Admiral refused, saying that their mission was to sail to Cathay, and he would do it. For two months he sailed on among the islands, discovering Cuba (which is so large that he became convinced it was the mainland) and another large island which he called Hispaniola. Then one morning the *Pinta* was found to be missing, gone without trace, and Columbus suspected that she might have steered for Spain; but he could do nothing to overtake her, for she was the swiftest ship in the fleet, and indeed a day or two after her departure a heavier blow befell the Admiral.

On Christmas Eve the two ships were sailing in very calm weather along the coast of Hispaniola and all the crew of the *Santa Maria* were asleep except for one young boy at the helm. This was contrary to the Admiral's direct order, but the ship's watch had neglected their duty. Unnoticed by the lad at the wheel, the ship had gone into a swift current making towards the shore, and suddenly, with a sickening crash, she drove into a sand-bank. All was confusion in the darkness as the Admiral leaped on to the deck and seized the useless wheel. She heeled in the rushing water, but she never responded to the helm, and the soft, treacherous sand took a grip upon her and would not let go, though the little *Nina* came as close as she could with ropes to tow her off. When morning came there was the *Santa Maria* in the death grip of the sands, with the breakers pounding her.

The ship could not be saved, but the people of the island came with tears of sympathy and offered help and shelter, and the Admiral moved out of the ship all the goods and a quantity of treasure, and all the crew were brought to the shore. Now only the *Nina* remained, an open caravel whose normal accommodation was for a crew of 18 men; a vessel not much bigger than a fishing smack such as may be seen in any small English port. But she was 3000 miles from home, in strange seas, with the worst of winter before her, and 70 men to sail in her, and all the cargo of gold and wonders to carry.

V

Columbus called his men together and he made a plan. Many of the seamen had thought these islands a paradise, after the desperate voyage from Spain, and some of them were willing to wait here until the Admiral could go back to Spain and then return. They built a stockade on a hill and set up a trading post to collect gold from the natives, and Columbus left them his stocks of beads and bells and other trifles, and he called the place La Navidad. The flag of Spain waved over the stockade, and so leaving the little colony, almost certainly the first white settlers in America, Columbus embarked in the *Nina* and sailed away, on January 4, 1493. Two days later, by chance, he fell in with the *Pinta*, and although he felt a deep distrust of her commander, Martin Pinzon, for his desertion, he kept this to himself so that the ships could start on the perilous return journey together. Pinzon had been trading among the islands, trying to make a cargo of gold for himself (for Columbus had decreed that all gold was to be the property of the Crown) but now, after taking in wood and water for the long voyage, the two ships began to beat out against the trade wind into the open sea. The south Atlantic in January is a cruel, relentless sea, but the Admiral set his course for Spain and the two little ships plunged and rocked and dipped into the green waves, and held doggedly on. For six weeks they sailed against contrary winds, or in a treacherous calm which hindered their progress so that they began to run short of supplies. Then, towards the end of February a terrible storm sprang up and raged for days, separating the ships and all but overwhelming them, so that Columbus and his men could do nothing as the ship drove under bare poles, and the light of the day never shone under the racing, rain-heavy clouds; and they prayed together, and made a vow to God that if he brought them to safety they would make a pilgrimage in his name. The storm never slackened, and the ship raced on, her decks awash, her people cold and famished; but she came safely to the island of St. Mary's, in the Azores, and dropped anchor at last in the lee of the land. This was a precarious safety, however, for St. Mary's was a possession of the Crown of Portugal, a power unfriendly to Spain.

The Governor arrested the first party of men ashore, and would not release them, despite protests from Columbus. He refused to acknowledge the Admiral's commission, and almost suggested that the ship was a pirate. For several days it seemed as if the expedition must lose its triumph, and its people lie for ever in a Portuguese jail, but at last the Governor was persuaded of Columbus's integrity, and of the great discoveries he had made; and he let them go. A week later the little ship sighted the coast of Portugal, still storm-tossed and in danger as she coasted the rocky shores. On March 4 she entered the Tagus, and rested at last.

VI

Columbus was kindly received by the King, and loaded with honours. But he distrusted King John, and he made his excuses, and begged to be allowed to go on to his own master, the King of Spain, and after a week or so the King reluctantly allowed him to go, and the *Nina* ran down the coast and came again at last to Palos, from which she had sailed those many months ago. That same evening the storm-shattered *Pinta* came limping in, and the joy of the townspeople was complete; but Martin Pinzon, conscious of the dishonour he had brought upon himself by his desertion of Columbus, and sick, kept his cabin until after the Admiral had departed to meet the King; and a little later, he died.

Now in his triumph Columbus was honoured and fêted at the Spanish court and new and splendid titles were heaped upon him, and new expeditions planned. Three other great voyages he made to the Americas, and he experienced in his later years the fickleness of Kings' favour, for like many princes Ferdinand soon forgot the service done and found new favourites to honour. In his last years, Columbus knew the bitterness of his service to Spain, for he saw younger men preferred and great enterprises attempted for which he was not called upon to serve or advise. Yet in all those years, from 1493 when he returned in triumph to Spain, until 1506 when he died at Valladolid, he never ceased to work to establish for Spain a rich and extensive empire in the new lands of the west; and he died still in the belief that somewhere just below that glittering horizon lay the splendours of Cathay.

We leave him in his moment of greatest triumph, displaying before the King and Queen of Spain the gold, the spices, and the tall, brown-skinned people he had brought from the western seas, from what was called in wonder, the New World.

Captain James Cook

NAVIGATOR OF THE SOUTHERN SEAS

Aubrey de Selincourt

I

IF you look at any map or chart drawn a few centuries ago, you will notice here and there, off stretches of coast or in the lonely spaces of sea, vivid little pictures of sea-monsters, great serpents with uplifted heads, or huge fish with manes like lions, tails curved high above the waves and nostrils spouting foam. Mariners in those days brought back strange stories. They had seen much, and fancied more during their long watches amid the silence of the sea. No seaman could go to sea on a long voyage without the chance, and the hope, of finding some unknown land or island, inhabited by strange creatures and barbarous men; and even as recently as 200 years ago geographers thought that far southward in the Pacific Ocean there lay an undiscovered continent—a fine, rich country, it well might be, and good for adventurous men to settle in and make their fortunes.

Naturally, the British would have liked to be the first to find this golden continent, and it so happened that in the year 1768 the British Admiralty sent off their finest seaman in a small sailing vessel, and with secret instructions in a sealed envelope, to look for it. That seaman was James Cook, and his ship was the famous *Endeavour*. Cook did not find the continent, because it does not exist, but in the course of looking for it, he found a lot of other things, and did his country service not less glorious, and perhaps even more lasting, than the great Nelson himself, his younger contemporary.

James Cook, the son of a farm labourer, was born in Yorkshire, at Marton in Cleveland on October 27, 1728. He left school at the age of thirteen and worked for eighteen months as a grocer's boy at Staithes, a fishing village near Whitby. The

92

grocery trade was not to his taste; more interesting than packets of rice and pounds of butter were the fishermen's boats in the little haven and the collier brigs which used the port of Whitby. He listened to sea talk whenever he could, and that was often, and it was not long before he had a mind to go to sea himself.

When Cook had a mind to anything, he invariably did it; for that is the sort of boy—and man—he was. When he was fourteen he got himself apprenticed to a firm of coal-shippers, in the coastal trade, and his life's work had begun.

Cook learned the hard way—the only way for a seaman; and he learned to handle ships in shallow coastal waters, where more dangers are to be met and more skill is required than in the open ocean a thousand miles from land. He quickly rose in his profession, and at the age of twenty-seven he was offered the command of a collier. To his employers' surprise he refused the command, and started all over again as an 'able-bodied seaman' in the Navy. Asked why, he smiled his sardonic smile and said he 'had a mind that way'.

In point of fact, Cook knew perfectly well what he was doing, and already foresaw the future much more clearly than the owners of the shipping firm with whom he had learned his trade. All the time he had been serving them, he had been working hard to perfect himself in the science of navigation, and by the time he volunteered for the Navy he knew as much about that tricky and mysterious art as anyone in His Majesty's fleet. He soon rose to the position of Master—the Warrant Officer, that is, who in those days was responsible for navigating the ship and determining her position on the sea.

His first chance to prove himself came in 1757, when his ship H.M.S. *Pembroke* was sent to the St. Lawrence River to take part in the operations against the French in Canada. Here in the following year, he assisted at the landing of General Wolfe's troops at Quebec. But that was routine work merely; his real service was of a different kind, and called for special abilities which Cook possessed in a higher degree than anybody else in the navy of his day. This was *marine surveying*. It does not sound very exciting, but if one imagines for a moment the peril and loss of life for men in ships on unknown and rock-bound coasts, or in river estuaries encumbered with hidden shoals and swept by fierce tides, when they have no adequate chart to guide them, it is at least easy to see that such work is important. Cook, with the simple means at his disposal, charted accurately the estuary of the St. Lawrence, and also on a subsequent voyage the entire coastline of Newfoundland. His charts of Newfoundland waters were so thorough and accurate that they began to be superseded only some thirty years ago. Nobody had taught Cook the complicated mathematical calculations which such work called for. He had had almost no formal education. He was, from the beginning, his own teacher.

III

Cook was now just on forty years old—a tough man, pickled by salt and sea-wind, over six feet tall, with a touch of sternness in the keen eyes under their jutting brows. He was a man to trust—and also to fear, by anyone who failed in his duty. He had been married for six years, and to the end of her life his wife, Elizabeth, took him as her standard in all things of right and wrong. "Mr. Cook," she used to say, "would never have done such a thing"; or, "That is how Mr. Cook would have behaved." She was to have many years of loneliness while her husband was at sea; but she bore them bravely, and brought up her children to honour and love their father, as she did herself.

It was at this time that the British Government decided to send a ship on a special mission into the Southern Ocean. The objects were to look for the Great Continent, to annex for Britain any other undiscovered lands or islands that might be met with, and to make certain important astronomical observations. Cook was chosen to command the expedition, and he set sail from Plymouth on August 25, 1758.

His ship, *Endeavour*, was quite small, of less than 400 tons. She was a brig, built a few years before at Whitby for the coal-carrying trade. Cook was offered other ships, ships from the Navy, and an East Indiaman; but he would have none but his collier brig. He *knew* the Whitby colliers, and he knew that one of them would serve his purpose best.

Before Cook's time one of the worst dangers of the sea was scurvy, that horrible disease which rotted a man's bones, turned his gums to jelly so that his teeth fell out, and then killed him. It was assumed that in any voyage of a year or more a half to three quarters of a ship's company would die of it. Cook, however, had a mind to prevent this disease, and as soon as *Endeavour* began to make her leisurely way southward down the Atlantic, he set about his task. The method was simple : scurvy is caused by the lack of vitamins to be found in fresh food, especially in vegetables and meat, and Cook ensured a supply of these whenever possible. At other times he forced his men, by threat of the lash, to eat pickled cabbage with their salt provisions. The men grumbled, but obeyed : indeed they could not help obeying, for Cook came to their mess at meal times, and glared at them till they swallowed it. Later, they were grateful ; for throughout the three years' voyage not a single man fell sick of the dreaded disease.

Endeavour rounded the Horn and struck north-westward into the Pacific. Eight months after leaving home she anchored at Tahiti, where the astronomers did their work, and then sailed westward into uncharted seas. Cook's next task was to chart (and name) the Society Islands, after which he continued to the westward until he fell in with the north island of New Zealand. The explorer Tasman, a century before, had found this land, and had supposed it to be a promontory of the Great Southern Continent. Cook proved it was not ; he sailed round, and charted, both islands—the first man ever to do so. Then he sailed west again, looking for Australia.

IV

The western half of Australia was already known, but the eastern half had never been explored, and it was generally believed that Australia and New Guinea formed a continuous mass of land. Once again Cook was to put the geographers right.

Twice during the voyage up the eastern coast of Australia the *Endeavour* was nearly lost. Threading her way amongst the islands and coral-heads inside the Great Barrier Reef, with a leadsman sounding day and night, suddenly, one moonlit night, a few seconds after the leadsman had called a depth of 17 fathoms, she ran hard aground. It was high water, and as the tide ebbed, the vessel heeled on her side. She was leaking badly. Guns, stores, all heavy gear that could possibly be spared, were thrown overboard to lighten the ship. The leak gained on the pumps. Every man worked like mad to haul her off the reef, not knowing whether, once she was off, she would float or sink. Happily, she floated; a sail was drawn under the damaged part of her bows, and she limped on, looking for somewhere to put into and effect repairs. The second occasion was even more alarming. They were just outside the Reef, when the wind dropped suddenly to a calm. There was a heavy swell, setting on to the reef, and with every wave *Endeavour* was swept nearer to it. Nothing could be done. It was too deep to anchor. Soon the ship was within the length of a single wave from the jagged coral. Every man aboard was certain that another minute would see the end of them—yet Green, the astronomer, calmly continued to take the lunar observation upon which he was engaged. Then, by luck, the ship got into an outward stream of tide from a gap in the reef. This gave her a breathing space and a few minutes later a breeze sprang up, and she was saved.

Having reached the northern limit of the coast *Endeavour* turned westward again, sailed through Torres Strait and made her slow way home round the Cape of Good Hope and up the Atlantic. Cook had added New Zealand to the map, half of the vast Australian continent, and countless islands in the Pacific. But he had not yet disproved the existence of the Great Southern Continent.

This, however, he was very soon to do; for after only a year at home with his wife in their modest house at Mile End, he was sent off on a second voyage. The Navy Board had no hesitation in choosing him for the task, as he had already proved himself by far the greatest of living navigators and explorers. This time he had two ships under his command, *Resolution*, in which he sailed himself, and *Adventure*, under the command of Captain Furneaux. His orders were to sail south as far as he could—till the Antarctic ice stopped him—and then to turn eastward and circumnavigate the globe. Thus, if he kept always as far south as the ice allowed, he would be bound, sooner or later, to fall in with the Southern Continent—if it existed.

The orders were carried out, and *Resolution* often in fierce gales and fog, and through drifting icebergs, sailed her perilous course around the world, passing right over the areas in which Dalrymple and other geographers had hopefully sketched-in the fancied outlines of the Terra Australis Incognita, as they named

96

it. But the Great Southern Continent was not only unknown, it was non-existent. Less exciting, perhaps, to read about, this second voyage was a harder, more dangerous and more important one even than the first. It fixed once and for all the southern limit of the habitable world. Incidentally, in the course of it Cook penetrated further south (70° 10′) than any man had been before.

V

On his return to England Cook was presented to King George III and received his captain's commission. He was appointed Captain of Greenwich Hospital, with a comfortable salary and an official residence. He might, had he wished, have lived the rest of his life in leisured ease, enjoying his fame. However—he had no mind that way.

The naval authorities were already planning a new voyage of discovery: this time, it was to find out if there was a north-west passage, round the unknown northern coast of Canada, from Europe to Asia. Cook, who, meanwhile, had been elected a Fellow of the Royal Society, was invited to dinner by Lord Sandwich and other distinguished officials of the Board of Admiralty in order to give his advice both on the conduct of the new voyage and on who should be asked to command it. Cook himself was by the far the most brilliant living seaman and far better qualified than anybody else for the work of discovery; but the authorities, having appointed him to the post at Greenwich Hospital, were unwilling to ask him to accept this further task, thinking, quite rightly, that he had already done enough to earn his rest. Cook, however, thought otherwise. Before dinner was over he rose to his feet. "Gentlemen," he said, "I will myself undertake this work, if you are willing to entrust it to me."

So once again Elizabeth was to be left alone. She was to say another good-bye to her husband, this time for ever.

In July, 1776, Cook sailed from Plymouth in his old ship *Resolution*, and was joined at the Cape the following November by Captain Clerke in the *Discovery*, and the two ships, from then on, sailed in company. They went first to New Zealand, then northward and eastward up through the Pacific to Tahiti. How did ships in those distant days find their way over the vast

97

spaces of ocean? For centuries past seamen had been able to find their latitude (that is, how far north or south of the Equator they were) by taking the altitude of the sun with a quadrant; but they had no means of exactly determining their longitude. To reach, say, some previously known island, it was necessary to get the ship on the right latitude and then sail along it until the island appeared. However, just before Cook's second voyage a man named Harrison had perfected a time-keeper (or chronometer) by means of which longitude could be accurately reckoned. Cook had one of these chronometers with him both on his second and third voyages. It proved a triumphant success, and marked the beginning of modern scientific navigation.

As the ships made their way north-eastward towards the American coast, many groups of islands in that island-studded ocean were discovered and charted by Cook, most notably the Hawaiian group. Then, falling in with the coast somewhere between San Francisco and Vancouver, Cook proceeded to follow it northward, round the Alaskan peninsula and into Bering Strait. He was able to chart the coastline on both sides of the approaches to Bering Strait, and, after exploring various deep inlets, to satisfy himself almost completely that there was no practicable passage through to the Atlantic. Winter was now upon him, so he sailed south again to Hawaii, meaning to return northwards the following spring and complete his work.

VI

After a couple of months spent in charting the island (Cook was nothing if not thorough), the two ships brought up in Kealakekua Bay, and the crews set about the usual business of filling up with wood, water and provisions. The natives were very friendly and anxious to please. Cook had a way with savages: he was prepared, as indeed he had to be, to use force if ever they threatened the lives of his own men, but it was seldom that he actually did so. He knew that to treat them with courtesy was not only the most humane but also the safest way. He rarely had trouble, except occasionally with the Maoris of New Zealand, who were an awkward lot, and cannibals at that. Here at Hawaii the brown-skinned islanders flocked to the ships with pigs and fruits and vegetables to give or to barter, and as day succeeded day their respect for the

White Chief grew and grew, until it began to seem that they looked upon him as something more than human. When he walked ashore men and women would fall on the ground as he passed, crying *"Orono! Orono!"* as if he were their own great King come alive again from the past to visit and protect them.

Cook shrugged his shoulders and smiled to himself a little grimly—but it was not for him to disillusion the islanders. For his men's sake he wanted their friendship and respect. For weeks the two ships were loaded with presents of food, far more than was needed, until the King of the islanders, a fine fat savage called Terreoboo, began to get anxious that supplies for his own people would run short.

Then Cook decided to sail, and Terreoboo, in spite of his reverence for the White Man was not sorry to say good-bye. Unfortunately, however, the ships had not been two days at sea when a violent gale struck them, one of *Resolution*'s masts was sprung, and they were forced to put back again.

This time they found the bay deserted. Not a single native canoe came to meet them. It was very odd—and a little sinister. Parties of men went ashore for the work of repairing the sprung mast; the islanders they met were cool, but not, it seemed, actually hostile. Then, one day, the *Discovery*'s cutter was stolen. The Hawaiians, like all the Pacific islanders, were inveterate thieves, but this theft was a serious one and could not be overlooked. Cook at once determined to take steps for the cutter's recovery. An officer entering his cabin found him loading his double-barrelled gun.

Early in the morning he stationed a cordon of boats across the mouth of the bay, to prevent any native canoes from escaping, and himself with a party of nine marines under their officer, Lieutenant Phillips made for the shore. Two other launches accompanied him, to cover his landing. He went with Phillips straight to the hut where Terreoboo was living; the marines were drawn up, ready for trouble, close to the water's edge.

Entering the hut he asked Terreoboo and his two sons to come back with him on board *Resolution*, intending to keep them as hostages until the stolen cutter was returned. Terreoboo at once consented; but as soon as he got to his feet,

Cook called to the boat-crews to cease firing
and pull into the beach

the women in the hut raised an outcry, clutched at his hands and clothes and begged him not to go.

Phillips glanced at his commander, but Cook shook his head. Nothing could be done without violence—and violence would be dangerous. The two men left the hut and walked slowly towards the beach, some forty paces distant, through a crowd of islanders which had collected as if from nowhere.

Suddenly from the bay a shot rang out, and with mysterious swiftness the news spread that an island chieftain had been killed by the white men. A murmur like a rising wind ran through the crowd. A native strode up to Cook and shook his fist in his face. All the islanders were putting on their war-mats. The native continued to threaten Cook, and Cook discharged one barrel of his gun at him. It was loaded with small shot, and did no serious harm. Then suddenly there was a rush for the marines who were lining the beach. Four of them were killed. The boat-crews off shore fired a volley. Cook was still facing the now furious mob of savages; then he turned, and called to the boat-crews to cease firing and pull in to the beach. That movement was his undoing. An islander, immediately Cook turned away, struck him on the head with a club; another stabbed him in the back. He fell forward into the water, and a dozen of the savages flung themselves upon his body, dragged it up the beach and hacked it to pieces.

Next day the two ships sailed, but without their great commander. Cook's work was unfinished; but he had done more in his 11 years of exploring than any other man before him. His fame before he died had spread over the world. It is good to remember that during his last voyage the governments of both France and America, who were then at war with England, had given orders to their ships that, if they met *Resolution* or *Discovery* on the high seas, they were not to molest them but to give them any assistance of which they might be in need.

Pierre and Marie Curie

DISCOVERERS OF RADIUM

Eileen Bigland

I

IN a miserable little glassed-in shed (rather like a miniature greenhouse) attached to the ground floor of the School of Chemistry and Physics in the Rue Lhomond, Paris, the French scientist Pierre Curie and his Polish wife Marie had been conducting a series of highly complicated experiments for six long years. Ever since Röntgen's discovery of X-rays scientists had been trying to determine if such rays were given out by fluorescent bodies under the action of light. Becquerel had found out that a rare metal, uranium, gave out the same sort of rays *spontaneously*, without being exposed to light, and in their researches the Curies had progressed still further—they had discovered that crude pitch-blende ore contained an entirely new and unknown element, which we now call radium.

But though their work went on ceaselessly, and under appalling conditions, they could not manage to isolate this element and, on an evening in 1902, they locked up their shack about six o'clock and returned to their little house in the Boulevard Kellermann where their small daughter Irène and Pierre's old father awaited them. Both the young Curies were exhausted by their labours and more than a little disconsolate. Would their efforts never be crowned with success, they wondered, would this mysterious element always elude them?

After their simple supper Marie went upstairs to sit with Irène until the child fell asleep; then she rejoined her husband in the living-room. For some strange reason she felt restless. "Pierre," she said nervously, "suppose we go down to the Rue Lhomond for a moment?"

As always, Pierre needed no second bidding to return to his beloved laboratory. Arm in arm the two sauntered through the

102

crowded streets, and as Pierre drew out his key Marie clutched at his arm excitedly. "Don't light the lamps," she whispered. "I have a feeling . . . Do you remember the day you said to me: 'I should like the element we have christened radium to have a beautiful colour'?" Then as the door creaked back on its rusty hinges she added breathlessly, "Look, Pierre, look!" From the row of test-tubes in their shelves on the wall came a bluish gleam. They glimmered like so many little glow-worms in the inky darkness of the shed. . . .

The Curies' heroic labour was ended. They had isolated radium.

II

The question has often been asked and has never been answered satisfactorily: If Marie Curie had never met or married Pierre Curie, would she have discovered radium by herself? She assuredly had the genius to do so, but perhaps if she had not had the love and inspiration of her equally gifted husband she would not have been able to accomplish her gruelling task. Certainly her discovery would have been greatly delayed, and when reading her many books and papers on the subject we find that she always wrote of 'our' work.

The youngest daughter of a Polish professor, Marya Sklodovska was born in Warsaw in 1867. Even in her 'teens she dreamed of science as a career but Polish students (especially girls) were frowned upon by the Russian Tsarist authorities who ruled the country, and she had to become a governess. Not until she was nearly twenty-four years old did she save enough money to come to Paris, where she stayed with her elder sister Bronya and her doctor husband and registered as a student at the famous Sorbonne University. For the next four years she studied frantically, living in the greatest poverty on a diet which barely sustained her—but she not only gained her Master's degree in Physics but was asked to make a study of the magnetic properties of various steels. A professor anxious to help this brilliant student, said: "I know a scientist of great merit, Pierre Curie, head of the Physics and Chemistry laboratory. Perhaps he might have a room available for you to work in."

Of course Marie knew the name; indeed she regarded Pierre

"Look, Pierre, look!" From the row of test-tubes came a bluish
gleam—they glimmered like so many little glow-worms

with awe because of the wonderful work he had done, first with the building of the ultra-sensitive 'Curie scale', and then with the research on magnetism which led to his discovery of a fundamental law, 'Curie's law'. And when they met at the house of the professor, both she and Pierre were immediately conscious of an overwhelming mutual attraction which had nothing to do with science.

They were married on July 26, 1895, and then began the unique partnership which was to be broken so tragically almost 11 years later.

III

It was after the birth of Irène in 1896 that Marie determined to make Becquerel's mysterious 'spontaneous rays' the subject of her doctor's thesis, and it was Pierre who wrested permission for her to use the shed from his reluctant director. It was a wretched place, icy cold in winter, burning hot in summer, and atrociously damp all the year round but the Curies did not care. From some Bohemian mines they requested several hundredweight of the residue of pitch-blende after uranium salts had been extracted from it, and the mine-owners promptly sent them the present of a ton, adding they must be lunatics to want the stuff! They stored the sacks in the courtyard and thereafter worked like navvies, shovelling the ore, staggering around with huge jars of the liquid they made from it, stirring the boiling stuff in a smelting basin.

By 1900 they were able to draw up a full report on 'radio-active substances', but while this caused immense interest among scientists both in Europe and America, Pierre's own country of France was remarkably backward in acknowledging their amazing contribution to scientific research.

With their actual isolation of radium, however, they leapt into fame. Wonderful radium! There seemed nothing the white crystals could not do. Radium gave off heat spontaneously. Its rays were so intense that they penetrated every substance except a thick sheet of lead. If kept in cottonwool radium reduced it to powder; if in test-tubes it stained the glass violet. It made the air around it a conductor of electricity. But it was also highly dangerous because it was as contagious as a disease. "The various objects used in a chemical laboratory, and those

105

which serve for experiments in physics, all become radio-active in a short time and act upon photographic plates through black paper. Dust, the air of the room, and one's clothes, all become radio-active," as the Curies stated in their note-books.

Not that the Curies cared about danger. In order to prove the doctors' contention that radium could cause grave injury when a person's skin was directly exposed to it, Pierre deliberately exposed his arm to the action of radium and was delighted when a lesion appeared. At the same time he realized that if radium was used *indirectly* it might help in cancer cases. We know now, of course, how many thousands of cancer sufferers it has helped.

The Curies lent their first precious gramme of radium to aid various experiments on both human beings and animals, and by 1904 they had published no fewer than 32 pamphlets about its properties. But despite their spreading fame the couple had many personal worries. Marie's beloved father died in far away Poland; Pierre began to suffer agonizing shooting pains in both legs; they were in chronic financial difficulties since the French authorities still refused to reward Pierre with the Professor's Chair which was his due. Worn out as they were by years of overwork, they found these things hard to bear, but gradually they overcame their depression and forced themselves to struggle on, and in June, 1903, Marie was accorded the title of Doctor of Science for her thesis on *Researches on Radio-active Substances.*

IV

Now foreign honours came thick and fast. In November the Curies were awarded the Davy Medal of the Royal Society of London, and a little later they were informed that "the Nobel Prize in Physics for the current year was awarded half to Henri Becquerel and half to M. and Mme Curie for their discoveries in radio-activity." Their share amounted to 70,000 gold francs, which they promptly paid into the bank together with 25,000 francs, Marie's half of the Osiris prize jointly awarded to Edouard Branley and herself. Characteristically the Curies spent a considerable amount of this money on their needy relatives and friends, and although they did instal a bath and re-paper one small bedroom in their home, there is no record in Marie's meticulously kept account books of any expenditure on new clothes—they did not even think of such frivolities.

Pierre was now able to give up his lecture post and devote himself entirely to experiments, but Marie insisted upon keeping on a teaching job she had at Sèvres. Only once, when he received a letter from America asking for information about radium, did Pierre suggest that they might patent their discovery and so assure themselves of rights over the production of radium throughout the world. Marie stared at him in amazement. "It is impossible. It is contrary to the scientific spirit." He smiled at her. "I think so too—but our life is hard, and it threatens to be hard for ever. Besides," he laughed, "we could build a fine laboratory, you know." For a minute or two they looked at each other; then simultaneously they agreed that to make any money out of something which was going to be of incalculable benefit to humanity in general was an impossible idea, and neither of them ever mentioned the subject again.

V

So the radium industry grew and expanded and the Curies laboured on with their experiments, though certainly their circumstances were a shade easier than in former days. In 1904 the University of Paris created a Chair of Physics for Pierre—but rather spoilt this gracious act by refusing to build a proper laboratory to go with it. Grudgingly they at last agreed to erect two rooms in the Rue Cuvier with the proviso that the cost of all installations be deducted from his yearly appropriation! Still, the rooms were a vast improvement on the shed, where they had latterly found it almost impossible to work owing to the presence of eager sightseers anxious to catch a glimpse of the famous scientists in their curious lair.

Invitations to luncheons, dinners, receptions, or to lecture to some learned Society kept pouring in, and while Pierre and Marie possessed generous natures and were only too glad to interest outsiders in radium, they were not a socially-minded pair and found these events extremely irksome. At one lecture, however, when they visited Stockholm in the summer of 1905, Pierre sounded a note of warning which must find an echo in our minds today. After pointing out the dangers of radium falling into criminal hands he wondered if humanity was ripe enough to gain anything by solving the secrets of nature. "The example of Nobel's discoveries is characteristic," he added. "Powerful explosives have permitted men to perform admirable work. They are also a terrible means of destruction in the hands of the great criminals who lead the peoples towards war."

Meanwhile, the Curies had had a second daughter, Eve, in December, 1904, and naturally her arrival meant much more work for Marie who had to run her home with the aid of a small maid. Moreover, she did not feel well herself and worried constantly about Pierre's leg pains which were growing steadily worse. "Pierre," she said one day, "if one of us disappeared ... the other should not survive ... we can't exist without each other, can we?" But Pierre shook his head. "A scientist has no right to forget her mission," he said sternly. "Whatever happens, even if one has to go on like a body without a soul, one must work just the same."

VI

In April, 1906, Marie remembered those words. She and Pierre had been striving to dose radium with precision by the amount of emanations it gave off, and they decided to spend the Easter break at a little house they had rented at St. Rémy-les-Chevreuse. On Easter Monday the weather turned very hot, and while Pierre la dozing in the meadow Irène chased butter-flies with her little green net and Marie tried to teach small Eve to walk. Presently Pierre sat up and stroked his wife's cheek. "Life has been sweet with you, Marie," he said. At the words a stab of fear struck her, but by the time they had walked through the Port-Royal woods gathering great branches of blossom and a bunch of water ranunculi she had managed to thrust anxiety out of her mind. The next day they returned to Paris and a sudden change in the weather, for it was raining heavily and a keen wind had sprung up. The following morning Marie said she had errands to do but would go to the laboratory in the afternoon, while Pierre said he must lunch with colleagues, call at his publishers to correct proofs, and visit the Physics Institute.

The luncheon over, he walked towards the Seine through streaming rain only to suffer a disappointment—owing to a printers' strike the publishers' office was closed. Rather crossly

108

he turned down the Rue Dauphiné, but found the pavements so crowded that he stepped into the roadway behind a cab. At the corner by the Pont Neuf he absent-mindedly thought he would like to cross to the far pavement, and as he came out from the shelter of the cab a heavy wagon drawn by two trotting horses bore heavily down upon him. Pierre struggled to grip the chest of the horse which had struck him, failed, and slipped on the muddy road. He lay there unhurt by the horses' hooves or the front wheels; but the wagon had a six-ton load, and one of the back wheels passed over him, crushing his skull like paper. Death was instantaneous.

Professor Appell and Professor Perrin, two of the dead man's colleagues, went to the house in the Boulevard Kellermann with the sad news, but not until six o'clock was Marie's key heard in the lock. Very gently Appell told her the facts. She stood so still that he repeated them twice, thinking she had not heard. But outwardly she seemed turned to stone, though tortured thoughts chased through her mind. Pierre was dead? Dead? Absolutely dead? Briefly she gave her friend precise instructions then walked past him into the sodden garden where she sat motionless on a bench, her head cupped in her hands.

VII

Less than a month later Marie was appointed to her husband's post—the first time any woman had ever been entrusted with such an important position. Still wrapped in that icy calm which had possessed her since his death she accepted the honour with a wry smile, remembering how long Pierre had worked and waited for recognition, remembering too the weary years in the Rue Lhomond shed. Then she thought of his words about going on with one's work and squared her shoulders. Truly, she was now "a body without a soul"—but before her stretched the prospect of ceaseless labour that was to be her fitting memorial to the husband she had adored.

Now fame pursued her more hotly than ever. She was the first woman professor in France and none more famous—doctorates, prizes and diplomas were showered on her from America, Britain, Switzerland, Holland and Imperial Russia—and in 1911 she was awarded the Nobel Prize in Chemistry.

109

A quiet, unassuming little figure in rusty black, distinguished only by her high forehead and finely chiselled features, she moved almost silently through all the functions she had to attend. She was interested in only two things in life, her work and her daughters.

Suddenly she was stricken with kidney trouble, and a severe operation had to be followed by a long convalescence, but even during that time she never relaxed her efforts for the building of a Radium Institute. At last the Sorbonne decided in favour of the suggestion. The Institute was to cost 400,000 gold francs and to be divided into two parts, a laboratory of radio-activity presided over by Marie, and a laboratory for biological research and Curie-therapy in charge of an eminent doctor, Professor Claude Regaud. On a bright summer day the building was at last ready and before she entered it for the first time Marie glanced up at the words cut into the white stone above the doorway: INSTITUT DU RADIUM, PAVILLON CURIE. How proud Pierre would have been! Under her breath she quoted a saying of Louis Pasteur: "They (labora-tories) are the temples of the future, of wealth and well-being. It is there that humanity grows bigger, strengthens and betters itself . . ." She did not notice the date on a wall calendar in the entrance hall. The month was July, 1914.

VIII

The outbreak of the First World War meant that the Radium Institute was to remain empty for four long years. For Marie they were years of ceaseless work among the Allied soldiers, for she travelled with X-ray apparatus to field hospitals and even to advanced dressing-stations. When the war ended she was over fifty and worn by a life of constant overstrain, but never once did she falter in her determination to honour Pierre's memory. In addition to a prodigious amount of work at the Radium Institute she undertook gruelling lecture tours—always an agony to one as shy and sensitive as she was—to America, to Rio de Janeiro, to Spain and many other countries, and on each tour she raised funds to buy grammes of precious radium. In the year 1932 came one visit which held a special appeal for her; she journeyed to Warsaw to open a Radium Institute there, and her abiding love for the city of her birth was shown in a letter to her daughter Eve: "There is a Cracow song in which they sing of the Vistula: 'This Polish water has within itself such a charm that those who are taken by it will love it even to the grave . . .'"

In 1923 Marie had all but lost her sight and had undergone an operation on her eyes. To everyone's astonishment she recovered sufficiently to undertake again the delicate precision work her researches demanded, but as the years went on she grew increasingly frail. Often when she returned to her flat in the Quai de Béthune on the Ile Saint-Louis she was so tired that she could barely crawl up the stairs—but still she laboured feverishly at the Institute. And every day she worked with radium, handled it, breathed in its gas. Her blood pressure became lower, her hands developed nasty sores, she developed singing noises in her ears, and in December, 1933, an X-ray showed the presence of a large stone in her gall-bladder. "It is nothing," she protested to her family and friends—and somehow she hoodwinked them into believing she was on the mend until the following May when, to her great joy, her daughter Irène and her husband, Frédéric Joliot, discovered *artificial* radio-activity.

But the sands were running out. Too weak now to argue, Marie consented to go to a sanatorium at Sancellemoz. Examination here proved that the real trouble, as her doctors had long suspected, was radium poisoning. She had pernicious anæmia in its worst form. One early morning, when the sun was rising above the mountains, they found Marie Curie lying still in her narrow bed, the white hair brushed back from the immense forehead, the deep-set grey eyes closed. She looked so gentle, so peaceful, so young. And on the coverlet lay the scarred hands that had brought the inestimable blessing of radium to thousands of sufferers.

The date was July 4, 1934.

Herr Daimler and Herr Benz

INVENTORS OF THE HORSELESS CARRIAGE

Egon Larsen

I

"In the name of the Law—open up!"

Half a dozen policemen's fists hammered at the door of No. 13, Taubenheimstrasse, in Cannstatt, an industrial town in Württemberg. A frightened female face appeared as the door was opened. The policemen marched right through the house and into the garden. There was a large shed at the bottom. The police officer in charge kicked the door open and said: "I have a search warrant. What's going on here?"

Two men looked up from the strange machine on which they had been working. "Are you sure you are at the right address?" the older one asked the officer politely. "My name is Gottlieb Daimler, and this is my friend, Wilhelm Maybach. We have nothing to hide."

"And what is this here?" asked the officer, pointing to the machine.

"We'll show you," Daimler said obligingly. "Maybach, crank her up!"

At the next moment, a deafening din filled the shed. The policemen, taken completely unawares, started back. The strange machine had become a live, thundering, sparking monster. The two men could not help laughing as they saw the intruder's perplexity. "It's our new petrol engine," explained Herr Daimler. "Quite harmless, really—there!" And he switched the terrible machine off with a flick of his hand.

The officer seemed rather embarrassed. He saluted. "Sorry, sir! There seems to have been a misunderstanding. You see, someone has informed the police that you are making forged money in your shed!"

II

Gottlieb Daimler was the son of a small-town baker in Württemberg, born in 1834—nearly forty years before that country became part of the German Empire. The baker wanted his son to be a civil servant, and made him go to the local grammar school. But Gottlieb had no talent for Latin and Greek; he had a technical mind, and he managed to persuade his father to let him leave school and become a gun-maker's apprentice at the age of fourteen.

The next stage in Gottlieb Daimler's career was a machine-tool factory near Strasbourg, where he tried to work in as many workshops as possible; at night he went to technical evening classes. Already at that time he must have burnt the candle of his life at both ends, an unfortunate habit that may have caused his premature death. However, he enjoyed that mode of life: "Hard work," he used to say, "is the greatest pleasure." He also saved much of what he earned, and as soon as he had enough he returned to Württemberg to take an engineer's course at the Stuttgart Polytechnic.

At the age of twenty-five young Daimler was a fully-fledged engineer. A wealthy patron who often encouraged promising technicians sent him on a study tour of England and France to see the latest methods in the machine-tool factories. A few years after his return he was already in charge of a large department in a large Karlsruhe engineering works and father of a fast-growing family.

He could have settled in this important and well-paid position, leaving it to others to experiment with new inventions and machines. However, when an inventor by the name of Nikolaus Otto founded a small factory for the production of his new internal-combustion gas engines—regarded with suspicion and ridicule by most traditionally-minded engineers—Daimler joined him, taking over the technical management of the enterprise and bringing with him a former fellow-student, Wilhelm Maybach, as chief constructor. That was in 1872.

What fascinated Daimler in that new and unconventional 'prime mover' as distinct from the well-tried steam engine were the immense possibilities he saw in it for the future. The steam engine, for all its reliability, was not adaptable either for

E   113

small workshops or for road vehicles. There was a great need for a light-weight engine, easy to control and economical, and safer than the steam engine with its open fire. Gas, which could be burnt internally and which expanded during combustion, seemed to be the right fuel; but Otto's depended on the gas mains for its fuel supply and was therefore not movable. However, Otto's engine was working on the right principle; like the steam engine it had cylinder and piston, but its cycle of operation was divided up into four strokes: suction, compression, ignition, and exhaustion. The third stroke, at which the gas was ignited, was the one which did the actual work.

It took Daimler and Maybach another ten years to realize that only some petroleum product could supply a kind of gas that would make the engine independent of the mains. Otto, however, would not see that the future of the internal-combustion engine lay in its independence and mobility; so they decided to separate, and Daimler undertook an exploratory journey to Russia to study the methods of oil production and refining in the Odessa region.

On his return he bought a house in Cannstatt, not far from Württemberg's capital Stuttgart; it had a large shed at the bottom of the garden, secluded from the curious gazes of the neighbours. Here, Daimler and Maybach built the first motor vehicle—a motor-cycle with a wooden frame and an air-cooled, one-cylinder petrol-engine.

That was the invention which gave rise to the rumours that the two men were forging money in the shed, and which prompted the police raid. The time had come to try it out: the year was 1885.

Little did Daimler know that only a short distance from Cannstatt another inventor, working on almost the same idea, had reached exactly the same stage at the same time.

III

Georg Benz was an engine-driver on the new railway from Heidelberg to Karlsruhe. In those days—the 1840s—the engine footplates were entirely unprotected, and one day, after working himself into a sweat, Benz caught pneumonia and died, leaving a widow and a two-year-old son, Karl.

There were no pension schemes for railway workers then,

and Karl had a miserable childhood. But Frau Benz had decided that he should go to the secondary school, and she achieved her ambition. In his spare time Karl helped her as much as he could, and found a way of adding a little to the household budget. His father, who had come from a watch-maker's family, had done watch repairs as a remunerative hobby, and left Karl five watches. The boy, who had a great flair for everything technical, took them to pieces to see what made them tick, and put them together again. Then he asked his schoolmates and the neighbours to entrust him with repairs. During all his years at the grammar school in Karlsruhe he helped his mother to keep the wolf from the door by repairing watches, and later, when he had bought a photographic camera (with wet plates and complicated developing equipment), by taking portraits and group pictures.

After the grammar school came the Polytechnic, but Karl did not like studying books. He wanted to do something prac-tical, and also earn money for his mother. So he became an ordinary locksmith in an engineering works.

Factory conditions in the 1860s were incredibly severe. The working day began at six o'clock in the morning and ended at seven in the evening, with only an hour's break at midday. Most jobs had to be done in very bad artificial light. Small wonder that young Karl Benz was dead tired at night, with blistered hands and a headache. Yet as soon as dinner was over he would climb up to the attic of the house which he had equipped as a little laboratory; and here he would make sketches for all kinds of horseless carriages.

Somehow the idea had got hold of him during his days at the Polytechnic. After drawing scores of sketches, most of them more imaginative than technically sound, he decided to get some practical experience in vehicle construction. He found a new job in a Mannheim railway coach factory.

At about that time his mother died, and he longed to have his own family. He married the pretty daughter of a carpenter. The marriage began under circumstances that were far from ideal. He had left the coach works, and rented a mechanic's workshop in a Mannheim back street; but customers were rare, and he spent most of his time tinkering with a gas-engine which he had built himself. He tried to find a financial backer, but

115

no one would hear of it. There came a time when Karl Benz could not give his wife enough money for a meal.

At last Chance took a hand. A court photographer, Herr Bühler, became Benz's customer; he needed highly polished steel plate-holders, which no other workshop had been able to make for him. Benz did the job within a week. The photographer was very enthusiastic about the young mechanic's skill, and Benz demonstrated his engine to him. Bühler agreed to invest some money in this invention, and became a 'sleeping partner' in Benz's firm.

At last things began to move. The general prejudice against the internal-combustion engine as a source of power in the factories was disappearing, and Benz was commissioned to make a number of stationary petrol engines for that purpose. They proved to be economical and reliable motors. Benz was able to enlarge his workshop, and founded a new company with more partners and a staff of forty mechanics.

At one of the first company meetings Benz let the cat out of the bag. What he was aiming at, he told his partners, was the construction of road vehicles powered by internal-combustion engines.

This revelation had a most distressing effect. He was treated like a madman planning a trip to the moon. The mere thought of such a mechanical vehicle racing through the streets of Mannheim seemed utterly ridiculous. "You had better not risk our money on such an impossible venture," Benz was told by his backers.

Secretly he went ahead with his construction of a three-wheeled 'carriage without horses'. But his backers found out; there was a noisy meeting, and the company folded up. However, an enterprising Mannheim businessman, Max Rose, came to his help, lending him enough money to build the vehicle. Benz completed it without using anybody else's ideas; every detail had to be thought out, every problem solved in his head and at the workbench—ignition, choice of fuel, carburettor, cooling system, power transmission, steering, springing. Only the differential gear which he embodied in his design was someone else's invention, that of an English engineer by the name of James Starley.

One spring morning in 1885 the little carriage was ready,

waiting for its first outing. Within the protecting walls of the workshop yard, hidden from the curious eyes of the Mannheimers, the vehicle described a few circles. It was the first test of the first motor-car.

IV

As soon as Benz felt that his vehicle was reliable enough he announced that he was going to demonstrate it in the streets of Mannheim. At the start, however, instead of driving out of the gate into the road he drove into a brick wall, and the great event had to be postponed for a week. When it took place at last the crowd of onlookers was so great that Benz was frightened he might run one of them over. The street arabs of Mannheim had the time of their lives. The journey ended, of course, with a technical mishap—the clutch failed to work. The whole town seemed to be on the road along which he pushed his carriage home.

The police did not like the thing at all and told him that they would invoke the laws against 'mechanically propelled vehicles' if he dared to drive through Mannheim again. He wrote to the Minister of the Interior of the Grand Duchy of Baden asking him for a general permission. The reply was that he could drive his car—at a maximum speed of seven miles an hour on the open road, and of four miles an hour in the towns!

Benz knew that if he had to comply with these restrictions it would be the end of the motor-car. So he summoned up all his courage, and invited the Minister for a ride!

No one was more surprised than Karl Benz when the mighty man accepted. Now the inventor went ahead with his own little plan. He persuaded a milkman to drive with his horse-van quickly past the motor-car, shouting derogatory remarks about the ridiculous snail's-pace of the horseless carriage.

The stratagem succeeded beautifully. The Minister took his seat beside the inventor, and they proceeded through the streets at the prescribed four miles an hour. The milkman drove past at top speed, shouting, "Hey, you two, can't you go faster with your Christmas cracker? Shall I come and push?"

The Minister went red with anger. "Can't you go faster, Herr Benz? This is quite infuriating!"

117

Benz grinned. "I could easily, Herr Minister, but your regulations don't permit it!"

"Hang the regulations!" cried the Minister. "Go as fast as you can—I'll take the responsibility!"

That was the beginning of the end of the four miles per hour regulation.

Karl Benz decided to show his invention at an exhibition in Munich. He built a new vehicle and took it there by railway. In the meantime, unknown to him, his first model which he had left in Mannheim became the 'hero' of a new chapter in the history of transport.

His two sons, Eugen, aged fifteen, and Richard, aged thirteen, were just as crazy about the car as their father, who had shown them how to handle it. He had hardly turned his back when they persuaded their mother to drive with them to Pforzheim, 60 miles to the south of Mannheim, where her family lived.

It was a momentous journey—not only the longest ever undertaken by the rickety little vehicle, but the first with two boys at the controls. There were innumerable hitches and minor breakdowns of every conceivable part of the car; yet the boys mended them all, resourcefully though not always the orthodox way—the short-circuit of an ignition cable, for instance, was repaired with the help of Frau Benz's garter, and a stopped-up petrol tube with her hatpin!

The country folk who saw that contraption for the first time seemed to think the devil himself was at large. Many made the sign of the cross, some collected their children and barricaded themselves in their houses, and a few village lads threw stones at the travellers. Horses shied at the unaccustomed sight, and some innkeepers refused to serve the boys and their mother. In a beer-garden where they had a meal some farmers started a rowdy dispute, which nearly turned into a fight, as to whether the carriage was being driven by steam or by clockwork. The boys opened the engine bonnet and explained.

Karl Benz pretended to be angry when he heard what his boys had done with his car. In fact, however, he was as proud as could be—not so much of Eugen and Richard, who had brought the car safely back from Pforzheim, as of his invention. For the boys had proved that driving a motor-car was, in the literal sense, child's play!

V

Meanwhile, Daimler in Cannstatt tried out his motor-cycle in the backyard of his house. He thought that country postmen might make good use of it, but for the time being he wanted to try out the engine in other means of transport to test its adaptibility. He built it into a boat and offered to all and sundry free trips on the river Neckar. But people were frightened of the unusual engine and feared the thing might blow up. In order to encourage them Daimler fixed porcelain knobs to the boat and stretched wires between them so that they should think it had an electric motor! But it was in vain, because now the good people of Cannstatt were afraid of getting electric shocks.

Next, Daimler and Maybach built a four-wheeled car, a horseless carriage in the true sense of the word because Daimler believed that one should be able to convert any horse-drawn coach into an 'automobile' just by taking away the horses and adding a petrol-engine. Thus, Daimler's first motor-car looked indeed like a coach without the horses. It was tried out on a trip to a neighbouring town one dark night, for Daimler shunned the ridicule of his fellow-citizens. The top speed he reached was over 11 miles an hour.

Yet he went on testing his petrol-engine for a number of purposes. He put it in the bogie of a sub-standard railway coach and let it haul a train, and he built it into a tramcar; then he provided the fire-brigade of Hanover with a pump driven by a petrol-engine. As early as 1886 a Daimler motor-boat took part in a regatta on the River Main at Frankfurt, and Bismarck ordered one for the lake on his estate.

For some years, Daimler and Maybach struggled with the designs for their motor-cars until they had to admit that the idea of the engine that could be built into any coach was fundamentally wrong, and that an 'automobile' had to be designed as a special-purpose vehicle right from the start. Such a motor-car, a motor-cycle, and a motor-boat, all from Daimler's workshop, were exhibited at the Paris exhibition of 1889, and created much more excitement than they had ever done in Germany. A French firm acquired from Daimler the licence to build cars from his designs; thus began France's quick growth into the world's first motor-car-minded country, long before a young mechanic by the name of Henry Ford put America on wheels.

The first motor-car race took place in 1894; the track was the road from Paris to Rouen and back. It was won by a Daimler car with an average speed of 20 miles per hour. A partner in the French firm which had the Daimler licence, a certain M. Jellinek, who was Austro-Hungarian consul at Nice, went to Cannstatt to discuss with Daimler his idea of building the prototype of a heavy new racing car; Daimler agreed to everything, but when Jellinek suggested that the new engine should develop 6 h.p. instead of the 4 h.p. of Daimler's standard engine, the engineer burst out, "Good heavens, what do we need six horses for—aren't our cars already fast enough with four?"

In the end, Jellinek won the day. He had also a special request. If a number of these new cars were to be introduced from Germany, there would be some opposition from the ranks of the French mechanics and motor enthusiasts. Therefore, said Jellinek, it might be wiser to drop the German name of Daimler for the new model and give it some fancy name, such as that of Jellinek's daughter who would be the first to own such a car—Mercedes.

That was the birth of the name of a car which is still among the most famous in the world.

Shortly after Jellinek's visit Daimler received another one, from a retired cavalry officer by the name of Count Zeppelin, who commissioned a number of engines for the dirigible airship he was planning to build. "Would you like to build not only the engines but the whole airship for me?" asked the Count. Daimler hesitated with his answer; eventually he said, "You see, the people think I'm a complete fool because I make motor-cars; if they heard that I was also building an airship they'd lock me up at once in a nuthouse!"

Zeppelin smiled and said, "Now I know what's in store for me."

Daimler did not live to see the miracle of 1900—the Zeppelin airship; neither did he live to see the Mercedes racing-car of 35 h.p. which was built in the same year. He died at the age of only sixty-six; he had driven himself too hard all his life.

VI

"Germany is the father of the motor-car, but France is its mother," Karl Benz used to say. Benz, too, exhibited his cars at the Paris exhibition of 1889; he, too, sold the licence to build his cars in France to a French firm of mechanics. Born ten years after Daimler he was still a man full of vigour when the age of the motor-car began in the 1890s; motoring in England, first held up by the notorious 'Man with the Red Flag', developed with great speed, and America followed in the early 1900s. By the way, the first motor-car ever to drive over an American road was a Benz model of 1888.

In 1905, Benz opened a new factory for his two sons, who had become fully-fledged engineers. Benz cars and Daimler-Mercedes cars appeared as rivals everywhere, but in 1924 the two companies were merged into one—Mercedes-Benz. Karl Benz, then eighty years old, made his last public appearance on that momentous occasion; five years later he died, mourned by all Germany and by motorists in many countries.

VII

Perhaps the strangest thing about Karl Benz and Gottlieb Daimler, the two fathers of the horseless carriage, is that they never met. Although they pursued the same idea at the same time, separated by only a hundred miles as the crow flies, they heard nothing of each other's efforts until the Paris exhibition of 1889; and even then they seemed to have little desire to make each other's acquaintance.

"It may sound strange that I heard nothing of the Daimler car until so long afterwards," Karl Benz wrote. "In the 1880s, the Press paid no attention yet to the motor-car, and there was little communication between the towns. I had no connections with Cannstatt, and I am sure that Daimler did not know anything about my invention until he read the patents."

One day in the 1890s, however, the two men nearly met in the streets of Berlin. Benz had made a business trip to the German capital and was walking along a busy street when a friend who accompanied him cried suddenly, "Look who's walking over there!"

121

"Gottlieb Daimler," said Karl Benz and smiled.
"Well, let's go and bid him a good morning."

Benz looked, but none of the many faces on the other side of the road was familiar to him. "Which of them am I supposed to know?" he asked his friend.

"There—can't you see? It's Gottlieb Daimler! Don't you want to say hallo to him?"

"Gottlieb Daimler," said Karl Benz and smiled. "You're right. It's about time we met."

The friend looked at Benz with his mouth open in surprise. "But don't you know him?"

"No, I don't. Well, let's go and bid him a good morning."

It took them a while before they were able to cross the road, which was full of coaches, horse buses, and handcarts. When they arrived on the other side the old gentleman with the grey, pointed beard had disappeared. They looked for him for a while, but could not find him.

Karl Benz laughed. "Well," he said, "I suppose we were not meant to meet. Perhaps Fate does not want Gottlieb Daimler and Karl Benz to shake hands. Just one of those things——"

Charles Robert Darwin

INTERPRETER OF THE PATTERN OF LIFE

John Crompton

I

THE students were assembled in the operating theatre of Edinburgh University. The patient, a child, lay on the table. All was ready. The operation began. Suddenly one of the students, white-faced and on the verge of collapse, rushed from the room. No doubt there was every excuse, the year was 1826, twenty years before anaesthetics came to be used, when operations, however serious, had to be performed on fully conscious patients. But students, if they hoped to become doctors, had to face up to this. This particular student, however, did *not* hope to become a doctor. He had had enough already. At the only other operation he had attended he had behaved in the sam way. Moreover, the ordinary routine, the bookwork and clas es, bored him. He took no interest in any aspect of medicine. So, at the early age of seventeen, he had to abandon his medical studies.

His father, Dr. Robert Darwin, a huge and domineering man, six feet two in height, twenty-five stone in weight, was bitterly disappointed. He was a well-known doctor and the son of an even better-known doctor, Erasmus Darwin, who had been offered, but refused, the post of physician to King George III. It was naturally taken for granted that Charles should follow in their footsteps.

Charles had disappointed the doctor even before this. He had done badly at school and his reports had caused his father to remark, "You will be a disgrace to yourself and all your family." Charles's only interests in life seemed to be shooting and collecting. As the shooting season approached he could think of nothing else, and he was like a jackdaw for collecting. He collected anything and everything: shells, pebbles, stamps,

124

coins, dead beetles, birds' eggs (though he had a solemn agreement with his sister never to take more than one egg from a
nest), wild flowers, leaves, and so on.

His father regarded the collecting as childish waste of time,
the passion for shooting he regarded more seriously. For of all
types of men Dr. Darwin most disliked the idle, sporting type,
and he saw his son developing into just that type.

That was why he had taken him from school and sent him,
at the unusually early age of sixteen, to begin his medical career.

Well, it seemed now to his father that the only opening left
for Charles was the Church. Charles was not averse to the idea
(it would have made no difference if he had been); as a country
parson he would still be able to shoot and collect. Before becoming a parson he had to get a degree. He was sent to Cambridge to get one.

He thoroughly enjoyed his three years at Cambridge. He
became a boon companion of the shooting, hunting, sporting
crowd and finished up most days with jovial dinners, singing
and card-playing. He attended only what lectures were necessary, but with the help of a tutor got his ordinary B.A. After
that he had to spend another two terms at Cambridge.

Though he had allowed his sporting proclivities full rein, he
was as keen as ever on collecting. But he was narrowing it down
and giving it more thought and observation. His pebbles and
bits of rock led him on to an interest in geology; his shells,
beetles, etc., to an interest in natural history. He sought advice
and his keenness aroused the interest of his teachers, particularly that of Henslow, Professor of Botany, and Sedgwick,
Professor of Geology. They showed him what to read and took
him on country expeditions.

Now about this time a ten-gun brig, H.M.S. *Beagle*, was
about to sail round the world to make a survey of the lesser-
known coast-lines and waters, and her commander, Captain
Vitzroy, had gained permission from the Admiralty to take a
naturalist (unpaid) with him. He asked Professor Henslow if
he could recommend one. The trip would take two years. Not
many graduates could waste so much time and money. Henslow
approached Charles, and told him he need not worry about his
disqualifications.

The idea filled Charles with such enthusiasm as he had never

125

known—not even before the partridge shooting season. A trip round the world visiting the places he was reading about in his geology and natural history books! Then his spirits dropped. What would his father say? And his father would not only have to permit the trip but finance it!

His father said what might have been expected. Now that Charles was at last able to start on a career he wanted to go gallivanting off on a pleasure trip for two years! Certainly not!

In despair, more to get consolation than from any hope, Charles went to his uncle, Josiah Wedgwood. Surprisingly, 'Uncle Jos' thought the idea a good one and even promised to talk to the doctor about it. Dr. Darwin had always admired Josiah as a shrewd business man and, more important, he liked him. Josiah told the doctor that in his opinion this trip would have a stabilising effect on Charles just at the time he needed it. It would be hard work and there would be no chances of getting into mischief under Navy discipline.

He won. Dr. Darwin agreed to the trip and agreed to pay Charles's expenses.

So it came about that, on December 27, 1831, H.M.S. *Beagle* sailed from Plymouth carrying on board an excited fledgling naturalist, who was shortly to be very sea-sick and who was to return in five, not two years.

II

The Galapagos Islands lie on the Equator, 500 miles west of South America. Formed of blackish grey lava, pock-marked with craters and lined with fissures, these Pacific islands are no place for a holiday. Except in the centre of some of the larger ones, the chief vegetation consists of thorn-trees, cacti and weed-like flowers. Everywhere is a faint, unpleasant smell. It is the home of crabs, lizards and huge tortoises. The latter weigh up to 400 lb. and probably attain an age of 300 to 400 years, but they are now on the verge of extinction. Naturally, if they can help it, ships never put in there, but on September 15, 1835, a brig might have been observed heading for Chatham Island, the most desolate of them all. It was the *Beagle*, looking the worse for wear and minus her lifeboat, which had been washed away in a gale.

The *Beagle* had spent all this time surveying up and down

off the east coast of South America and then up and down off the west coast until, after nearly four years, she had turned her bows west and started on the long voyage home.

In those days ocean surveying and sounding took a great deal of time so the *Beagle*'s naturalist was often able to spend long periods on shore, making journeys into the interior, writing voluminous notes and collecting specimens. Trust Charles to collect specimens! He collected so many that they would almost have sunk the *Beagle* several times over had he not been able fairly frequently to ship them home from various ports. The specimens varied from huge fossils and slabs of rock to mice, insects, spiders and water animals.

But Charles was not now just collecting, he was beginning to think as well, and the more he collected the more he thought. He noticed that the species of plants and animals changed as he went from one part of the continent to another, and yet that they often possessed remarkable similarities. He paid as much attention to geology as to natural history. He was surprised to find deep-sea shells on the highest mountains, hundreds of miles from the sea, showing that these mountains had once been fathoms deep under the ocean. This and other things forced him to conclude that the land all over the globe was continually, though infinitely slowly, rising and falling, at one time connecting continents and islands, making possible the spread of animals and plants, at others separating them by great tracts of water.

And here, just for a moment, we must leave Charles to make a note of the attitude of the scientists of those days towards life generally. Everyone knows what a species is. The bear, for instance, has only a few—the brown bear, the grizzly bear, the polar bear, and one or two others. Moths and butterflies have very many more, as those who collect them, and even those who do not, are aware. Spiders, too, have thousands of species, many very much alike. Now, scientists in those days believed that each species had been specially created in the beginning by the Creator and that these species never changed and never would change. Practically everybody else believed this too. And, of course, species never *do* seem to change.

Charles was as firm a believer in this as anyone else, but after his truly vast examination of innumerable species in South

America he was a little puzzled as to why the Creator had made so many that were so similar and yet dissimilar. It seemed a waste of creative power. If, of course, over a long period, species changed as they spread from one territory to another, or even changed while they remained in one place, it would explain a lot. But species did not change.

Back now to the *Beagle*. After anchorage, Charles, bronzed and wiry, viewed Chatham Island without enthusiasm but he was soon ashore watching the crabs and lizards and coming unexpectedly upon two of the giant tortoises going along a path they had worn by continual passage. They viewed him without fear and almost without interest. Exuberant at being able to stretch his legs again, and fit for any pranks, Charles jumped on to the back of one of them and whacked the hind part of its shell. It rose obediently and waddled forward. Its pace was not much more than a yard a minute but all the same Charles fell off. He tried several times during his stay in the islands without ever managing to stick on.

But his interest in these animals was not confined to having 'donkey rides' on them. He had seen from the first that they were a species known nowhere else. And yet they were strangely like some of the tortoises found on the American mainland. Later, he found it was the same with the birds and plants of the islands. Half of them were peculiar to the islands and yet had resemblances to certain finches and plants of America. He was still more intrigued when he found out that the tortoises on the various islands were different, very much alike but definitely different species. And it was the same with many of the birds and plants.

To Charles it seemed that there could only be one explanation: at a remote period the ancestors of these animals and plants had got over from distant places to the Galapagos—and there were several ways in which they could have done so. Once there they had gradually changed and branched out into a number of different species. Which meant that species *did* change. And if that were so, it was even possible that all life had originated from one, or just a few very small beginnings.

That is what he was thinking when the *Beagle* at last set sail from the Galapagos and the giant turtles—but he kept his thoughts to himself.

Darwin jumped on to the back of one of the tortoises
and whacked the hind part of its shell

New Zealand, Australia, the Indian Ocean with its coral islands, South Africa, then the long run home. Charles was no longer enjoying the trip. He was sea-sick again, sea-sick and very homesick. "I loathe, I abhor the sea and all ships which sail on it," he wrote in his diary.

On the afternoon of October 2, 1836, the *Beagle*, her sheets worn, her bottom foul, sailed into Falmouth Harbour and anchored. Her naturalist wasted no time. He took the night coach for Shropshire and never left Britain again for the rest of his life.

III

Not far from Bromley, Kent, in the typically English country-side that is now fast disappearing, lay the village of Down, a few hamlets clustered round an old stone church. Quarter of a mile away was a country residence, a large, brick three-storey house surrounded by spacious lawns, flower beds, flowering shrubs and long avenues of limes. Here, every day, a tall, thin man pottered about attending to plants or visiting his pigeons and rabbits. He had a bald dome and a brow that jutted out over his eyes like a cliff overhanging caves below. No one could possibly have connected this oldish-looking man with the young, pleasant-faced Charles Darwin who had sailed on the *Beagle* twenty years before, but it was he.

It had been intended, you will remember, that he should become a clergyman on his return, but he had abandoned that idea years ago. This does not mean that he had fallen into those ways of sporting idleness that his father had dreaded— the trip on the *Beagle* had cured him of that once and for all. He had left England a mere dabbler in science; he had returned an experienced naturalist and geologist. The specimens and the notes that he had sent home from time to time had attracted the attention of several scientists of high standing, and within a few years he occupied a distinguished place amongst them. Many of them were his personal friends.

At first he had lived in London, taking on much work in connection with various societies, but soon he became affected by a mysterious illness which forced him to get away from London and live a quiet life. So he had found Down House and gone there with his family. And he stayed there all his life.

No one ever found out the nature of this illness. He looked fit, took long walks, and lived to old age, but half an hour's conversation would exhaust him, and even the prospect of a journey, however short, would bring on headaches, nausea and stomach pains. It was obviously a 'worry' illness. There was nothing to worry him in his home life, though there was in his work. He was engaged in very controversial matters and he shrank from attack and adverse criticism. He was not a fighter like his friend, Professor Huxley.

He was working now on the masses of notes he had made and the specimens he had collected during the voyage. He was busy, too, making further collections and studies. The result of this vast labour was to appear in a book he was writing, called *The Origin of Species.*

All his work so far had confirmed his views about the change-ability of species, but one thing had puzzled him: species changed, but what *controlled* these changes? Why did new species 'take over' from other species, rising to predominance and then themselves giving place to others? In the case of domestic animals man, of course, was the controlling force. Charles kept pigeons and he knew that his pouters, tumblers, fantails and the rest had all come originally from one pair of wild birds. By selecting from the types he wanted, aided by variations, man had brought about the different species. But there was no selection in nature.

The answer to the puzzle, when it came to him, seemed very simple. There *is* selection in nature—'the survival of the fittest'. Any species that comes to have even slight advantages over other strains must in the battle for existence, inevitably oust those strains, probably to be ousted itself later. He called this process Natural Selection.

Twenty years had gone by and Charles was still working on his book. His friends urged him to publish it lest someone step in before him. He took no notice. His subject was a never-ending one really, for it was life itself. Probably *The Origin of Species* never *would* have been published had not Charles received a letter one morning from a man named A. R. Wallace enclosing a paper he had written. In this paper were

131

summed up all the conclusions about species at which Charles had arrived after so many years of laborious work. His friends had been right. He had been forestalled.

Charles offered to withdraw his own book in favour of Wallace. But it was obvious that he had arrived at his theories long before Wallace, and in the end the matter was settled amicably.

But there must be no more delay. Charles worked as never before. *The Origin of Species* was published in 1859. It had a mixed reception, mostly hostile. The fireworks were to come later.

IV

They came the following June at a scientific meeting in Oxford. Scenting a row, so many people assembled (over 700) that a large hall had to be obtained to contain them. Charles (luckily for him) was too ill to go. In his absence Huxley bore the brunt of the attack that developed.

The one thing Darwin had been hoping to avoid was mention of man. Man, of course, was included in his theory of evolution but there was little data to go on at that time. The so-called 'missing links' had not yet come to hand. Needless to say, man *was* mentioned.

Speaker after speaker attacked Darwin. Then rose Samuel Wilberforce, the urbane Bishop of Oxford (disrespectfully known to undergraduates as 'Soapy Sam'). For half an hour he ridiculed Darwin and Huxley, then turned to Huxley and asked him with an ironic smile if he claimed descent from an ape on his grandfather's or grandmother's side.

There was clapping and cheering. The meeting was almost solidly against Darwin. With dramatic timing Huxley delayed his reply until people were beginning to wonder if he was going to speak at all. Then he rose. He tore all the Bishop's arguments to shreds and finally stated (to give only the gist of what he said) that he would sooner have an ape for an ancestor than a man who, instead of attending to his proper duties, interfered in scientific matters of which he knew nothing: in other words that he would sooner have an ape for a foreparent than the Bishop of Oxford.

At this insult to a cleric pandemonium broke out. It looked

almost as if the little group of Darwinites would be physically attacked. A woman fainted and had to be carried out. Amongst the shouting mob was Charles's old friend, Captain Fitzroy of the *Beagle*, waving a Bible aloft and referring to Charles as "that viper I once harboured on my ship". The Bishop sat with a strained smile.

As it happened, this disorderly meeting did good. It attracted publicity and brought the whole matter into the open. In ten years time there was hardly a scientist who did not believe in evolution. Most of the clergy, too, came to reconcile it with their religion.

V

In a kind of general knowledge test a class was asked, "What do you know about Darwin?" and a bright youngster replied, "He discovered evolution." More or less the same reply would be given by most people. But it is incorrect. Darwin's own grandfather believed in a sort of evolution and had written verse about it. A man called Chambers had also written about it, while a Frenchman, Lamarck, a famous zoologist born sixty-five years before Darwin, had held the same views and had carefully expounded them.

So the idea of evolution can be said to have been 'in the air' in the 19th century. Yet speculative ideas, unsupported by facts and upsetting to old beliefs, are easily ignored. Then Darwin came and by a mass of observations, a lifetime of careful research, proved that evolution was more than an idea—it was the pattern of life itself.

Charles Dickens

THE LIFE OF THE IMAGINATION

John Bayley

CHARLES DICKENS was born in 1812, the year of Napoleon's retreat from Moscow. The war against France was at its height; England was maintaining an enormous fleet at sea; and Charles Dickens's father was a clerk in the Navy Pay Office. He seems to have been a feckless and inefficient sort of man, although with a warm heart and a certain stylishness and swagger, qualities that endeared him to his son, who was afterwards to immortalize both his good and bad qualities in the Mr. Micawber of *David Copperfield.*

The young Dickens had one sister, Fanny, two years older than he, who afterwards became an actress and to whom he remained greatly attached. Dickens senior was stationed near Rochester for some time, and his son came to have a particular affection for the district and returned to it again and again as a background in his novels, for although Dickens, unlike Hardy, has no very strong rural connections, he has a great knack for hitting off the feel and spirit of a place, the slums of London in *Oliver Twist*, the fens of Lincolnshire in *Bleak House*, and above all the Thames estuary and the town of Rochester itself, a cheerful town in *Pickwick*, and a haunting, crumbling, and sinister one in *Edwin Drood*, his last unfinished novel. Equally memorable is his evocation of the Thames-side marshes in *Great Expectations*, and the convict who roams there and who is finally caught and taken back to the convict hulk, an old man-of-war of Nelson's day which Dickens must often have seen as he went up the river with his father in the naval pay yacht.

When the boy was eleven his family went to live in South London, and it was then the blow fell which so much blighted his adolescence and shook his confidence in the happiness and security of life. His father's finances were in a desperate state, and because he could no longer afford to keep his son at school he sent him out to work at a small factory run by a relation, which made shoe polish. Here it was Dickens's task to screw the lids on the tins of polish and stick on the labels. He felt utterly depressed by the sense of wasted time and by the thought of being condemned for life to the gloomy rat-haunted warehouse where he worked. Not all was waste, however, because in his free time he wandered through the colourful London around him—Soho and Seven Dials—storing up impressions, odd figures, and even odd names—(the name Pickwick he claimed later to have seen over a shop)—which were to be of the greatest value to him in the future. Their value was all the greater because of the emotional state which his employment caused, for Dickens could never write about anything which he had seen in a calm and detached way—his genius was essentially of the emotional kind and had to be supplied with feelings, misery, joy, indignation, pathos, before it was able to create. During the vital seven weeks that he spent at the blacking factory such emotions had full play, with a certain vitality and cheerfulness always breaking through, even when the shilling a day he had to feed himself on was spent and there was 'nothing for it but to take a turn in Covent Garden and stare at the pineapples'. And there was the joy, perhaps the most intense of his whole life when his father's debts were temporarily settled and he was able to go back to school. Perhaps his most powerful and vivid piece of writing describes David Copperfield's experiences at a similar factory, but we must remember that in Dickens's case the experience was much shorter, though no doubt no less intense, than in the case of his imaginary hero.

II

Money troubles were by no means over, for although his father had been released from the Marshalsea, the debtor's prison which Dickens describes in *Little Dorrit*, he had been dismissed from naval employment as a result of his insolvency, and he remained a financial burden to his son for the rest of his life. Dickens meanwhile had become a lawyer's clerk, a job which brought him into contact with all the entrenched peculiarities of the legal profession, peculiarities which he was to satirize mercilessly in his novels. The hero of *Bleak House* is ruined by a protracted lawsuit in the Court of Chancery; and Serjeant Buzfuz is a miracle of absurd pomposity in the case of Bardell *v.* Pickwick. It has often been observed that the Law is the only profession which Dickens makes a real part of his characters: the doctors, clergymen or landowners exist in his pages quite independently of their business lives.

Bureaucracy was another of Dickens's bugbears of which he obtained a vivid glimpse at this time and later held up to ridicule in his picture of the 'Circumlocution Office' in *Little Dorrit*. This is one abuse that is always with us, and whereas Dickens's portraits of certain Victorian evils have lost their relevance today, his account of civil service red tape and muddle remains as amusing and meaningful today as it was in 1857.

He is almost equally severe with parliamentary procedure and the voting system, which he came to know intimately when in 1832 he took up parliamentary reporting. The great Reform Bill was just in process of being passed, but Dickens, sitting in the Reporters' Gallery in the House of Commons and watching the debates upon it, was by no means convinced of the marvellous benefits which were claimed for it. He even wrote a little satire, in the manner of the Arabian Nights, in which the beautiful damsel called Reefawm is enthusiastically received into the English harem but turns out to be as faithless and unsatisfactory as all her predecessors! Although Dickens had such faith in the virtues of family life and in the warmth and goodness of common people, he was sceptical about the possibilities of good government and never really bothered to familiarize himself with the progress towards a better society which the reformers of his day were making. About elections he was particularly scathing. As a reporter for the *Morning Chronicle* he covered several elections, and the fruit is his superb account of the Eatanswill election in *The Pickwick Papers*.

While working under full pressure as a reporter Dickens was also writing sketches of London life, one of which he sent anonymously to a magazine and had the pleasure of seeing it printed. Booksellers began to compete for his work, and the publishers Chapman and Hall asked him to write a series of stories, to appear monthly and to be concerned with the adven-

While working as a reporter, Dickens also
wrote sketches of London life

tures of a band of sportsmen who had formed themselves into a club. Dickens knew nothing of sport but he promised to try and oblige, and the result became *The Posthumous Papers of the Pickwick Club.* It was not an immediate success, but as soon as the talented young artist Hablot Brown began to draw the pictures in the monthly numbers and created the fat, bespectacled and benevolent Mr. Pickwick whom we all know, the sales began to mount. Dickens was lucky in his illustrators. The celebrated George Cruikshank had illustrated his first *Sketches by Boz,* and now Boz and 'Phiz', as young Hablot Brown called himself, were to become as famous a pair of collaborators as Gilbert and Sullivan. Dickens took his early pen name of Boz, incidentally, from his younger brother's nickname: the family called him Moses, but as he always had a cold in the head he pronounced this 'Boses', and the family shortened it to Boz.

III

About this time (1836) after an early and hopeless though passionate love affair with the daughter of a banker, Maria Beadnell, whom he never forgot and who subsequently furnished the character of Dora in *David Copperfield,* Dickens fell in love with all three daughters of a journalist called Hogarth, and soon married the eldest, Kate. Her younger sister Mary, to whom Dickens was very much attached, died suddenly at the age of seventeen, and he felt the blow so keenly that the tragic and pathetic deaths of the young, like Little Nell and Paul Dombey, were to become some of the most affecting scenes in his works, which he himself wrote with the tears streaming down his face, and which threw into mourning the whole reading public of the country. We often say nowadays that Dickens is sentimental, but we must remember that the sentiment is always genuine and was felt acutely by the author. We must also remember that the Victorians were much more demonstrative than we are, and liked to give vent both to their joy and their grief in what would strike us as the most extravagant ways. It is this that Dickens understood so well and mirrors so faithfully in his novels. The same applies to his apparent exaggeration. We are more reserved and controlled today, more self-conscious and afraid of making fools of ourselves, but beneath it our essential selves, our vanities, obsessions and daydreams, are perhaps just as grotesque as those to which Dickens gives full play in his characters, and those which the Victorians themselves expressed more openly. "If you think I exaggerate, just try looking around you," Dickens would say to his friends, and certainly many of us would recognize the timeless accuracy of—say—Mrs. Skewton's fatuous admiration of the Middle Ages:

"Those darling bygone times, Mr Carker, with their delicious fortresses and their dear old dungeons and their delightful places of torture and their picturesque assaults and sieges and everything that makes life truly charming! How dreadfully we have degenerated!"

"Yes, we have fallen off deplorably," said Mr Carker.

(*Dombey and Son*)

Dickens himself was no admirer of the past and wrote a *Child's History of England*, which is both unfair and inaccurate about such controversial characters as Henry VIII and Bloody Mary. Even in *The Tale of Two Cities*, his novel about the French Revolution, he is more interested in the human and fantastic side of his subject than in the historical. No one, perhaps, could be so perfect as Sydney Carton, just as no one could be so pure and so self-sacrificing as Little Nell or Little Dorrit, but these are conventional heroes and heroines who were never as much Dickens's strong point as his incidental characters. If you think that no one could be so hypocritical as Mr. Pecksniff in *Martin Chuzzlewit*, or so pompous and self-righteous as Mr. Pumblechook in *Great Expectations*, or Mr. Sapsea, the auctioneer of *Edwin Drood*, try looking more closely at the people with whom you come in contact and you may get a surprise!

With the success of *Pickwick* Dickens settled down to the life of a writer and each new book added to his reputation and helped to establish him as the foremost English novelist of the time. *Oliver Twist* followed *Pickwick*, appearing in a magazine, *Bentley's Miscellany* (1837–8), and then came *Nicholas Nickleby*, with its famous and terrifying picture of life in what must surely be the worst school in the world, Dotheboys Hall, kept by the terrible Mr. Squeers. *The Old Curiosity Shop* and *Barnaby*

Rudge were next to appear (1840–1), and in 1842 Dickens went to America, where he was fêted as a great man but did not take so kindly as he expected to American manners, and made himself unpopular by speaking in favour of an International Copyright Law; for his own books and those of other English authors were being published in America without any payment being made to the man who wrote them. On returning home he put many of his impressions of America into *Martin Chuzzlewit* (1843). In the same year he wrote *A Christmas Carol*, the first of a series of popular books appearing each Christmas. He then travelled on the continent where he wrote *Dombey and Son* (1848), and in 1850 started a weekly periodical, *Household Words*. *David Copperfield* appeared in the same year and *Bleak House* in 1852, followed by *Hard Times*, a short novel depicting the industrial miseries of 'Coketown', a typical Midlands manufacturing centre. Dickens's next four novels were *Little Dorrit, A Tale of Two Cities, Great Expectations*, and *Our Mutual Friend*, which came out in 1864.

IV

Meanwhile his family had grown and he now had ten children; they lived at a large London house, in Bloomsbury, where the Dickenses entertai ed the most famous people of the day. Inspired perhaps by her husband's enormous output of novels, Mrs. Dickens had herself written one work, a cookery book with the engaging title, *What Shall We Have for Dinner?* She made no secret of the fact that her husband's favourite menus were included, and her book gives a fascinating sidelight on the Victorian appetite, and perhaps a clue as well to the gusto and vitality that abound in Dickens's pages with their hearty descriptions of food and drink. An average Dickens dinner consisted of the following: Carrot Soup, Turbot with Shrimp Sauce, Lobster Patties, Stewed Kidneys, Roast Saddle of Lamb, Boiled Turkey, Knuckle of Ham, Mashed and Brown potatoes, Stewed Onions, Cabinet Pudding, Blancmange and Cream, and Macaroni. Like the inventory of the water rat's picnic in *The Wind in the Willows*, it is a list to take one's breath away. One imagines Dickens and his large family tucking into it and then settling down to private theatricals in the large studio of their house.

For Dickens adored the theatre, and was never so happy as when he was producing some play, usually a farce or comedy, but sometimes a melodrama like *The Frozen Deep*, whose subject was Franklin's tragic expedition to the Arctic. In addition to producing and writing much of the play himself he would also take two or three parts in it, and had he lived in the Elizabethan age he would undoubtedly, like Shakespeare, have been an actor-manager and writer of plays. As he grew older his urge to perform came to dominate him more and more, and in 1858 he began to give readings from his works to large audiences, making them laugh and weep with his astonishing dramatic power as he acted out the scenes of Fagin's execution or Winkle's duel. His other great interest in these later days was the detective story, and here his great friend and associate was Wilkie Collins, author of *The Woman in White*, the first English 'whodunit', which had appeared in *Household Words*. Under his influence Dickens began to write his last novel, *Edwin Drood*, but his public readings had exhausted him, and he died suddenly in May, 1870, leaving the book unfinished in mid-sentence. In some ways it is the most fascinating as it is the most tantalizing of all his novels. It is impossible to be sure how Dickens would have continued it, though many conjectures have been made, and it is well worth reading to see if one can decide for oneself how it might have ended.

Had he lived, Dickens might have developed the Novel still further, but in any event he had achieved much; his characters, with all their vitality, richness, and humour had become indeed 'household words', as they still are today, and when he was buried in Westminster Abbey the number of mourners showed that his novels had reached all kinds and classes of people and that the whole of England felt what a great writer he had been.

Sir Francis Drake

SCOURGE OF SPAIN

Eric Williams

I

I T was Whit Saturday, May 24, 1572, and there was a fair wind in the English Channel. Francis Drake gave the order and his two ships, *Pasha* under his command and *Swan* captained by his brother John, cast off from the quayside of the Barbican in Plymouth.

The galleons' sails filled and they swept out of the Sound past the small island which is now called Drake's. As a child of eight he had taken refuge on this island with his parents and his young brothers and sisters, after a Catholic mob had driven them from their farm cottage up at Crowndale near Tavistock. They had camped out on the island until the father, a seaman-turned-evangelist, was appointed preacher to the new Navy shipyard at Chatham, and moved his large family to live on a rotting hulk in the River Medway.

What little book-schooling Francis had, he had from his father. In his early 'teens he had been apprenticed to the captain of a small ship which traded with Holland across the North Sea. The boy soon proved his mettle and his seamanship, and the skipper took a strong liking to the tough, stocky, round-faced youngster who never accepted defeat nor let the cold North Sea storms damp his lively spirits. When the old man died, Francis inherited the tramp. He sold her to go back to Plymouth, to join John Hawkins who was engaged in the profitable slave trade between Africa and the Spanish West Indies.

He took part in two such expeditions, first as a junior officer and finally in command of the bark *Judith*, and on both occasions the voyages ended in disaster for the English adventurers, due to Spanish treachery.

Young Captain Drake, with the magnificent pride of the

142

fighting Englishman, then declared a private war on Spain. That the Spanish King Philip was intolerant of Protestants and tortured any of them he could lay hands on added zest to the battle, but primarily Francis Drake was out to recoup his losses a thousandfold, to make a name for himself and, incidentally, to serve his Queen, Elizabeth the First, and establish England as a Great Sea Power.

Quietly he made two voyages of reconnaissance to Panama and the Spanish Main. Now, not yet thirty years old, he was heading out into the Atlantic again on the buccaneering expedition which was to make his fortune and his name. His crew of 73 were all Devon men and boys, and only one of them was older than their Captain. They were resolved to intercept, on land or on sea, the Spanish gold convoy on its way from the mines of Peru to the coffers of King Philip.

II

Seven weeks later *Pasha* and *Swan* floated cautiously into the concealed natural harbour of Port Pheasant on the Isthmus of Panama. Drake had discovered the place on his last voyage, and had provisioned it as a base for his attack on Nombre de Dios, where the gold was embarked. The jungle he had cleared had grown in his absence. Worse, the Spaniards had discovered the hide-out and removed his stores.

Drake took a risk, and stayed. He also took precautions and built a stockade round his camp, where he assembled the three fast pinnaces he had shipped in sections. This done, he set sail for the Isle of Pines, nearer to Nombre de Dios. There he found some Cimaroons, escaped negro slaves who hated their cruel Spanish masters and who always repaid Drake's kindness with information and effective help.

Leaving *Pasha* and *Swan* at anchor Drake set out in the pinnaces to attack the city. He had timed the assault for dawn, but the strain of waiting began to tell on his young followers. It was part of Drake's genius that he could change his plan to overcome setbacks, and as the rising moon lightened the coast-line he cried, "It is dawn!" and the pinnaces sped silently in to attack.

There was a merchant ship in the harbour, but they chased it away. They swarmed over the sea wall, seized the defending

143

cannon, and tumbled them off their carriages. Leaving sixteen men to guard the boats, Drake sent his brother with half the remaining force to encircle the town and make for the market place from the east. He and the rest, drum playing, trumpet blowing, firehead arrows blazing, marched straight down the main street to meet them. Within minutes the town was theirs.

A thunderstorm broke, and they took shelter to keep their flintlocks and their bowstrings dry. When they moved off again Drake fainted, and his crew saw that where he had been standing was a pool of blood from a deep leg wound he had received in the fighting. Instead of breaking into the King's Treasure House and seizing the gold and pearls they had come for, they hoisted their captain on their shoulders and, despite his furious protests, re-embarked. Pausing only to remove the cargo of Canary wine from the ship they had disturbed, they sailed out of the harbour and found sanctuary on an island beyond gunshot of the town.

Drake recovered strength rapidly, and royally entertained a Spanish officer who had come under a flag of truce to inquire whether he was the dreaded 'El Draque' and whether the arrows his men had used were poisoned. Delightedly he acknowledged the first and indignantly denied the second. Jovially he warned the officer that the Governor should "open his eye, for with God's help I will reap some of that harvest that is sent into Spain to trouble the earth".

III

But Nombre de Dios had been alerted, and Drake decided to attack the mule treasure trains on their way across the Isthmus. As a feint he first harried shipping along the coast and among the islands, and even removed a captured ship in full daylight from the strongly fortified harbour of Cartagena.

With the three pinnaces in commission as well as *Pasha* and *Swan* he had not enough men for all his craft. He called Thomas Moone, *Swan*'s carpenter, to his cabin secretly one night and told him to bore three holes with his spike gimlet as near the keel as possible, during the second watch.

Thomas Moone was appalled. "But why? She is a good ship, new and strong, which has served you well on your last two voyages. Your brother John and my shipmates would kill me."

Drake explained the necessity, and that he did not want to cause his brother grief. Moone was persuaded.

The next morning being hot and still, Francis rowed across to *Swan* and called to John to come fishing. As they put off again from the ship's side he said, as though he had just noticed it, "The *Swan* is low in the water!"

John leaped back aboard and ordered his men to the pumps, refusing Francis's offered help and telling him to bring back plenty of fish. By the time Francis returned it was obviously hopeless. John and his crew took off their gear and set fire to their beloved ship. To comfort his brother, Francis made one of those generous gestures which help to explain his men's devotion: he put John in command of his own *Pasha*, and himself voyaged in a small uncomfortable pinnace.

IV

Pasha was anchored in another sheltered cove they called Port Plenty, and while John and his crew hunted ashore for pig and deer and looked for friendly Cimaroons, Francis and his men made more forays against Spanish shipping. Unhappily John was not content to leave all the fighting to his brother and during an attack on a passing Spanish vessel he was killed. Soon afterwards fever swept through the camp. Many of the seamen, including another brother named Joseph, died. Francis with intelligence in advance of those superstitious days, ordered the ship's surgeon to conduct an autopsy on Joseph's body, but they did not discover the cause of the fever. Later the surgeon too died, from the effects of a new drug which he had tried out on himself.

At last the Cimaroons reported that another load of the King of Spain's treasure was about to cross the Isthmus. It was again time for action. With 18 Englishmen and 30 Cimaroons Drake marched inland and climbed the mountain range. At the highest point Pedro, the Cimaroon leader, led Drake to a great tree and bade him climb the steps which were cut into the trunk.

From a platform in the branches Drake gazed for the first time on the Pacific Ocean. He was the first Englishman to see it. For him this glimpse of the other side of the world was an inspiration. He prayed God to give him 'life and leave to sail an English ship in those waters'. Years later he was to realize his ambition and return to England with a greater prize than the millions of pounds of treasure concealed in his hold—a successful circumnavigation of the globe, which opened up the rich trade of the East Indies to English merchants. It was the foundation of England's prosperity.

But the present treasure would not wait while he dreamed. He led his men down the Pacific watershed and hid them in long pampas grass to await the mule train which a Cimaroon had reported on its way. He ordered them to cover their doublets with their white shirts for easy recognition, issued each man with a tot of brandy, and forbade them to attack until he whistled.

One man, who had had more than his quota to drink, did not wait for the whistle but leaped up at the sound of a horse. A Cimaroon dragged him down, but it was too late. The Spanish horseman had seen the white-shirted figure, and gave warning. When the convoy reached the ambush and was captured Drake found that the treasure had been turned back and he was the richer by only a few stores.

Drake and his men recrossed the Isthmus, once more empty-handed but still undeterred. Again he harried Spanish shipping, captured cargo vessels, removing them to safety, emptying their holds and—if he did not need them—turning them loose with their crews. Unlike his enemies, he treated prisoners with a courtesy which was unusual in those days, and often sent them away with presents (after he had relieved them of all their possessions).

He was now shorthanded, and when he fell in with a French ship he bargained a half share of the plunder for the use of her best fighting men. Thus reinforced he was ready for another attempt at the treasure.

This time he decided to capture the convoy just before it reached Nombre de Dios, when the muleteers would be tired after their long trek across the Isthmus and less watchful as they neared their goal. The pinnaces sailed away to shelter after landing Drake, the French captain, and their men on the banks of a river 20 miles from the town. Pedro and his Cimaroons then guided the raiding party through the vast forest to the chosen spot.

146

The convoy, 200 mules laden with gold and silver, was guarded by 45 Spanish soldiers. It was a larger force than Drake's, but he had the advantage of surprise. After a fierce hand-to-hand battle the Spaniards fled, and Drake's voyage was, to use his own phrase, 'made'.

But the French captain was wounded. After burying the silver which they could not carry, Drake left two men to look after him and hurried away with the gold to the rendezvous he had made with the pinnaces.

When he arrived at the meeting-place the pinnaces were nowhere to be seen, and Spanish shipping was ominously near. Although they had just finished a forced march of 40 miles and were exhausted from the excitement of the battle, Drake did not despair. He found the strength to rally his men, help them fell trees and construct a rough raft. Telling the main party to remain hidden among the trees, he with three others paddled the half-submerged raft downriver to the sea where they found the pinnaces, which had been forced to move anchorage because of the enemy ships.

Tired as he was he could not resist a joke. He scrambled on board and to the eager question, "How did you fare?" he replied coldly, "Well"—his usual answer when things went ill! Then he relented and pulled a gold quoit from his doublet.

They went straight back to meet the rest of the party and then on to pick up the French captain and the buried silver. They found that the three Frenchmen had been killed by the Spaniards, and the silver was gone. The district was no longer safe and it was 'high time to think of homewards'. After paying the French crew their share of the gold (more than half a million pounds in today's money), Drake broke up the pinnaces and gave their precious ironwork to the Cimaroons. He offered Pedro whatever he wanted as a parting gift, and grinned stoically when the Cimaroon leader chose his most cherished sword which had once belonged to Henry of Navarre. He then provisioned his ships from shore and set sail for home.

On a Sunday morning in August, 17 months after he had embarked, he sailed *Pasha* with only 31 of his 73 young men into the Sound. The citizens of Plymouth tumbled out of church and raced to the Hoe. They could hear parson preach next Sunday, but Drake was home today.

147

V

Plymouth fêted the victorious seaman, but Queen Elizabeth did not. To the despair of her advisers she blew now hot, now cold, to Philip of Spain. Courageous herself, she was ever fearful of the danger of war for her subjects, and closed her eyes to Philip's scheming and avowed intention to secure the English throne. At the moment Philip was her beloved cousin and Drake, flaunting his Spanish wealth and conquests, a sore embarrassment. The Queen's Secretary advised him to disappear, and he spent the next two years in Ireland.

Then the wind of the Queen's favour changed and she even took shares in the expedition to the Southern Sea on which Drake had set his heart. She granted him an audience and told him frankly, "I would gladly be revenged on the King of Spain for divers injuries that I have received." The plan was as before, to torment the King of Spain and to seize his ships and his treasure, but in a different ocean and with royal sanction.

In December, 1577, Drake left Falmouth with a fleet of five ships: *Pelican, Elizabeth, Marigold, Benedict* and another *Swan*. Two years and ten months later he returned with one ship only the *Golden Hind* (as he had re-christened the *Pelican* before he passed through the Straits of Magellan). In that time he had quelled a mutiny with rough justice, and given the common seaman a Bill of Rights by declaring that 'the gentlemen must haul and draw with the mariners and the mariners with the gentlemen'. He had discovered that the land to the South of the Straits was not a great continent as Magellan had thought, but small islands in a limitless ocean. He had captured Philip's biggest treasure galleon off the coast of Peru, landed on the western mainland of North America and claimed it as 'New Albion' for Elizabeth, and tried for the fabled non-existent North-west Passage home. He had stuck firmly on a reef as he navigated the East Indian Archipelago, and it was only by a ruthless jettisoning of half the guns and a small fortune in spices, and with luck in a changing wind, that he had refloated the *Golden Hind* and brought her safely home round the Cape.

Again he found Elizabeth flirting with Spain, but she forgot Philip in her joy at Drake's achievement and at her share of the treasure. She visited the *Golden Hind* at Deptford, decreed

148

that the ship should be preserved, and knighted its Master. Knighthoods were rare in those days, and the honour, fame and fortune delighted the Devon boy brought up in the rough school of the sea. Although the courtiers were jealous of his advancement, the common people adored him. Like Winston Churchill in a later war he embodied the spirit of England.

In 1585 Drake, now an Admiral in the growing Navy, commanded another expedition to the Spanish Main. This time he missed the treasure fleet, but sacked the chief ports and captured 240 cannon. This completely demoralized the Spaniards and caused a serious setback to Philip who was busy amassing his Armada in the harbours of Spain and Portugal.

Drake did not rest on his laurels. A year later he was off to 'singe the King of Spain's beard' with a bold attack on the Armada which lay waiting for men and stores in Cadiz harbour. He set sail in a hurry, fearing that the Queen would change her mind. She did—but the pinnace she sent with all speed after him, to cancel his orders, met with 'foul winds' and could not catch him, although the wind for Drake was fair.

In the confined harbour of Cadiz Drake played havoc with the Armada and claimed that he sank 37 of its ships in all. He stormed Cape St. Vincent, the south-western point of Portugal, and used it as a base to blockade the supply line to Philip's ships gathered in Lisbon. He had the satisfaction of capturing the King's own treasure ship, before he sailed for home.

VI

Philip was still determined on the conquest of England. He meant to restore the Catholic church, burn Elizabeth as a heretic and, now that Mary Queen of Scots had died a traitor's death, he meant to have the English crown himself. With the zeal of a fanatic he mustered another Armada of 160 ships and 20,000 men, and in 1588 he despatched them across the Bay of Biscay on the 'Enterprise of England'.

On July 19 the huge fleet was sighted off the Lizard, and warning bonfires were soon aflame on every headland. Drake, who was playing a game of bowls on Plymouth Hoe when he heard the news, declared 'There is plenty of time to win this game, and to thrash the Spaniards too.' He was right. Thanks largely to his insistence, the English ships were no longer slow

Drake did not rest on his laurels. A year later he was
off to "singe the King of Spain's beard!"

and top-heavy like their enemies. They relied on gun battles across the water rather than grappling and boarding—and losing as many men as they killed in the close fighting.

Howard, the English Lord High Admiral, with his Vice-Admirals Drake, Hawkins and Frobisher, followed the slow Spanish galleons in tight formation up the Channel to Calais, at an average speed of two knots. They attacked when they could, anxious at all costs to prevent the enemy force from landing. There were small engagements off Plymouth, Start Point and Portland Bill, and a larger one in which the English ships pushed the Spaniards safely past the vulnerable Isle of Wight. The two fleets neared Calais on July 27, eight days after the Spaniards had first been sighted.

The English Navy was now full strength, and the wind was in its favour. Quickly the Admirals selected eight small ships, one of which was Drake's personal property. Skeleton crews sailed them close to the crowded Armada, set fire to them, took to their dinghies, and let the wind do the rest. The unhandy Spanish galleons made desperate attempts to avoid the flaming wrecks, but their Captains had been outwitted. They scattered in confusion, and the English completed the victory in the Battle of Gravelines two days later. The proud Armada was put to flight in the North Sea, and less than half of it limped home after a stormy voyage round the inhospitable coasts of Scotland and Ireland.

The Queen, exhilarated by victory, now agreed that Drake should carry the war back into Spanish waters; but she was not content to leave the conduct of the campaigns to him. She plied him with orders and counter-orders, and divided his command with first a General and then another Admiral who contested Drake's every decision. She allowed her gentlemen courtiers to embark as amateurs, and inevitably they got in his way.

He made two more expeditions, one to Spain and Portugal and one to Panama. Both were doomed to failure from the start, and finally his luck gave out. On his last attempt to win more gold from Philip's treasure-trove in the Indies, he went down with dysentery. On January 28, 1596, he died as his ship lay anchored off Puerto Bello, and on the next day he was buried at sea.

Thomas Alva Edison

THE MAN OF PRACTICAL GENIUS

Egon Larsen

I

ONE morning in September, 1869, a young man of twenty-two stepped from the steamboat that had brought him from Boston to New York. All his luggage was a small bag, and he had no more than one dollar in his pocket. Yet he brought with him the determination to conquer that great, crowded, busy city.

New York, however, took little notice of the young man. Everybody seemed preoccupied with his own affairs. There was an urgent problem to be solved: how could he get some breakfast without sacrificing his last 'buck'?

Absent-mindedly, he watched a tea taster sipping from a row of steaming cups at a warehouse. The tea taster saw the young man's hungry face and offered him a cup. That was his first 'meal' in New York.

He went on tramping through the streets in search of a friend who had gone to the big city before him. Surely that man would help him, perhaps offer him a job, lend him some money. ... At last the young man found his friend.

"Thomas Alva Edison! What on earth are you doing in New York?"

"I don't know yet!" said young Edison. "I've only just arrived. As a matter of fact, I wanted to ask you——"

"Look, Al. Here's a little cash. It'll get some food into you. And if you want a roof over your head—I've got a job as a telegraphist with the Gold Indicator Company in Wall Street. I guess nobody will notice if you sleep in the cellar room where the batteries are. Just for a few nights, of course, until you find work."

That night Edison slept in the battery room. The next day he strolled around the building. The Gold Indicator Company operated a few hundred 'tickers'—little telegraph receivers installed in the stockbrokers' officers around Wall Street for reporting the latest gold prices. The whole ticker network was a result of the American Civil War, which had cost the country so much money that the government had to issue enormous amounts of banknotes and suspend their exchange into gold coins. Thus the American currency split into gold and paper dollars, and the country fell victim to an alarming runaway inflation.

The only people who profited from it were the speculators. As the gold price rocketed and the value of the paper dollar sank, the stockbrokers had a good time buying and selling. A Gold Exchange had been established in Wall Street, and Mr. Laws, a former president of the Stock Exchange, established his ticker network operating from a central transmitter so that the stockbrokers would not have to send their messengers to learn the latest gold price.

Edison had been sheltering in the battery room for three days when suddenly pandemonium broke loose. Three hundred messenger boys from the stockbrokers stormed into the building, shouting that the tickers were not working. Behind them appeared some of their bosses, with sinister faces, for they suspected that some trick was being played on them.

But the breakdown was genuine; the transmitter had stopped, everybody was crowding around it, and the technicians were unable to find what was wrong. Mr. Laws was tearing his hair. "Get it going again, you numskulls!" he cried. "They'll be lynching us if you don't!"

"I think I can fix it," said a quiet voice behind him. Mr. Laws turned round to face a young man he had never seen before. "All right," he cried, "get it going again if you can!"

The machine was new to Edison, but for three days he had had a chance to look at it. He set to work. A small contact spring was broken—he had suspected something like this. He repaired it in a short time and without much difficulty, and the transmitter started up again.

Mr. Laws called him into his office. "I don't know who you are and I don't care," he said, "but this place needs a technical supervisor, and I am offering the job to you. Will you take it?"

153

The young man just nodded, overwhelmed. Mr. Laws shook him by the hand. 'Now sit down, Mr.—Mr.——"
"Edison."
"Glad to meet you, Mr. Edison. Now tell me something about yourself. Where do you come from? Where do you live? How did you acquire your technical experience?"
The young man told him his story.

II

Stolid fishermen and sailors for many a generation, the Edisons had emigrated from Holland to Canada because they were Quakers and wanted to live in religious freedom. One of them stood against the British in the Canadian rebellion, which was crushed; he fled across the United States border, and settled with his wife in the little town of Milan, on the shore of Lake Erie. One of his children was Thomas Alva, 'Al' for short, born in 1847.

He was an intelligent boy; but when once his teacher had dared to suggest that Alva had an 'addled brain', Al's mother was so furious that she took him out of that school and taught him herself—for she, too, had been a teacher before her marriage. About that time, too, the little town in which they lived was by-passed by a new railway line connecting Port Huron to Detroit. The disaster for Milan was a gain for Port Huron, and Al's father decided to set up a grain business there.

After the family had settled in Port Huron the railway line was soon playing a most important part in the boy's life. At the age of eleven he had started his first business venture— growing vegetables in the kitchen garden, and selling them to neighbours. The demand far exceeded what Al could supply, and he decided to go by train to Detroit every few days, and buy vegetables there for his customers. With his earnings, he bought books on chemistry and equipment for chemical experiments.

This went on for a few years. But Al soon extended his activities substantially by using the time he spent on the train. First he took copies of the Detroit newspapers with him on the way back, and sold them during the stops at the stations all along the line to Port Huron. Then he hit on the idea of producing his own newspaper in the luggage van of the train where he used to travel with his vegetables.

And so, at the age of fifteen, Al became the owner, reporter, editor, printer, publisher, and newsvendor of what even *The Times* in faraway London declared to be "the first newspaper to be printed on a train". It was called the *Weekly Herald*, a two-page sheet with local news from the towns along the line, some editorial musings by the young journalist, and a good deal of gossip. In its heyday, the paper had a circulation of 400 copies at three cents each. The luggage van was cluttered up with compositor's cases, printing press, books, chemicals, and vegetables. The railwaymen found this quite amusing; after all, the boy did no harm.

One day, however, the train was late, and the driver went faster than usual to make up for lost time. The coaches swayed wildly, and a stick of phosphorus fell off the rack in the luggage van. Within a few seconds, the van was on fire. The conductor stopped the train; with the help of the driver, the brakesman, and some passengers he put the fire out.

The next thing poor Al knew was that the conductor was throwing out all his belongings—printing press and test-tubes, newspapers and vegetables, books and chemicals; and finally it was Al himself who was sent flying from the train with a tremendous box on the ear.

He felt a sharp pain; he reeled and fell among the wreckage. What he did not at first realize was that the box on the ear had burst the drum. He was hard of hearing for the rest of his life.

He refused to be discouraged by his misfortune, however. He salvaged the printing equipment and published his news sheet from his home. Indeed, Al's journalistic career came to an end only when a big, strong man who had felt himself misrepresented in Al's gossip column caught the editor by the scruff of his neck and threw him into the river.

But Al had already decided that telegraphy was to be his career in life. Only he had not been able to find a telegraphist who would introduce him into the mysteries of that invention. One day, however, he happened to be waiting for a train in Mount Clemens station when he saw the station-master's child strolling in front of an approaching goods truck. He jumped on to the line and snatched the child out of danger—it missed being run over by a hair's breadth. One of the wheels actually grazed Al's boot. The station-master asked him how he could show his gratitude, and Al said that he would like to be taught telegraphy.

III

Four months later, at the age of sixteen, young Edison got his first job as a telegraphist on the Grand Trunk Railroad, and it was in this capacity that he made his first invention. It arose not so much from ambition to invent as from his desire to sleep without being disturbed. To make sure that the night staff was awake and alert, the company required them to send the Morse signal '6' from every station all along the line to headquarters punctually every hour. And punctually, Edison's hourly '6s' arrived at headquarters from the small station to which he had been posted. Once, for some reason, however, headquarters called him back by telegraph just after they had received his signal, '6'. There was no reply. An inspector was sent to see what was wrong. He found Al sound asleep on the couch. The ingenious young man had fixed an apparatus to the station clock that made it give the signal automatically every hour.

"We don't want inventors, we want telegraphists," Al was told, and was fired

But there were several railroad companies and many stations. Edison worked up and down the country, training himself to be one of the fastest telegraphists. Eventually he settled in Boston, with the Western Union company. When he had finished with his daily work in the telegraph office he went into a small workshop which he shared with another mechanic, and tinkered with all kinds of gadgets and inventions.

His first patent, granted in 1868, was a 'Voting Recorder', which he hoped to sell to the Washington authorities for use in the House of Representatives. It was meant to make the voting procedure easier, faster, and fool-proof. All the Representative would have to do was to press a button on his desk either for 'Aye' or 'No', and the apparatus would then count the votes automatically.

The chairman of the committee which tested the machine sent for the inventor. "Young man," he said, "if ever there was an undesirable invention it is this one. You probably don't know that the minority party in the House has only one effective weapon to prevent the passing of a bill by the majority, and that is by questioning the accuracy of the voting figures. Your machine works too well; it's too reliable. In short: we don't want it!"

IV

Much of this story he told Mr. Laws. At the end of the interview he heard that his new job of technical supervisor would bring him 70 dollars per week. As he walked down the stairs to his 'home' in the battery room, he felt queer at the very thought of so much money.

Yet this was only the beginning. A year later, when the Gold Indicator Company merged with a rival firm, the new president, General Lefferts, commissioned him to design an entirely new ticker system. He did so, and the General asked him how much he would want for the patent rights in the machine. Edison thought that 5000 dollars would be wonderful, but he was prepared to accept 3000. However, he feared that if he asked for so much money he might be thrown out. "I leave it to you, sir," he said.

"Would you be satisfied," said the General, "with forty thousand?"

Much later, Edison confessed in his memoirs that at that moment "I came as near fainting as I ever got." Three days later the contract was signed, and he received the first cheque he had ever held in his hands. He went to the bank and handed it to the cashier. The latter said something which Edison, in his deafness, could not understand, and shoved the cheque back at him. So it was all a practical joke the General had played on him, and the 'cheque' was a worthless piece of paper! Edison crumpled it up and put it in his pocket. Back in General Lefferts's office, he began to complain about having been tricked when the General started laughing. "My dear young friend," he said to the inventor, "all the cashier wanted to tell you was that you should endorse the cheque with your name!"

Edison was back at the bank like a shot. The cashier, however, really played a joke on him by paying out the entire sum in small banknotes. Edison stuffed them in his pockets until the seams nearly burst. He lay awake all night for fear that a

157

burglar might come and steal the money. The next day he asked General Lefferts for advice. "Have you never heard of a bank account?" asked the General. And back to the bank went Edison to open the first bank account in his life.

With the money he had earned he opened a large laboratory in Newark, and for the next few years he worked on a number of improvements in the field of telegraphy—automatic transmission, the printing of Roman characters insteads of dots and dashes, multiple telegraphy over a single line, and other inventions, many of which are still in everyday use. He got married to a charming girl who worked in his laboratory, a shocking idea in those days when girls were meant to stay at home until they became engaged. But Edison liked her just for that reason—because she had a mind as unconventional as his own.

v

In 1876, when he was twenty-nine, he built himself a whole village of laboratories at Menlo Park in New Jersey, an hour's train ride from New York. It was the year of the great Centennial Exhibition at Philadelphia where many fascinating new inventions were shown, including Alexander Graham Bell's telephone. Edison immediately pounced on it to improve it; he invented a better contrivance than Bell's for turning sound waves into electric impulses. Edison used carbon dust because its particles responded quickly and reliably to the sound waves by variations of their electrical resistance. He called his gadget the 'microphone'.

One day in 1877 he was working on a machine designed to record telegraphic signals on a wax cylinder. He was busy adjusting the needle which he used to impress the dots and dashes in the wax, talking to a mechanic at the same time—when suddenly he felt a sharp pain in his finger. The needle had pricked it at a certain sound coming from his lips!

Edison dropped everything he was working on and at once made a rough sketch of one of the strangest gadgets he had ever asked his mechanics to build. It was to be a metal cylinder with a handle and an ear-trumpet with a parchment membrane and a needle at its end, mounted on a pivot above the cylinder. It was a machine for recording and reproducing sounds!

The machine was ready within a day or two. Edison spread

a sheet of tinfoil round the cylinder, turned the handle, and spoke the first words that came to his mind into the ear-trumpet: "Mary had a little lamb, its fleece was white as snow . . ."

Then he put the needle back at the starting point and turned the handle again. "I was never so taken aback in my life," he wrote later. For there came the faint but clear words out of the machine: "Mary had a little lamb . . ." A human voice had been captured for the first time in history.

VI

The 'phonograph', as Edison called his machine, had a sensational success. It made his name famous the world over within a few weeks. The newspapers called him 'The Wizard of Menlo Park'. Everybody wanted to buy a phonograph. But the craze was soon over; the machine was still too imperfect and too difficult to handle. And with the public, the inventor himself lost interest in his amazing machine. Only ten years later he took it from the shelf, worked on it for five days and nights (Edison ignored the clock when he was concentrating on a job), and turned it into a fool-proof little penny-in-the-slot machine for fun arcades. It made a fortune for him. Other inventors, however, gave the sound-reproducing machine its present form, replacing Edison's revolving cylinder by a flat disc from which any number of copies could be made. That was the birth of the 'gramophone'.

Despite the financial success which Edison achieved with his inventions he never cared to see that they were commercially exploited. It was the problem that fascinated him, not the reward which its solution might yield; and he was prepared to spend his bottom dollar to find that solution. Once, after pursuing an idea for many months, he had to admit that he was beaten— which he did with this characteristic remark to his fellow workers: "Well, the money's all gone, but wasn't it fun spending it?"

After the first success of the phonograph his mind soon turned to another problem, which scientists and inventors in many countries had been unable to solve—the problem of electric light. He had seen an arc-light installation using carbon plates to produce an unpleasant, wasteful, flickering, bluish light; and he decided to invent something cheaper, more practical, and less harmful to the eyes. He had noticed that strips

159

of carbonized paper glowed for a few seconds with a bright, incandescent light when an electric current was passed through them. If some more suitable material were placed in a vacuum tube, without oxygen so that it would not burn up, surely the light would shine much longer, he thought.

He searched for that material with infinite patience and resourcefulness. It had to be carbonized first to be made to glow in the vacuum bulb. He carbonized everything he could lay hands on—from coconut shells to the red hair of a casual visitor to Menlo Park. He even employed a Japanese farmer to grow a certain kind of bamboo for him, and sent an expedition up the Amazon River in search of rare plants that might perhaps be suitable.

One night in October, 1879, he sat at his desk, wondering what to carbonize next. His eye fell on a button on his jacket that was coming loose. Absent-mindedly, he pulled it off, and fingered the bit of thread still hanging from the jacket. "Why not try sewing thread?" he thought and went out into the laboratory.

The thread was carbonized and carefully placed in a vacuum bulb. Edison switched the current on. The sewing thread began to glow with a pleasant, yellowish light . . . and continued to glow. Bets were laid by everybody in the laboratory: how long would it glow? A minute? An hour perhaps?

It glowed for 40 hours. The incandescent lamp was invented.

VII

Within a year, Edison had developed his lamp so well that it burnt for 500 hours and could be mass-produced at a reasonable price. Then came the greatest venture of his life: after conquering almost insuperable difficulties—technical as well as financial—he succeeded in turning a whole district of New York into the first electrically-lit area in the world. On September 4, 1882, 14,000 Edison lamps in 900 houses "burst into a bright and mellow brilliance as the switch was pulled at a signal from the famous inventor"—so wrote the *New York Herald.* "Lo and behold, the dim flicker of gas was supplanted by a steady beam, under which one could sit down and write for hours. What his critics said was impossible the Wizard of Menlo Park has made an everyday reality!"

It was inevitable that Edison should have tried his hand at

Edison switched on the current. The sewing thread began to
glow with a pleasant, yellowish light . . . and continued to glow

solving another problem that was in the air: that of making photographs come to life. The marketing of a new photographic material, the celluloid film, prompted him to build a camera for the recording of continuous movement. Curiously enough, however, he did not adapt a magic lantern to project these pictures before a large audience, but built a peep-show for one person only. He combined the 'kinetoscope', as he called it, and the phonograph into a new attraction for the fun arcades: you put a penny in the slot, turned a handle, and saw a scene in motion through the eyepieces while a phonograph was playing. The kinetoscope was one of Edison's most popular achievements, but he did not go on to invent the cinema.

Work never ceased for Edison. His staff at Menlo Park worked in shifts around the clock. When he was 'up to something' he did not go home for days on end, taking short naps on a laboratory table with a couple of books for a pillow. At midnight he and his fellow-workers would have a meal; someone would play a piece on the harmonium and they would all sing. Then they would go back to their jobs. Edison's only 'vices' were heavy cigars and strong black coffee.

There is hardly a technical or scientific field to which he did not apply his fertile brain, from Portland cement to wireless telegraphy. He had already become a legendary figure when he left his laboratories on America's entering the First World War, in order to work for the United States Government without pay, building chemical factories and developing substitutes for drugs and dyes which had been obtained from Germany before the war.

He once said that genius was only 1 per cent inspiration—and 99 per cent perspiration. It was certainly an enormous amount of perspiration which helped him to take out no fewer than 2,500 patents, American and foreign. He was actively at work almost to the day of his death in October, 1931, a happy man and a lucky one, for he had earned a rich reward for his labours.

We shall never see a universal inventor of his stature again; for during the few decades since his lifetime Science has become so specialized that no single human mind could do more than forge ahead on a narrow sector of scientific research—not even the mind of a genius such as Thomas Alva Edison.

Elizabeth I

THE QUEEN WITH THE HEART OF A KING

Peggy Chambers

I

A T ten o'clock on the morning of Palm Sunday, 1554, Elizabeth Tudor landed by barge at the stairs of Traitors' Gate in the Tower of London. Looking up at the high grey walls, she thought fearfully of the many people who had been brought here as prisoners, as she was today, and who had never come out alive.

She had left a city bearing all the gruesome proofs of Sir Thomas Wyatt's rebellion against her half-sister, Queen Mary. The latter had been on the throne only a few months, but this was the second uprising of her reign. She had had to defeat the first one in order to gain her crown. Before his death in 1553, the boy king, Edward VI (son of Henry VIII and his third wife, Jane Seymour), had altered his will, naming his cousin, Lady Jane Grey, as his successor and cutting out his sisters, Mary and Elizabeth.

He had no right to do this, but had been 'persuaded' by the Duke of Northumberland, the most powerful nobleman of the time, who had taken care to have Lady Jane married to his own son. Jane, the granddaughter of Henry VIII's younger sister Mary, was a brilliant and studious girl who had not the slightest desire for a crown, but was merely a tool in the hands of the Duke and her parents who shared his ambition. When Edward died she was proclaimed Queen.

The people of England, however, would not accept her. They had nothing against Lady Jane herself, but they recognized the injustice done to Mary and rallied to her cause. The hated Northumberland was defeated, and the unwilling Queen of nine days sent to the Tower.

Mary, joyfully welcomed by her people, treated the rebels—

except Northumberland who was executed—very leniently, and Lady Jane and her husband were not kept in strict confinement. No doubt they would have been freed if a second rebellion had not forced Mary to sterner measures.

It was Mary's ambition to restore England, now mostly Protestant, to the Catholic faith of her mother, Catherine of Aragon, Henry VIII's first wife. Because she had borne no son, Henry, after twenty years of marriage, divorced her (though the Church of Rome never recognized this). He had then married one of her maids of honour, the dark-eyed, quick-tongued Anne Boleyn, who became the mother of Elizabeth I. Within three years Anne had been accused of unfaithfulness to the King and sent on her last frightening journey to Traitors' Gate. It was not unnatural that Mary, daughter of Catherine, should grow up to hate Elizabeth, daughter of Anne; and though her earlier hatred of her young half-sister, the Protestant Elizabeth, had softened considerably, feelings between them were still very strained.

Mary's early popularity did not last long. Although she had some support from her older subjects for her religious crusade, she had none at all for her proposed marriage to Philip of Spain, for that would have meant for every Englishman the possibility of foreign domination.

In January, 1554, revolt against Mary flared up in several places, but chiefly in Kent, where it was led by Sir Thomas Wyatt. With typical Tudor courage, Mary spoke to her people from the Guildhall in London, and they rallied to her again. Wyatt was captured, and Lady Jane and her husband, innocent themselves, but likely to supplant Mary if the rebels had their way, were executed.

For most of her sister's reign Elizabeth had remained at one or other of the royal manors. But to Simon Renard, the Spanish Ambassador, Elizabeth was a far more dangerous threat to Mary's throne than Jane had been. Wyatt, it was said, had written incriminating letters to her. She must be brought to London and questioned. She came, and it was small wonder that her foot was not quite steady as she stepped upon the rain-polished stairs at Traitors' Gate that morning.

"Lord," she cried, "I never thought to have come in here as prisoner."

II

At Whitehall Renard was urging Mary to action.

"The Lady Elizabeth must be questioned, Madam."

"She will have her answers ready, never fear, Master Renard," retorted Mary. "She is long practised in argument."

Renard persisted. "She is a threat to your Grace's person and your throne, as was the Lady Jane."

"Poor Jane!" said Mary softly. "She was so young. She had no ill intent towards us. She was used by others."

"As the Lady Elizabeth might be," Renard pointed out.

Mary smiled wryly. "I hardly think the Lady Elizabeth will let herself be used by anyone. The temper of the people is high in her favour."

Renard recalled some of the people's recent demonstrations against his masters—the ambassadors arriving from Spain to complete the marriage treaty had been snowballed by London schoolboys. "You are Queen, Madam," he reminded her. "You will want your capital cleared of rebels before July."

July! Mary sighed! Philip was coming to be her husband. She prayed they would have a son to succeed to her throne—a Catholic son, to save her people from Elizabeth and Protestantism. But Elizabeth *was* her sister, and nothing had been proved against her yet. Wyatt had been tried and awaited death. Except for her faith Mary did not like shedding blood.

"Elizabeth shall be questioned again," she told Renard and would promise nothing more.

III

Elizabeth was brought before the councillors, but they got nothing out of her. When Wyatt was taken for execution in April he declared her innocent from the scaffold, and London rang with shouts of "God save the Lady Elizabeth!"

After much debating, Mary packed her off to one of the country manors again and her journey there was like a royal progress. But Elizabeth did not forget that she had stood near to death. She would wait for what the future would bring. She was good at waiting.

Mary's unhappy life dragged to its frustrated end in 1558. Elizabeth was at Hatfield when, on November 17, Sir William

165

Cecil came to tell her that she was Queen. She rose to her feet. "This is the Lord's doing," she said, "and it is marvellous in our eyes." England was hers at last.

True, it was a poor enough legacy, but she read challenge in its very disaster. Cecil, who, after being Secretary to Somerset, Protector of Edward VI, had steered his diplomatic genius safely through the reigns of both Jane and Mary, became her Secretary, and later Treasurer.

"The judgment I have of you," she told him, "is that you will not be corrupted with any manner of gift, and that you will be faithful to the State; and that without respect to my private will you will give me that counsel which you think best."

For forty years he maintained her trust. They wrangled, schemed and planned for England throughout that long, loyal partnership. Unobtrusive, he was there when needed, and she called him 'Sir Spirit'.

He summed up her inheritance thus: "The Queen poor, the realm exhausted, the nobles poor and decayed; good captains and soldiers wanting; the people out of order; justice not executed; the justices not meet for their offices; all things dear; division among ourselves; war with France and Scotland; the French King bestriding the realm, having one foot in Calais and the other in Scotland; steadfast enmity but no steadfast friendship abroad."

It was not much of a Merrie England. Her first task, delicate indeed, was the composition of the new Council; but, having made a few appointments, she left the rest of the seats empty. It would not hurt their aspirants to wait for a while. On her first public document, instead of flourishing 'Head of the Church' at the end of her titles, she added a noncommittal 'etcetera', which kept both faiths wondering. She was the first sovereign to conduct her own foreign affairs. A fine scholar and versed in Latin, French, and Italian, she needed no interpreter when interviewing ambassadors, and her genius in argument defeated them at that game of deception called diplomacy.

Heavy as were the economies she had to make, she gloried in satisfying her people's appetite for pageantry. During the first weeks of her reign she rode through London or passed down river by barge, courting her people's love which she valued above all jewels, and which, having captured, she never lost.

Her coronation was planned for January 15, 1559. The day before, dressed in cloth of gold, she was carried in an open litter through the City to Westminster, her attendants wearing crimson damask and velvet with the Tudor Rose in silver on back and front of their jerkins. The streets were hung with tapestries and swinging with banners, and the packed crowds craned to see her pass.

She had the quick eye of her mother and the affable good-fellowship of her father, and she dispensed this woven gracious-ness with such impartiality that the acclamations dimmed the bells and drums and gunfire. But mostly they were won by her smiling thanks for the flowers tossed to her, her personal greeting of those who shed tears of ecstasy, her assurance to the Lord Mayor that she would if necessary 'spend her blood for her people'.

When she was crowned at Westminster a foreign envoy com-mented acidly on the informality with which she tempered the pomp and ritual. But throughout her reign she judged the feelings of her people perfectly. Thus Elizabeth, at her most royal, could touch the common heart.

IV

But she was equally aware of the danger of enmity in more powerful minds. Mary, Queen of Scots, granddaughter of Henry VIII's elder sister Margaret was, in Catholic eyes, heir to Mary Tudor's throne, for to them Elizabeth was illegitimate. Indeed, on Mary Tudor's death, she had assumed the title of Queen of England. Now that she was married to the Dauphin of France, her father-in-law might be tempted to use his influence with the Pope against Elizabeth, even to deposing her.

In Spain King Philip had inherited the greatest empire the world had seen since the days of imperial Rome, with the most powerful army and navy and tremendous wealth on land and sea. He certainly did not want France to dominate England, but Elizabeth well knew that his own aim was to impose his religious beliefs upon the world. For some years, along with other suitors, she let him court her. Thus dangled, he was not likely to make war on her.

167

Queen Elizabeth I rode through London or passed down
river by barge, courting her people's love

Mary, Queen of Scots, became Queen of France as well in 1559, but a few months later her husband died and, at the age of nineteen, she returned to Scotland. The question of who would succeed Elizabeth, vexed by Elizabeth's ability to keep her own suitors in suspense, was further complicated when, in 1565, Mary married her cousin, Henry Stuart, Lord Darnley, also descended from Margaret Tudor by her marriage to the Earl of Angus. The English Catholics looked upon Darnley, as he himself did, as First Prince of the Blood in England. Thus Mary's position was considerably strengthened.

But he was weak and vicious, and the only happiness the marriage brought Mary was the birth of her son James. In 1567 Darnley was murdered. A few weeks later Mary married the Earl of Bothwell who, with herself, was suspected of complicity in the crime, and whose own wife had been speedily granted a divorce. The nobles had no love for Darnley, but they had even less for the arrogance of Bothwell. They revolted, Bothwell fled, and Mary was brought to Edinburgh, where the people in the streets demanded her death by fire or water. Imprisoned in the island castle of Loch Leven, she was induced to renounce her throne in favour of her son.

Elizabeth, though not condoning the Bothwell affair, expressed herself vehemently against the Scottish nobles. Emphatically she did not want the French to interfere—it was suggested that the baby prince be sent to France—but she had a strong sense of rank, and when her own Council sided with the Scots, she lost her temper.

"They have neither warrant nor authority by the law of God or man to be as superiors, judges, or vindicators over their prince or sovereign, howsoever they do gather or conceive matter against her," she stormed.

Cecil and the others shook their heads. "If the Lords speak not English," they pointed out, "they will speak French."

But Elizabeth raged on and insisted that they come to an understanding with Mary. Then, after ten months, Mary escaped. Elizabeth wrote congratulating her and offering to mediate between her and her people, but warning her not to seek aid from France as that might lead to war. "Those who have two strings to their bow may shoot stronger," she said, "but they rarely shoot straight."

But the letter was never delivered. Mary's army was routed at Langside and on May 16, 1568, she fled over the Border to beg Elizabeth's protection. This made matters doubly difficult for Elizabeth. If she sent Mary back to Scotland, the Scots would demand her life. She would not send her to France. But neither would she risk the Church of England. There was no other course but to keep her as a prisoner, honoured, but still a prisoner. She remained one for nineteen years.

Country houses acquired a new legend if she stayed there, as others did if Elizabeth slept in them. In some cases there was more legend than truth, for Elizabeth, in spite of the fame of her progresses, did not go beyond Dover, Southampton, Bristol, Worcester, Stafford and Norwich. It was an unfortunate omission for, with her gift of winning people's hearts, she would most likely have captured their loyalty, religion or not. As it was, she never visited the northern half of England and this remained true to Mary, whose romantic person excited sympathy wherever she went, no matter how her past might offend religious scruples.

Year after year conspiracies were woven in her cause. In 1569, the North rose for her but was put down. In 1570 the Ridolfi plot, led by an Italian banker with Spanish aid and the sympathy of the aged Duke of Norfolk, their intention being to rescue Mary and arrest Elizabeth, was exposed by Cecil. Norfolk, who had been allowed parole after the Northern rising, was now arrested for treason, but Elizabeth hated signing a death warrant even for a traitor, and several months passed before she did so.

Although Elizabeth paid £52 a week towards the cost of Mary's household, Mary, in the intervals of sending her exquisite samples of needlework, used the money allowed her as Dowager Queen of France to pay her spies. Elizabeth, who would no doubt have done exactly the same, was quite aware of this.

"You have much secret communication with the Queen of Scotland," she wrote the French ambassador, "but, believe me, I know all that goes on in my kingdom. I myself was a prisoner in the days of the Queen, my sister, and am aware of the artifices that prisoners use to win over servants and obtain secret intelligence."

170

Still the intrigues went on, but it was not until the Babington plot in 1586 was exposed by Walsingham, Elizabeth's Secretary, proving beyond doubt that Mary was party to a conspiracy to bring an army to England, that Elizabeth could hold out no longer. In all her long queenship she hated nothing so much as sending Mary to her death, but for twenty years Mary's life had endangered hers.

Mary was tried at Fotheringay Castle in Northamptonshire. On February 8, 1587, she died calmly on the black-draped scaffold erected in the hall. Imprisonment and rheumatism had sapped the beauty of her face and figure, and her grey-cropped hair was covered with an auburn wig, but her courage and dignity did not falter. She had set aside her own son, who was a Protestant, from the succession to her rights in England, and named Philip of Spain as her heir. London went mad with joy, but Elizabeth could neither eat nor sleep.

V

If Elizabeth was looked upon as leader of the Protestants, Philip was head of a vast number of Catholics. Under his domination the Inquisition, which tortured men for having a different faith, operated in Spain, Italy, and the Netherlands. Now he had one ambition, which he regarded as a duty to his faith—to break the power of England and humble Elizabeth. Admittedly he was further incensed by the plundering of his ships by her seamen. From 1585 he had directed his whole energies towards preparing what he called the Most Fortunate and Invincible Armada, and a harvest of galleons was being garnered in the Spanish ports.

England was as usual harried for money. Elizabeth could not afford to keep both army and navy mobilized and, moreover, she hated war. But she, who could pay the waiting game so brilliantly as long as it suited her, knew better than anyone else when to strike.

She had fine seamen at her command, albeit that some of them were known to engage in piracy and slavery. Sir John Hawkins had been Treasurer of the navy since 1577 and was in favour of the new methods of warfare. Henry VIII, founder of the modern navy, had had port holes cut in the sides of his ships and guns mounted to fire through them nearer to the water line. The latest ships were no longer unwieldy tubs, but slimmer and faster. Captains and sailors had no fear of the Spaniards, provided they had the ships to go out and meet them. Spain was taking a long time to assemble hers, however, and waiting cost money. In 1587 Drake, who did not like inaction, set out to prove that attack was the best method of defence.

With a small squadron he sailed into Cadiz harbour and brazenly destroyed thousands of tons of shipping and stores. He stormed San Domingo and Santiago, and took Cape St. Vincent. Lisbon was too well defended for him to repeat the effrontery, so, instead of wasting his ammunition, he sat at anchor watching the port with a cool impudence the Spaniards must have found infuriating.

The Pope, who had even been moved to compliment Elizabeth on her statesmanship at one time or another, rubbed salt in the wounds. "Just look at Drake. What forces has he? We are sorry to say it, but we have a poor opinion of this Spanish Armada, and fear some disaster."

Humiliated by their own lack of action, the Spaniards called Drake, among other things, the Dragon. "He is no man," they cried, "but a devil. He works by witchcraft. He gives orders to the wind and waves."

Drake, not caring what they said, seized £114,000 worth of booty off the Azores on the way home and thus, in his own words, singed the King of Spain's beard; the invasion was postponed until, presumably, it grew trim again.

Meanwhile, England, given a breathing space, was making sacrifices in order to swell the navy into a fleet of 191. The largest ship was only of 1000 tons, but it was called The Triumph.

It was May, 1588, before the Armada, sped by the prayers of Spain and blessed by the Pope, in spite of his misgivings, set sail from the Tagus. It carried 22,000 men, as well as 180 priests bearing the apparatus of torture which was to convert England to the old faith. Six inquisitors had already been appointed, and Elizabeth was to be burnt alive. The fleet planned to call at Dunkirk, where the Duke of Parma was waiting with his army, which had marched there from the Netherlands, and convoy his troops across in flat-bottomed barges. England determined to prevent this, but had soldiers posted along the east coast as far north as the Wash in case of emergency.

On July 19, with an air appropriate to that of a Spanish grandee, the Armada moved up the Channel, the great galleons looking like floating baronial halls. Admiral Lord Howard of Effingham was playing an after-dinner game of bowls on Plymouth Hoe with some of his officers when Captain Fleming of the *Golden Hind* rushed up to tell them that it had been sighted off the Lizard. The players turned at once to Vice-Admiral Sir Francis Drake, who paused, wood in hand.

"There is plenty of time," he said, "to win this game, and to thrash the Spaniards too."

He spoke, not out of bravado, but as an experienced seaman. The wind had slackened, the tide was running up-Channel, and he knew that they could not move the English ships from where they were in those conditions.

The fleets met on July 21. Now the slimmer English ships came into their own. They nosed among the galleons, closed on them, drew off, moved twice as fast, shot four to one, and, on July 27, after a running fight, the Armada, driven past hope of contact with Parma, took shelter in Calais roads. That night Howard sent fire ships among them and spread panic in flame. The English closed in again next day and scattered what was left. Even the wind, blowing up-Channel, opposed the Spaniards and they had to escape round the Orkney Islands. Here storm and tempest dealt them further blows, the island shores were strewn with the bodies of sailors, and only 53 wounded ships limped home to Corunna.

VI

Elizabeth's majesty had towered to the occasion. Two armies had been formed, one to guard her at St. James's, the other to wait at Tilbury in case of a possible landing by Parma. She drove by coach to Tilbury, there mounted a white horse and, with a marshal's baton in her hand, rode up and down the lines of her troops. Her words to them have become immortal:

"... Let tyrants fear. I have always so behaved myself that, under God, I have placed my chiefest strength and safeguard in the loyal hearts and goodwill of my subjects; and therefore I am come amongst you, as you see, at this time, nor for my recreation and disport, but being resolved, in the midst and heat of the battle, to live or die amongst you all, to lay down for my God, and for my kingdom, and for my people, my honour and my blood, even in the dust. I know I have the body of a weak and feeble woman, but I have the heart and stomach of a king, and of a king of England, too, and think foul scorn that Parma or Spain, or any prince of Europe should dare to invade the borders of my realm; to which, rather than any dishonour shall grow by me, I myself will take up arms, I myself will be your general, judge, and rewarder of every one of your virtues in the field. I know, already for your forwardness you have deserved rewards and crowns; and we do assure you, in the word of a prince, they shall be duly paid you."

The men fell on their knees before her as she ended: "Lord bless you all."

While Philip prayed alone in his Escorial, Elizabeth rode triumphantly through London. A service of thanksgiving was held at St. Paul's Cross, and the captured banners of Spain waved in the English breeze. We had not lost a single ship.

The battle cost England £161,000. It cost Spain immeasurably more in blood and pride. Philip swore he would try again if he had to melt down the silver candlesticks on his table, but his power was broken.

VII

Elizabeth once said that she "had a great longing to do some act that would make her fame spread abroad in her lifetime and, after, occasion memorial for ever". Her whole reign did that. She raised her country from the depths to the heights by statesmanship which, obedient to tradition, men believed impossible in a woman.

They were still cruel times—humanity's Renaissance did not come until the 19th century—there was poverty, corruption, unemployment, but far less at the end than at the beginning of her reign. The long period of peace which she and her ministers gave England provided time and room for the growth of trade, for the voyages which opened up new lands and markets, and, above all, for the flowering of that incomparable garden of dramatic and poetic genius headed by William Shakespeare.

Whatever her faults—her vanity, her temper, her unscrupulousness (which was, after all, the craft of diplomacy), her parsimony in finance, her extravagance in display—all were tuned to the service of her country. No foreign name was ever written across Elizabeth's heart. For nearly forty-five years she and England were one.

On January 21, 1603, the Court moved to Richmond in bad weather. A few weeks later the death of an old friend brought on a recurrence of the melancholy common to old age which has been bereaved of its contemporaries. She could not throw it off. Her body, which had so magnificently carried its burden of sovereignty, was failing, but her heart was still great. When a hint to name her successor was ventured, she retorted, "Who shall succeed me but a king?"

Over the Border the King waited—James VI of Scotland. On March 24, between the hours of two and three in the morning, a light went out in a window of Richmond Palace . . . and out of England.

Jean Henri Fabre

EXPLORER OF THE INSECT WORLD

John Crompton

I

TIMES were hard. A worried-looking French peasant sat discussing the situation with his wife.

"We might get some ducks," he said. "The tallow-maker reared some and sold them for a good price. They grow quickly. The big, black hen is broody. We could put some eggs under her, and when they hatch Jean can look after them."

A small boy of five, pretending to be asleep on his straw in the corner, heard and felt pleased. He would enjoy looking after ducklings.

A neighbour had a brown hen that was broody and offered to lend it them, so two dozen duck eggs were procured and twelve put under each hen.

When the eggs hatched the brown hen was returned. The black hen could look after them all, for an extra hen needs extra feeding.

As they grow up ducklings also need extra feeding. Again the peasant had a consultation with his wife. There was a large, shallow pond up the valley. It was full of water-weeds and worms and things, and nobody ever went there. On this pond the ducklings could look after themselves and would need no feeding; nor would they be interfered with. Yes, that was the solution. Jean could drive the ducklings there in the morning.

They started early, the bare-footed Jean carrying a switch and driving the ducklings. But progress was slow. Jean had a blister on his heel, and the ground was rough and stony. The sun grew hot. The ducklings, as tender-footed as Jean, stumbled and panted. Every few minutes they had to rest. But at last, foot-sore and weary, the little band reached the pond.

What a change came then! Quacking loudly, the ducklings

176

tumbled into the water. They splashed over the surface, flapped their stumpy wings, up-ended themselves and dug in the bottom. The terrible journey was forgotten.

Jean, too, was happy. He paddled and went about exploring. He found the stream that fed the pond and made a little water-wheel out of sticks and pieces of straw. He found stones containing shining minerals which he thought were precious jewels and which he put into his pockets thinking they might relieve the poverty at home. And then—— What was that?

Something had darted down and hidden in the mud. He tried to get it out, but failed. Then he saw other little creatures. The pond was full of them; tiny things that swam or wriggled or dived to the bottom, beetles, worms, tadpoles, mosquito larvae, water-boatmen, caddis-worms, newts and other things.

What were they, and what were they doing?

It was time to be going back, there was work for him at home. But the boy never even gave it a passing thought. He was trying to catch those little creatures and examine them more closely. Most eluded him, but he got a few of the slower movers and, having no tin or jar, put them in his pockets. He also got sopping wet.

Only the failing light made him realize that the day was gone. He went home. The blister was almost forgotten. He seemed to walk on air. He had seen wonderful things.

But he came down to earth with a bump when he reached home. "Where have you been?" shouted his furious parents. "What have you been doing? What are those stones that have broken your pockets open? What are those horrible slimy things?"

"Throw the whole lot away!" roared his father.

"A nice thing," moaned his mother, "bringing up children to have them turn out like this. You'll bring me to my grave—tearing your pockets with stones and carrying horrible creatures that will bite and poison you. There's no doubt—someone has thrown a spell over you!"

And a spell *had* been thrown over the boy from that day on, for the boy was Jean Henri Fabre, the greatest naturalist the world has known. Statues were to be erected to him, princes were to honour him—but not for very, very many years.

Jean Fabre was happy; he paddled and went about
exploring, found the stream that fed the pond and
made a little water-wheel

II

When he was seven Jean went to the village school. There was only one master and he had to teach boys of all ages. All they really learnt was to chant in chorus the multiplication table up to twelve times twelve (for at that time France had not adopted the metric system). Jean taught himself to read only because his father gave him a coloured card of letters with pictures of animals on it—A standing for Ape, Z for Zebra, and so on. Later, at a school at Carpentras, he learnt Latin and came to excel at it because he found that Vergil had written fascinating accounts of the bee, the cicada, the turtle-dove, the crow, and the nanny-goat.

While still in his 'teens he became a teacher in a primary school, where his class contained boys older than himself, whose one ambition was to play tricks on their youthful master.

He was determined to rise above the level of a primary school, and studied hard in his spare time. He taught himself algebra, mathematics, physics, chemistry and an amazing number of other subjects, passed exams, got his certificates and diplomas, and finished up by becoming a professor at the University of Avignon.

In those days for an impecunious peasant to rise to such a position was remarkable. It meant giving all his spare time to study. That did not worry him; in fact he liked it. What did worry him in his earlier years can best be expressed in one word —insects. He had bought a large book containing the pictures and names of many insects and he was always finding himself studying it when he ought to have been studying mathematics or some similar subject. Also, instead of keeping to his desk on holidays or off-hours, he found himself going off into the country to search out these insects and see what they were doing.

Finally he decided that insects might well ruin his career. He would give them up. Into the bottom of his trunk went the book and when he met an insect he looked the other way. He kept to this arrangement for some time, but he had attempted the impossible. Fabre could no more give up insects than a drug addict can give up dope. He had to give in in the end and he compromised: he would give half his spare time to his studies and the other half to insects.

179

III

The years went by and, as we know, Fabre rose in his scholastic career. He also became known as a naturalist. His accounts of his studies of various insects gave pleasure to many, but on the whole he was regarded as just another of those who like to potter about with a lens and a collecting box whenever they have the time. The starting point of his rise to fame came from reading an essay by Léon Dufour on the habits of a certain hunting wasp.

Léon Dufour was the leading entomologist of those days . . . but before going on with this story I am afraid it is necessary to say a word or two about hunting wasps in general. These are not the wasps that plague us in summer by buzzing around and getting into the marmalade and fruit but solitary wasps of different shapes and colouring and habits from the social wasps. There are many species, but in the main all work on a similar plan. The female makes a tunnel in the earth (or elsewhere) at the end of which she hollows out a chamber. She then flies off and kills some prey which she carries or drags to the hole and deposits in the chamber. There she lays a single egg on the corpse, and goes off and gets another. When the chamber is full of corpses she seals up the entrance hole and flies somewhere else and repeats the process.

Meanwhile, inside the chamber, the egg hatches into a grub and feeds on the body on which it was laid. When it has eaten that it goes to the next, then to the next and the next until it has eaten the whole lot, after which it pupates and emerges the following year as a fully-developed hunting wasp.

Some species store beetles for their young, some caterpillars, some spiders, etc., but they never mix them: the species that goes in for beetles goes in for nothing else, and it is the same with the hunters of caterpillars, spiders and the rest.

And now that that small item of natural history knowledge had been imparted we can get on. Dufour's essay dealt with a beetle-hunting wasp called *Cerceris*. Dufour saw one of these wasps going into a hole, dug into the hole with a trowel, and . . . "I could not believe my eyes!" he wrote dramatically.

What he found looked like a heap of jewels gleaming red, green, blue and yellow in the sun. They were beetles, slain and stored by the wasp and belonging to the genus *Buprestis*, many of which have metallic sheens that reflect gorgeous colours.

Dufour kept some and after a couple of days dissected them. To his surprise the bodies were as fresh as if they had been newly killed. Later he found some more of these nests, and always the dead beetles were fresh, though the weather was hot. He pondered over the problem.

Another thing puzzled him: the beetles killed by these wasps were all of one kind, *Buprestis*, though it was a kind not common in that region. There were beetles of other kinds running about in abundance but the wasps stored only this rather rare sort. Why?

Dufour never solved the last problem, but he solved the first to his own satisfaction and that of all other naturalists except one. The reason the corpses kept fresh, he explained in his essay, was because the wasp when stinging the beetle to death also injected an antiseptic fluid that preserved the tissues from decay. This was necessary because wasp grubs cannot live on bad, or even tainted, meat.

IV

Fabre knew practically nothing about hunting wasps and was extremely interested in this essay. He read and re-read it, but always when he came to the part about the wasp injecting an antiseptic he frowned and shook his head. How could a wasp, with a sting finer than any hair, inject enough fluid to get to all the parts of a beetle considerably larger than itself? Still, the fact remained that these corpses evidently *did* keep fresh, so there must be some reason for it, and the only one seemed to be that put forward by Dufour. After all, Dufour was the acknowledged 'Master' amongst natural scientists.

Fabre was on fire with curiosity. He would go and see these wonders for himself. He would find some of these beetles and, if possible, discover how they were stung. He eventually found a place where beetle-hunting wasps were fairly common but were of a different species from those observed by Dufour. Those had hunted *Buprestis* beetles, these hunted weevils. He managed to get several weevil corpses, both by digging into the wasps' chambers and by snatching them from between the legs of wasps carrying them home.

181

He made many experiments. Some corpses he kept in dry heat and others in moist heat. Normally the first ought to have gone dry and the others putrid in a few hours. They did not do so even though he kept them for over a month. Then he dissected these more-than-a-month-old bodies: the organs were as fresh as those of living insects.

The truth suddenly came to him. The beetles *were* alive. They were as much alive as they ever had been but they had been deprived for ever of the power of movement.

How could this be proved? He tried various ways. He treated fortnight-old weevil corpses, taken from wasps, with liquid irritants and other chemicals but they never moved. At last he tried a Voltaic battery, passing the current through the bodies. Immediately the legs were drawn up. Lest this should be due purely to reflex action he made the same experiment on beetles he killed himself. No movement was induced.

He felt sure now. The beetles had been paralysed—that is to say, the nervous system controlling movement had been put out of action. To do this without otherwise injuring the patient it would be necessary for the wasp to operate on each one of the movement-controlling nerve centres, or ganglia.

Before he could go any further Fabre realized that it was necessary for him to witness a hunting wasp stinging a beetle —a thing never observed before.

It was not easy. Indeed, it seemed impossible. The event takes place on trees or grass and is over in a second—and no preliminary notice is given of the time or place! Fabre stalked about through woods and fields all day, but never saw a wasp or a weevil, let alone a murder.

So he would have to fix it some other way. If he caught a live weevil and then found a hunting wasp's burrow—that ought to work. The wasp would come to its den carrying its paralysed weevil, go inside, deposit the weevil, and then come out. While it was inside Fabre would put his live weevil just outside the hole. Then the wasp would come out, but instead of having to fly away and get another weevil she would find one right on her doorstep. He would thus be able to see just how a hunting wasp paralysed her prey.

So Fabre arranged this. He got a weevil and found a wasps' hole, and sat down and waited. Sure enough, along came a wasp with a dead weevil which she dragged into her burrow. Immediately Fabre put his own weevil an inch from the hole —and kept it from running away by heading it off with a bit of stick.

Out came the wasp. Fabre gnawed at his fingers. Would she see his weevil? She did—she ran straight into it. Fabre leant forward; he must see exactly where the sting went in. The wasp brushed past the weevil, ran on a little, then, in the fussy way these wasps have, ran back to the hole to make some adjustments to the entrance so that it would be the right size to admit her next victim. Three times she went backwards and forwards—walking over the weevil's back each time! Then she flew off to get another victim.

Fabre was dumbfounded. His scheme had failed. Why had the wasp taken no notice of his weevil? Perhaps, in her hurry, she had not really noticed it. Very well, he would *make* her notice it. So he caught a wasp and another weevil and put them in a bottle. Another disappointment: it was the weevil that chivvied and chased the wasp, not the wasp the weevil!

Real naturalists never give up. (It was to take Fabre twenty years to find out how a grasshopper-hunting wasp killed its prey.) He put on his thinking cap again. Supposing, when a wasp arrived at her front door, he snatched her prey from her, and immediately put down his own weevil. The wasp might then think that it *was* her weevil, miraculously restored to life, and give it a second treatment. It was worth trying, anyway.

Again he found a fresh weevil and a wasp's burrow, and waited. The wasp arrived, and when she alighted opposite her burrow Fabre snatched her prey from her with his forceps and immediately threw down his weevil.

The wasp wheeled round, jumped on the weevil and clasped it to take it into her burrow. What was this? The creature was moving! Well, she would soon remedy that.

So Fabre saw—and was the first naturalist to do so—the paralysing of a beetle by a hunting wasp. The wasp held the weevil by the snout, pressed upon its back with her forefeet so as to force open the prothorax joint between the first and second pair of legs, and inserted her sting into that spot.

The effect was instantaneous. Without one convulsive movement the weevil fell, deprived of movement for ever.

183

Fabre repeated the experiment with other weevils and other wasps, with the same result; the wasp always inserted her sting into precisely the same spot.

Actually, because of a beetle's armour plating, it was about the only spot a wasp could penetrate with her sting. But why did it have such a tremendous effect? Only anatomy could supply the answer, and Fabre had but little knowledge of anatomy. Therefore he got a large book on the subject and studied it. He found that beetles possess three nerve ganglia that control movement. In most beetles these nerve centres are widely separated and situated in places where a wasp's sting cannot penetrate. But in the *Buprestis* and the weevils, the three ganglia are in one spot and practically touching, so that a single sting would put all three out of action. And this spot is just underneath the joint where Fabre saw the sting inserted.

So Fabre now knew why the beetle-hunting wasps confine themselves either to *Buprestis* or weevils and never interfere with others.

This was the beginning of Fabre's famous studies of hunting wasps, which made his name famous and occupied him all his life. And there was much to find out, for, as you know, there are many species, each treating different types of prey and using different methods. For instance, in contra-distinction to the beetle-hunting wasp, Fabre found that the caterpillar-hunting wasp has to stab its victim in about thirteen different places— for the caterpillar possesses thirteen nerve centres, none of which are close together.

V

His preoccupation with hunting wasps in no way made Fabre neglect other insects. *Any* insect intrigued him. More than once, while talking with a university colleague, he would stop in mid-sentence and dash away, leaving the colleague staring after him open-mouthed. He had seen some fly or other creature. No wonder his friends thought him mad!

Others thought him mad too. Like all great naturalists he had inexhaustible patience. Once during the holidays, very early in the morning, he set off for a place in some woods where, the day before, he had seen a certain fly emerge from a hole in a bank. He wanted to study that fly. He knelt down by the

184

spot and waited. Presently, along a footpath close by, came three peasant women on their way to work in the vineyards. As they passed they saw him crouching there, staring at the bank. That evening, when the light was beginning to fail, the women returned—and saw him still kneeling in the same place and gazing at the same spot. They hesitated and looked nervously at each other. Then one of them tapped her forehead and murmured a word meaning a harmless as distinct from a dangerous lunatic, and the three crossed themselves and hurried quickly by.

Darwin called him 'The Incomparable Observer': he was also a gifted writer. His accounts of his observations are not the dry-as-dust treatises usually associated with entomological records, but vivid stories as easily read by children as adults.

VI

The end of his scholastic career came with startling suddenness. Free classes for girls were opened in the old abbey of Saint-Martial at Avignon, and Fabre volunteered his services. He taught the girls physical and natural science—why a man breathes, how his body operates, how flowers produce seeds, what causes the lightning, subjects like that.

But in those narrow-minded days it was thought that girls should not be taught such things. The clergy and his university colleagues, as well as the ladies in the town, got up in arms. A lot Fabre cared. He went on lecturing. He was a good lecturer and his classes became more and more popular, until the abbey, at the times he lectured, was always full to overflowing. This pleased his enemies still less, and a plot was hatched.

Fabre rented a house but had no agreement in writing. One day his landlady told him he would have to go, and go at once. If he did not, his goods and chattels would be thrown into the street. He tried to find another house, but no one would have him. He was forced to resign his professorship and go elsewhere. So, with his wife, children and cats he went to distant Orange, from where he secured a house near the village of Sérignan, in Provence, to which he retired.

He was in his late fifties. All seemed over. Actually, all was beginning. This apparent disaster was one of the most fortunate things that could have happened.

The house at Sérignan had a very large garden (if it could be called by that name) overgrown with thistles and weeds of every sort. And it remained like that; not a weed was pulled up, not a blade of grass cut. For to this wilderness came insects of every sort—hunting wasps, mason bees, tarantulas, beetles, and a veritable host of others. There was a large pond, too, so Fabre could renew his acquaintance with the creatures that had so intrigued him as a boy.

He could now devote his whole time to the study of natural history, and it was from this house that came the bulk of those insect stories that have so enlarged our knowledge. For Fabre lived to a great age and spent thirty-six years at Serignan.

This was lucky in more ways than one, for he very nearly did not live to go there at all. One winter, in Orange, shortly after his enforced retirement, he got pneumonia, sank rapidly, until the end was plainly approaching and hope was given up. He writes about it himself, and says, "Being able to do no other sort of observing, I observed myself dying."

He passed the critical period but did not seem to rally. Then his son, Émile, found some *Halicti* (mining bees) insects his father had been studying before his illness, dug them up, and put them on the bed. In the warmth they gradually lost their torpor and began to crawl about on the cover. Fabre watched them with his 'failing eyes'. Whether or not it was due to these insects we cannot say, but from that time his recovery was speedy.

He had eight children and all were eager collaborators, so he did not lack assistants. One of them died when a boy and as time went on the rest married or went away to earn their living. His wife died, so Fabre was a lonely man when sheer old age claimed him at the age of ninety-two.

Not as lonely as one might think, perhaps: Fabre could never be really lonely whilst there were insects about.

Throughout his life Fabre was a shy man, ill at ease with adults but happy with children. He often took them with him on insect-hunting expeditions. His relationship with his pupils is summed up in his account of one such expedition at Avignon: "There were five or six of us: I was the oldest, their master, but still more their companion and their friend."

Francis of Assisi

THE UPSIDE-DOWN SAINT

Violet Needham

I

I N the province of Umbria in Italy the town of Perugia stands high on a mountain and overlooks the valley of the Tiber, here in its infant stages, and opposite on another hill stands Assisi. Perugia looks today probably much as it looked in 1182, but a great change has come over Assisi. In 1182 it was a small town and in that year was born Francis, the son of Pietro Bernadone. No great portents marked the day, neither his parents nor anyone in the town could have guessed that the new-born child was going to stir the heart of the Christian world by the way he chose to live.

Pietro Bernadone was a prosperous merchant and in the simple way of life of those days he sold his merchandise at a stall in the market place of Assisi. As his son grew up he followed his father's trade and took his place in the army that the town raised to carry on a continual strife with its more important neighbour, Perugia. All over Italy small states were for ever warring with one another and in this restless condition of strife produced some of the world's greatest poets, painters, sculptors and architects and in this year of 1182 one of the most beloved of the Christian saints. The boy, Francis, showed no particular sign of holiness, no special addiction to religious services or concern with any ritualistic aspects of religion, but he seems to have had early in life a sympathy with the poor, a sympathy that expressed itself in a quite indiscriminate charity. It happened one day when Francis was in charge of the stall, that he was attending to a customer when a poor man came asking for alms. Francis, busy with his customer, ignored the beggar, and when his business was done the man had gone. Francis left the stall, rushed round the town and when he had

187

found the beggar gave him all the takings of the day. What his father thought about this business we do not know.

II

At about this time he fell ill and when he recovered joined the army that was going to fight Perugia and left his home asserting that he would return as a great prince. This ambition was not satisfied. He fell ill again and, during his convalescence, he rode out into the country and on his way met a leper. He seems to have realized that this was not a chance meeting but a crucial test, the determining factor of his life; and, leaping from his horse with his usual impetuosity, he threw his arms round the leper and gave him such money as he had and then rode on. When he looked back he could see no one on the road.

His illness had wrecked his hope of distinguishing himself in the war and he was at a loose end, depressed and wretched. One day he was praying by a crucifix in the ruined Abbey of St. Damain trying to rid himself of his deep sense of disillusionment when he heard a voice saying:

"Francis, seest thou not that my house is in ruins? Go and restore it for me."

Again his impetuosity urged him to immediate action; he sold his horse and several bales of his father's cloth to raise money, regardless of the fact that the cloth did not belong to him. Pietro Bernadone instead of remonstrating with his son, locked him up as a common thief and the townspeople were indignant with a young man who could behave in such wise. He was summoned with his father before the bishop's court and told that he must restore the money and goods. The reply the young man made was unexpected.

"Till now I have called Pietro Bernadone father, but now I am the servant of God. Not only the money but everything that can be called his I will restore to my father, even the clothes he has given me."

With that he tore off all his garments but one and that was a hair shirt. He went out into the snow and as he went he burst into song.

Soon he resumed his work of re-building the church of St. Damain, and having no money nor possessions nor any credit, he rebuilt it literally by collecting stones and begging anyone, he met to give him more stones. In this effort to rebuild a church single-handed he was presently joined by two other volunteers. Bernard of Quintaville and Peter, a canon of a neighbouring church. During this period he lived presumably by begging. For clothing he had a brown tunic tied with a rope round his waist. He and his companions called themselves the 'Jongleurs de Dieu', possibly to indicate that they had had a spiritual reversal of the ordinary way of life. *Jongleur* was literally a tumbler and tumblers, standing on their heads, saw the world upside down. In the Middle Ages, however, *Jongleur* also meant a wandering minstrel; so they may equally well have thought of themselves as 'God's wandering minstrels'.

III

Francis was also a poet as is proved by his hymn "The Canticle of the Sun", the song that he sang wandering in the Umbrian meadows, a song full of the freshness of a re-born life, expressing his love of all creation.

That he placed courtesy amongst the chief virtues is shown by his address to the live fire that was used to cauterize his eyes when he was growing blind. "Brother Fire," he said. "God made you beautiful and strong and useful: I pray you be courteous with me." It was part of the secret of his power, that courtesy; he treated all men as lords of creation—as kings; and the animals and birds were his brothers and sisters to whom he preached of the love of God.

The three companions were presently joined by a fourth, Egidio, a poor man whom Francis met in the little hermitage of the Portiuncula and invited to enter. He did not call himself and his few followers monks, but Little Brothers. Probably he feared that a community of monks would entail an Abbot and so disprove his theory of the equality of men; but his companions had to take the three monastic vows of poverty, chastity and obedience. Another difference in his community from that of a monastery was that they were not to be stationary, they must not live in a house; they must travel and mix with the world or they could not preach their faith. Moreover there was another great obstacle to a monastery in the mind of Francis. "If," he said, "we had houses and possessions we should need weapons and laws to defend them."

189

The animals and birds were Francis's brothers and sisters
to whom he preached of the love of God

IV

It was when he had collected 11 others to join him that he resolved to go to Rome and see the Pope (at that time Innocent III), and found a Franciscan Order. He accosted Innocent without any introduction whilst the Pope was walking on the terrace of St. John Lateran, and the Pope took him to be some peasant and got rid of him quickly. However that night Innocent had a dream in which he saw the great church of St. John Lateran leaning crooked and tottering against the sky and one human figure holding it up. The figure was that of the peasant he had so abruptly dismissed, and he forthwith summoned Francis to him and heard his plea for the foundation of a Franciscan Order. This was strongly backed by Cardinal Giovanni di San Paola at a later meeting of Cardinals.

The story of the founding of the Second Order of Franciscans is as strange and beautiful as most of the events in the life of St. Francis: A girl, Clare, of a noble family had a deep desire to enter a convent. She was only seventeen years old, but in the 12th century that was considered a mature age when a young woman might be supposed to know her own mind and Clare did know her own mind. She knew she wanted to live the life of a cloistered nun, but her parents objected and arranged a suitable marriage for her. How she came to know St. Francis is immaterial, but there is no doubt that he encouraged her in her purpose and assisted her escape. The tale is as romantic as any of the Troubadour songs. Clare escaped through a hole in the wall and fled through the woods to the Portiuncula and was received by St. Francis and his 11 brethren at midnight by the light of torches. It is recorded that one night the people of Assisi thought the house of St. Francis and his companions was on fire; they rushed to the spot eager to extinguish the flames. They found no scene of disaster— only St. Francis and St. Clare breaking bread together and talking of the love of God. Their faith and enthusiasm had kindled the very air and set it flaming. with divine love. Such was the origin of the second order of the Franciscans.

The Third Order is, I suppose, unique. It consists of men and women following their ordinary lives in a normal fashion: no one meeting them on their daily business would suspect that they belonged to a religious order as exacting in its way as that of a cloistered community. King Louis IX of France was one of them; one of the greatest of poets, Dante, was another and the scientist who gave the world the secret of electricity, Galvani, was a third. The Franciscan ideal, a truly Christian one, embraced all sorts and conditions of men from the highest to the lowest and does still.

V

It could not be supposed that Francis was unmoved by the tremendous enterprise of his day, the first Crusade, the original attempt to wrest the Holy Land from the Moslems. The Christian army, composed of men of all nations, had marched to Palestine under the leadership of Godefroi de Bouillon to drive the Saracens from the country and place the Holy Land in the hands of the Christians. St. Francis was entirely in agreement with the object of the Crusaders, but not with their methods. The use of physical force was alien to his nature and faith, and he resolved to go to Palestine and use his own way to achieve the liberation of the Holy Land. He had in mind to do this not by killing the Saracens but by converting them.

He no sooner conceived the idea than he took steps to carry it out; he never hesitated once his mind was made up as to what was the right thing to do. On this occasion he simply boarded a ship sailing for Palestine as a stowaway. Unfortunately storms forced a return to Italy, but quite undeterred by this misadventure he started again. This time he reached his destination and went on, certainly with no companion and apparently without any introduction, to interview the Soldan. The result of the interview was negative—nothing happened at all. But the fact remained that he reached the Soldan and returned to the Crusaders' camp without let or hindrance, a fact in itself astonishing.

VI

If in the East Francis had made no impression, in Italy his Order made great strides; so powerful had it become that at Bologna a mission house had arisen as beautiful and majestic as Italian building of the period is wont to be. Francis viewed it with indignation. Since when, he asked, had Our Lady of Poverty been insulted with the luxury of palaces?

It was probably soon after this that he went to Monte Feltro, where for some occasion great festivities were being held. Probably he went to ask for alms and he began to tell the company the story of the Christian faith. Amongst those who heard him was one Orlando of Chuisi, who was so moved by the Saint's words that he made him a present of a mountain. The rules of the Order forbade a Franciscan to receive money, but apparently a mountain did not come under the ban of property. At any rate Francis accepted it and retired there when he wished to concentrate on prayer and meditation. The mountain was called Monte Alverno, and it was there that St. Francis had his vision of the seraph with wings stretched out like a cross. What actually he saw, what actually happened no one can tell, that it was some profound spiritual experience is unquestionable, and when dawn came after that night of sublime mystery the marks of the nails of the Cross were in his hands. It is easy to say that the vision was only imagination stimulated by fasting and penances; it is less easy to dispose of the physical fact of the mark of the nails, attested by reputable witnesses.

It was after his experience on Monte Alverno that Francis's blindness became accentuated and that his health began to fail; he still travelled through Italy preaching, but he had to be carried from place to place; and when on returning from Cortona—his last journey—he saw from a hill-top the church of the Portiuncula he cried out: "Never, never give up this place. If you would go anywhere, or make any pilgrimage, return always to your home, for this is the holy house of God."

When he knew himself to be dying he asked to be laid on the ground and his brethren gathered round him. There was Bernard, the first of those who had joined him, and Angelo, who had been his secretary, and Elias, who became his successor as head of the order. Those three watched beside him, murmuring prayers. And presently in the House of the Portiuncula there was a great silence. The spirit of St. Francis had gone home.

Sir John Franklin

EXPLORER OF ARCTIC CANADA

G. F. Lamb

I

WALKING in Canadian snowshoes can be a painful business if you are not used to it. Five British sailors who slogged their way through northern Canada, nearly 150 years ago, endured agonies. It was like having heavy weights fastened to the feet. Terrible sores were caused, and these were rubbed and rubbed again at every step.

"Our tracks are marked with blood," one of the sailors wrote in his diary.

At this time the northern coast of Canada was quite unexplored. Four British naval officers, with a seaman as attendant, had been sent out to discover where it met the sea and to map as much of the coast as they could. They were led by Lieutenant John Franklin, a thirty-three-year-old Lincolnshire man who had already been in the Royal Navy for 19 years. He was a man of wide experience. He had been engaged in two great naval battles under Admiral Nelson, and had helped his uncle-by-marriage, Captain Flinders, to map most of the coastline of Australia. Then, more recently still, he had been second-in-command of an expedition sent out by the Admiralty to try to reach the North Pole.

His present task was to find the source of a river known as the Coppermine (which only one white man had ever before seen), follow it to its mouth, and then start to explore the coastline. In order to reach the Coppermine he and his party were compelled to travel on foot across hundreds of miles of snow. This was how they came to be struggling along in unfamiliar snowshoes. What made things worse was that they were led for part of the way by Canadian '*voyageurs*'—men whose job it was to carry goods across the barren land between the scat-

194

tered trading-posts of two famous Companies, the Hudson's Bay and the North-West. Franklin had been instructed by the Admiralty to hire some of these men to help him. They themselves were well used to showshoes, and never thought of slowing their pace for the benefit of their British companions.

However, the injured ankles and feet gradually healed, and as time went on the officers became hardened to this way of travelling. The last of the trading-posts, Fort Providence, was reached. Now the journey had to be continued through completely unknown country.

At this stage, Red Indians were invited to join the small number of *voyageurs* who had volunteered for the coastal journey. The Indians were accustomed to shoot deer for the two Companies, and it was therefore natural that they should be asked to keep Franklin's party supplied with meat. They agreed to do so.

A special camp was built 160 miles beyond Fort Providence. It consisted of three big log-houses, and was called Fort Enterprise. Then, when winter had passed, the whole party set off into the unknown.

II

Franklin's courage and leadership were soon tested, for most of his very mixed party were casual helpers with no idea of discipline and little interest in exploration. The Indians were shockingly careless with the ammunition they had been given, and had to be constantly watched. The *voyageurs*, too, were sometimes troublesome, and were inclined to go on strike for more food, even when they knew it was not available. Franklin had to be firm with them.

When the Arctic Sea was at last reached, the Indians returned to their hunting grounds, promising faithfully to leave supplies of meat at various places, especially at Fort Enterprise. Franklin would need these on his return.

The tracing of the coast was to be done from the sea, the party travelling eastward in two large open canoes. None of the *voyageurs* had ever seen the sea before. The sight of great waves crashing on the shore terrified them, and it must be admitted that the two canoes were not really strong enough for their task. Heavy seas more than once damaged them severely.

195

None the less, they made a good deal of progress. Franklin carefully mapped the coastline as they proceeded. After covering exactly 555 miles in the canoes, he decided to return to Fort Enterprise, as their food supplies had almost gone. He gave their furthest point the suitable name of Cape Turnagain.

III

The journey back was one of the most dramatic in the history of exploration. It was decided to make the return by land, instead of by sea, in the hope that deer, or other animals, might be shot for food. But in fact there were hardly any animals to be seen. At an early stage of the journey, the *voyageurs* secretly threw away the fishing-nets in order to lighten the loads they carried, so even when they came to rivers and lakes they were unable to obtain fish.

Never have men come closer to sheer starvation for so long. Day after day they struggled through the snow with nothing to eat but some moss scraped off the frozen rocks, and some bits of leather cut from their shoes and fried into a sort of charcoal.

Nor was lack of food their only problem. There were rivers to be crossed. At first they used the canoes, which had been cut down in order to make them lighter. But the *voyageurs*, with their stomachs empty, found even these smaller boats difficult to carry. One man presently broke them to pieces, pretending that the damage was due to an accidental fall. The bits had to be used for firewood.

A month after the return had started, the party reached a branch of the Coppermine River. Fort Enterprise was now only 40 miles away, in a direct line. But how were they to cross the river to get to it?

"I'll try to make a raft," one of the cleverest of the *voyageurs* suggested.

He did so, using some branches of willow which were fortunately growing near. But the faggots were not buoyant enough to float easily, and the raft could not be paddled. They could not get it across the river.

Then Dr. Richardson, Franklin's second-in-command, had an idea.

"I'll swim across with a line. Then we can pull the raft

196

backwards and forwards across the river with one man at a time on it."

He stripped, as thin as a skeleton, and plunged in, a line tied to his waist. But the icy water was too much for him in his starved condition. Just before he could reach the further bank he lost consciousness, and had to be dragged back. He was rolled in blankets and placed in front of a big fire, but he lost all feeling on one side for several months.

The river was crossed at last, after some tent canvas had been fastened round the willows. Everyone was delighted.

The terrible journey across the barren land, it seemed, was now almost over. In a few days they would be at Fort Enterprise, where the Indians would have left ample supplies of meat.

IV

But if only they had known it, the worst experiences of the journey were still before them. Lack of food and the effort of crossing this last river had taken more out of them than they realized. Two men dropped behind, quite exhausted, and collapsed in the snow. One of them was never found. The other could not be roused to go on, though Dr. Richardson went back and did his best.

A little farther on, the party divided. Two or three of the strongest, under an officer, were sent ahead to look for Indians. Franklin's other officer, Midshipman Hood, found himself too weak to keep up with the others. It was decided that Richardson and the British seaman should stay to look after him at a place where there was some moss, while Franklin did his best to push on to Fort Enterprise. He agreed with the greatest reluctance to leave his companions behind, but it seemed the best thing to do for the survival of them all.

"I'll send back food from Fort Enterprise without delay if I ever reach it," he assured them. "And I'll get the most reliable of the *voyageurs* to promise that if I die on the way they won't leave you in the lurch."

The next day three of Franklin's *voyageurs* decided to go back, too, and stay with Richardson and Hood until help came.

"We cannot move any farther," they groaned.

With the four remaining *voyageurs*, Franklin went ahead.

197

For most of the time they had no food at all, but on one day they were able to gather some more of the unappetizing moss.

At last the log-houses of Fort Enterprise came into view. The terrible journey was ended. The agonies of starvation were over. . . .

Or so they thought. But when they staggered through the doorways of the deserted log-houses they made a ghastly discovery. The houses were completely bare! The Indians had not left a scrap of meat in them.

Perhaps this was the worst moment of the whole expedition. Franklin, however, was never a man to give way to despair. A small group, as we have seen, had already gone in search of the Indians. In case this effort failed, Franklin now decided to make a supreme effort to reach Fort Providence, 160 miles to the south.

His intention was defeated by an accident to his showshoes. He had to return to Fort Enterprise, where three of the *voyageurs*, who felt themselves too weak to travel, were still lying in despair.

Franklin himself was almost done. A short, heavily-built man, he was more affected than almost anyone else by the lack of food. But his will-power was tremendous. He managed to inspire his depressed companions to keep going. They all scratched about in the snow for discarded pieces of deerskin, which they scraped and boiled for food. For firewood they chopped down parts of the houses.

Three terrible weeks passed in this way. Then voices were heard.

"The Indians!" they croaked. Weakness had almost robbed them of the power of speech.

It was not the Indians, however. It was Richardson and the seaman. A dreadful story they had to tell. One of the three *voyageurs* who had left Franklin to join Richardson's party had been an Iroquois Indian. Hunger had turned his thoughts to cannibalism. After killing his two fellow *voyageurs* and feeding on their bodies, he had murdered Midshipman Hood, and seemed likely to attack the remaining two men. In self-defence Richardson had shot him through the head.

Enlarged by the addition of these two survivors, the little party at Fort Enterprise somehow managed to go on living, growing feebler and feebler. After a while they barely had strength to cut the wood, and the labour of scraping the hair from the deerskins became so exhausting that sometimes they just could not make the effort. A number of the skins, moreover, were so decayed that even starving men could not attempt to eat them.

Soon they were victims of the horrible and often fatal disease, scurvy. Their limbs became so swollen that they could hardly move. Now only spiritual courage could keep them alive.

Two of the three *voyageurs*, though probably stronger physically than the Englishmen, were in despair.

"If the Indians do not arrive before the end of October," one of them murmured, "I shall give up expecting them."

October 31 came, and still there was no sign of the Indians. The next day the two *voyageurs* lay down in the hut and died. They had lost the courage to go on living.

For another week the Englishmen and the remaining *voyageur* fought to keep death away; and on the last day of that week their courage was rewarded. The Indians came, bringing food with them.

At first the meat made the explorers ill, for their stomachs were not used to solid food. After a few days, however, they were strong enough to travel. Fort Enterprise was evacuated, and the journey home began. Franklin arrived back in England after an absence of nearly three and a half years.

V

Franklin's success in mapping the unknown coastline, together with the fearful hardships he and his party had undergone, attracted wide attention. He was promoted to Captain, and elected a member of the Royal Geographical Society.

In spite of his terrible experiences, he was soon arranging to go out to the Arctic again to continue mapping the coast of northern Canada. This time the journey was to be made in the other direction—towards the west instead of towards the east.

Something had been learnt from the disasters of the previous expedition. The Admiralty now realized that an effective exploring party could never be formed by hiring Canadian *voyageurs* and Indian huntsmen. Explorers need to have a real interest in the work they are doing. This time, in addition to three officers, Franklin was given a band of British seamen to take with him, all of them volunteers eager to take part in the expedition. They were provided with three strong open boats.

A camp was built on the shores of Great Bear Lake as an expedition base. The officers named it Fort Franklin in honour of their leader. Here preparations for the journey to the coast were made.

Very little use was made of Indian hunters. This time the expedition had brought far more food from England, and more reliance was placed on catching fish. Great Bear Lake was a fine place for fishing, and at suitable times up to 800 fish a day were caught. The Indians proved a nuisance rather than a help. They clustered round the camp, using up Franklin's stores, and sometimes stealing the fish. Great efforts were needed to persuade them to go to a fishing-ground of their own.

The journey to the coast was made in the summer of 1826. The party travelled down a great river known as the Mackenzie. Near the mouth a separation was made. Dr. Richardson took one of the boats east to trace the coastline as far as the River Coppermine, thus linking up with the first expedition. The other two boats, under Franklin's command, were to travel in the other direction as far as they could.

Richardson's party had a fairly straightforward journey on the whole, but Franklin met with a difficulty very early on. An Eskimo camp was seen on an island near the mouth of the Mackenzie. The Admiralty's instructions were that every effort should be made to get on friendly terms with any Eskimos who were met, and an Eskimo named Augustus was, in fact, included in the party to act as interpreter.

This man spoke to the Eskimos on the island.

"The white men have come to make friends with you. They will bring you good trade."

The Eskimos seemed friendly at first, though rather excited. But in reality they were a dangerous tribe of thieves, known and feared by all other Eskimos in the region.

Unfortunately the water near the island was very shallow at low tide, and the two boats stuck. The Eskimos, though still pretending to be friendly, dragged them ashore, and began stealing everything they could find. The seamen tried to keep them off with the butts of their muskets, but it was impossible

The Eskimos dragged Franklin's boats ashore, and
began stealing everything they could find

to cope with the enormous throng that crowded round the boats. A box of important instruments was saved only by being fastened to the leg of an enterprising seaman.

After several hours of struggle, strong measures had to be taken. Some of the Eskimos were beginning to use their knives as weapons. At the same time the tide began to come in, and one of the boats was refloated. At the command of its officer, Lieutenant George Back, rifles were raised. The Eskimos promptly dashed for cover!

Both boats were now able to get away. When the Eskimos next morning showed signs of following in their canoes, they were frightened off by the firing of a volley over their heads.

No other unfriendly Eskimos were encountered. The chief dangers of the voyage along the coast were ice and fog. The travellers had constantly to force their way through great blocks of ice. Sometimes these were dashed against the shore by heavy seas. Sometimes solid ice stretched so far out to sea that it was impossible for the boats to get by. The explorers had to wait until the ice was broken up by the wind and waves.

Fog was a great nuisance. It hindered their advance along the unknown coast, and prevented them, when ice held them up, from seeing where they might reach open water. At length it brought them to a halt. They were delayed for so long on a little island—they called it Foggy Island—that Franklin had to turn back to avoid being caught by the winter. If their boats had been completely frozen in, the men would have stood little chance of surviving, for they had not nearly enough supplies to last throughout the long Arctic winter.

Both parties got back to Fort Franklin without serious mishap. Although Franklin had not been able to reach as far as he would have liked, his expedition was very successful. His own party had covered altogether over 2000 miles, and Richardson had been nearly as far. More than 1200 miles of unknown coastline were discovered and mapped.

VI

Franklin had married after returning from his first expedition, but his wife had died soon afterwards. He now married again, and a little later he received his knighthood. For a time he was stationed in the Mediterranean Sea, near Greece, as the British naval commander. Here he was successful in preventing trouble during a change of government in Greece.

A little later, in 1836, he was appointed Governor of Van Diemen's Land, which we now know as Tasmania. He remained here for six years; but it was not an entirely happy period in his life.

In those days the island was used by the British Government as a place for sending convicts sentenced to transportation. Nearly half the population consisted of these men and women. Franklin, with his long experience as a naval officer and explorer, might have made an excellent Governor. But he was not in real control. The British Government at home were too ready to give directions without really knowing the conditions. Moreover, Franklin was hampered by the jealousy and ambition of one or two of his officials.

He was in many ways glad to be relieved of his office, though the people as a whole were sorry to see him go. A dense crowd lined the streets and cheered as he walked to the ship which was to take him back to England.

VII

The experience in Van Diemen's Land made him all the more eager to get back to the Arctic. When he learnt that a sea expedition was shortly to be sent out to find how to pass through the Arctic Sea from east to west (the famous North-West Passage) he was madly keen to command it.

The First Lord of the Admiralty was doubtful.

"You are not so young as you were," he told the explorer. "Remember you are fifty-nine."

"Oh no, my lord," Franklin said quickly. "I am only fifty-eight!"

Fifty-eight or not (he was in fact two months short of fifty-nine), Franklin was really too old for the arduous voyage. But his enthusiasm carried all before it. He was appointed to lead the expedition, which consisted of two sailing-ships with auxiliary steam engines, the *Erebus* and the *Terror*, and 129 men.

The expedition set off with high hopes and in splendid spirits. Franklin was very popular with his crews.

"We are very happy, and very fond of Sir John," one of his

senior officers wrote in a letter sent home from their last port of call, an outpost in western Greenland.

The *Erebus* and the *Terror* never returned. Many ships were sent out at different times in search of the lost expedition. A vast amount of the unknown Arctic was thus explored, but Franklin's ships remained undiscovered. Not until nine years had passed was the mystery partly solved. A final search expedition sent out by Lady Franklin discovered on a barren island less than 200 miles from the mainland, a brief message scribbled on a printed form. It had been put for safety in a tin canister on top of a cairn of stones.

The message revealed at any rate part of the truth. After a successful first season, the *Erebus* and the *Terror* had been caught in one of the worst ice-traps in the Arctic. Ultimately the whole party abandoned them, and tried to make for safety by starting a tremendous march to the south, hoping to find deer or other animals to kill for food.

The attempt met with disaster. Animal life was particularly scarce that year, and the sailors, in any case, were in no fit condition to undergo the terrible hardships of the journey. The whole party perished before even reaching the mainland.

Franklin himself was spared the agony of this tragedy. He died, probably in iis cabin, before the ships were abandoned, and while there w .s still a hope that they might get free from the ice. The date of his death was given in the scribbled message —June 11, 1847. He was just over sixty-one. Very likely a grave was cut in the ice and his body lowered into the Arctic Sea.

His last expedition, then, ended in disaster, after his death. But his record is far from being one of failure. Not only was he the first man to put on the map the coast of northern Canada —the land of the 'Mounties'—and the first explorer to find a North-West Passage. His steady persistence, his refusal ever to give up no matter what the difficulties might be, were an inspiration to many later explorers in many parts of the world.

Galileo

GREATEST OF EARLY SCIENTISTS

Gilbert Harding

I

I HAVE no wish to go to the moon. I pity the boy who delights in space-helmets and reads so-called 'science fiction' until his eyes pop; these accounts of daring, or demon, scientists have a horrible fascination and are, no doubt, eminently readable. But I deplore nearly all such books and magazine stories for what I think are two very good reasons. This earth upon which we are all placed is surely interesting enough; there are still so many fascinating things to be learnt about it. And all this stuff about 'rockets to the moon', all the stories of flying saucers, men from Mars, space-ships, and so on, are likely to make a boy, who has a genuine interest in things scientific, believe that no exciting discoveries can be made unless he has £500,000 to spend on a rocket or he is given a heaven-sent chance to be sent heavenwards as a cabin-boy or stowaway on some space-ship. And all the atomic work done today, too, adds to the impression that research of any kind is costly beyond the dreams of princes and certainly beyond the means of a schoolboy who has only his pocket money.

What nonsense! I am sure that a boy or girl with an inquiring turn of mind can have more genuine excitement with a not-too-costly microscope or telescope than all space books, all the so-called science fiction, could possibly provide.

The man who was largely responsible for inventing the telescope—an instrument that can wander and probe further into the secrets of space than any space-ship—was an Italian, Galileo Galilei, born at Pisa in Italy in the year 1564.

There was an incident in this great man's youth that I think is particularly encouraging to any young would-be scientist. When he was nineteen and a student in the university of Pisa,

Galileo used to go to church in that lovely cathedral with the perilously leaning tower. (It was leaning in Galileo's day, nearly 400 years ago, and it is leaning still.) Now I don't suppose he was the first young man, and I am certain he was not the last, to allow his attention to wander during a church service. Perhaps the preacher was a dull dog. Whatever the reason may have been for Galileo's wandering attention, wander it did.

He found himself watching one of the candelabra hanging down from the high roof of the cathedral, probably upon a lengthy, strong chain. And as he watched it, young Galileo noticed that it was swinging slightly from side to side.

Nineteen seems an unlikely age, and the inside of a cathedral seems a most unlikely place, to make a discovery of outstanding importance to all mankind. I don't say that such things can be done by every young man who is not paying all the attention he should to a preacher, but there is no knowing. A quick eye, a lively mind ever asking the question, 'Why?' is much more worth having than all the space-suits and trappings of a dreamy, bogus kind of science.

Galileo watched the candelabrum swinging. He was struck by the fact that the oscillations, no matter what their range, were accomplished in equal times. Ever resourceful (for young men did not carry watches in those days) he checked this observation by feeling that reasonably reliable 'clock' there is inside all of us, his pulse. He timed the swings against his pulse. Galileo concluded that the simple pendulum, by means of this equality of oscillation, might be made an invaluable agent in the exact measurement of time. In other words, that is how grandfather clocks were born.

In fact Galileo did not apply this momentous discovery, so important in the accurate, or more accurate, measurement of time, until a good deal later in his long and crowded life. But that morning in the cathedral was one of the important moments in the world's history. All great inventions seem so simple—after the first genius has thought of them. (At least *some* great inventions seem simple: so many of the new things of today—radar, mechanical brains—I cannot understand and, what's more, I cannot understand the men who understand them, either.)

206

So much depends upon the careful measurement of time: it is a thing we take for granted today as we take, say, another divinely simple but wonderfully useful invention, the wheel. Galileo's conclusions from his observation of the swinging candelabrum were about as momentous as the flash of genius that prompted some great unknown in the dawn of history, to say to another hairy, skin-clad man, "Look here, cock, I'm sure we'd shift this great lump a whole lot quicker if we put a round tree-trunk underneath and *rolled* it!"

II

If Galileo had made no further contribution to world knowledge than his observations and application of the swinging pendulum, he would have been remarkable and remembered. But the young man had an irrepressible interest in experiments and great ingenuity in mechanical constructions. He became professor of Mathematics at the University of Pisa.

At that time science and medicine had taken few steps forward since the days of Aristotle, the Greek philosopher. Far too much value was placed upon what the ancients had said; far too little importance was given to checking their dogmas against what the keen and experimental eye could see. Galileo was among the first men to ask questions, and to question what the 'authorities' laid down with such authority and, often, pig-headedness. "Aristotle said so, did he? Well, he may be right but let us see for ourselves," was the way—the revolutionary way—in which Galileo approached all things.

As you may well imagine, Galileo was not even in the running for the title of the most popular professor in that university. He aroused much hostility among the teachers and much enthusiasm, too, among the students; students have ever delighted in seeing the pompous, the windy, the pig-headed, cast down from their seats and made to look foolish.

Aristotle had laid it down that a heavier object must fall faster than a lighter body in proportion to its weight. It does seem more plausible, I must say, that if you and I, by some grave mischance, were both to fall from a high window I, with my undoubted greater girth, would deservedly travel more rapidly to my doom.

Galileo found that the Leaning Tower of Pisa was an
ideal place from which to drop things

But Galileo wasn't so certain. That leaning tower of the cathedral at Pisa was to hand, an ideal place from which to drop things. He carried out a number of experiments and proved to his satisfaction, and the discomfort of the Aristotelians, that falling objects, great or small, descend with equal velocity.

For the first, and not for the last time, Galileo was to learn that to be right could be dangerous and that some men love other things more than they love the truth and hate with a deep and passionate hatred the man who dares to upset their treasured and long-held illusions.

In 1591, when he was twenty-seven, and not long after his successful experiments from the leaning tower, he deemed it prudent, in the face of the enmity and bitterness he had provoked, to give up his university post and move on to the University of Padua, where he was to teach and work for eighteen years from 1592 until 1610.

I do not think there is much doubt that Galileo brought some of his troubles down upon his own head because (like me) he found it difficult to rule his tongue when provoked. He was right, but he was horribly right, maddeningly right; what was more, he said so perhaps a little too often and the bitterness of the discomforted Aristotelians was exacerbated by his telling taunts and cutting sarcasm.

III

When he was at the University of Padua, at the height of his powers, a man in the thirties and early forties, Galileo made his most important discovery. He opened up all the vastness of the heavens to the eye of man by his 'discovery' of the telescope.

I hate to use the word 'discovery' and the word 'invention' because no single man really discovers or invents anything unaided, out of the blue. All scientists are dependent one upon the other, and upon those who have worked in similar fields before them. Science only flourishes where there is a free, world-wide exchange of knowledge. One man advances from where others have left off, rarely from the very beginning: scientists are like boys, climbing one upon the back of the other, until the chap at the top can see something over a wall.

When Galileo was in Venice in May 1609 he heard an account of an instrument for enlarging distant objects upon which a Dutchman was working. What he heard was enough to fire his inventive imagination and, after much thought and work, Galileo made an instrument, the first telescope of any consequence.

With it he was able to scan the night sky, examine the Milky Way, and even look into the disc of the sun itself.

Those warm, cloudless Italian nights when Galileo sat in his observatory, the first man prying into space, must have been nights of unbelievable triumph. Columbus, high in the shrouds of his cockle-shell boat, looked out only over a great new continent. Galileo was seeing all the planets in their splendour, exploring the mysterious moon. But they must also have been nights of great struggle and mental upheaval for what he saw did not accord with what he had been taught and what he himself, until that moment had believed and taught.

He, too, was wrong.

The moon was not, as he had believed, a self-luminous and perfectly smooth sphere. The Milky Way was a tract of countless separate stars. When, by day, he had examined the sun, he saw the moving spots and, by observing them, he reached the conclusion that the sun rotated in about twenty-seven days.

These truths he accepted upon the evidence of his own privileged eyes. He taught and published them. Galileo might have enjoyed a more peaceful old age if he had not been so aggressive in his attitude to those who, like himself, believed otherwise but, quite unlike himself, found it harder to abandon older preconceptions.

IV

In February 1616 Galileo promised to obey Pope Paul V's injunction and undertook thenceforward not to 'hold, teach or defend' the newer doctrines, a step it is hard to understand. It produced peace of a kind, however, for until 1632, when he was seventy, Galileo was not involved in any major conflict with the ecclesiastic authorities. Indeed, he seems to have been regarded with high favour by Pope Urban VIII.

But in 1632 trouble came after the publication of a book, in dialogue form, in which the 'System of the World' was discussed. It gave as much or more offence for the way things were stated as it did for the theories it propounded.

The old Galileo was summoned before the Inquisition. After a long, wrangling trial—during which the sun continued to rotate and the moon to reflect the sun's glory and light—the old man was condemned to abjure by oath on his knees the truth of his scientific discoveries, and his prime revelation that the sun and the earth were not fixed but were, as all is, in constant flux and movement.

He knelt. He muttered the words he had been compelled to utter but, after his recantation, we can well imagine him adding quietly: "*Nevertheless it does move!*"

From the court he went for an indefinite term of imprisonment to the narrow dungeons of the Inquisition, an old, ill, defiant man. Happily (I like happy endings) the story of his life does not close with the closing of a dungeon door and death coming to him where he could see only a bright star or two through prison bars. Manfully he faced that terrible prospect. But Pope Urban commuted his sentence and Galileo was given permission to reside at Siena and finally at Florence.

At the age of seventy-three, however, he entered a darker world than any dungeon and a lonelier one than any prison cell: he became blind and deaf. Yet, for five more years, so brightly did his spirit burn within him, Galileo continued his researches with unflagging ardour, in freedom.

Galileo had an irascible nature and a tongue like a whip; he had, however, an equally quick capacity to forget and forgive and, what is much more important, to make atonement where he felt that it was necessary. He was the pattern for the scientists who were to come after him and explore the human body, the nature of the atom, and the very substances of the stars, because he resolutely refused to accept statements on the authority of others. He was no negative bone-head. He insisted upon the need to look, see, and experiment.

Galileo was the father of modern scientific method. He lived his life with energy and courage, and made an enormous contribution to our understanding of the world around us.

Owen Glendower

HERO OF THE FIGHTING WELSH

Geoffrey Trease

I

"MY lord," advised the Bishop anxiously, "you would do well to hear his case. This man could be . . . dangerous. I know the Welsh."

But Henry Bolingbroke—for the past few months King Henry the Fourth of England, more by might than right—was in no mood to listen. He stood there, a stocky, thickset, russet-bearded man, almost dumpy in the long belted gown whose immense sleeves brushed the floor.

At this moment in the spring of 1400 he had so many bigger things on his mind. He was meeting his first Parliament—and not all its members were friendly. He had enemies everywhere. Some refused to believe that Richard the Second was dead. Others wanted to know how and why—awkward questions which Henry preferred not to answer. Nowhere had Richard been more popular than in Wales. Henry disliked the Welsh, and he was not going to lift a finger to help them against one of his own English barons.

It was no good the Bishop of St. Asaph's going on about this case—after all, he was a Welshman himself, even though Henry normally trusted him and followed his advice. The dispute seemed to be about some stretch of wild mountain pasture between the valleys of the Clwyd and the Dee in North Wales. It was claimed by Lord Grey of Ruthin and by Owen Glendower. Lord Grey's men had occupied it years ago, but Glendower had taken the case to court, in London, and the judges had decided in his favour. That had been in Richard's time. A very different King was on the throne now. Grey had not lost a moment. He had taken possession of the land again

212

—and here was Glendower in London once more, asking for another verdict against him.

It sounded simple enough, as the Bishop put it. But (as Henry was painfully aware) once one started digging into the past and inquiring about men's rights to this and that, nobody could be sure where it would finish. No, he said sharply, he was not going into the case; he had no time for it. Then, possibly, the Bishop went a little too far, by reminding him how popular Glendower was with the Welsh, and how dangerous it might be to offend him. Whatever else he was, Henry was no coward. His temper was apt to be short. Now he lost it. He rapped out, contemptuously:

"What do *we* care for the barefoot rascals?"

It was a stupid insult, and he was doomed to pay dearly for it.

II

No one could have looked less like a 'barefoot rascal' than the tall distinguished gentleman who stood there, silent and dignified under the King's outburst. He was about forty at that time, ten years older than Henry, and the two men had known each other well for a long time. Owen, after first serving as squire to the Earl of Arundel, had been in the service of Henry himself while he was still only Earl of Derby. Henry knew perfectly well that, although Owen might not be as rich as the English barons (like Lord Grey) whose castles were so thickly dotted over Wales, he was at least one of the wealthiest of the native Welsh landowners. As for nobility—if one reckoned the ancient Welsh princes from whom Owen was descended on both sides of his family, his blood was quite as royal as Henry's own. And finally, if it came to education and culture, Owen was a much-travelled and learned man, who had studied both at Oxford and at the Inns of Court in London.

It was unwise of Henry to speak of 'barefoot rascals'. He was not the only man to have his pride—but there were others who had patience as well, and more power to control their temper.

Owen Glendower stroked the handsome forked beard which marked him out among the other courtiers. He swallowed the insult from the man he had once served faithfully, and went back to the valleys he loved in the heart of Wales.

No one could have looked less like a barefoot rascal
than that tall distinguished gentleman

He had two fine estates there, besides smaller ones inherited from his mother in South Wales where he himself had been born. There was Glyndyfrdwy in the upper valley of the Dee, between Llangollen and Corwen—it was this estate which included Croesau Common, which Lord Grey had seized—and ten miles or so to the south, across the rolling ridges of the Berwyn Hills, was the place he loved most of all, Sycharth, quiet and peaceful in the lee of the wooded hillside.

Here, particularly, he kept open house to his friends and neighbours. There was always a specially warm welcome for the bards, the wandering minstrels and poets of his country. Long ago, they had been honoured men in Wales, and the people had contributed a tax, the *cwmwrth*, to support them. Then Edward the First had conquered Wales, planting it with English castles and giving the title, 'Prince of Wales', to his own son. He had done his best to stamp out patriotic feeling and he had abolished the tax, so that the bards since then had been forced to wander over the countryside like beggars.

Sycharth was a favourite gathering-place for them. There, in Owen's dining-hall, they kept alive the old songs and stories— the tale of Branwen, the Trials of Dyfed, the legend of Lleu and the Flowerface—along with the more recent and historical exploits of Llewellyn the Great and other heroes who had fought the English. Not that Owen himself had any hatred of the English as a people. He had many friends among them, and, though he had married a Welsh girl himself, Margaret Hanmer, daughter of an eminent judge of the King's Bench, he arranged English husbands for four of his five daughters.

They were a big family when they were all at home at Sycharth. Red Iolo, the bard, made up a poem about them. He called his hostess:

> "*Illustrious lady of a knightly family,*
> *Most honoured, noble, and benevolent.*
> *Two and two her children step forward,*
> *Beautiful her brood of chieftains.*"

The five girls were Isabel, Elizabeth, Janet, Jane and Margaret. There were five boys, Griffith, Meredith, Madoc, Thomas and John.

Red Iolo also described the castle, for such it almost was, with its inner and outer moats and its strong gate house, even though it did not compare with the massive fortresses of the English barons. (It was closest perhaps to the fortified manor-houses of the Border country.) The main building had nine big halls or rooms, each with a wardrobe well stocked with clothing for the household, and there was a separate guest-house nearby, timber-built and tiled, with eight bed-chambers. There was also a chapel, planned in the shape of a cross.

There was a pigeon-house to guarantee pigeon-pie when winter made fresh meat unprocurable; a fish-pond so that fish should not fail on Fridays or in Lent, a warren swarming with rabbits, orchards, even a vineyard, for in those days it was quite usual to grow grapes in Britain . . . There were wiry hill-ponies in the stables, so that Owen and his sons could range the hills with their hunting dogs or fly their falcons after smaller game. When dusk fell they came back to find the trestle-tables set up in the hall, laden with great joints of beef and venison and mutton, and with pasties of all sorts, the crust golden brown upon them . . . and when they could eat no more, a harp would begin to twangle in the fire-glow, and the voice of Red Iolo or some other bard would begin to recite.

It was a good life. Owen had no wish to change it. He had seen plenty of the world—he had seen something of war as well as peace, he had known Westminster as well as Wales. Forty was a greater age then than it is now. Owen, with some of his daughters already married, felt almost old. 'Barefoot rascal' had been the King's phrase? Never mind. Ignore the insult. Henry knew perfectly well, really, what a respectable career he had had. He had done nothing notable, of course. The bards would never sing about him in years to come, and his name would not occur in the histories. But at forty the active part of a man's life was over. If there had been no adventures yet, there were not likely to be any adventures in the future.

Owen Glendower was never more mistaken.

IV

Lord Grey of Ruthin was not satisfied with the piece of land he had seized: he was determined, if he got the chance, to ruin Owen altogether. Then there would be no fear of revenge from the Welshman, and, with luck, more of his land might come into Lord Grey's possession.

Henry was mustering an army to fight the Scots. Owen's name was put down on the list for service, and it became Lord Grey's duty, as chief Lord Marcher in North Wales, to notify him. This was the baron's chance. He deliberately failed to send Owen this 'call-up' summons until it was too late for him either to join the King's forces or even to let Henry know the reason. There had previously been some disorders in Wales and, though Owen had taken no part in them, Henry jumped to the conclusion (aided by a little malicious suggestion from Lord Grey) that he was among the trouble-makers and was therefore refusing to come. Lord Grey got the authority he had schemed for: leave to use force against Owen Glendower, now named among the 'rebels', and to seize his estates in the King's name. Things would have to go very badly, Lord Grey calculated, if some of those estates did not end as part of his own domain.

Owen had no idea of what was brewing. Lord Grey's next move took him utterly by surprise.

He had only the briefest warning. Lord Grey was out with his men, riding hard for Sycharth, already near at hand . . .

There was no time to arm and muster his own followers. To stay would have meant death or capture, useless bloodshed, Sycharth perhaps burnt about his ears. Owen slipped away into the woods, knowing that there he could outwit any Englishman who tried to find him. Lord Grey found the bird had flown, and rode away again, grumbling and empty-handed.

v

This incident forced Owen to make up his mind.

His fellow Welshmen were simmering with revolt. Some had already urged him to be their leader. He had hesitated long enough. He was a peace-loving man, his whole training and background had given him a respect for the law—but he had another side to his character, which the bards could touch with their passionate reminders of bygone heroes. This side of him now came uppermost. Owen saw his destiny as the man who was to free Wales from her English masters and restore the glory of her past.

He gathered his Sycharth men and rode over the hills to his

217

other house beside the Dee. There the old flag of Wales was unfurled—the red dragon on the white ground—and the armed bands came streaming in from all the surrounding valleys. The bards whipped up the general enthusiasm. They led in the various detachments, carrying (besides their harps) the bent bows which signified a state of war. Bow and spear were the Welsh weapons. They were well but lightly equipped, so that they could fight in mountainous country. Even the leaders fought usually on foot, though they had ponies for journeys. Heavy war-horses, like heavy armour, were useless in the hills.

A few months before, the King had made his son Prince of Wales. Owen's followers retorted by giving that title to their own leader. Gathered under the Red Dragon, the little army cheered and brandished their weapons. Red Iolo plucked his harp-strings and sang his praise.

It was fair-time with the English settlers in Lord Grey's town of Ruthin on the other side of Llantysilio Mountain. Owen had not the siege-engines needed for an attack on the castle itself, but he swept down upon the market-place, his followers looting and burning as they pleased. Lord Grey, it seemed, was not at home. At any rate, there was no serious opposition. Owen led his band triumphantly eastwards, raiding into England almost as far as Shrewsbury.

News of his victories spread throughout Wales—and beyond. Welsh students in Oxford left their lecture-halls to join the movement. Other Welshmen, who had gone into the towns and villages of England to seek a living, downed tools and hurried home to take up arms. Owen flew his Red Dragon from the summit of Plynlimon, that grassy boggy mountain which is the mother of the Severn and Wye. From that rounded green top, nearly 2500 feet above the blue expanse of Cardigan Bay, the army could look down upon almost the whole of the land they were fighting to free—hill-wrinkled and river-veined, shaggy with woodland and jewelled with lakes. And they could look across the sea towards Ireland, whence they hoped that help would come from their brother Celts.

Owen's title, 'Prince of Wales', was to be no idle phrase. He had a seal made, showing his own fork-bearded portrait. He sent out letters to the King of Scotland and the lords of Ireland and the King of France, addressing them as equals.

The King of France had refused to recognize Henry as King of England, and was quite disposed to be friendly, though it was a long time before he gave Owen any practical help. From Scotland and Ireland Owen got none of the troops and supplies he had hoped for. He began to see that he must fight alone.

VI

At first all went well. Owen was fighting in the country he knew and loved, in the way his men understood. He proved himself a master of guerrilla tactics. His wiliness gave the Welsh a new legend. Tales were told of the ways in which he tricked his old enemy, Lord Grey—luring him into an ambush by making dummy soldiers of helmets set up on stakes, or reversing his horseshoes to make the footprints point in the wrong direction. Lord Grey's forces were surrounded and wiped out. The baron himself was carried off into the wilds of the Snowdon range, to the lonely castle of Dolbadarn between the Llanberis lakes, where rescue was impossible. There he stayed for a year, until he could raise the tremendous ransom of 10,000 marks and promised never to bear arms against Glendower for the rest of his life. In another fierce battle a lieutenant of Owen's routed the English under Sir Edmund Mortimer, who was taken prisoner and so kindly treated that a few months later he married one of Owen's daughters.

Castle after castle fell to the Welsh patriots. Those which held out against them did so with the utmost difficulty—the luckiest garrisons were those on the coast, who could sometimes be reached by supply-ships from Bristol. Time after time King Henry himself crossed the Severn with his army, but never could he come to grips with his shadowy opponent. The weather fought against him, flooding the rivers so that the fords were impassable, wreathing the hills in dank mist and breaking the spirit of his soldiers.

Owen thrived on the rough weather. Nothing pleased him better than to pounce on the English out of the storm—it was little wonder that the story went round that Glendower was a Welsh wizard, who could conjure up the rain and the wind, thunder and lightning, to be his allies.

He was an inspired guerrilla leader—but he needed to be more if he was to establish the independent Wales he dreamed of.

219

He could harry the English, he could hold most of the country against them, but Wales could not give him the armies he needed to strike Henry a knockdown blow. So, season after season, the English came back against him—and it was not always the Welsh who had the best of it.

In 1403 Owen missed his greatest chance. He was in the south, besieging Carmarthen, when the North of England revolted under Henry Hotspur. If Hotspur (who knew him well) had only consulted him, they might have acted together, bringing in the Scots as allies, and overthrown the King. Instead, Hotspur fought alone at Shrewsbury against hopeless odds, and was one of the 4000 who were killed. A few years later Owen made a pact with Mortimer and the Earl of Northumberland, by which they should divide most of England and Owen should rule an enlarged Wales stretching into Worcestershire and Staffordshire. But nothing came of it. Hotspur, alone, could have carried it through and he was dead.

Once only, Owen received sufficient help from outside to invade England with a full-scale army. A French invasion fleet of 140 vessels sailed from Brest in the summer of 1405 and landed a force of perhaps 5000 fighting men at Milford Haven. Owen joined them with 10,000 Welshmen, and the combined army marched to within a few miles of Worcester. There the King met them—but there was no battle. The two sides looked at each other warily for the space of a week, neither anxious to risk the first move, and after a number of skirmishes in which several hundred men were killed the Welsh and French retreated with their plunder and the King moved cautiously after them.

VII

After this only the most optimistic of Owen's followers could believe in an independent Wales which England would leave to govern herself. It was all very well to keep court in Harlech Castle and call a Parliament in Machynlleth, to dream of a new university to be founded in North Wales and another in the South. It was more to the point that the countryside had been laid waste by these years of marching and counter-marching. Everywhere stood the blackened ruins of houses—and even of churches and monasteries. And no man could see the end of it.

Owen suffered with his people. Sycharth and his other home, Glyndyfrdwy, had long ago been utterly destroyed by Prince Henry. Now, during his absence, Harlech Castle fell and his wife, his daughter Jane, and her children, were carried off to London as prisoners. Little by little Owen lost his supporters, until soon he was no more than an outlaw chief, a kind of Welsh Robin Hood, flitting elusively through the birchwoods and bracken of his native hills.

Once, when the chase was growing hot, he went unarmed with a single companion to Coity Castle in Glamorganshire, and, speaking French, asked Sir Laurence Berkrolles for a night's lodging. Sir Laurence found his conversation so entertaining that he pressed the unknown visitor to stay for several days. "If you wait," Sir Laurence said, "you may be lucky enough to see the great Owen Glendower brought in as a prisoner—he is in these parts and all my tenants are out looking for him." Owen smiled and answered: "It would be well to get hold of that man—if any one could!" When he took his leave, a few days later, he told Sir Laurence who he was, and gave his oath that neither he nor his followers would ever harm him. The coolness of this promise, added to the impudence of the whole adventure, so took the Englishman's breath away that Owen and his companion rode off unhindered.

The English never caught him. When the King died, and his son came to the throne as Henry the Fifth, a general pardon was issued to all Welsh rebels, and, when Owen did not accept it, special messages were twice sent to him by name. The young Englishman wanted to let bygones be bygones. But Owen did not trust his promises, or he could not make peace with a nation which had recently brought in so many fierce new laws against his own.

At last, it is said, Owen disguised himself as a shepherd and made his way to one of his married daughters, Alice Scudamore, and spent his last years peacefully at her home in Herefordshire. Perhaps his wife, freed from captivity, was also living there. The other members of the family who had been taken prisoner with her had long since died in London. Just when and where Owen himself died remains a mystery to this day. He had lived like a shadow on the hills, and like a shadow he faded from history.

Joan of Arc

THE SAINT WHO FREED FRANCE

Violet Needham

I

O N one of my visits to France I went to stay with friends at the Château de Bourlemont. The castle is very old with walls eleven feet thick and from the window of my room I could see a chapel that I was taken to visit the next day. It is small and unpretentious; on either side of the altar are flagstaffs and the pennons meet across the altar. One is the Tricolor of France, the other is the Union Jack and they bear outstanding witness to the Entente Cordiale for the chapel is at Domrémy and is dedicated to St. Joan of Arc. Here England and France together pay homage to the woman who defeated England and saved France, and no more beautiful and significant symbol of peace between the enemies of centuries could be imagined.

What sort of woman was she, this saint? Just a peasant's daughter, a peasant in prosperous conditions, owning his own land; his wife a good, sensible woman who taught Joan to spin and sew and saw that she learnt her catechism from the parish priest. Joan was always devout, but not given to any extravagant show of religion. She was a great tall girl, very handsome with black hair and grey eyes that looked everyone candidly in the face and she was by nature gay. As a child she ran races and played games with the other children of the village. It was not till she was about thirteen years old that she began to see visions and to hear the Voices that for the rest of her life dictated her actions.

France was at that time torn by contending parties; the English held the north, the Burgundians, in alliance with the English, fought and plundered in the east and the young king, Charles VII could call very little of the country he was supposed to rule his own.

II

It was the distress of France, which was apparent to Joan as to everyone else, that urged her to follow the bidding of her Voices. They told her to seek out the Dauphin and take him to Rheims to be crowned. To reach the Dauphin from her remote village must have appeared an almost impossible task for he was at Chinon, one of his castles on the Loire, some 450 miles away from Domrémy. Much of the country she would have to travel through was in the hands either of the English or the Burgundians and in any case the roads were unsafe on account of the many robber bands that infested the district.

Joan applied to the nearest military commander, Robert de Baudricourt, who held Vaucouleurs for the Dauphin. Her father had had dealings with him on various matters concerning the village, so she knew him personally and approached him in May, 1428. She asked him quite simply to send a message to the Dauphin to the effect that he was not to engage in a battle yet, for the Lord would send him succour by mid-Lent and that by God's will she herself would lead him to be crowned. Baudricourt was not impressed, but in the following year, in the month of February, Joan appealed to him again with the words: "In God's name you are too slow in sending me, for this day near Orleans a great disaster has befallen the gentle Dauphin and worse fortune he will have unless you send me to him." Baudricourt remembered these words when soon after he had news that the French had been heavily defeated at Rouvray and probably this determined him to send Joan to Chinon with an escort of men-at-arms.

It was suggested to the girl that she would be wise to travel in men's clothes and she saw the sense of the advice. She set forth on her journey clad in breeches and high boots; the people of Vaucouleurs bought her a horse; Baudricourt himself gave her a sword and bade her farewell with the words: "*Allez et vienne que pourra.*" ("Go and happen what may.")

III

The journey apparently was uneventful and when she reached Chinon Joan seems to have had no difficulty in getting an audience of the King. She called him the Dauphin because she said he would not really be King until he had been crowned at Rheims and had taken an oath to reign in all godliness. Charles accepted her at once as an ally in what appeared to most people a lost cause; the clergy on the other hand viewed her with the gravest suspicion and indeed one can hardly blame them. Her simplicity and faith overcame every prejudice and every obstacle; she was lodged in the tower of Coudray and a page, Louis de Coutes, was given her as her attendant. As she had yearned to go to Chinon, now she besought everyone to send her to Orleans, besieged by the English and she reproached the Dauphin for his hesitations. "You hold so many and such long councils," she complained. It was at Chinon that Joan met the King's brother, the Duc d'Alençon, who was to be her firm friend to the end.

IV

The doubts of the clergy as to Joan's conviction that she was sent to accomplish a divine mission induced Charles to send her to Poitiers to be examined by various learned ecclesiastics. The girl fretted under these endless delays, she only wanted to get to Orleans and relieve the beleaguered town and the foolish questions asked her made her answer impatiently at times as when they enquired in what language her Voices spoke to her. Her answer to one, Professor Seguin, who enquired thus was: "The Voice speaks a better language than yours." Seguin was a Limousin and their dialect was the laughing stock of the rest of France . . . Eventually she convinced everyone of her honesty of intention and perfect faith. She was sent to Tours whilst arms and armour were prepared for her and it was there that she received her mystic sword.

It was she herself who sent for this weapon. It was to be found, she said, in the church of St. Catherine at Fierbois where it would be behind the altar, all rusty. It had five crosses on it and she knew of it through her Voices. The clergy of Fierbois gave her a sheath for the sword, the people of Tours gave her two, one of red velvet, one of cloth of gold. With her usual commonsense Joan had one made of strong leather. At long last she was able to set forth to the relief of Orleans and when she reached her destination she was met by the young and chivalrous commander, Dunois. "I bring you," she told him,

224

"better rescue than ever came to knight or town, the succour of the King of Heaven." She made good her words, the siege was lifted, and it was the beginning of the end of the long domination of England in France.

After this success Joan was determined to take Charles to Rheims to be crowned. Every conceivable obstacle was put in her way by people round the Dauphin who only wanted to further their own interests and by others, more reputable, who pointed out that the strong towns of Auxerre and Troyes would first have to be subdued, but Joan had her way. Events justified her; the French army by-passed Auxerre and Troyes surrendered. The citizens were so impressed by the energetic and sensible measures that Joan took to commence the siege that they took fright and found it more profitable to surrender. The Archbishop of Rheims thereupon wrote to his people in Rheims, bidding them submit and when Charles and the Maid reached the town the citizens were busy preparing for the coronation. Charles was crowned on July 19, 1429.

V

The rest of Joan's life is a sorry story. The jealousies and intrigues of the men round Charles, and the divided loyalties of French and Burgundians made havoc of the Maid's wise counsel and brilliant military strategy. She was a born soldier and her enemy the Duke of Bedford knew it; hence his determination to get rid of her.

The end of her active career came at the siege of Compiégne. One day at about five o'clock Joan made a sortie from the town; she rode a grey horse and wore a scarlet and gold embroidered surcoat. She scattered the men of the outpost that she had attacked but reinforcements came and most of her own men fled. The drawbridge of the town was raised to prevent the English entering the town, but Joan had not been able to reach the drawbridge in time. She was surrounded and dragged from her horse by a troop of Burgundians. She was summoned to surrender but refused, hoping to be killed, for her Voices had warned her of disaster and had thereafter ceased to speak to her. Burgundy had abandoned the English and become the ally of France so no one raised a hand to help her. The Archbishop of Rheims observed acidly that Joan would

Joan was surrounded and dragged from her horse
by a troop of Burgundians

226

never take advice, but did as she chose. King Charles said he would go to the help of Compiégne, but did nothing.

The Burgundians sold Joan to the English and she was moved from prison to prison and finally brought to Rouen, shut up in a dark cell and fettered in heavy irons.

Her trial was a mockery of justice for which English and French bear equal blame. She was abused and ill-treated whilst a prisoner and her evidence and defence at her trial twisted and turned into a confession of heresy. It was a French judge and French court that condemned her to be burnt alive, but the English could either have commuted or altered her sentence if they had had the generosity to recognize the valour and nobility of her character and life. She was at least allowed the final consolation of receiving the Sacrament. To one of the priests with her just before she was led to her death she said: "Master Pierre, where shall I be this evening?" He replied: "Have you not good faith in the Lord?" And Joan returned: "I have, and by God's grace I shall be in Paradise."

On the scaffold she asked for a cross to gaze on in her agony and an English soldier made a little cross of two bits of wood and gave it to her. The last word she uttered was "Jesus," and an Englishman is reported to have muttered: "We have killed a Saint!"

The town where Joan met her death is today in ruins, shattered by the violence of war and only beginning to rebuild itself into the mighty city it was before 1939, but the martyrdom of Joan of Arc was a greater tragedy than the sufferings of a city that endured nobly in a just war. It was a tragedy and crime for which England and France bear equal blame.

Leonardo da Vinci

THE MAN OF MANY MINDS

Michael Levey

I

IN the autumn of 1517 a party of Italian visitors arrived in the small French town of Amboise, one of the favourite seats of the young king, François I. The party was headed by the Cardinal Luigi of Aragon, and like all visitors the Cardinal took the opportunity of seeing the local sights.

Not far from the town, in a small Gothic manor house of brick and white stone, was living one at whose presence there the King of France felt proud. On October 10 the Cardinal and his suite set out for the manor house at Cloux. Conveniently, his secretary accompanied him and later made some notes about their host of that day: "Messer Lunardo Vinci, an old Florentine . . . the most eminent painter of our time."

Autumn was a suitably symbolic season for their visit to Leonardo. The painter was growing old in a foreign country—he seemed more than seventy though he was some years less; he was ailing and his right hand had become paralysed; it was unlikely he would ever paint again. But he aroused himself for his fellow countrymen. He showed them some pictures he had painted before paralysis. He opened the many volumes of his manuscript notebooks which covered so many subjects: anatomy, hydraulics, geology, botany, mathematics. The Cardinal and his suite must have seen also the very small group of friends and pupils about Leonardo. And there was Leonardo himself, still an impressive figure, with the long beard of a great magician or a Victorian father, settled at last in the security of his eight-roomed manor which he was not to quit until death.

His life had consisted of many journeys, of serving under different patrons, owing no allegiance to anything but his genius: a life lonely and self-contained, elegant without wealth, famous but not always successful. Some at least of these strands

228

went back no doubt to his childhood without a mother and to the circumstances of his birth. He was the illegitimate son of a peasant girl, Caterina, and a successful lawyer, Ser Piero. Probably he was brought up in the Tuscan countryside, near the small town of Vinci (whence his name), for it was in this district, at the village of Anchiano, that he was born in 1452.

II

Quite early he displayed such ability in drawing that his father showed some of his sketches to an artist friend, Andrea Verrocchio. Presumably at Verrocchio's suggestion, Leonardo entered his studio at Florence. Verrocchio's studio was a busy place, occupied not only with painting but with goldsmith's work and sculpture in bronze and stone. It was in painting, however, that Leonardo declared himself, by painting an angel in Verrocchio's *Baptism of Christ* which, so legend says— was so good that Verrocchio, sulking at his pupil's talent, never painted again. Fortunately the picture survives at Florence and from the style it is clear that the angel at the furthest left is by a different hand—that of the young Leonardo.

In these early years Leonardo began to make his mark not only as a painter but as a personality. The immense glamour about his name is no recent cult and there has been no period when his genius has been neglected or forgotten. In the rather simple life of everyday Florence, where the artists divided their spare time between quarrels and practical jokes, Leonardo's aristocracy of spirit marked him off as different from the average artist. He was aloof, graceful, elegant and cultured. In addition to ability, he had great personal beauty. Vivid brief echoes of his character come down to us: of his brilliant conversation, his talent as a musician, his love of clothes. He would wear a short rose-coloured cloak at a time when most people wore long cloaks. He loved horses and birds—often he went and bought caged birds (still for sale today in the streets of Florence) and freed them. All forms of life he respected, probably to the point of avoiding eating animal flesh.

This person was clearly not going to enjoy the steady work-aday existence of the average painter or sculptor. Indeed Leonardo has left on record his scorn for sculpture and the sculptor who gets covered with sweat and dust and chips when chiselling the stone. The painter, on the other hand, he thinks of in romantic terms as painting in fine clothes, listening while he works to the sound of music or to a book being read aloud. Dreaming of some such existence, Leonardo seems to have been allured from the prosaic life of Florence by the softer air of Milan. In Florence the virtual ruler of the city and great patron of artists, Lorenzo de' Medici, does not seem ever to have employed him. And when Leonardo went off to Milan it was, an early writer tells, as a musician, carrying a marvellous silver lute of his own design shaped like a horse's head.

III

At Milan the Duke Lodovico Sforza was attempting to create out of the duchy he had seized a cultured, magnificent and impregnable city. Leonardo believed he could be of use to the Duke in all these ways and he drew up a letter of self-recommendation eminently practical and without any mention of silver lutes. In this he sets out at length his qualifications and his proposals as a military engineer, the instruments of war he can construct and the terror he can cause. Leonardo, so passionate for a bird's liberty, describes dispassionately his machine for bombardment; and this curious coldness can be detected again and again in his comments and in his drawings. He dissected a body without repugnance and drew the face of a freak apparently without pity. At the end of his letter to Lodovico Sforza Leonardo mentions, almost casually, that he hopes to be of use in a time of peace as architect, engineer, sculptor and painter.

The Duke seems to have been impressed. At the age of just over thirty, Leonardo was working in Milan. Yet the promise of the place was never quite fulfilled; Leonardo, too, was perhaps never fulfilled. His years at Milan were far from idle, but many of his occupations were trivial, others unfinished, others doomed to early decay. Already there was a Hamlet-like flaw in the centre of his activity. His desire for the best often resulted in nothing being accomplished. His dreams were divine but incoherent. His experiments both scientific and artistic fascinated him but seldom justified themselves in practice.

When he left Florence he probably left behind unfinished an altar-piece, *The Adoration of the Kings*, for some monks who patiently but vainly waited fifteen years for him to complete it. In Milan, Leonardo's first task was to paint an altar-piece, *The Madonna of the Rocks*; this time his failure to complete the picture resulted in a long and complicated lawsuit not settled for more than twenty years—during which time the picture remained half completed. There are two versions of this famous composition, in Paris and in London; the London version remains even now not quite finished.

For the Duke, Leonardo began a sculpture called 'the Horse' to be a monument to the Duke's father. Of this only the preliminary model was completed and set up. Later when the French invaded Milan their archers used it as a target. Nothing has survived of it but Leonardo's many preliminary sketches.

One task Leonardo did after delays complete: the fresco of the *Last Supper* for the refectory of the monastery of Santa Maria delle Grazie at Milan. But in this instance he experimented with the medium he used and, on the damp wall, the fresco began to deteriorate during his lifetime. Again and again it has been restored, the last time quite recently; but nothing can bring back what is lost and the wreck on the wall today is a faint shadow of Leonardo's fresco.

The prior of Santa Maria delle Grazie had a young nephew who used often to see Leonardo and years later he remembered how the painter could occasionally be seen walking the hot empty streets of Milan at midday, coming to paint—or just to gaze at—his fresco. Sometimes Leonardo would climb the scaffolding, give a few touches to the wall with his brush, then leave the building for the rest of the day. At other times he came but did no painting—simply stood considering the composition for some hours.

He aimed so high that the execution of anything never quite satisfied him. Nothing was simple, and each fact led him on to another, until he was an eternal Sherlock Holmes forever pursuing a vital clue which always eluded him. He himself was well aware of this. Across many of his drawings he wrote, "Tell me if anything was ever finished." And this refrain occurs again and again: "Tell me, tell me if ever . . ." he scribbles over the paper, leaving the sentence itself unfinished.

Leonardo was not only a great painter, but scientist,
inventor, architect and engineer as well

IV

Painting was only one part of his task at the Sforza court. Like all Renaissance artists he had to be a handyman, needed as pageant master and scene designer, architect and engineer. Over a question of heating the Duchess's bathroom he was called in; over a play acted at court; over fortification of the Duke's castle. It was perhaps all this variety of job which prompted him to start his vast series of notebooks, packed with hundreds of his observations, recorded by writing and drawings. The notes are jumbled together: whole passages of books read, observations on anatomy, on clouds, on faces seen in the street, accounts of how much he has spent on food or on clothing one of his servants, drafts of letters written, plans for cities, diagrams and drawings of prodigal beauty. Better than anything else, these books map the extent of Leonardo's studies and demonstrate their colossal range.

Outwardly he showed no vulgar signs of activity. He appeared to dawdle over projects. He remained elegant and handsome and self-absorbed. His studio was full of young men —lists of their names occur among his notes—who worked for him and loved him. Some, like his favourite, Salai, behaved badly; he notes Salai's behaviour, but he fondly buys him green and silver clothes in which Salai can ape his master's exquisiteness.

Perhaps Leonardo would never have left Milan, but events compelled him. As time passed the Duke grew dilatory. The glamour of his duchy dimmed as the threat of French invasion became imminent. He had soon no time for artistic affairs. In the autumn of 1499 he was deposed and in December Leonardo carried away his genius, and his pupils, from Milan. No loyalty held him. He drifted about Northern Italy: now at Mantua, now at Venice. Then, after eighteen years absence, he turned to Florence.

V

Lorenzo the Magnificent was dead and the city had declared itself a republic. But the old passion for art remained. It was as a great artist that Leonardo returned home and soon the crowds were pressing into the room where for two days was exhibited his drawing of the *Madonna and Child with Saint Anne*. This is said to have been sent later to France. It is typical of Leonardo's refusal to be committed in political loyalties that he had already found patrons among Lodovico Sforza's enemies and after his return to Florence he was busy with a painting for the secretary of the King of France.

As usual, however, painting did not satisfy him for long. He had not been back many weeks before he lost patience with his brush. Instead he was occupied studying geometry. Then he widened his activities beyond abstract science. A friend of his was serving as captain in the army of the Pope's war-like son, Cesare Borgia. Leonardo joined the staff as military engineer.

The Borgia prince was Fortinbras to the Hamlet of Leonardo. Ambitious, audacious, practical, he had embarked upon a conquest of all Italy. Under him Leonardo was to find action at last—but action as dangerous as it was exciting. First he made maps for Cesare; then he accompanied him to besiege a city; during a rare respite from war he drew the prince's portrait. Suddenly, on the last day of the year 1502, Leonardo's friend and Cesare's captain was strangled—on Cesare's orders. Perhaps Leonardo felt some portent. Surprisingly soon he was off the staff and back in Florence where life, if duller, was safer.

Here he resumed painting, with a portrait which has become almost too famous. The second wife of an ordinary citizen Francesco del Giocondo sat for her portrait and the result was the *Mona Lisa*. Early the picture was the object of stories: how Leonardo worked at it four years and to preserve the sitter's smile had music played and jesters to perform (though the jokes must have been better than most samples of Florentine wit which have come down to us). Although the *Mona Lisa* began as a simple portrait of an ordinary woman, it changed under Leonardo's hand until it became the strangely smiling image in the Louvre today. Heavy varnish and repainting have helped the mystery and obscured a face which originally possessed—and perhaps underneath still does possess—startling lifelikeness and vivid colour.

As well as private commissions Leonardo now received a public commission from the city council. He was to paint a patriotic fresco of a Florentine victory, the *Battle of Anghiari* for a hall in the Palazzo Vecchio; a short while afterwards his younger rival Michelangelo, was commissioned to paint a fresco opposite in the same room. The two great artists were too temperamentally contrasted for there to be any sympathy at all between them and the idea of cooping them up together in the same room was audacious. Their rivalry should have resulted in the Florentine government gaining two splendid works of art. Unfortunately neither painter ever came near finishing his fresco. Michelangelo was summoned away by the Pope. Leonardo experimented, as was his way, and the process again went wrong. He did not proceed. Then the French governor of Milan asked to borrow him and he, too, left Florence. But the Florentines pressed hard for his return, yet when he came it was only because of a law suit resulting from his father's death. He did not touch the *Battle of Anghiari*, a portion of which remained for some years on the wall and then was obliterated.

The King of France now asked that Leonardo should return to Milan; and for the French for some years he designed pageants, planned engineering feats, projected statues.

VI

Five or six years later, however, found him in Rome, where the younger son of Lorenzo the Magnificent had recently been elected Pope. Indolent, pleasure-loving, good-tempered and artistic, Leo X was the perfect patron and from everywhere Italian artists migrated to Rome to enjoy the Papal favours. Leonardo and his pupils were housed in the Vatican and it seemed that the Medici family was at last to patronise the ageing painter. The Pope's brother became his protector and the Pope himself ordered a picture.

But Rome was a centre of artistic rivalry as well as activity. Younger men, like Michelangelo and Raphael, were already employed and were already famous. Leonardo could emulate neither Michelangelo's titanic energy nor Raphael's graceful facility. His methods were complex, intricate, so pondered upon that even the Pope's good nature rebelled. "He thinks of the end before the beginning!" Leo exclaimed on hearing that Leonardo was considering a new recipe for varnish before even

235

starting a painting. And, it seems true, that the picture was never completed—perhaps was never begun.

Leonardo could not satisfy a vulgar demand for results; the person he wished to satisfy was himself. He withdrew into isolation, playing with toys of his own invention, dabbling at various things but achieving nothing. He had a pet lizard which he equipped with false wings and horns to make out of it a dragon to frighten people; he amused himself by studying and experimenting with mirrors. One or two paintings, now lost, are recorded at this time, but probably he painted little during the three years or so of his stay in Rome. While Raphael drove himself towards premature death and Michelangelo drove himself to premature old age, Leonardo idled. Even when he tried to work there would be trivial but annoying hindrances. One of his craftsmen, a German, played truant and would not work, would not learn Italian, preferred to go out shooting with the soldiers. Leonardo drafted time-consuming letters of complaint on the whole subject to the Pope's brother. Then his patron left for France where he was to be married, and afterwards came news of his sudden death.

VII

Leonardo appe red to be deserted on every side, but a last patron, perhaps . .s most devoted, summoned him. This was the new king of France, François I, flashy, handsome, fond of jewels and women—and artists. Like so many Renaissance princes, he wanted the glory of having employed great men. In Rome was a genius at leisure, an old magician whose prestige in France had not lessened. And at the court of François, Leonardo would be honoured and welcomed and safely lodged for life.

He set out on one final journey, to France. The king gave him the manor of Cloux, close to Amboise where he himself often stayed. The presence of Leonardo was enough; he seems to have been employed on little, but the king came many times to talk with him, and years later said that he thought no other man knew so much about the arts as Leonardo. The conversations of the old artist and the young monarch have been lost to us. We hear however of one final fantastic spark of Leonardesque ingenuity in the machinery of a lion that he designed. At a court masque this advanced upon the king as if to attack him, and then its head opened to reveal the lilies of France upon a blue background.

Even this piece of pageantry was behind Leonardo when the Cardinal of Aragon came to see him. From the next year survives a broken sentence, written on St. John's day 1518. This is the great Florentine feast because St. John is patron of the city and Leonardo writes down, as if to note the strangeness of being so far away on such a day: "in the palace of Cloux at Amboise."

It was his last St. John's day. On May 2, 1519 Leonardo died at Cloux. Some time before he had made his will, stating the masses to be sung for his soul, the poor men who were to carry torches at his funeral. He remembered his half-brothers at Florence and a French servant, perhaps his housekeeper, at Cloux. To Francesco Melzi, his faithful Milanese pupil, he left those notebooks which contained so much of his personality.

There he had sketched solutions to problems which seemed uninteresting or ridiculous to most of his contemporaries. He nearly anticipated Harvey's discovery of the circulation of the blood. From fascination in the idea of flight evolved his plans for machines with wings so that men could fly like birds. In his beautiful backward-sloping handwriting—for he was left-handed and wrote in that way—he noted his observations on anatomy, optics, geology. Implicitly he had grasped the theory of evolution. And all these interests were illustrated by the myriad drawings—in pen, or silver pointed pencil, or crayon. This was his testament, his justification for the years of procrastination.

His loss, Melzi wrote sorrowfully, is a grief to everyone, for it is not in the power of nature to reproduce such a man.

Abraham Lincoln

THE PRESIDENT WHO FREED THE SLAVES

Peggy Chambers

I

NEW ORLEANS on a humid day in the spring of 1828! Two young men have sailed a flatboat, loaded with flour, corn, bacon, and pork, from Anderson Creek, Indiana, more than a thousand miles down the Ohio and Mississippi Rivers to the port. At the southern tip of the State of Illinois, where the two rivers met, the Mississippi widened hugely and, it seemed, to one of the young men who had hitherto known only the raw life of the frontier villages, symbolically. A new world opened before him.

Having sold their goods, they stood for a while looking at the concentration of activity around them. All movement along the cobbled streets was swift and purposeful. Goods were being carted to warehouses to await reloading. Even the moored boats nudged the waterfront impatiently as if anxious to be away on the next job. The wharves were piled with barrels and sacks and bales. From the torn corners of some of the sacks the contents escaped in a white froth. The young men recognized it—raw cotton, picked by Negro slaves on southern plantations.

They walked on and saw fine houses and gardens about the city, and a tall cathedral overlooking the roofs; theatres and gambling dens and concert halls, for many thousands of people lived in New Orleans—white, black, and (a mixture of both), mulatto, freeman and slave.

An advertisement on a street corner placard read: "I will pay the highest cash prices for Negroes of every description and will attend to the sale of Negroes on commission, having a jail and yard fitted up expressly for boarding them." Another one announced a reward for the return of a mulatto slave named Sam, who was white enough to be mistaken for a free white man.

Young Abraham Lincoln paused and stared at them. He had heard of this sort of thing but, except for a remote childish memory, this was his first encounter with it in, so to speak, black and white. It did not seem right to buy and sell one's fellow creatures. He returned home richer in experience than dollars.

II

He had been born in a log cabin on February 12, 1809, at Nolin Creek, near Hodgensville, Kentucky, on the edge of the forest which had to be cleared before they could plough and hoe and set their Indian corn, and where they had to hunt and kill before they had food to eat or clothes to wear.

In 1811 his family moved north to Knob Creek where there was better farming land and more life. The old Cumberland Trail from Louisville to Nashville passed near to their door. Every year pioneers were opening up trails to the west and the covered wagons lumbered by, sometimes with a family's whole possessions inside and the livestock following. They were brave people, these frontiersmen and women, for the great American continent challenged them with every hardship in nature— forest, plain, swamp, and desert—and some were beaten and died by the wayside, but others came, determined to conquer and use this hard-won land. Occasionally a chain of slaves straggled behind an overseer, but few people owned enough land round Knob Creek to employ them.

Thomas Lincoln, farmer, carpenter, odd-job man, had little use for books and put his son to work as soon as he could hold a tool, but his mother, Nancy, wanted him to learn to read and write, so Abe and his sister Sarah, two years older, sometimes went to school two miles away.

Five years later they crossed the Ohio River into Indiana and set themselves once more to the hard labour of the land. School was now nine miles away and it was not often that the children could be spared. Thomas shot and skinned and Nancy sewed. Abe shot one wild turkey and shot no more. He hated blood-shed.

In 1818 his mother died and a year later Thomas married a widow with three children. Abe loved her and she saw that he went to school as often as possible, but life was primitive and, all in all, his formal education lasted barely a year. Nevertheless, he wanted to learn and he devoured what books he could get hold of—*Pilgrim's Progress*, Aesop's *Fables*, *The Life of Washington*, *The History of the United States*, the Declaration of Independence.

"There must have been something more than common," he said, "that those men struggled for."

The axe toughened his muscles to steel and he became the best athlete in the district. He grew tall, thin, and angular, with a face which looked as if it had been carved, not born of flesh and blood, with high forehead, big ears, a beak of a nose, and a jutting underlip—a rough-hewn face above an unkempt figure, at the end of whose long arms dangled hands as big as a scarecrow's gloves. But the grey, questioning eyes were kind, and the drawling voice gentle, for the man himself looked and spoke through them, a man who thought more than he said; yet he was a born story-teller, and any company gathered around him could expect a warm wit spiced with the broad humour of the backwoods.

In 1830 the Lincolns moved west into Illinois, but this was Abe's last trek with them. He made another trip down the Mississippi for a storekeeper named Offutt, and on his return became his clerk in the village of New Salem. Having time on his hands, he began to study. Between customers he would lie full length on the counter with his head on a roll of calico, reading law or the Constitution of the United States. He wrestled, wrote letters for people who could not write, and joined the local debating society. In the latter he startled the assembly, who had expected a lively anecdote or two, with the force and clarity of his arguments.

"I don't feel easy," he would say, "until I have turned my thoughts all round—north, south, east, and west."

His friends encouraged him to take up politics. In those days a candidate for the State Legislature (Government of the State) merely had to announce in the local papers that he was willing to stand. Having done this, Lincoln made known his policy and told his readers: "Every man is said to have his peculiar ambition. Whether it be true or not, I can say for one that I have no other so great as that of being truly esteemed of my fellow men, by rendering myself worthy of their esteem."

About this time Offutt's store failed, so it was rather convenient for Abe that the last Indian rising in Illinois, led by Black Hawk, broke out. He enlisted and his company chose him as captain, which election he always regarded as the greatest honour of his life. Inexperienced, however, he could not always remember orders and once when his company, twenty abreast, had to pass through a narrow gate, he halted them and shouted, "This company will break rank and reform on the other side of that gate." Which was as effective if not as neat as single file.

They never saw a feather of Black Hawk and his men, except for one old Indian who strayed into camp one day with a safe-conduct pass. The men wanted to kill him, but Lincoln defied them to lay a hand on him. Lincoln had first enlisted for thirty days, but after this incident he did so again for another thirty, and the man who mustered him in was Lieutenant Robert Anderson. They were to hear of each other again in a greater war.

After serving eighty days in all he returned to New Salem to continue his election campaign. He was defeated but his appetite for politics had been sharpened. To earn his living he worked as rail-splitter, mill hand, farm hand, deputy surveyor, and postmaster. In 1834 he offered himself again and was elected. Encouraged by a young Springfield lawyer named Stuart, he began to study law, and in 1836 passed his bar examination and received his licence to practise.

He often carried his humour into the court-room. Once he defended an assault case in which it was necessary to decide who attacked first. "My client," he said, "was in the position of a man walking along the road with a pitchfork on his shoulder, when a savage dog suddenly attacked him. To save himself, the man killed the dog with the pitchfork.

"'Why did you kill my dog?' cried the angry farmer.

"'Why did the dog try to bite me?' retorted the man.

"'Why didn't you fend him off with the blunt end?'

"'Why didn't your dog go for me with his blunt end?'"

His appropriate actions amused the jury and he won the case. He may not have known all the complications in law, but he understood human nature.

III

In the two-yearly elections he was returned in both 1838 and 1840. Two years later he married, but it was not to his first and perhaps only real love. Years ago he had loved Ann Rutledge, daughter of the mill owner at New Salem, and they became engaged. But the gentle Ann died of fever when only twenty-two. Her death hit him hard and deepened the melancholy which was already part of his nature.

Eighteen months later a half-hearted love affair with Mary Owens petered out for want of enthusiasm on both sides, and in April, 1837, he left New Salem for Springfield, the new capital of Illinois. Here he found lodgings with a storekeeper named Joshua Speed, who became his friend.

One of the leaders of Springfield's social life was Mrs. Ninian Edwards, whose sister, Mary Todd, was staying with her, and it was at her house that Lincoln and Stephen Douglas, already his rival in politics, became rivals in love. Douglas, so short, bull-necked and belligerent in appearance that he was known as the Little Giant, was also a lawyer, smooth of tongue and manner, and of intellectual background. Nevertheless, it was to Lincoln that Mary Todd gave her attention.

The Todds were an aristocratic Kentucky family and Mary was attractive, lively, a good talker, and witty, but her charm hid an iron core of ambition and personal vanity. Her people did not approve of a match with Lincoln who, aware as he was of his own social shortcomings, had his own ideas about the aristocracy.

"One 'd' is good enough for God," he observed drily, "but the Todds have to have two."

They became engaged, but the courtship was stormy and he did not feel happy about the partnership. Indeed, he did not turn up on the day the wedding was to be held. Now he was more miserable at the thought of having let her down, and his health suffered. Fortunately his friend Speed took him off for a holiday and he recovered his spirits a little, but he could still write: "I have done nothing to make any human being remember that I have lived. Yet what I wish to live for is to connect my name with the events of my day and generation, to link my name with something which will be of interest to my fellow men."

The crisis passed. Through a friend they met again and were married on November 4, 1842. They were not a well-matched pair. Her possessiveness was hurt by his moods, and her ambition angered by his careless dress and disregard of the social graces. Once when she was changing her dress, two ladies called. Her husband opened the door to them and said, "Come in, my wife will be down when she's got her trotting harness on."

Bad headaches drove her into unreasonable tempers which became more uncontrollable as she grew older, and did eventually end in mental illness. But there was sincere affection between her and Lincoln and, though he sometimes shut himself in his study to escape her, and thought perhaps of the gentle Ann who would have walked quietly beside him without pushing, he was grateful to Mary for her efforts to help him in his career.

IV

After eight years in the Illinois Legislature he aimed higher and was elected to the House of Representatives (the Lower House of the Government in Washington). He sat from 1847–48 but was not renominated at the end of the session, so he returned to his law practice in Springfield.

Meanwhile, America was growing, pushing the frontier further and further west, and as each new territory applied for statehood, the overriding question was—should it be a slave state or a free? The South was economically dependent upon slave labour, but it was not allowed in the North.

In 1820 a law had been passed known as the Missouri Compromise which banned slavery north of a certain line; in 1854 Stephen Douglas got this repealed, which meant that new states coming into the Union could please themselves about accepting or rejecting slavery. The publication in 1852 of Harriet Beecher Stowe's book, *Uncle Tom's Cabin*, had angered the South and delighted the Abolitionists. Though it perhaps emphasised cruelty to the Negroes more than was justified, it also maintained that they were human beings with rights, a view not held by their owners.

During the 1830s one slave owner had taken a Negro into Illinois, a free state. The Negro, Dred Scott, brought a lawsuit claiming his freedom and, eventually, won his case. In 1857 the United States Supreme Court reversed the judgment and held that, as a slave, he had no right to bring a suit at all; also that, according to the Constitution, no man may be deprived of his property. What else was a slave but property? The South agreed, but the North was furious. Slavery must be stamped out.

The repeal of the Missouri Compromise hastened the formation of the Republican Party, opposing slavery. Douglas, a Democrat, had no moral objection to it, and no humanitarian feelings whatever about the Negro. In 1858 his debates with Lincoln during an electoral campaign for a seat in the Senate (the Upper House at Washington) extended Lincoln's fame far beyond the boundaries of Illinois. One of the latter's speeches, contained the words, "A house divided against itself cannot stand. . . . I believe this government cannot endure permanently half slave and half free"—a speech that swept the country. Douglas was elected, however, but the nation had listened to Abraham Lincoln and in 1860 he was nominated by the Republicans for the highest office of all and won. He was President of the United States, and his aim was to keep them united.

V

Much as he hated slavery, he would not have shed blood for its abolition, preferring, if possible, to educate its supporters into seeing the wrong of it. But within a few days of his election in November, South Carolina seceded from the Union. Other Southern States soon followed. Five weeks after his inauguration the following March, South Carolina fired on a ship entering Charleston Harbour with supplies for the garrison of Fort Sumter. The Fort's Commander, Major Robert Anderson (of the Black Hawk War) held out for thirty-three hours, then surrendered, taking the torn United States flag with him. Now Lincoln called for 75,000 volunteers.

Like all civil wars, it was a conflict between brother and brother. The Confederate States (those seceded) set up their own president, Jefferson Davis, and men fought for their own territory no matter what their beliefs. The father of two young men, one of whom died for the North, the other for the South, raised a monument over their graves inscribed, "God knows which was right."

Lincoln himself got little co-operation at first, even from his own ministers. His world torn, and his heart with it, he could see from his office window in the White House, the broad waters of the Potomac River. South of it his countrymen were preparing to fight those to the North. The South regarded themselves as aristocrats and despised the 'mechanics' and 'moonstruck theorists' of the North. They were gentlemen, accustomed to giving orders and receiving service, though they had called the new President names not in keeping with their code of courtesy—'gorilla' was one of them. He did not care about that, but he did care that millions of young men were donning uniforms, the Blue or the Grey, and preparing to kill one another. No doubt, in time, the slaves would have been freed without war, but time is long when you live in bondage.

It was to be no quick victory. The North had greater numbers but the South, at first, had more brilliant generals, and several times the troops in grey came perilously near to Washington. In September, 1862, Lincoln issued the Emancipation Proclamation which, from January 1, 1863, set free "all persons held as slaves within any state". Its first aim was to make the slaves available for the Union Army, but Lincoln wanted no revolt on their part against the South and begged the Negroes to refrain from violence. Many stayed where they were (uneducated, they could scarcely fend for themselves in such circumstances), but wherever the Northern armies penetrated the South, many more fled to the Union camps. Some had been deserted by their masters. By the end of the war 186,000 coloured troops had joined the Union Army.

In July, 1863, two great victories turned the tide for the North. Vicksburg, in Mississippi, surrendered to General Grant, whom someone once described as a common fellow.

"Friend," replied Lincoln, "the Lord prefers common people. That's why he made so many of 'em."

Another Northern army won the greatest battle of the war at Gettysburg in Pennsylvania. Four months later Lincoln dedicated the National Cemetery on the battlefield in memory of those who ". . . gave their last full measure of devotion", ending his speech with the words: ". . . we here highly resolve that these dead shall not have died in vain—that this nation, under God, shall have a new birth of freedom—and that government of the people, by the people, for the people, shall not perish from the earth."

VI

In November, 1864, he was re-elected President for a second term, and the following March gave his inaugural address: ". . . With malice towards none; with charity for all; with firmness in the right, as God gives us to see the right, let us strive on to finish the work we are in; to bind up the nation's wounds; to care for him who shall have borne the battle, and for his widow and for his orphan—to do all which may achieve and cherish a just and lasting peace among ourselves and with all nations."

Abraham Lincoln had become the greatest orator the United States has ever had.

Next January Congress passed, amid scenes of hysterical joy, a Thirteenth Amendment to the Constitution, abolishing slavery for ever. When Lincoln visited Richmond, the Federal capital in Virginia, Negroes kissed his feet.

"Don't kneel to me," he said gently. "Kneel to God only . . ."

"Yes, Mars'," replied one of them, "but after bein' so many years in de desert widout water, it's mighty pleasant to be lookin' at last on our spring of life."

VII

The war ended in May but Lincoln was to see only the assurance of victory. On April 14, 1865, he went to the theatre with his wife. John Wilkes Booth, an actor who had won fame by romantic appeal rather than ability, went, too. He loved the south but hitherto had let others do the fighting.

The play had reached the third act when the audience saw him leap from the President's box on to the stage. His spur caught in the Union flag which decorated the front, and he broke his ankle as he fell. Shouting "The South is avenged!" he dragged his way out of the theatre. A slow tail of smoke drifted from the box.

After a moment's stunned silence the audience broke into pandemonium. The unconscious Lincoln was carried to a

When Lincoln visited Richmond, Negroes kissed his feet.
"Don't kneel to me," he said gently. "Kneel to God only."

house nearby and laid across a bed—he was too tall to lie straight—but the doctors could do little, and he died at half past seven next morning.

They took him home to Springfield to bury him, and for twelve days his body passed through the mourning country while bells tolled for this man who had come from the back-woods to the White House, yet never lost his simplicity; who had no formal religion but who could say, "I have been driven many times upon my knees by the overwhelming conviction that I had nowhere else to go," and quote an Indian's epitaph to justify his clemency:

> "*Here lies poor Johnny Kongapod,*
> *Have mercy on him gracious God,*
> *As he would do if he was God,*
> *And you were Johnny Kongapod.*"

This man who, loving freedom, said, "Whenever I hear any-one arguing for slavery, I feel a strong impulse to see it tried on him personally"; who knew little personal happiness throughout his life but who so richly upheld the doctrine embodied in the Declaration of Independence—"We hold these truths to be self-evident: that all men are created equal; that they are endowed by their creator with certain inalienable rights; that among these are life, liberty, and the pursuit of happiness"; this man who was America's greatest President—Abraham Lincoln.

David Livingstone

THE MISSIONARY EXPLORER

Kenneth Hopkins

I

We have at last entered the town. There are hundreds of people around me—I might say thousands, without exaggeration. It seems to me it is a great triumphal procession. As we move, they move; all eyes are drawn towards us. The expedition at last comes to a halt, the journey is ended for a time, but I alone have a few more steps to take. There is a group of the most respectable Arabs; and as I come nearer, I see the white face of an old man among them. He has a cap with a gold band around it; his dress is a short jacket of red blanket cloth; and his pants—well, I didn't observe. I am shaking hands with him. We raise our hats, and I say, "Dr. Livingstone, I presume?" and he says, "Yes".

"DR. LIVINGSTONE, I presume?"—these words record one of the most celebrated meetings between two men that have occurred in modern times, for the old man in the red jacket stood in the heart of Africa, many hundreds of miles from another white man or a civilized settlement, and the young journalist, H. M. Stanley, had come half across the world to find him; and by a miracle had succeeded.

It was October, 1871, and the place was Ujiji, a native port and slave market on the shores of Lake Tanganyika, which Livingstone had reached only a few days earlier, after a journey through unknown Africa which had lasted five years. Stanley's journey was the shorter, for he had come direct to Ujiji from Zanzibar in a little over eight months. I have called their meeting a miracle, and so it was; for the journalist had only the vaguest idea where in the huge unexplored depths of the continent Livingstone might be found, and there was very strong evidence to suggest that the famous explorer was already

249

dead. And yet, here they were shaking hands and raising their hats to one another, for all the world as if this were the shady side of Pall Mall one sunny Sunday morning! Who was this Livingstone, and why was H. M. Stanley looking for him? The answer to that question makes almost a history of exploration in central Africa, and at the same time it is a story of courage and self-sacrifice which is one of Scotland's glories—for David Livingstone was a Scot.

II

He was born on March 19, 1813, at the village of Blantyre, not far from Glasgow. Neil Livingstone, his father, was a grocer, but not a very prosperous one, and it became necessary for young David to go to work as soon as he was old enough. After a year or two in the village school the lad was sent along to the great cotton mills which employed almost all the people of the district, and there at the age of ten he commenced work at six o'clock every morning and remained at the works until eight at night. This was in 1823, when work was hard and long for poor people.

But Scotland is a land in which the poorest lad can enjoy a college education, if he will make the effort. David had bought a little cheap school-book of Latin with part of the first week's wages he ever received, and from his intention to make time for learning—even after a fourteen-hour working day—the boy never departed. After a few years he had saved enough to afford the fees for a winter at Glasgow University, and every day, rain or shine, he walked nine miles from his father's house to the university, and nine miles home again when the day's study was over. He was learning to be a doctor, and already he had made up his mind what his real life's work was to be. The cotton mills should know him no more, and he would be a missionary. He wanted to preach the gospel in China.

In 1838 Livingstone was called to London to be interviewed at the London Missionary Society, and he spent almost two years in further study and training (including taking his degree as a Doctor of Medicine) before sailing for Cape Town in December, 1840. To his great disappointment, the Society had not offered him a post in China, where at that time there was little missionary activity because of the war with England. But Livingstone entered into the task he had been given with loyalty and energy, and at once commenced the task of spreading Christianity, health, and civilization, where only ignorance, disease, and poverty had been masters. He journeyed to the missionary post established in Bechuanaland twenty years earlier by another great Scot, Robert Moffat, and from there he began a series of journeys into unexplored regions to find a suitable place at which to establish a missionary settlement of his own.

III

Africa has long been called 'the dark continent', and in 1840 the name was wholly justified, for only a handful of white men had ever made extensive explorations in that mysterious interior of forests, deserts, and high mountains. Huge rivers wound for hundreds of miles through swamps and jungle, or dashed through dreadful ravines and over stupendous cliffs with the sound of thunder; dangerous beasts roamed at large, lion and elephant and rhinoceros; poisonous snakes and spiders lurked in the trees, great crocodiles swarmed in the waters; and the warring tribes confronted one another ever with spear in hand. Into this place full of hatred, suspicion and unrest the missionaries had come with their news of a loving God, but for one tribesman that believed there were a hundred to mock, and many to hear and forget.

David Livingstone soon learned this for himself. He considered it futile to 'convert' a few scores of natives, most of whom would return to their old tribal gods as soon as the white man went away, and he decided that the true work of the missionary lay as much in ministering to their bodies as to their minds. The people of Africa laboured under many evils—a crippling burden of diseases—leprosy, fever, sleeping sickness, and a dozen others. They were constantly at war among themselves, burning crops, stealing cattle, destroying villages and killing, always killing. And they were frightfully beset every year by the miseries of slavery. The evil traders of Zanzibar made regular journeys into the heart of the continent, buying up the captives of war, and the unwanted children, and driving them like wild beasts to the coast to be shipped off to Egypt, Arabia, and the

251

east. Up to 20,000 wretched captives passed through the port of Zanzibar each year, and no one could compute how many died by the way. On the north and west coasts of Africa other great slave markets supplied the demands of Turkey and eastern Europe, and the southern states of America. This vile trade Livingstone determined to bring to an end if he possibly could; and at the same time he set his face against disease and war. It was in a real sense the Church militant that Livingstone repre-sented. He set up his first post 200 miles north of Moffat's, and here he built himself a house and brought his bride. He had married Mary Moffat, Robert Moffat's daughter, a woman of tremendous personality and courage who shared in much of his work until her early death in 1862.

Livingstone had not long been in Africa when he had a practical and nearly fatal demonstration of the dangers of every-day life there. He went out with a party of natives to hunt a group of lions that had been making off with the cattle. The great beasts were traced to a thicket, and surrounded. Livingstone fired at one, and at the same moment another rushed at him from behind:

Starting and looking half round (Livingstone writes), I saw the lion just in t e act of springing upon me. I was upon a little height. He caug t my shoulder as he sprang, and we both came to the ground below together. Growling horribly close to my ear, he shook me as a terrier does a rat. The shock produced a stupor . . . It caused a sort of dreaminess in which there was no sense of pain nor feeling of terror, though quite conscious of all that was happening . . . Turning round to relieve myself of the weight, as he had one paw on the back of my head, I saw his eyes directed at Mebalwe, who was trying to shoot him at a distance of ten or fifteen yards. His gun, a flint one, missed fire in both barrels; the lion immediately left me, and attacking Mebalwe, bit his thigh. Another man . . . attempted to spear the lion while he was biting Mebalwe; he left Mabalwe and caught this man by the shoulder, but at that moment the bullets he had received took effect, and he fell down dead. Besides crunching the bone into splinters, he left eleven teeth wounds in my arm.

The result of this injury was felt throughout the rest of Livingstone's life, and after his death the injured arm was a

He caught David Livingstone's shoulder as he sprang
and they both came to the ground together

means whereby his body was identified when it came into the hands of his friends.

For ten years Livingstone laboured at Mabotsa and at other missions which he established within the area, teaching and ministering to the natives and winning their confidence and love. He found some chieftains ready to welcome his message and spread it among their people, but he met with opposition too, even in the charitable work of his mission. The Dutch farmers —Boers, as they were called—were implacably opposed to the missionary work, and in 1852 an army of 600 Boers and 700 of their native followers attacked the town near which Livingstone had his settlement, killing many of the people, and destroying the Doctor's books, medicines and missionary station. At this time he was absent from home, and when he returned to its desolation he at once set out, not for the south, where he would have found friends and helpers, but to the north, where almost single-handed he established a new post. Whatever the adversity, Livingstone never turned his back on it.

IV

The first part of Livingstone's career came to a close in 1852, when he returned to Cape Town and saw his wife and children on ship for England. He then for a time gave up the practical missionary work of preaching, teaching, and healing the sick in one place, and began the first of his great African journeys as an explorer. This he did because of his conviction that only by opening up the country to white travellers and a white influence could the worst of its evils—slavery—be overcome. He had already—in 1848—made a crossing of the Kalahari desert with two English hunters for company, and they had reached Lake Ngami, the first white men to do so. Now Livingstone attempted something much more ambitious; he set off alone— except for his faithful native guides and bearers—on a journey into unexplored territory which was to last two and a half years, and result in important discoveries.

Think for a moment what this meant, all those years ago. To begin with, there was no radio and there were no aircraft. Once out of sight of the outposts of civilization, Livingstone would be quite alone and cut off from the world, unless he sent a messenger back along the trackless ways they had come. Apart from occasional native paths, there were no roads. There were no maps, except such as the explorer made as he went along— and today, much of what is on the map of central Africa is unchanged from the maps that Livingstone made. Behind, with every days' march, there existed a thin thread of known land, sometimes hardly wider than the path he had forced through the jungle. In front lay a great question mark : what would he find?

As for the journey : imagine to yourself some wood or piece of commonland near your home. Imagine yourself leaving the road, and beginning to cross it, and imagine that from that point you would be cut off from your friends and from all help until you reached the other side. The way lies through forests, over mountains, across rivers, and most of the time you have to walk. You are going to be walking for two and a half years before you come out again among white men. You will probably die on the way. That is what exploring Africa meant, in 1855. And here is an example of the chanciness of contact with the outside world : when Livingstone had been absent some time, his father-in-law Dr. Moffat, from his missionary station far to the south, tried to send him letters and parcels of supplies. These were carried north by a party of Matabele warriors, sworn enemies of the tribes in whose territory Livingstone was travelling. At a point far up the turbulent Zambesi river the party halted, and tried to parley with their enemies, the Makololo, on the opposite bank. "They are goods for the great white Doctor," the Matabele cried, but the Makololo feared to take them, thinking that there was treachery. So the Matabele dumped the packages, and returned home. Then the timid Makololo came and carried the parcels to a small island, and built a little hut around them, and left them. When Livingstone came that way a year later the parcels were intact, but much of their contents had become spoiled—the food supplies in particular. The explorer found here the first letters he had received from his family for three years—and that, surely, shows how isolated a man might be, in the dark continent.

In scientific information the results of this journey were of such value that, at one stride, Livingstone became the greatest of central African explorers; for, whatever the difficulties—and he was stricken by disease many times—he never failed to cram his notebooks with details of the country, the habits of the

255

people, the names of tribes and rivers and hills, sketches of animals, insects, flowers, and astonishingly accurate observations on latitude, longitude, altitudes, and all the particulars required in making maps. He had long since learned the native languages, and had made friends with chieftains and warriors whose normal instinct would always be to kill a traveller first and inquire his business afterwards. But Livingstone was so loved and respected by the chiefs and their people that they consulted him even in such private matters as choosing husbands for their daughters!

And then, in November, 1855, Livingstone made the most spectacular of his discoveries.

He had heard from the Makololo of a place where there was 'a smoke that sounds', along the Zambesi river, then unexplored for more than half its 2000 miles of length. Accompanied by Sekeletu, the Chief, and 200 of the Makololo, the explorer set out to visit this great mystery, and on November 17th he came to the place called Mosi-oa-Tunya, the 'smoke that thunders'. He found the bed of the river suddenly split across by a great fissure, into which the water plunged with a continuous, earth-shaking roar. The great falls were a mile wide, and almost 400 feet deep, and the spray rose into the air for hundreds of feet like smoke . . . here, indeed, was a smoke that thundered. Below, the boiling river was forced through a narrow cleft in the rocks, to leap and struggle for thirty miles through a tall, winding gorge, crowned with dense forest, until it reached the level plain again, to follow more placidly on to the sea. The Victoria Falls, Livingstone called this stupendous sight, and today his statue stands overlooking the plunging waters.

With this smoky thunder sounding in his ears Livingstone now turned his face towards the east and six months later, much broken in health, he arrived at the seaport of Quilimane, on the coast of East Africa, after a 'walk' of some 4000 miles. By the end of the year he was back in England, for the first time since setting forth sixteen years earlier. Then, he was an obscure missionary; now, he was the world's most famous explorer.

V

The next eighteen months were eventful, although Livingstone was in England, where little exploring remains to be done!

He received high honours from the Royal Geographical Society, and the promise of aid in his next expedition. He wrote and published his first and best book, *Missionary Travels and Researches in South Africa*. And, most significant, he severed his connection with the London Missionary Society. This he did, not because of any dispute, but because he now felt certain that the task of establishing and administering mission stations was not for him, important though such work might be. He wanted to keep on the move. And even more important at that time than spreading Christianity was the need to put down slavery, he thought.

Early in 1858 the Government organized an expedition to explore the country about the Zambesi, and appointed Livingstone its commander, with the title of 'Her Majesty's Consul at Quilimane'. So off Livingstone went, this time with quite a big company of white men under his command. These included his brother Charles, and John Kirk, a young man who later became a famous explorer. The expedition landed in Africa in May, 1858, and spent the rest of the year examining country through which Livingstone had already passed on his earlier travels. There was still much to be learned there, and to a great extent the work of the expedition lay in increasing our knowledge of known territories, rather than in opening up entirely new ground. But one notable new thing was done: Livingstone had brought with him a steam-launch, named the *Ma-Robert* after the native name for Mrs. Livingstone, and in this they explored a number of rivers and lakes, among which was the discovery of Lake Nyasa, a great inland sea 350 miles long. Livingstone had quickly learned the art of commanding his little steamer, and Dr. Kirk gives us an amusing glimpse of him on board ship a little later, when he was voyaging in a new launch, the *Pioneer*. Livingstone, more used to being quite alone, liked to take the whole responsibility himself, and we can imagine him pacing the deck, one eye on the weather, grappling with the expedition's many problems: "When the weather gets foul or anything begins to go wrong," says Kirk, "it is well to give Dr. L. a wide berth, most especially when he sings to himself. But the kind of air is some indication. If it is *The Happy Land*, then look out for squalls and stand clear. If it is *Scots wha hae* then there is some grand vision of discovery

257

before his mind. But on all occasions humming of airs is a bad omen!"

The fact is, the expedition was not running smoothly. Some of the explorers proved unequal to the work, because they had been chosen by Livingstone without proper regard for their qualifications, perhaps because he credited all men with his own outstanding powers, or perhaps because his many years of travelling alone had weakened in him the ability to judge a white man's character. But, besides this, Livingstone himself was found wanting as a commander, again no doubt because he had become accustomed to solitude. He seldom consulted his companions, and hardly ever took them into his confidence. He gave orders, and did not see that they were efficiently carried out. He allowed himself to be unjust and intolerant, two qualities no leader can afford to display. Moreover, towards the close of the expedition a great trouble came upon Livingstone.

In 1861 the party had been joined by Bishop C. F. Mackenzie and a group of missionaries, whom Livingstone had promised to guide into the interior and assist in establishing a mission, and this work took the rest of the year, when Mrs. Livingstone and the mission ladies landed from England. The long journey up to Bishop Mackenzie's mission ended in disaster, for on arrival they found the Bishop and another missionary had died of fever. A few weeks later the same deadly scourge took Mrs. Livingstone.

Livingstone threw himself more and more into the work of his expedition, but he was once again broken in health, and his lieutenant, Kirk, was in the same case. A letter from England officially recalling the expedition reached them late in 1863, and by the following April the party were home again. They had accomplished much, but Livingstone was deeply conscious that it might have been so much more. His account of the expedition, *Narrative of an Expedition to the Zambesi and its Tributaries* has little of the zest of his earlier book. He was conscious of failure more particularly because the journey had shown him the full extent of the horrible traffic in slaves, and yet had left him powerless to prevent it. He determined to try again, being convinced that if his explorations could open up the way for legitimate trade the slave trade would come to an end, because profits from trading in goods were much more solid, and more certain, that those from the traffic in slaves. One more object Livingstone had before him: he was not yet satisfied that the discoveries of J. H. Speke and his companion, Grant, had finally settled the age-old question of the source of the Nile. That great river had been proved by Speke to have its principal source in Lake Victoria, far to the north of Lakes Nyasa and Tanganyika; but Livingstone believed there was some waterway probably connecting all these great lakes, and he hoped to find it. We now know he was mistaken.

VI

This time, once again, he travelled without white companions. He had at the outset nearly forty bearers, some of them Indians from Bombay, and in addition he set out with six camels, three buffaloes, two mules, four donkeys, a calf, and four goats. This mixed company of animals he took in order to learn which of them, if any, could withstand the bite of the dreaded tsetse fly, whose presence makes vast tracts of fertile African country uninhabitable by cattle. On April 4, 1866 Livingstone turned his back on civilization, and set his footsteps once more towards the darkest part of Africa. This was a journey lasting seven years, and ending in death.

For a time the outer world heard little of his activities, except for an occasional letter carried back by messengers taking months over the journey. Then came a long silence, and the report of the explorer's death. It was a false report, but it seemed true at the time, for the men who brought it claimed to have been eye-witnesses. I have before me as I write a *Life of Livingstone* published in 1868 which gives the facts in detail; and yet they were entirely untrue. This shows how difficult it was in those days of slow communications, ever to be certain of accurate news. Some of Livingstone's friends were not convinced, despite the wealth of detail given—that he had been killed by a blow of an axe, and buried by his surviving bearers after a fight with hostile natives. So great was the national feeling of alarm and sadness that the Government sent an expedition to learn the truth, and although it did not find Livingstone (who had travelled hundreds of miles further on by now) it did establish that he was alive.

It is impossible to follow the great Doctor through those last

259

long years of wandering, for we have only his *Journals* to describe them and a few of his letters. The *Journals* contain a wealth of scientific observation, but Livingstone was not a man given to describing adventures; after some hair-raising experience he will refer to it in half a dozen words—"Today I shot a mad elephant", perhaps—and so the full story of one of the greatest journeys in the world can never be told.

VII

In 1871 fears for Livingstone again became a grave public preoccupation, but the Government refused to send a further expedition in search of him and it was left to the Royal Geographical Society and public subscriptions to undertake this. At the same time, a great American newspaper owner, James Gordon Bennett of the *New York Herald*, determined to send one of his correspondents, Henry M. Stanley, on a private expedition with the same object. Stanley has left an account of his interview with Bennett in a Paris hotel, when the American calmly ordered him off to Africa to 'find Livingstone'. It would cost a fortune, Stanley told him.

"What will it cost?" Bennett asked abruptly.

"I fear it cannot be done under £2500," Stanley said.

And Bennett replied, "Draw a £1000 now; and when you you have gone through that, draw another £1000; and when that is spent, draw another £1000; and when you have finished that, draw another £1000; and so on, but—*find Livingstone!*"

Stanley was to start at once, but not go straight to Africa. His employer wanted him to take in the ceremony of opening the new Suez Canal first, and send an account of it to the newspaper in New York; then he was to have a look at the Nile, go across to Jerusalem, pay a visit to Constantinople, make a detour to the Crimean battlefields, and finally proceed through Russia to India, taking in Persia and Baghdad on the way. If, after all that, Livingstone had not turned up, Stanley was to cross from India to east Africa and set to work and find him. Stanley began to see that drawing 'a £1000' and then 'another £1000' might be his employment for years! However, Bennett was the boss and Stanley set about obeying him. It was January, 1871, before he reached Zanzibar, after travelling half-way over

Asia to get there. There was still no authentic news of Livingstone, and Stanley began to organize his relief expedition.

All this time Livingstone had been journeying through unknown lands north and west of Lake Nyasa, filling his notebooks with priceless scientific information and ceaselessly preaching to the tribes about the evils of slavery and the advantages of trade. His resources were now reduced to nothing—no cloth, no beads, no 'wire' for giving the presents every petty chieftain demanded. At the last he had to beg his way from place to place, but he never forgot to enter in his journal the details of the country through which he passed, even when fever had struck him and his few faithful companions had to carry him in a litter. In this way, he entered Ujiji, almost dead, on October 13, 1872, and at once began his most famous account of the horrors of the slave trade, an account which shocked England when it was received, and did much to bring about the trade's final suppression. Livingstone told how he had watched a massacre of 'unwanted' or 'unsaleable' slaves, when the Arab traders without warning came into the great market at Lualaba and shot the helpless women and children by hundreds.

At Ujiji Livingstone found the stores he had ordered to be sent there had been stolen. He was ill, helpless, destitute. And then, out of the blue, Stanley arrived with his richly-laden expedition and his famous greeting, "Dr. Livingstone, I presume?"

Why did Livingstone not return home to England with Stanley? We cannot be sure. We only know that after regaining some part of his strength, and journeying with Stanley for a time, he turned his face once again to the north, and his strange quest for the sources of the Nile, and so passed for ever from the sight of his friends. We last see him alive 'winding up his watch with difficulty' on the night of April 30, 1873, stricken with fever somewhere in the lower swamps of Lake Bangweuld, 600 miles inside the Dark Continent. In the morning his men found him kneeling by his bed, as if at prayer. But he was dead.

Wolfgang Amadeus Mozart

THE PRODIGY WHOSE GENIUS WAS FULFILLED

Helen Henschel

I

When Mozart was a tiny boy,
A scoffer, wishing to annoy
Dared him to play a wide-spaced chord
Upon his father's harpsichord.
Of course his hands were far too small,
The thing could not be done at all.
But, much to his papa's delight,
He played the top half with his right,
While with his left he struck the bass,
A smile upon his pretty face.
There still remained between the two
A middle note—what would he do?

Yes, it is just as you suppose,
He played it with his little nose.

FROM these light verses you can see at once, first, that Mozart was an extremely clever and resourceful little boy, and secondly that he was obviously accomplished far beyond his years in the art of music. In fact, he was one of the great musical miracles, for it seemed that he arrived in this world ready and able to compose beautiful music when other children are usually still playing with woolly toys.

But except for his extraordinary gifts in music, Mozart was as gay and full of fun as any other small boy; what is more, that some gaiety and sense of fun stayed with him almost to the end of his very short life—(he was only thirty-five when he died).

One can enjoy music more completely if one knows at any rate a little about the people who wrote it, and I hope that the few things I can tell you here will make you feel you would like

262

to know more about Mozart. His letters are particularly delightful; he was a great letter-writer, and as he was often away on
concert tours for months and even years at a time, he had lots
to 'write home about', as you can imagine.

(One of my favourite Mozart letters, written to his sister when
he was thirteen, ends thus: "*Addio* my children. I kiss Mama's
hand a thousand times and imprint one hundred little kisses on
that wonderful horse face of thine.")

II

Many of the great composers were unlucky in being
born into unmusical families, and having to fight hard to be
allowed to become musicians instead of lawyers or business-
men like their fathers. Mozart was not among these; he was the
son of a very good musician called Leopold Mozart, whose
great ability as a violinist sent him into the private orchestra of
the Archbishop of Salzburg, and later to the post of Court
Composer to this Prince of the Church.

In those 18th-century days the high dignitaries of the Church
lived in great state and had their own Court and retinue of
servants. The musicians attached to these Courts, I am sorry
to say, were usually treated as servants too, and were obliged to
be at the beck and call of their employers, just like lackeys.

So little Wolfgang never had any trouble about being allowed
to take up a musical career. Quite on the contrary. Leopold
was a very good business man, and soon realized that a great
deal of money could be made out of his two wonderful children.

Yes, there were two of them, and so we must now stop and
get some details about the family in general.

Wolfgang Amadeus Mozart was born on January 27, 1756,
the youngest child of Leopold and Anna-Maria Mozart, in the
lovely Austrian town of Salzburg. Their eldest child had been a
girl whom they named Maria Anna, but who was always known
as 'Nannerl'. There were five other children, but only the
eldest and the youngest, Wolfgang, survived. Sometimes one
wonders if the five who died would have been such musical
prodigies as the first and the last; for Nannerl was just as
remarkable a harpsichordist as her wonderful brother.

'Little Wolferl' (as he was called at home) really did
absorb music 'from the cradle,' because when he was in bed he

263

could hear his father giving Nannerl her music lessons. He wasn't more than three years old before he began picking out pieces on the harpsichord, and he actually began to compose some pieces of his own when he was only five. These are not only pretty tunes, but are also perfectly correct in form and construction; all the technical side of music would seem to have been born in Wolfgang too, because he could hardly have had harmony lessons 'in the cradle'! Those of you who learn the piano might be interested to get these compositions by Mozart —a set of minuets—and play them yourselves. They are not difficult but they are very charming.

Nannerl was really as good a musician as her brother, though all her music went into her ten fingers on the harpsichord and not into composition. So, when she was eleven and Wolferl six, Leopold began to take his two children on concert tours. After a start at the Court in Munich, they went on to the Imperial Court in Vienna. Here the children made a tremendous impression, being received with amazement and delight by the Royal Family and everyone else who heard them. Little Wolferl completely captivated the Empress and the princesses; there is a well-known story of how, when he slipped and fell on the polished floor, the Archduchess Marie-Antoinette—who was only a very little older than he—picked him up and petted him. "You are good, and I will marry you," cried the little boy. Poor Marie-Antoinette. She might have been happier as Mozart's wife than as the ill-fated Queen of France.

Though most people delighted in Wolferl's charm and cleverness, some of Leopold's fellow musicians were jealous, and tried to make out that Wolferl was not as wonderful as people thought. It was one of those rather curmudgeonly people who was responsible for the incident described in verse at the beginning of my story.

It was not only disagreeable German musicians who could not get the better of little Mozart; a few years later his father brought him and Nannerl to London, where they were summoned to Court. King George III tried hard to 'stump' Wolferl by giving him all sorts of extremely difficult pieces to play at sight on the harpsichord, but he sailed through them all with perfect ease, and later accompanied the Queen in some songs. Mustn't it have been lovely to have been there?

264

Mozart began to compose some pieces of his own when he
was only five, and soon was playing before kings and queens

Mozart came to London several times in his life; in fact it was in London that he first began to compose symphonies. The family had moved to Chelsea—then a quiet little village—for Leopold to recover from a serious illness; Wolfgang would not practise for fear of disturbing his father, and thus began his series of symphonies. There are over forty of these altogether, all beautiful, but four of them at least are among the greatest works ever written by anybody.

If you are ever near Victoria Station, you might have a walk down Ebury Street, and there you can see, marked by a little notice on the gate, the house where Mozart spent so much of his time in London.

III

By 1766 the children had been away from home for three years; just imagine three years of touring for a little boy between seven and ten years! And it wasn't as if travelling was as easy and quiet as it is now; small stuffy Channel boats (the children were often sea-sick), and long bumpy coach journeys cannot have been very agreeable. So it is hardly surprising that the children were often ill. For instance, 1765 was a very bad year for them both: they had just left London and were on their way to Holland, when Wolfgang fell ill in Paris; and no sooner had the concerts in Holland begun with the usual success, than Nannerl became so dreadfully ill that she very nearly died. As soon as she recovered, Wolfgang fell ill again. All the same, the concerts went on, and the Dutch people were as enchanted as everyone else.

As time went on, however, and the children paid return visits to the various Courts, they found themselves less rapturously received than before. In Vienna, though the Empress Maria Theresa was just as cordial, there was now an Emperor, Joseph, on the throne, and he was not willing to spend much money on the arts, being of an economical turn of mind. But he did do one thing which turned out to be very important, indeed: he invited Mozart to write an opera, and told the manager of his theatre that he wanted the work performed. Well, the opera (called *La Finta Semplice*) was written, but not performed, because of all sorts of jealousies and intrigues among the musicians and singers and publishers. However, the important thing was that it started Mozart writing operas. The first one that came to be heard was a delicious little work, full of fun and lovely music, called *Bastien and Bastienne*. Mozart was barely *thirteen* when he wrote it.

Another good thing that emerged from this second year in Vienna was that Mozart was asked to write a Mass for the dedication of the chapel of an orphan asylum; a very grand occasion, because the Imperial family and a lot of high church dignitaries were present. A contemporary newspaper reported: "The entire music was composed by Wolfgang Amadeus Mozart, of Salzburg—a boy of twelve years old, well-known for his extraordinary talent. It was conducted by the composer with the utmost precision and accuracy, and was received with universal applause and admiration."

IV

On his return to Salzburg his patron the Archbishop arranged a performance of the Mass, and was so impressed with it that he made Wolfgang—aged twelve—the regular *Kapellmeister* (director of music) at his Court.

I think Mozart must have been glad of a comparatively peaceful time at home after all this rushing about, but his father did not allow him to rest very long. Leopold had always wanted to visit Italy, in those days still the most famous country for music, and so, in 1769, he set off for Florence with his thirteen-year-old son, leaving Nannerl at home this time. Suffice it to say that Mozart created as much excitement here as everywhere else, but perhaps most of all in Rome, for it was here that he performed the following astounding feat of memory, which has become historic:

Having arrived in Holy Week, the Mozarts hastened to the Sistine Chapel to hear the Vatican Choir, then the greatest in the world. There was a certain *Miserere* by Allegri sung on this occasion, which for some reason was kept only for performance in the Sistine, and nobody was allowed to have a copy; even the choristers were forbidden to take the parts home to study. But Mozart wrote the whole work out at first hearing, and on Good Friday took his manuscript back to the chapel inside his hat and corrected it at second hearing.

The secret eventually leaked out, and though the monks were

angry at their treasure being no longer their own, they were even more amazed at the boy's extraordinary feat, and his celebrity grew all the greater.

In this connection I would like to say something in general about specially gifted children. In these days of radio and television we often enough hear and see very young boys and girls (chiefly boys) who can play the piano every bit as well—sometimes better—than many grown-up professionals. This sort of talent amounts almost to genius, but genius in one direction: that of 'executive' talent, or ability *to play some instrument* extremely well. Why Mozart's genius was so very much beyond this is because it was 'creative', and that means that he was able to create, or invent, beautiful music out of his own mind and thought—a gift that no one so very young has ever had before or since. There have been other composers who began to write when they were in their later 'teens, but only Mozart seems to have had almost a man's musical genius in his baby head.

Luckily this 'grown-up-ness' was only in his music; in every other way he was as young and gay of heart as could be, almost to the end of his life. And he badly needed this light-heartedness as time went on.

During the yea s between boyhood and manhood, Mozart continued his tours, mostly in Italy, but as I have said, money did not pour in as it had when he was a child, and so he had to enter the service of the Prince Archbishop like his father before him, and this servitude cannot have made for his happiness, as you can imagine.

v

When on a visit to Mannheim in 1877, Mozart met a very musical family called Weber, who were very kind to him. Wolfgang fell in love with one of their daughters, named Aloysia; she was an opera singer, and Mozart took a lot of trouble to get her an engagement at the Salzburg Opera House. But she was most ungrateful, and threw him over as a reward! Finally he married her younger sister, Constanze. This was hardly a romantic affair, if we can judge by Mozart's own words. In a letter to his father he wrote: "Constanze is not ugly, though anything but beautiful. Her whole beauty consists of two small

268

black eyes and a handsome figure. She has no wit, but enough sound commonsense to fulfil her duties as wife and mother."

It cannot be said that she showed much of that commonsense after her marriage, but she certainly 'fulfilled her duties as wife and mother', for she had no fewer than six children, (of whom only two survived), and she grew ill and fretful in consequence. Constant anxiety about his wife's health and the heavy expenses connected with her many visits to health resorts added to Mozart's worries, and he became ill himself.

VI

But there were still highlights against this sombre background. In 1786 Mozart's opera *The Marriage of Figaro* (one of his most enchanting works, which you should see and hear whenever you get the chance) was produced in Vienna. The principal tenor was an Irishman named Michael Kelly, who wrote to a friend describing the first night. . . . ". . . never was anything more complete than the triumph of *Figaro*. I shall never forget Mozart's little animated countenance when lit up by the glowing rays of genius; it is as impossible to describe as it would be to paint sunbeams."

Luckily such moments must always come to the creators of beauty in any form, however sad and difficult the rest of their lives may be, and Mozart's high spirits and love of fun came uppermost often enough. For instance, there is a place in *Don Giovanni*, another (and possibly the greatest) of Mozart's operas, where one of the characters—a girl who is being ill-treated by the villain of the piece—has to utter a piercing scream offstage for people on the stage to hear. The lady who was taking this part could not (or would not) scream loud enough, so one day Mozart crept up behind her as she was waiting behind the scenes to do her scream and gave her a jolly good pinch; whereat she shrieked most realistically, afterwards laughing heartily with Mozart at his little joke.

VII

But the end of Mozart's life was very sad. His growing struggle with poverty, the lack of appreciation and the endless hard work played havoc with his health; his body grew weaker and weaker, though his spirit remained unconquerable to the last.

Mozart was engaged on his final opera *The Magic Flute* when he received a private commission to compose a *Requiem Mass*. Sir Hubert Parry tells us in his very interesting book *Studies of Great Composers* how ". . . he worked at it with unusual preoccupation and excitement; according to his wife's account he began to be possessed with the feeling that he was writing the *Requiem* for himself."

By now he was desperately tired as well as ill, but from his bed he continued to dictate the music to the pupils gathered round him.

It is hardly surprising that the struggle was too great, and on December 4, 1791, he died with the glorious work unfinished. The saddest thing of all is that there was no money to pay for his funeral, and so, on a day of storm and snow, he was buried in a pauper's grave; the blizzard was so blinding that the few friends who started to follow the coffin had to turn back; unknown hands lowered it into the earth, and nothing marks the spot where his body lies.

But we do not need a grave to 'mark the spot where he lies'.

He lies enshrined in the hearts of us all, and surely the love and gratitude of succeeding generations everywhere in the world is the finest and most enduring monument of all.

Horatio Nelson

HERO OF THE FLEET

Admiral Lord Mountevans, K.C.B., D.S.O.

I

O N a chilly day in March, 1771, a blue-eyed auburn-haired lad stood forlornly on the quarter deck of H.M.S. *Raisonnable.* His father, the Rev. Edmund Nelson of Burnham Thorpe, Norfolk, had travelled to London with him but had left him to make the last part of the journey to Chatham on his own. Although he had been appointed as a midshipman to his uncle's ship, nobody had been notified of his coming and he was left for the best part of a day before he was taken below deck to the midshipmen's mess. It was not a bright start nor did the frail, sickly-looking Horatio Nelson look a promising candidate for the sea. His uncle, did not think much of him: "What has poor little Horatio done . . . that he above all the rest should be sent to rough it out at sea . . . A cannonball may knock off his head and provide for him at once." Moreover he hated cold and damp and was terribly liable to seasickness!

Such, however, was his courage and his passion for the sea that the twelve-year-old boy soon established himself in the wild and savage life of a naval ship in the 18th century. Even in peacetime, the ratings suffered atrociously; they were badly fed, under-paid, kept without leave, and savagely flogged for the slightest offence. Too often the officers looked on the men as sub-human animals, to be kept under by brutal punishment, rather than as fellow-Englishmen risking their lives in the service of their country. Horatio was not particularly young for a midshipman; boys of still more tender years endured the bad food and worse treatment of the orlop deck, the lowest deck above the hold, where they had their quarters.

Nelson did not forget those early days. Always considerate

271

of his subordinates, he had a particularly soft spot for midshipmen. As a lordly captain, he encouraged a trembling child, scared to go aloft. "Well, sir, I am going a race to the mast-head, and beg I may meet you there."

II

His early experience included a trip to the West Indies in a merchant ship and he then joined an arctic expedition. The Admiralty rules stated that boys should not be taken, but he persuaded Captain Lutwidge of the *Carcass* to enrol him as his coxswain. It was pretty cool for a boy of fifteen! On this expedition, entirely against orders, he took a friend bear-hunting. They ran out of ammunition and Nelson was seen, fiercely striking with the butt-end of his musket at a bear which was fortunately separated from him by a strip of water.

Next there followed service in the Caribbean where he caught the malaria which dogged him for the rest of his life. In 1793 war broke out with France and Nelson received his first command, the 64-gun *Agamemnon*. He was thirty-five. Next year he led a landing operation against Calvi in Napoleon's birth-place of Corsica, and lost the sight of his right eye when an enemy shot kicked up a shower of gravel in his face. He did not once go off duty.

Nelson then came under the command of Sir John Jervis who appointed him to the 74-gun *Captain*. Although Jervis was a martinet of the old school who ruled by fear and not love, he recognized the great qualities of the young captain and treated him more like an equal than a junior officer. In February, 1797, Jervis with 15 sail of the line engaged a fleet of 27 Spanish warships; as the battle was joined, the enemy broke and fled. The British fleet was moving towards them in line ahead and Nelson saw that the escape route must be blocked at once. without waiting for orders, he turned out of the line of British ships and grappled with the *San Nicolas*. In the wild confusion, a much larger Spanish ship, the *San Josef*, collided with the *San Nicolas*. Calling for boarders, Nelson led the attack. He captured both ships. The British fleet was delighted and spoke of Nelson's patent bridge for boarding first raters, the patent bridge being of course the *San Nicolas*.

Jervis was generous in his praise. Fainting with fatigue,

272

blackened with powder, his clothes in ribbons, the young captain stood proudly on the admiral's quarterdeck. He would not have changed places with anyone living. A grateful country made Sir John Jervis, Earl St. Vincent and Horatio Nelson, Sir Horatio Nelson, K.B.

III

His next command was the *Theseus*. In this he joined the fleet off Cadiz which was maintaining a blockade on the French and Spanish ports and thus remorselessly squeezing out the life of Napoleon's vast land empire. The *Theseus* had a bad reputation; some of its crew were believed to have contacts with the mutineers of the *Nore* whose revolt had recently endangered the safety of their country.

Nelson was merciless in dealing with treason and mutiny but he knew too well that the men were often shamefully treated. He himself paid for the discharge of two seamen who were clearly unfit for service but had been put in irons as suspected malingerers. Nelson led rather than drove; he saw to the comfort and health of his men and knew the value of filling in their spare time with such things as amateur dramatics. The *Theseus* became a better ship. One night a piece of paper was dropped on the quarterdeck:

> Success attend Admiral Nelson! God bless Captain Miller! We thank them for the officers they have placed over us. We are happy and comfortable, and will shed every drop of blood in our veins to support them, the name of the *Theseus* shall be immortalized as high as the Captain's.—Ship's Company.

Nelson suffered his second mutilation in another landing operation, this time against Santa Cruz, the harbour of Teneriffe. The attack failed and Nelson was taken back to the *Theseus*, with his shoulder shattered. He refused a chair but hauled himself aboard by means of a rope and went below to the cockpit, where the surgeons were at their bloody work. With amazing stoicism he endured an amputation, noting the coldness of the knife as it cut through the muscles. Afterwards, he insisted that hot water should be kept handy so that operating knives could be warmed before use!

K   273

IV

The loss of an arm did not check his career. In 1798 he was sent in the *Vanguard* to command a force meant to counter any Mediterranean movement made by Napoleon who was then in the full flush of his land victories. In which direction would he move? Nelson had neither aircraft nor radar; he relied on the fast-sailing frigates, the eyes of the fleet. They failed to make contact and Nelson trusted his instinct that Napoleon had gone to Egypt, intending ultimately to attack British India. Nelson sighted Alexandria without seeing the French and turned east. Everybody was in despair, convinced that the French had given them the slip. Then came the great news: "Sir, a signal is just now made that the Enemy is in Aboukir Bay and moored in a line of Battle."

British naval tactics were simple and effective. They attacked the enemy in two lines ahead and brought an overwhelming force to bear on the windward part of the enemy line by cutting it in half and overwhelming it before the leeward section could get round to its help. The French fleet at Aboukir, however, was anchored close to the shore, on the edge of shoal water. The southernmost ship, the *Guerrier*, had just enough room to swing freely at anchor and therefore there was just enough room for a British ship to get through. The French admiral, however, did not dream that such a risky move would be tried and the guns on the shoreward side of the French ships were not even cleared for action. With consummate skill, the leading English ships slipped between the shore and the enemy who were battered on both sides.

Nelson himself was struck on the head and fell, blinded and convinced that he was dying. The wound, however, was only superficial; a flap of flesh had fallen across his one good eye and obscured the sight. Hastily patched up by the surgeons, he was put in a store-room with orders to rest. Instead, he sent for his secretary, Comyn, and began to dictate his dispatches. Terrified by the firing and appalled by the shrieks of the wounded, Comyn trembled so much that he could not write. Nelson snatched the pen from him and began to write with his left hand.

V

Nelson returned home, to be raised to the peerage and to be fêted as the hero of the hour. His next major service was in 1801 when he was sent to the Baltic as second-in-command to Sir Hyde Parker. Russia and Denmark had proclaimed armed neutrality against the British and refused the right to search neutral ships which England has always claimed. Moreover the French were putting pressure on these states in the hope that they would join in the war and use their powerful fleets against England. The English government wished to prevent this, but was uncertain whether to do so merely by a display of force or by an outright attack on them before they could strike us. Much discretion was left to the commander, Sir Hyde Parker, who was old and cautious and afraid of his brilliant and unconventional second-in-command. The story goes that he steadily refused to see Nelson until the latter had the brilliant idea of sending him a gift of turbot. It was Sir Hyde Parker's favourite dish and he asked Nelson to share it. After that, Nelson's personality carried all before him in conference!

The position at Copenhagen was not dissimilar to that at Aboukir. The Danish ships were moored close to shore, protected by a fort at one end and shoals at the other. Nelson persuaded Sir Hyde Parker to bombard the fort whilst he led an attack on the other end of the Danish line. It was a long, savage and bloody battle. At one point Sir Hyde Parker flew the signal for recall. "Leave off action," said Nelson. "Now damn me if I do!" He began to waggle the stump of his right arm—working his fin' as his men called it—a sure sign of agitation. Then he made up his mind. Exclaiming that with only one eye he had a right to be blind sometimes, he clapped the glass to his right eye and directed it to the flagship. "I really do not see the signal," he grinned.

The Danish fleet was beaten, a truce made, and the danger of intervention on the French side was past. Nelson's wonderful physical courage was equalled by his moral courage in disobeying an order he felt to be wrong. Had he failed, he faced utter disgrace.

Nelson returned to England to enjoy the short period of peace ushered in by the Treaty of Amiens. In 1803, however, war broke out again and Nelson resumed the long blockade of the

French and Spanish coasts. He never showed more genius in the management of ships and men than in this long and exhausting work. Of the *Victory*'s crew of 840, hardly any reported sick. This would be a source of pride to a modern ship; in the navy of Nelson's day it was a miracle. Nelson's amazing success was based on physical and moral grounds; he paid the utmost care to diet and thus avoided the dreaded disease of scurvy, and he treated his men not as the scum of the earth but as his 'poor brave fellows' as dear to him as his officers, 'the band of brothers' who commanded them. He was universally loved.

VI

We draw now to the close of this great life. Napoleon planned to land an army in England; he decided to draw off the main part of the British fleet by a raid on the West Indies and then pass his army across the channel whilst the British command of the sea was temporarily weakened. Villeneuve avoided Nelson and sailed westwards across the Atlantic. Nelson followed but just missed him; Villeneuve then re-crossed the Atlantic but was sighted by other English ships and Napoleon's plan was never put into operation. Nelson arrived back in Portsmouth in August 1805, and spent 25 days leave at his home in Merton in Surrey. On September 28 he rejoined the ships cruising off Cadiz.

The fleet was delighted to have their hero back, and at a conference of senior officers he explained the Nelson touch. The effect, said Nelson, was like an electric shock. Harsh martinets like Collingwood wept. How wonderful was the influence of this sickly little cripple on the tough sea dogs he commanded! The Nelson touch *in tactics* was not new; it meant concentrating overwhelming force on the first enemy ships before the rest could help them. What stirred them so deeply was the Nelson touch *in morale*. Signals may be hard to read but "No captain can do very wrong," he said, "if he places his ship alongside that of an enemy."

On October 19 Villeneuve at last brought out the combined French and Spanish fleets. As they left Cadiz, they turned for Gibraltar. It was the hour of trial. At dawn on October 21 the enemy fleets were at last in sight and Nelson wrote in his diary: ". . . I commit my life to Him who made me."

276

Nelson in the *Victory* grappled with the *Redoutable*, whose
captain had crowded his fighting tops with marksmen

Nelson's plan to break the enemy line and encircle part of it was frustrated by the wind dropping. Instead, as the two British lines moved slowly towards the enemy, the leading ships were vulnerable to every enemy ship within range before they closed with the enemy. The English captains knew that the leading English ships would suffer appalling casualties, and the *Temeraire* tried to overhaul the *Victory* so that Nelson should be less exposed to danger. As she drew level, Nelson called out clearly, "I'll thank you, Captain Harvey, to keep in your proper station which is astern of the *Victory*."

Nelson was in the state of calm exultation in which he always faced battle. Turning to the signals officer, he said, "Suppose we telegraph 'Nelson confides that every man will do his duty'". The signals officer suggested that 'confides' would have to be spelt in full whereas there was a signal for *'expects'*. He also suggested 'England' for 'Nelson'. The famous signal was run up. It had a magical effect. Collingwood, that cold and efficient martinet, saw the signal and said irritably: "I wish Nelson would make no more signals. We all know what we have to do." Then, when he heard what the signal was, he, too, was touched by the Nelson fire and announced the signal to his ship's company. They greeted it with a round of thunder and cheers. Within a few minutes six hundred of them were killed and wounded.

The *Victory* grappled with the *Redoutable* whose captain had crowded his fighting tops with marksmen. These snipers spattered the poop and quarterdeck of the *Victory* with musket bullets. Hardy saw Nelson sinking slowly to his knees, his backbone shot through from left to right. They carried him to the dreadful cockpit where the surgeons were at their grim work. He sent message after message for Hardy but his faithful friend could not leave the quarterdeck. Nelson lay dying for about half an hour. During that time the fate of Europe was decided. At last Hardy came down, to say that eighteen enemy ships had surrendered. "I bargained for twenty," whispered Nelson. Then, still more feebly, "Kiss me, Hardy." The big sea captain knelt down and kissed the forehead of his beloved chief. Nelson died in the moment of supreme triumph. His last words were: "Thank God, I have done my duty."

Florence Nightingale

THE WOMAN WHO BROUGHT HELP TO MEN

Violet Needham

I

A LITTLE girl sat on the floor in her nursery bandaging a doll's arm. When this was done and the doll put to bed, the child took another doll and bandaged its head and it in turn was put to bed. An odd game for a child the nurse thought, though she could not but admire the skill of the bandaging. The house was Embley Park, the home of Mr. Nightingale and the little girl was his younger daughter, Florence, a name that was to become famous throughout the whole civilized world.

The child had been named Florence after the lovely city of her birth, but her childhood was spent chiefly at Embley. She led a healthy outdoor life, ran about the garden at Embley and made friends with all the animals on the place. One day she met a shepherd in distress over his dog that had broken its leg; Florence rose to the occasion and bandaged the broken limb efficiently. These two incidents of her childhood were indications of her future vocation, though no one could have guessed from them the scope and value of her work.

At the age of eighteen she went to London to be presented at Court like other young ladies, but, unlike other young ladies, society made no appeal to her. Parties and balls she avoided, partly no doubt because she was agonizingly shy, partly because she was already attracted to the profession that was to become her major occupation in life. She began visiting hospitals and Nursing Institutes and it must have been disconcerting to her parents who no doubt expected her to enjoy the normal amusements of her age and station, but they put no obstacles in her way, perhaps because they realized it would be a waste of energy for she was a young woman of great determination.

Not content with visiting English hospitals she went abroad to see foreign institutions and probably found them better organized than English ones for England was very much behindhand in health services. Being eminently practical she realized that the first essential in reforms was practical knowledge; vague ideals would be useless, so she took a course of training at the Institute of Protestant Deaconesses at Kaiserswerth. She then visited the hospital of the Sisters of St. Vincent de Paul in Paris, and did another course of training there. Her grasp of the necessity for adequate knowledge and the need of discipline in hospital staffs made its impression on the authorities. England was ringing with accounts of the deplorable conditions in the military hospital at Scutari during the Crimean War and Miss Nightingale received a letter from the Minister of War, Sydney Herbert, asking her to go out there and organize the hospital service. The letter, curiously enough, crossed one from her offering her services.

She must, if contemporary portraits are accurate, have been a good-looking woman, wearing her hair parted down the middle according to the fashion of the day and looped up on either side of her face over her ears. Her eyebrows were strongly marked in a beautiful curve over eyes that in her portraits have a singularly penetrating and yet serene expression. Probably they were serene because she knew what she wanted; she never indulged in wishful and muddled thinking and sentimental vapours, so what she set her mind to achieve she usually accomplished. That was her true greatness which is often obscured by the picture inevitably called up by the title of 'the Lady of the Lamp'. Not that that picture is one of false sentimentality; it was both beautiful and true. The gracious figure moving so quietly, with her lamp carefully shaded, through the hospital wards at night to see for herself that all the patients were tended with the skill, thoroughness and gentleness that she deemed necessary for their welfare was the indelible picture imprinted in the minds of hundreds of men who had never known, nor probably imagined, such care before. She brought them not only skilful nursing, but a sympathy that was just as valuable, if not more so. It raised their morale and convinced them that the privations they went through were rated at their true worth and counted as much as their courage and endurance in the

280

field. In her presence each man became an individual, not merely a number in a regiment—a necessary asset in war, who when disabled through sickness or wounds was of no account and deserving of no consideration.

II

When Florence Nightingale started for the Crimea she took with her thirty-seven other women all of whom had some sort of training, either in nursing or dispensing, and everyone was amazed that so large a number was prepared to face the risks of such an unprecedented venture. It does not appear an impressive number now-a-days when one considers the work undertaken and compared with the army of trained nurses and members of Voluntary Aid Detachments that went to France in 1914 and 1939, but nurses in those days were rare. Nursing was barely a profession and was often undertaken by women with no training. Some of them were nurses out of the kindness of their hearts, some because they could not earn a living any other way; few of them had any skill or real knowledge of the elementary principles of their profession and such knowledge as they had was often misapplied.

When Miss Nightingale arrived with her contingent of nurses in the Crimea she was faced with conditions in the hospitals that were shocking even in those days. The dirt, the squalor, the overcrowding was appalling and the doctors had neither the energy, nor apparently the will to improve matters. They regarded Florence Nightingale with suspicion and jealousy. What was an even greater handicap in carrying out her task was the open hostility of the officers in command. They viewed the arrival of women in the hospitals as a precedent that must be combated with all the power and influence at their command and that was considerable. They put every conceivable obstacle in her way to prevent the fulfilment of her mission. Women, they thought, might be all very well in civilian hospitals, but women in military hospitals, especially at the seat of war, could be nothing but a nuisance. They would succumb to the hardships of active service, or if they were robust enough to withstand the rigours of war they would make exorbitant demands on supplies (which proved true). They would never be able to distinguish between the malingerer and the genuinely sick and

Florence Nightingale had the love, almost the adoration,
of her patients from the beginning

would be in everybody's way. Many thought that women would never be physically capable of enduring the hardships of the work and the climate.

The question of supplies Miss Nightingale dealt with immediately by ordering a consignment to be sent out immediately at her own expense to enable her to start her mission of mercy and reform. The hostility of the commanders she could not dispose of so easily and she only overcame it by degrees, but her determination never to appear as a rebel and always to acquire the necessary authority for her sweeping reforms gradually enabled her to obtain not only the consent of the higher command but a whole-hearted co-operation. A difficulty that she had not foreseen was the discord that at once broke out amongst the nurses themselves, the squabbling and wrangling that proved more wearing than any of the hardships of the situation. However, the hospitals were started on the lines Miss Nightingale laid down, though only by degrees for it was a Herculean task. Her patience, her determination and persistence achieved it and behind her she had the unswerving loyalty and authority of Sydney Herbert. The love, almost the adoration, of her patients she had from the beginning and when in a few weeks the death rate in the hospitals dropped from approximately 42 per cent to 2 per cent it became difficult for anyone to raise objections to Miss Nightingale's presence at the front.

III

Her achievement was all the more remarkable from the fact that she was of a retiring disposition, not only did she not want to be in the limelight, but she took great pains to avoid it. Her work in the Crimea had made her not only beloved, but famous; she had become a celebrated woman all the world over. Her work was the subject of newspaper articles in every civilized country and she found this publicity very trying. When after a year's work at Scutari she was going home, the government sent a man-of-war to bring her back and London prepared a tremendous reception. The crew of the ship must have been disconcerted to find that the illustrious passenger they expected had already slipped away unnoticed in a French liner and she concealed her arrival in London so successfully that she reached her home at Embley without anyone being aware that she was in England.

Her arduous work in the Crimea had undermined her health; she had not been content with re-organizing the hospitals, she had also taken part in the work. No operation was performed without her being there to support the patient by her presence, and she frequently worked for twenty hours on end. No constitution could stand such a strain for so long and though she lived to a great age—she was ninety when she died—she was from the time of her return always ailing and spent most of her time in bed. But though she was exhausted physically, her mind was as active as ever and nothing checked her urge for work.

Having re-organized the hospitals at the front, she now turned her attention to the military hospitals at home and she drew up a system that comprised startling innovations. She left Sidney Herbert no peace till her reforms were carried out, and so persistent were her demands that the unfortunate Minister of War is said to have died from the overwhelming amount of work forced on him by his indomitable ally, Florence Nightingale. There is an element of truth in the accusation. She admitted it herself and reproached herself bitterly when it was too late. She had not realized the difference in their situations, for she lay in bed ministered to by an army of devoted servants and secretaries whilst he had the whole burden of a Minister of State to bear and had to lead the life of a man of the world as well.

But Miss Nightingale knew her limitations; she was quite aware as she had been at Scutari that she could do nothing on her own authority and she never produced wild cat schemes, hoping vaguely that they would come off. Everything was carefully thought out, provision made for every eventuality and then put forward for the Minister's approval. However much her reforms might be delayed by this procedure it was perfectly correct. Her work was built up on solid foundations, it always had the backing of the competent authority.

IV

Having carried out her reforms in the military hospitals she turned her attention to civilian establishments that were also in need of a change of method and a drastic overhauling. Her

284

work in the Crimea had not only moved the country to senti-mental applause, the people's admiration had taken the practical form of a nation-wide collection and she was presented with the sum of £50,000. She had realized as soon as she began her investigations of the civil hospitals that their trouble was the lack of an adequately trained staff and that the training of the few nurses available was lacking in what she considered essential principles. As a first step she wrote a book in 1858 laying down what she considered the basic necessities for good nursing, but with her usual practical sense she was aware that books are of less use than training. The money that the country in its spon-taneous gratitude had subscribed gave her the means to put into practice a scheme that she had for some time been considering. She founded the Nightingale Home for Training Nurses at St. Thomas's and King's College Hospitals and here the students were impressed with what she considered the basic necessities for good nursing.

She had by this time become bed-ridden, though what her actual complaint was her doctors did not seem able to diagnose. Some people blamed the physicians, but it has been said that her ill-health was purely imaginary and that overwork and over-strain had induced chronic hysteria. If she had had to work for her living, perhaps she would have been perfectly well. There is probably a grain of truth in this theory. Her experiences in the Crimea were enough to affect her nervous system, but they had left her mental vigour untouched.

V

In her book on nursing she had laid down the principles of good nursing and in the Nightingale Home these were empha-sized. The first was fresh air—a considerable shock to the old school. Warmth and quiet were the next. Warmth must have been difficult in those days when there were no systems of central heating. On the other hand coal and labour were cheap and plentiful. Quiet was probably easier; there was nothing like the volume of traffic that roars along the streets nowadays.

All these activities were directed from her bed with a good sense that brought forth universal admiration and with a vigour that dismayed all those working under her. It was impossible to keep up with the demands she made on her devoted friends and servants, but her spirit never flagged till she was about eighty years old. She lived another ten years, but it was mere existence; her great spirit had consumed her vitality and during those last years the flame of life only flickered in her worn-out body.

It is difficult for us to realize the magnitude of the work she accomplished in these days when nursing has become a profession second only to that of doctors in its importance, but the name of Florence Nightingale will always be remembered with admiration and gratitude. The name by which she was, and still is loved, will always be 'The Lady of the Lamp'.

Louis Pasteur

SCIENCE IN THE SERVICE OF MAN

William E. Dick

I

ONE July day in 1885 a little Alsatian lad named Joseph Meister was wending his way to school when suddenly a mad dog sprang out upon him. Joseph was only nine years old and too small to be able to ward off the savage attack; all he could do was to throw up his hands to protect his face. Fortunately a bricklayer saw the incident. He rushed to the boy's rescue and beat off the dog with an iron bar he was carrying. Then he gently picked up the badly mauled child and carried him to the nearest doctor's surgery.

Meantime the dog had returned to his master, the village grocer, whom he bit. Whereupon the grocer seized his gun and shot the rabid beast. Afterwards a post-mortem examination was carried out and the dog's stomach was found to be full of hay, straw and bits of wood. There was no doubt about it now: the dog was suffering from rabies, which can be transmitted to human beings, causing the dreadful disease called hydrophobia —in which the sufferer has a most terrible thirst but cannot bring himself to touch water.

Now at that time there was no cure for hydrophobia, and, as mad dogs were not uncommon then, everyone dreaded the effects of their bite. The doctor who examined the wounded boy could do little beyond washing the bites with carbolic acid. He knew that wounds like these inflicted by a mad dog were commonly fatal, and to the parents of young Joseph he could offer small hope that their son would recover. He told them there was only one chance, and that a very forlorn one. This was that the mother should take the boy to Paris with all speed and seek out a scientist called Louis Pasteur. He explained that Pasteur was not a medical man. At that time there was not a doctor in all

287

France—nor even in the whole world—who knew how to cure rabies, but Pasteur had been experimenting with a vaccine which had worked successfully on dogs. After vaccination the dogs could be bitten by mad dogs without the usual dire results—they had become immune from hydrophobia. The vaccine, however, had not yet been tested on any human being.

So it was that Joseph, accompanied by his mother and by the grocer who had owned the mad dog, arrived at Pasteur's laboratory on July 6, 1885. Pasteur was shocked when he examined the lad and saw the fourteen ugly wounds on his body. He was told that two days had elapsed since little Joseph had been bitten, and Madame Meister then asked him whether he could do anything for her child. Pasteur was unable to give her an immediate answer, for he did not feel sure that he could risk treating the boy with the vaccine which had never yet been tested on a human being. He could do nothing until he had discussed the matter with Professor Vulpian of the French Government's Rabies Commission. The professor had been extremely impressed with the power of the vaccine to protect dogs and he expressed the opinion that it would be just as successful with human patients. After examining Joseph, he told Pasteur that the boy would almost certainly die unless he received the vaccine. And so the decision was taken to innoculate little Joseph Meister. With a hypodermic syringe a few drops of vaccine were injected into his side. It was a good omen that Joseph stopped crying almost immediately after the injection; he dried his tears when he realized that the slight prick from the hypodermic needle was all that he would feel with vaccination. It was not long before the child sat up and began to take notice of his surroundings. To a child Pasteur's laboratory was paradise, and young Joseph lost little time before he was playing happily with the experimental animals—the rabbits, white mice and guinea pigs—which belonged to his friend, dear Monsieur Pasteur, as he called the scientist.

Ten days after his arrival in the laboratory Joseph was given the last of a series of fourteen inoculations. Pasteur was beginning to believe that the experiment was going to be a success. "Perhaps one of the great medical events of the century is going to take place," he wrote. By day Pasteur was optimistic; this could be the beginning of a new era in which rabies could be cured. But at night he was a prey to his worst fears and his sleep was troubled with visions of the child suffocating in the last throes of hydrophobia, like a child he had seen die of the disease some years before.

Then came the final test—the injection which would prove whether the child was now immune against the disease. He was injected with a culture of virus strong enough to produce rabies inside seven days when it was given to a rabbit. If the boy took this injection without harm, then the treatment was complete. To the great joy of everyone the boy remained in perfect health. His wounds had healed and he was now well enough to go back to school. Alike to the parents of Joseph Meister and to the greatest medical men in France, this was a miracle.

Pasteur's name now became a household word in France, and in the remote parts of the world new hope was born. Rabies could be cured. Pasteur's development of the anti-rabies vaccine came as the climax of a great career. Rabies was not the first disease he had vanquished by vaccination, but it was his greatest triumph in the field of human disease. From all over France people who had been bitten by rabid dogs came to his laboratory; doctors in countries as far apart as Russia and America started sending him patients. The miracle was repeated over and over again, and nearly every single patient out of the hundreds who came for his treatment recovered perfectly. His 'hydrophobia service' became his main occupation, and until this had been organized on a big scale Pasteur's researches had to come to a full stop.

So there came into existence the Pasteur Institute in Paris. From all over France, from all over the world, subscriptions poured in towards the cost of setting up this great humanitarian centre; millionaires sent hundreds of pounds, and poor people sent their pennies. The subscription list from Alsace-Lorraine included the name of little Joseph Meister—the first human being to be brought back from the jaws of a rabid death. As Pasteur's friend Professor Vulpian said: "This new benefit adds to the number of those which our illustrious Pasteur has already rendered to humanity. Our works and our names will soon be buried under the rising tide of oblivion: the name and the works of Monsieur Pasteur, however, will continue to stand on heights too great to be reached by its sullen waves."

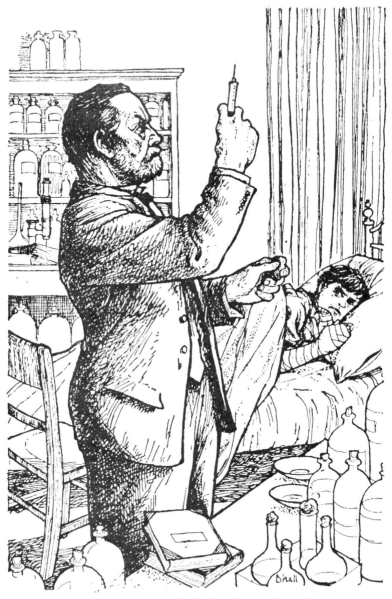

And so Pasteur took the decision to inoculate
little Joseph Meister

How true were those words of Professor Vulpian. The name of Pasteur is indeed immortal. In many cities there are Pasteur Institututes, and we also recall this great French scientist every time we use such terms as *pasteurization*, which is the method of food preservation which he perfected. His esteem among fellow scientists was beautifully expressed in this tribute from an English surgeon: "He was, it seems to me, the most perfect man who has ever entered the kingdom of Science. Here was a life, within the limits of humanity, well-nigh perfect. He worked incessantly; he lived to see his doctrines enthroned, his methods applied to a thousand affairs of manufacture and agriculture, his science put in practice by all doctors and surgeons, his name praised and blessed by mankind; and the very animals, if they could speak would say the same."

II

Although Pasteur's work revolutionized medicine, and opened up new realms of biological thought, he started his career neither as doctor nor biologist. His first researches belonged to chemistry. But he was a pioneer in every field he touched; indeed, when Fleming discovered penicillin it turned out that Pasteur had already discovered the first antibiotic, as long ago as 1877.

Louis Pasteur was born on December 27, 1822. His birthplace was Dôle in the eastern part of France. His father, Jean Joseph, had served as a conscript in Napoleon's army and had fought through the Peninsular War against Wellington's troops. He belonged to the Third Regiment of the Line—'the bravest among the brave', as one historian described it. Back in France his division fought with great courage against a force that outnumbered them five to one and Jean Pasteur, now a sergeant, was awarded the cross of the Legion of Honour. Came Waterloo and the cessation of hostilities, and Pasteur's father went back to his pre-war trade—that of a tanner. Always he kept his sabre as a reminder of the military glory of France's First Empire, and he never tired of recounting his army adventures to young Louis, who, as ardent a patriot as his father, was to add to the glory of France in no uncertain fashion.

There was nothing precocious about Louis; his boyhood was

not exceptional and it gave no hint of the rich streak of genius which was to emerge later. The earliest talent which he showed was not for science at all, but for art; his pastel drawings were quite remarkable and he would certainly have made his mark as an artist. It was the headmaster of the college at Arbois who first realized there was a hidden spark in the conscientious and hardworking schoolboy. At that time his caution obscured his underlying brilliance. As a boy he never affirmed anything of which he was not absolutely sure—an invaluable trait for the future scientist, for it is a scientific axiom that 'it is better to be sure than sorry'. (No scientist can afford to guess; he must always be quite certain.) Pasteur's headmaster inspired him with the ambition to become a professor, a prospect which made his father extremely proud. "If you can become a professor at Arbois, I shall be the happiest man on earth," he told young Louis. In 1840 he obtained his bachelor's degree and the examiners reported that he was 'very good in elementary science'. His target now was to enter the Ecole Normale Supérieure in Paris, the great college that Napoleon had founded in 1808 for the training of young professors. The entrance examination was a stiff one and required months of intensive study; at that time Pasteur found the physics and chemistry which he had to learn most interesting, but he was not so happy about the mathematics, which he found both dry and exhausting. He entered the Ecole Normale in 1843. Paris was then the most important scientific centre in the world and Pasteur came under the influence of some of the great masters.

III

Chemistry became his passion and his first great discovery was made in that field. He had tackled a problem that had baffled scientists for years. This was concerned with the substance called tartaric acid, which was prepared commercially from tartar, the crust or sediment which accumulates in wine casks. Chemists had discovered that this acid exists in two quite different forms; the first was *tartaric acid* proper, and the other they called *racemic acid* or para-tartaric acid. These two acids had exactly the same composition; they contained exactly the same variety of atoms (namely carbon, hydrogen and oxygen) and these were present in identical proportions in both acids—namely four carbon atoms to six hydrogen atoms to six oxygen atoms, the formula being $C_4H_6O_6$. From the two acids, salts were easily prepared and crystals of these salts collected. The two sets of crystals—one set from tartaric acid and the other from racemic acid—looked as though they had precisely the same shape. Yet when the solutions of the one and of the other were tested in an instrument called a saccharimeter (which measures the amount of sugar in a solution by the extent to which the solution rotates a beam of polarized light) they behaved quite differently. The solution of tartrate twisted the light to the right, yet there was no twist at all when Pasteur repeated the experiment with racemic acid solution in his saccharimeter; to use the proper expression, the racemic was 'optically inactive'. Pasteur then proceeded to examine the crystals of the racemic more closely and found that they were not all of the same kind—some were right-handed crystals and the rest left-handed, the first class of crystal obviously being the mirror-image of the second class. (You can visualize this by thinking of the two different gloves that make up a pair.) So, patiently, by hand, Pasteur picked out all the right-handed crystals and put them in one pile and then he collected a pile containing nothing but left-handed crystals. When he dissolved the right-handed crystals he found that the solution twisted polarized light to the right; with the second set of crystals he obtained a rotation to the left. His 'right' tartrate performed in exactly the same way as the tartrate which he prepared from proper tartaric acid.

Next Pasteur put equal quantities of the 'right' and 'left' tartrate solutions together in his saccharimeter. This time there was no rotation of the polarized light; the twist which the 'right' tartrate would have produced was exactly balanced by the twist in the opposite direction imposed by the 'left' tartrate. In other words he had succeeded in re-combining the two optically active tartrates to produce the optically inactive racemate. Pasteur's discovery became the talk of the scientific world and won him the friendship of Monsieur Biot, one of the elder statesmen of French science. Largely through his friend's influence he received the red ribbon of the Legion of Honour in 1853, when he was only thirty.

In spite of his obvious talents for research, Pasteur was posted to the University of Strasburg as professor of chemistry. There he married Marie, the daughter of the university's rector, and of Madame Pasteur it has been said that "she was more than an incomparable companion; she was his best collaborator", acting as his scientific secretary as well as looking after their home and family.

IV

His next great triumph was the synthesis of racemic acid, which he made by transforming the compound called cinchonin tartrate at a high temperature. This won him a prize of 1500 francs awarded by the Pharmaceutical Society of Paris, and most of this money he used to equip his laboratory at Strasbourg. His interest in the asymmetry of tartrate crystals was now to lead him far away from conventional chemistry and into the field of microbiology, where he was to eclipse all his previous work and gain the nickname of 'the Christopher Columbus of microbes'. The abrupt switch that happened to his career came about in this way. He happened to be studying what occurs when a solution of a tartrate like ammonium tartrate ferments. He was working with a species of blue-green mould called *Penicillium glaucum*—which is a cousin of the mould that produces penicillin—and he fed the fungus both ordinary ammonium tartrate and ammonium racemate to see what would happen. The mould thrived on ammonium racemate, but the result was quite unexpected; the left-handed tartrate appeared, so evidently what was happening was that the mould was fermenting the right-handed tartrate and leaving the other tartrate entirely alone! Pasteur recommended this as the best way of preparing left-handed tartrate.

By now he was developing vivid and exciting ideas about asymmetrical substances which were optically active, and the part that such substances played in the chemistry of living organisms. It emerged that many organisms can distinguish between left-handed and right-handed molecules; for example 'left' tartaric acid is twice as poisonous to guinea-pigs as the 'right' acid; the 'right' form of asparagine possesses a sweet taste whereas you cannot taste the 'left' form at all. Pasteur figured that asymmetrical compounds are inseparable from life,

294

and the researches of generations of organic chemists and biochemists have revealed how right he was in this idea.

V

His next university appointment was at Lille. This was the richest centre of industrial activity in Northern France, and the university placed special emphasis on training young men to become foremen and industrial managers. Pasteur entered a new and exciting world. He realized the great part which science could play in industry, and the inspired view which he showed to local manufacturers and to his students alike can be glimpsed in these remarks of Pasteur on applied science: "Where in your families will you find a young man whose curiosity and interest will not immediately be awakened when you put into his hands a potato, when with that potato he can produce sugar, with that sugar alcohol, with that alcohol ether and vinegar? What student would not be happy to tell his family in the evening that he has just been working on an electric telegraph? And be convinced of this: such practical work is seldom if ever forgotten." It was men like Pasteur who started up the laboratories in colleges and schools that are so indispensable to the teaching of science. But while Pasteur spoke to industrialists of the practical value of science, he was at great pains to stress that *pure* research—knowledge for its own sake—is essential to the progress of science. "What is the use of a pure scientific discovery?" he was asked. He regarded the question as fatuous and quick as a flash he came back with the counter-question: "What use is a new-born baby?" That settled the argument.

Local industry quickly took to consulting Pasteur on their problems. There was, for example, the manufacturer who brewed alcohol for industrial purposes from sugar beet; initially he had obtained a good yield but for some unaccountable reason the process had gone wrong. Pasteur's first move was to examine the brew under a microscope, the instrument which symbolized his series of great studies on the phenomena of fermentation. Later it was he who introduced the microscope into English breweries! The microscope showed him that a good alcoholic brew contained nothing but round globules—the cells of the yeast plant. When the fermentation went awry, then

295

along with the yeast the microscope revealed small rod-shaped bodies—the bacillus which converted sugar into lactic acid. As a chemist Pasteur proceeded to dig far deeper into the chemistry of fermentation than anyone had before. He soon discovered, for example, that ordinary alcoholic fermentation produces quite significant amounts of two other chemicals— glycerine and succinic acid. The upshot of his researches in this field was that all the industries that used fermentation in making their products could now be re-organized on a scientific basis, a step which improved their output and the quality of their products. Not only did this affect brewing and bread-making (both of which involve the use of yeasts), but also such things as the manufacture of cheese and the curing of tobacco. Today all kinds of chemicals can be made by fermenting such materials as sugar and starch; such substances include acetone, citric acid, and the various antibiotics (including penicillin).

VI

Pasteur established the principle that there is 'no fermentation without life'. In other words, all fermentations are the result of the activity of microbes. As logical as Pasteur's move from tartaric acid crystals to ferments was his next switch—to the great biological question of what is called 'spontaneous generation'. This had been a riddle for hundreds of years. A few wise men had reached the conclusion that only living things can beget living things; but the majority believed the opposite— that living organisms—plants and animals—could suddenly, spontaneously, appear. For example one first-class scientist, van Helmont, maintained that he could produce mice by putting some cheese on a pile of dirty linen and leaving the mysterious force of spontaneous generation to conjure forth baby mice. Another classic delusion was the belief that driftwood spontaneously produced barnacles (the kind called 'goose barnacles') and that these changed spontaneously into butterflies, which in turn were transformed into birds.

Once in a long while someone would do a scientific experiment that clearly contradicted this faith in spontaneous generation. There was the Italian naturalist Francesco Redi who did not accept the current view that meat spontaneously generated maggots. They were, he said, nothing but the larvae of flies.

To prove his case he protected some meat with a piece of gauze that excluded the flies; so long as the flies were unable to get at the meat and lay their eggs on it, the meat never turned maggoty. (This was, of course, the origin of the still familiar meat safe.) Men like Redi disproved the theory of spontaneous generation and substituted the rule that 'like begets like'—in other words, a mouse can only be derived from other mice and cannot come into existence in any other way.

But when the miscroscope was invented and a new world—the world of microbes—was discovered a new race of believers in spontaneous generation came on the scene. They honestly believed that the apparently simple microbes can suddenly materialize in such liquids as broth, milk and sugar solution. Pasteur realized that there would be no progress in microbiology unless this question was settled once and for all. The spontaneous generationists believed that life could be conjured up out of thin air. Pasteur pondered upon this idea and came to an entirely different conclusion. Suppose that the air was not thin at all; suppose the atmosphere contained microbes or the seeds (*spores*) of microbes. Then if you put down a saucer or bottle of milk, surely some of those microbes or their spores will soon get in the milk and proceed to multiply until the milk is stiff with them. So Pasteur first boiled some milk in a flask to kill any microbes already in it. Then he plugged the neck of the flask with a plug of cotton-wool which had been singed in a flame to destroy any microbes in it. This simple device incidentally would allow air to reach the milk but that air would be filtered, any microbes being trapped by the cotton-wool. What was the result? Instead of going bad as milk normally would, it remained fresh indefinitely; it did not ferment and no microbes appeared in it.

In London's Royal Institution a British physicist, John Tyndall, did similar experiments and the results he obtained fitted in perfectly with Pasteur's. These two men did hundreds of tests and always obtained the same results, but still the theory of spontaneous generation survived. Their cleverest opponent, a Frenchman called Pouchet, had produced one very awkward fact on which the spontaneous generationists made their last great stand. Pouchet had brewed an infusion of hay but when he sterilized this liquor according to Pasteur's method and plugged the flask with a sterile filter the hay liquor still proceeded to go bad! One fact like that can destroy a scientific theory, as both Pasteur and Tyndall knew all too well. It was Tyndall who found the correct explanation. He repeated Pouchet's experiment; even after boiling the hay infusion for eight solid hours, Tyndall could still not get it to keep. One up to Pouchet, but Tyndall struck back with a new series of experiments which gave the final death-blow to spontaneous generation. He proved that the heating killed only the living hay bacteria. Their *spores* on the other hand could survive being boiled! To kill the whole lot it was necessary to boil once, allow the liquor to cool, let the spores germinate and produce living bacteria, and then boil a second time. The second boiling did the trick and proved effective even if it lasted for only a fraction of a second. (This method of 'discontinuous heating' is known as *tyndallization* and is complementary to *pasteurization*.)

These techniques of sterilization were soon applied to industry. Pasteur perfected a method of preserving wine, beer and other liquors that can go bad by heating them for a few minutes at 50 degrees Centigrade or so. This method—now universally known as pasteurization—is used all over the world; most milk in Britain nowadays is pasteurized.

VII

No scientist has ever possessed a more wide-ranging brain than Pasteur's. After he had realized that microbes bring about the decay of dead tissue—butcher's meat, for instance—he started thinking about what microbes might do to the bodies of living animals. Particular kinds of fermentation were due to particular kinds of microbes; was it possible that the contagious diseases of man and other animals were due to specific micro-organisms? This was Pasteur's germ theory of disease which was to revolutionize medicine.

The first infectious disease he tackled was *pébrine*. This is a disease of silkworms that was ruining the French silk industry. Pasteur discovered that this was due to a microbe (called *Nosema bombycis*). He showed also that the disease was propagated by healthy silkworms eating with their food the frass of infected caterpillars; the moths from infected cater-

298

pillars laid infected eggs. He then taught the silkworm culti-vators how to obtain uninfected eggs and so he saved this industry.

The time was ripe for Pasteur's incursion into medicine. The introduction of anaesthetics had made it possible for surgeons to perform complicated and time-consuming opera-tions successfully. But too many patients died after the opera-tions because little could be done to protect them against blood poisoning. As one surgeon said of the surgical wards of that period, "Pus seemed to germinate everywhere, as if it had been sown by the surgeon." There was almost complete ignorance about the mechanism whereby a cut became infected and pro-ceeded to suppurate. A few daring surgeons tried sterilizing the flesh with such things as hot brandy and the bandages they used with an antiseptic mixture of alcohol and water. The results were most encouraging and one of these surgeons, Alphonse Guerin, teamed up with Pasteur in 1873 with the aim of improving his antiseptic methods. Pasteur had another vigorous disciple in Britain—Joseph Lister (1827–1912), who worked out his principles of antiseptic surgery in Glasgow and Edinburgh. Before the onslaught of these men 'the evil of putrefaction' as Lister called it practically disappeared from the surgical wards and the mortality after operations dropped to a tenth of what it had been. The French Government now recognized the great achievements of Pasteur by giving him a life pension.

German scientists, too, had become imbued with Pasteur's ideas about germs and one of them—Robert Koch (1843–1910) —gave the new science of medical bacteriology a flying start by discovering the full details of the life history of the anthrax bacillus. He followed that up by two other vitally important discoveries—the isolation of the bacteria that cause tuber-culosis and cholera. Then followed the golden era of medical bacteriology; inside the next twenty years the things that cause most bacterial diseases were identified and studied.

VIII

The next problem which Pasteur tackled was the question of immunity to disease. Could the immunity of human beings to attack by specific germs be produced by any artificial means?

Edward Jenner had immunized people against smallpox by vaccinating them with the mild form of the disease known as cowpox; that was back in 1798, and no other useful vaccine had been discovered since.

The first vaccine which Pasteur produced was the result of a lucky accident, the kind of accident which the brilliantly prepared minds of master scientists exploit to the full. In 1879 an epidemic disease was crippling poultry keeping in France. Pasteur turned his attention to this disease. He showed that the germ of this chicken cholera could be grown on broth prepared from chicken gristle. By accident a culture of this microbe on broth was lost. Some weeks later it came to light again and Pasteur carried out a routine test on it, injecting it into some hens to see whether it was still infectious. The hens fell sick as usual—but then, to everyone's delighted surprise, they began to recover. The stale culture was an effective vaccine. But how could he produce the vaccine again when he wanted it? Pasteur discovered that the strength of a cholera culture could be reduced by starving the bacteria of air; the weakened culture—*attentuated culture* is the technical term for this— protected the hens which Pasteur vaccinated with it.

The most serio"s disease of farm animals at that time was anthrax—or *charl n* as the French called it. He found he could grow the germ—*bacillus anthracis*—in sterile urine and broth. Pasteur's next problem was to attenuate the bacillus to produce a safe and effective vaccine. He knew that at 45 degrees Centigrade this bacillus cannot grow at all; it should therefore be possible to pick a somewhat lower temperature that would enable the bacillus to multiply but provide a culture rather weaker than normal. Attentuation by heat proved successful and Pasteur achieved the much-needed vaccine. In May 1881 he demonstrated the power of his anthrax vaccination. An agricultural society put at his disposal a farm at Pouilly le Fort and 60 sheep. Pasteur vaccinated 25 sheep, keeping another batch of 25 animals unvaccinated for the sake of comparison. Then he injected all the sheep with virulent anthrax. Almost all of the unvaccinated sheep died but, exactly as Pasteur predicted, every single vaccinated sheep survived. "No success had ever been greater than Pasteur's," wrote his biographer. "The veterinary surgeons, until then the most sceptical, now convinced, desired to become the apostles of his doctrine (of vaccination)." The vaccine caught on like wildfire and in a matter of a fortnight Pasteur and his assistants, Roux and Chamberland, treated no less than 20,000 sheep, with complete success. Anthrax was conquered, one of the four animal diseases for which Pasteur perfected vaccines in the incredibly short period of four years.

The scientist had been working on rabies which medical men had always regarded as incurable. By 1885 he had been able to produce a vaccine that gave protection to dogs. Pasteur worried about making the final test that was necessary—the trial of his vaccine on a human being. The effects of this disease in humans were horrifying in the extreme and Pasteur could not forget the case of rabies he had once seen in hospital. He hesitated to take the plunge; as he wrote on March 28, 1885, "I have not yet dared to treat human beings, but the time is not far off, and I am much inclined to begin by myself—inoculating myself with rabies and then arresting the consequences." Pasteur had never lacked courage and had never hesitated to come in contact with the most dangerous of the contagious diseases; now he was prepared to take the ultimate risk. But it never became necessary, because of the arrival of little Joseph Meister, the lad from Alsace, at his laboratory. The test as you know was made on the boy and saved his life.

The story of Pasteur's life, which began in 1822 and ended in 1895 is now complete. No scientist ever achieved more in a lifetime and I hope you will want to read more about Pasteur; if so, there is a wonderful biography about him, *The Life of Pasteur* by René Vallery-Radot, his son-in-law.

Anna Pavlova

PRIMA BALLERINA

Noel Streatfeild

I

ANNA PAVLOVA was born in St. Petersburg, which is now called Leningrad. The exact date of her birth is not known, but it was either late January or early February 1881 or 1882. Anna was a seven months' baby, so frail that she was expected to die. In those days there were no incubators or other modern aids to keep premature babies alive, but there was cotton wool. Rolled in it the tiny flame of life was kept burning, and the baby lived.

Anna's home was not a good one in which to bring up a delicate child. Her father died when she was two years old and left her mother with no money. For days together the only food which came into the house was rye bread, and cabbage of which soup was made. To add to the anxieties of bringing Anna up she managed not only to catch most of the infectious illnesses at an early age but to have worse attacks of them than most children. So, frail to start with, she had to spend many of her early days in her bed.

Although it must have been a terrible sacrifice to part with Anna, while she was still very young, her mother sent her away from home to live with her grandmother in the country, at a little place called Ligovo. Living in Ligovo had a great effect on Anna. Not only in the country air did she grow much stronger, but the cold purity of the countryside in a northern Russian winter made a lasting impression on her. So perhaps too did the loneliness of the life. Anna was devoted to her grandmother, and the grandmother to her; but much of the child's time was spent alone, her amusements and playthings being those which belonged to the season and to the countryside. Children who learn at an early age to be happy by themselves often grow up

302

with an unusual store of self-sufficiency, so it could be Ligovo helped Anna to grow up to be such a person.

II

When Anna was eight, as a Christmas treat, her mother took her to see The Imperial Russian Ballet dance *The Sleeping Beauty*. Her reaction was one that many little girls who later become dancers experience. She was utterly carried away, and knew with every sense in her body that she too must dance. But where Anna differed from most small girls enthralled by their first sight of ballet was in what she said. When her mother, delighted at her obvious pleasure, asked her if she wished she were one of the dancers, Anna answered without hesitation that when she danced it would not be with others, but by herself, like Sleeping Beauty.

This statement showed that even when she was eight Anna already possessed a quality she never lost, certainty in her destiny. This gave her the strength to make her mother, who took a great deal of persuading, take her to The Imperial Ballet School to ask if she could be a pupil. But that time all the determination in Anna was of no use, for The Imperial Ballet School said that she was too young and application should be made for her in two years' time.

Anna's mother was convinced it was most unlikely that at any time would Anna become a pupil of The Imperial Ballet School. For one quality every child selected had to have was perfect health. What chance then had Anna, who, though she was stronger, still looked so noticeably frail? However, two years later application was made, and Anna was ordered to attend a preliminary examination.

The very sight of the school must have been intimidating for the would-be pupils, for the door was opened to them by a beadle in the Czar's livery. Then they assembled in a room on the first floor, where they were looked over by the directress and the governess before being marched two by two into the next room for the first stage of their examination. There the children were called out in groups to the middle of the room where the examiners could walk round them, studying how they were made. Presently they were ordered to walk, then to run, and finally their knees were looked at. Only a certain number of the candidates got through this preliminary examination, but one of them was Anna. The next stage was for her even more frightening, for it was the medical examination. Miraculously, for the examination was very thorough, again Anna got through. For her frail appearance was deceptive; it was the way she was made; there was nothing physical the matter with her.

The medical examination was followed by tea and sandwiches; then the children were tested for musicality, and in the three Rs. Again many candidates were weeded out, but Anna was still not one of them. Even then there were too many children for the vacancies in the school. Back the remainder were marched to appear again before the original examiners. This was the last part of the audition; the select few were picked and Anna was one of them. Stage one of her career had begun.

III

Almost from the beginning of her training it became clear to her teachers that Anna had the makings of an outstanding dancer. Then, as now, no teacher would dare prophesy the future of a pupil, for so much can go wrong with a dancer, but they probably said to each other in the phrase that covers so much: "Little Pavlova has a something." That she had 'something' became more certain after her fourteenth birthday, when she made her first public appearance in a school performance, and soon afterwards danced at The Maryinsky Theatre. But though it was hoped there would be a brilliant future for Anna there were those who wondered if she might be unable to live up to her promise; this was because of the nature of the dancing at that time most admired, and the figure at that moment fashionable.

An Italian dancer called Legnani had visited St. Petersburg, and had performed 32 *fouettés* in succession. The Russian dancers trained in the stylized French manner were amazed, and a burning determination filled every heart to be able to do the same. Because Legnani's 32 *fouettés* and other showy acrobatic dancing achievements were admired, her rather solid figure was accepted amongst her fellow dancers as ideal. Pavlova, so frail and delicately built, was by this standard far from ideal. How, asked many of those watching her progress, could that piece of porcelain find the strength for the difficult Italian steps?

Luckily for Anna, her teacher, Guerdt, was not blinded by the craze for virtuosity. He saw in Anna a dancer of rare quality. "Don't," he said in effect, "bother with all this acrobatic nonsense, for that is not where your gifts lie." Although presumably Anna, like all the other students in the school, practised *fouettés*, Guerdt's counsel was in line with her own taste, and she did not overstrain herself attempting feats for which she was not built. For from the beginning of her career, both as a dancer and in her private life, Anna abhorred ostentation and was incapable of even a tinge of vulgarity.

In 1899 Anna's schooldays finished. At her final examination Guerdt arranged ballets which would show off her qualities, and she immediately attracted attention. She was, Valerian Svetlov writes: "delicate, svelte, and pliant as a reed . . . she was graceful and fragile as a piece of Sèvres porcelain."

After leaving school Anna's career was like that of a rocket. The balletomanes of St. Petersburg were on the whole a discerning lot, and her qualities were at once appreciated. In 1902 she became a second soloist, in 1903 a first soloist, and in 1905 a ballerina, a word totally misused today, for in Russia it was a title only granted to dancers of great distinction.

IV

What was Pavlova like? What had the school done to the character of the little Anna who had played alone at Ligovo, or to the eight-year-old who had said: "I shall dance by myself like Sleeping Beauty"? I cannot find a description of her in those formative years. All that is on view is what came out of the school. From her earliest public appearance she was in the highest sense a dedicated dancer. She probably accepted quite simply that she had been endowed with exceptional gifts, but at no time did she consider this a matter for vainglory, for her gifts were to her a sacred trust. She was a religious girl, and probably looked upon her dancing as a vocation just as another girl might accept a vocation to become a nun. From the beginning she was quite uninfluenced by applause, for the dancer in her knew perfection, even when she was far from being able to attain it, and, if a performance of hers was below her standard, applause became an aggravation. All through her life there are stories of her displeasure, even rage, at being cheered and clapped when she knew by her standards her performance had not merited it.

In the year that she became a ballerina Pavlova first danced *The Dying Swan*, it was arranged for her by Fokine. It was one of those miraculous fusings of talent at the right moment which makes history. Fokine's choreography, the music of Saint-Saëns, and Pavlova to dance. It probably seemed to Fokine, when he designed it, a simple dance, yet from its first performance it was clear something perfect had been born. It is never possible to define genius, exactly what quality lifts an artiste to Olympus. Pavlova had fine technique, but no finer than many others. She was, except for her hands which were on the large side, though she used them so perfectly few could have guessed it, exquisitely built for a dancer, with beautiful legs and perfect insteps. I only saw her dance once, and that was at the end of her life. In those days I did not know much about ballet, but if I shut my eyes I can still see her dancing *Gavotte*. It was, I think, a charming dance, nothing more, and all I can write to explain her is that she had a quality that belonged only to her, for she made that simple little dance something so perfect my breath was caught just as it can be caught today by the perfection of a laburnum in full flower. I never saw her dance *The Dying Swan*, but evidently it was the ideal vehicle for her. For not only was she to make it famous throughout the world, but from the moment she danced it, that she was a very rare dancer was accepted in the ballet world of Russia, and it was not long after that a high honour was granted her, for she became a prima ballerina.

V

Pavlova was an individualist. Perhaps the self-sufficiency bred in her at Ligovo helped, but it became clear to her she must live her artistic life in her own way, and not as others dictated. In Czarist Russia it was the custom for the leading dancers to ask for, and obtain, permission to dance abroad during the summer months. Pavlova took advantage of this arrangement, and in successive summers danced in Germany, Sweden, Denmark, with Diaghilev in Paris, and for a month in New York. Her need for artistic independence came to a head when she danced a second season, this time in London, with Diaghilev. She was an immense success, dancing *Giselle* amongst other rôles, and she must have been a superb Giselle, but she could not stay with Diaghilev. Knowing all we know of that great company today, this seems at first sight extraordinary, for from many points of view working with Diaghilev must have given the dancers great artistic satisfaction. But it made Pavlova feel it was increasingly impossible for her to be part of the whole, she had to be the person round whom everything else was built. With Diaghilev, who believed each ballet must be the work of a team, such a personality as hers was completely out of place. In any case it is doubtful if two such individualists as Diaghilev and Pavlova could ever have got on for long together, for to work for either was to accept that you were serving a god, and who can argue with the gods?

In 1911 Pavlova bought Ivy House in Hampstead. That house now has been made to sound a dream home, where she lived like a princess, surrounded by swans. It is true there were swans, and a charming garden which she loved, but Pavlova was an exceedingly good business woman, and, more important than swans and gardens, Ivy House had a room large enough to work in, and there was storage space for costumes and scenery not in use. It was fortunate she bought Ivy House, for three years later the first world war broke out, and it became her only home. When the war started Pavlova was dancing in Germany, but she got out and came home to Ivy House, but stayed there only long enough to collect a company together before she sailed for the U.S.A.

For the next five years Pavlova and her company of 22 danced all over North and South America. The company she took to America during the war was not her first; she had formed several small companies to dance with her during her seasons abroad. At first she had employed dancers from The Imperial Theatres, but such dancers were free only in the summer months, and so she had turned her attention to English dancers, and it was a largely English *corps de ballet* that, braving submarines, went with her to America.

The war over, and travel again possible, Pavlova still with a largely English company, began those tours of the world which she continued until she died. What an exhausting undertaking those tours must have been. It is said she travelled during her life time 500,000 miles, and it is likely enough to be true. It must have seemed sometimes as if she was possessed—why else would a great artiste wear herself out, moving, ever moving, often staying only one night in a place? She was successful beyond our understanding today. We are used to a world which is largely ballet-minded; she came as the first true dancer many of her audience had ever seen. The ballets she danced were largely simple and undistinguished, but what did that matter? To every rôle she brought herself, and though she seldom pleased herself, to her audience she was the stuff dreams are made of.

Was Pavlova satisfied with dancing to fill her life? It is certain she could no more have given up dancing and settled down than the wind could give up blowing and settle down. But there were, and she knew it, things that she missed. She never saw enough of her friends. She would have liked longer periods at Ivy House. Above all she would have worshipped children of her own. She loved children, and stories of her kindness and tact to would-be dancers brought to her by fond mammas are innumerable. In the fragments of leisure that were hers, between her work in the theatre, the social life which was a part of her great position, and her journeys, she almost always saw such children, and, however grieved and shocked she was at what had been done to them by ignorant dancing teachers, the children never knew, for she was charming to them. In Paris she expressed her love for the children she could never find time to have, by founding a home for White Russian orphans, which she not only supported until her death but which became one of her few interests outside her company.

VI

Fortunately there are a great many people about who knew and worked with Pavlova, and it is on their testimony that the best pictures of her are obtained. She was fabulous, but she was still a human being. To read contemporary papers you might doubt that, for it is hard to see a real person through the superlatives. I turned for help to one of the Pavlova girls, as they were called. What was she like as a person, I asked? What was she like to work with?

The years rolled back and I was able to see what Pavlova meant to dancers in the years following the first world war. At that time there was no English ballet, so there was almost no stage on which would-be dancers could dance. To be accepted as a dancer it was usual to take a foreign name, as did Alicia Marks—whom we know as Markova, and Ninette de Valois—who was born Edris Stannus. But Pavlova, and Pavlova almost alone, believed that English girls had talent for dancing, and had no need to hide behind foreign names, so she took them into her company, where they danced under their own names and their confidence in themselves was built up because she stated publicly on every possible occasion that she was proud of her English dancers. Not that Pavlova was not frequently infuriated by her girls, she was. She was a temperamental Russian by birth, and a ballerina, a temperamental creature whatever country she belongs to, by profession, so it is fair to say she would have been infuriated whatever the nationality of her dancers, only had they not been English she would have been infuriated by different faults.

Every description of Pavlova's tours states not only how hard she herself worked, but how hard her girls worked. But it is doubtful if Pavlova's company were worked any harder than the great directors of ballet work their companies today. What made life for Pavlova herself and for her company exceptionally tiring was that she never stopped travelling, and there were so many one-night stands on her tours. No one who has not experienced one-night stands in a foreign country with the normal discomforts due to change of climate and unusual food has any conception what stamina is needed. If not staying in hotels the company would climb on to their private train after the performance and bump and jolt to the next town, which they would reach perhaps only a short while before the rise of the curtain. But no matter at what time they arrived Pavlova always went to the theatre to practise, and expected her company to do the same. Quite often, perhaps after an eight-hour journey, she would call a rehearsal. On occasion there would even be a rehearsal after the show, while the train waited for them. But there is nothing unusual in this, those who direct ballet

309

companies are ruthless in working for perfection, and today's dancers are just as willing to be sacrificed on the altar of perfection as were Pavlova's girls.

VII

What made working for Pavlova a unique experience was the awe which her girls felt for her. When she raged at one or other until they were sobbing, it was not because technically they could not do what she wanted, but that they could not understand what was in her mind—what she wished them to do. So the sobs, though partly frustration, were largely grief because Pavlova found them wanting. For none of them ever disputed her greatness, and still today hold in their minds pictures of her, the way she moved, the beauty of her arabesque, which somehow, unlike any other arabesque, seemed to stretch to infinity. Those of her girls who teach know they have forever a vision to be aimed at, and sometimes for a brief moment, when watching a pupil, think 'that is near'.

Off-stage Pavlova chaperoned her girls rigorously. At no time were any of them on terms of intimacy with her. In fact, off-stage as on, she awed them and they dreaded her disapproval. But respect was their over-riding feeling for her, she was a creature set apart, aloof, unapproachable, ageless. Not that Pavlova did not take a vivid personal interest in each of her girls. She did, thinking and planning for their good, but her approach to them was that of a sovereign to a member of her household. And not only did she know there was this great gulf between herself and the members of her company, but it was a gulf which she believed should exist. For on one occasion, when one of her dancers who had been with her for some time happened to club together with two new girls to give her flowers for Easter, she did not like it at all. "You should not be on such terms with new members of my company," she explained. "They should feel to you as you feel to me."

Pavlova set immense value on propriety. Even at rehearsals her girls had to sit in such a way that they did not show too much leg. Not for them the Degas widespread knees; they had to pull the rather long tunics in which they practised over their knees, and place their feet neatly. On the long sea voyages, which were part of each tour, even the mildest flirtation was

Pavlova was a creature set apart—a great gulf existed
between her and the members of her company

311

frowned upon, and one look from Pavlova and young men were hurriedly dismissed with "Goodness. I'd better go to bed." No detail of her girls' appearance missed her; to one whom she thought it time she should use a little lipstick she sent a powder compact, to another there was a call from Pavlova's husband, suggesting tactfully that less make-up off-stage would be more becoming. She was extraordinarily generous, but probably remembering her own childhood could be parsimonious. She paid her company highly, but expected her girls to save, only spending when really necessary, and considered she had the right to criticize, and even to punish extravagance. She watched the friends her girls made, and to one who was hurt because a solo had been taken from her she said: "I do not like you now, because I do not like the people you are with. Now you are angry, but some day you will thank me for telling you this." Years later the girl saw what Pavlova had meant, the friends she had at that time were not right for her.

No picture of Pavlova with her company would be complete without a word about her men partners. A male dancer with few exceptions is badly treated by fame, it is the ballerina who is noticed, not the cavalier. Leading male dancers are every bit, if not more temperamental than ballerinas, so they need tactful handling. Pavlova, following her vision, regardless of anybody, was not the person to be continually sensitive about the feelings of her partners, and there were royal rows, noticeably with a brilliant dancer called Mordkin. Nevertheless in all her long career she had only four cavaliers, for though Pavlova might be difficult at times, she was lovable, and it was an honour to partner her.

VIII

Pavlova was touring Holland when on January 23, 1931, she died. It is not an exaggeration to say the whole world mourned. More words were written about her, and more tears shed than would be devoted to any artiste today. Although she was only about fifty, an early age to die, it is doubtful, studying her as a person, if perhaps her dying when she did was not kind to her. Even her inexhaustible energy was flagging, not on the stage, but, jolted on trains and rocked on boats in every corner of the world, she had in the two years preceding her death had passing thoughts on retirement. But could she have retired? Could that dynamic personality have been happy living a normal life in Ivy House? Could she have existed without dancing? It is unlikely. There are those who must do what they do to their lives' end; Pavlova was such a person.

Pavlova died on a Sunday, and that night The Camargo Society, a godmother of our present Royal Ballet, was giving a performance. It seemed to the dancers appalling to be asked to dance on the night Pavlova had died. So to comfort them, and honour Pavlova, a tribute was planned. That evening the orchestra played Saint-Saëns's music for her Dying Swan solo. Slowly the curtain rose on a dark stage. Then a tiny spotlight fell on the centre where she might have danced. The effect was moving past bearing. As if it was pre-arranged, the whole audience rose to their feet, and stood until the music ended. Then the curtain dropped, and in dropping seemed to say: "Good-bye Pavlova."

Pablo Picasso

PAINTER OF AN EPOCH

Michael Levey

I

Whenen Picasso was seventy-five an exhibition was held in London. It was an exhibition very different from those usually concerned with painters; it consisted not of Picasso's paintings but of material connected with his life and art, recorded chiefly in photographs. It was a piece of homage to the most famous painter of the day, and the most photographed.

Amid the photographs was a painting by Picasso's young son, Claude. And suitably enough it was dedicated by the artist to his father. Young as he might seem for a painter—he was then only eight or nine—Claude Picasso was old compared with his father's age when he first started to paint and draw. Picasso himself was also a painter's son. He was born making drawings—it has been said of him—not the drawings of a child but the drawings of a painter.

Picasso not only began early; he continued throughout his career to squander his prodigal gifts, and then to be endowed with further gifts, right up to his old age. Late in life he suddenly began to amuse himself with designing pottery, and when he stopped the fashion went on. In fact it is still percolating down even to suburban china shops in England, and since these have hardly altered their wares for forty years the implied compliment to Picasso is considerable. More importantly, Picasso was the subject of flattering and unflattering attention for many years. Thousands of articles were written about him; at least fifty books were devoted entirely to his life and work. In the 1950s a film was made with him as subject and principal performer.

Picasso himself gave the whole affair a good deal of

attention, sometimes ironically. He obligingly dated many of his pictures not only with the year but with the month and day as well; he provided with scrupulous accuracy the detail of his birth hour: 9.30 p.m. He kindly answered many questions, and even the stupid ones sometimes had a reply—of sorts; since he was witty as well as talented, the replies were often more interesting, and certainly more amusing, than the questions. His private life was turned into public property—as happens to the very famous but seldom to the very great, the two being rarely the same. The women he had known, the children he had, the name of his dog (it was Kasbek) were all solemnly recorded. We know, for instance, that though he was called simply Pablo Picasso his baptismal names were a long and saintly string: Pablo Diego José Francisco de Paula Joan Nepomuceno Crispin Crispiniano de la Santisima Trinidad. And, so his secretary once said, Picasso thought everybody had as many names as he had.

After those names it is hardly surprising that Picasso was a Spaniard—one transposed to France for most of his life, but remaining nonetheless Spanish. He was born at Malaga, on the Mediterranean coast of Spain, on October 25, 1881. From the first he followed his father's career and painted. The rooms of the family flat in Malaga were fortunately large; they served not only as studio for Picasso's father but also as aviary for the many pigeons he kept. These served as the subject of his pictures and the pictures served as rent. When, finally, his father gave up painting Picasso took over the subject of pigeons and his own rooms in Paris were, many years later, also full of pigeons.

Don José, Picasso's father, moved his family to Corunna when his son was about ten. Here the family grew miserable in the constant wet weather, and Don José grew bored. He was tired of painting, tired even of his favourite pastime— going to bull-fights. In the end he handed over his brushes and paints to Picasso and after that gesture did not paint again. Picasso painted busily. A number of his pictures from this very early period survive, some of them in his own collection for he was said to hate throwing anything away. Along with trivial fragments of his past these have been stored up and they show how early he achieved a marvellous competence. There is

315

nothing startling or exciting about these pictures, which are often of Spanish beggars, except that they were painted by a boy of fourteen. They refute, already, any theory that Picasso's later pictures were drawn by someone who could not draw. So great was his technical ability that he could pass in a day entrance examinations for schools of art, examinations for which, owing to their difficulty, the usual period was a month.

II

When he was fifteen his family moved to Barcelona where his father had a professorship at the Academy of Fine Arts. Into the same academy Picasso passed one day, and a few months later he repeated his performance at the Academy in Madrid. Other members of his family had become interested in him, partly as a financial asset it seems, and his trip to Madrid was sponsored by their money. However, Picasso disappointed their expectations and ignored the academic standards. He saw the masterpieces of the Prado Museum (of which he was one day to be created director), but otherwise Madrid and the atmosphere of the Academy there bored him and soon he was back in Barcelona.

More lively than Madrid, the city offered Picasso a congenial café life where artists and writers met and drank and argued. The centre of this activity was the café *Els 4 Gats*—the Four Cats—and Picasso frequented it. The youngest of the group of writers and painters with whom he now became friendly, he was also among the most active. At this time he still signed his work P. Ruiz Picasso, the first being his father's name, the second his mother's. Later he dropped the first, which is a common Spanish surname, and retained the name by which he is famous. At The Four Cats Picasso held his first exhibition—in 1897— and the first newspaper article on him was published. A room in the café was set aside and the painter and his friends hung it with his pictures and drawings, most of which were portraits. The idea was to interest the public of Barcelona, but such public as came were largely the subjects of the portraits. They came, as usual, to the café, drank coffee and gossiped.

Of this group a number were already looking beyond Spain to France. Some in fact had already left for Paris and soon Picasso persuaded his parents to allow him to go there too,

316

provided he returned to Barcelona within a few months. In the autumn of 1900 he made his first trip, returning to Spain in time for Christmas. Although he was poor and could not yet speak French, he at least managed to sell some of his pictures: the first sale of his work in France. Three sketches of bull-fights were bought by a Montmartre dealer, Berthe Weill. And the next year, after a brief stay in Madrid, Picasso was back in Paris. He set to work. In the autumn his friend, Jaime Sabartés (later to become his secretary), arrived and saw the new pictures—pictures so different from Picasso's Spanish work that he was amazed and perturbed. In a brief space of time Picasso had leapt beyond Sabartés' comprehension. And Picasso, as Sabartés was later to record, went through life taking such leaps. No sooner did he shock by one thing than it was replaced by something so much more astounding as to make the first seem quite ordinary and familiar.

III

The pictures he showed his friend in 1901 were chiefly painted in a pervasive blue tone which went with their gloomy and limited subject matter. Many of the pictures of this period, which is inevitably called Picasso's 'Blue Period', are painted in a blue monochrome. They show people who are usually alone and sad: a woman in a bare blue room, a blind beggar; sometimes in despair a nude man and woman twine their arms together for consolation, modern Adam and Eve expelled from the paradise of warmth and security. Picasso's interest was with people, with the poor whom he, being poor, knew so well—and with the unhappy.

The reasons for his use of blue paint at this time have been learnedly and fruitlessly discussed. Basically, Picasso used blue because he wanted to, and this is reason enough. His own life at the period could not fail to make him attracted by melancholy subjects and by melancholy colour. All art, he is said to have believed then, emanates from sadness and pain. He painted a self portrait, which shows him bearded and pale, with a face like a convalescent after a serious illness; and he must have very nearly been ill, living in a lampless room, dining off rotten sausages and, once, setting fire to his own sheets of drawings so as to have a fire. He returned home briefly to

317

Spain, but was again in Paris in 1902 sharing the hotel room of his poet friend, Max Jacob. There by day he slept as Jacob was out working; by night he painted and Jacob slept.

Despite these facts of existence, Picasso settled finally in Paris in 1904. He had a room in a dilapidated tenement in Montmartre—a house nicknamed 'the floating laundry' and crammed with all sorts of people, actors, poets, impoverished clerks, painters. Picasso lived a drifting life, now poor, now suddenly and momentarily affluent through a sale of some paintings. One of the women who knew him well at this time, Fernande Olivier, has described very vividly the Picasso of those days: experimenting with opium, carrying a revolver, sitting at cafés—and paying frequent visits to the circus.

IV

It was there that he discovered new subject matter and a new manner. Through the gradually predominating use of terra-cotta pink in his pictures at this time the period has been named 'Rose'. Blue was replaced by this and the pathos of his earlier work was replaced by tender and more intimate scenes of circus life. For the first time Picasso fully revealed his capacity for drawing: his line became delicate but finer and stronger, marking the sensitive faces of harlequins above their spangled finery, the litheness of acrobats, the tented interiors behind the circus ring where clowns and their wives and children are touchingly at home.

The instant appeal of such pictures helped Picasso to become —if not yet famous, at least well-known. He found patrons and patrons discovered him. One of the largest pictures painted at this period is the *Family of Saltimbanques* (travelling performers) where in an empty sand-coloured landscape the family are seen, resting perhaps on their travels—a brief pause before they pick up their bundles and again take the road. The poignancy of these people who are about to vanish—eternally performing and eternally wandering on—is so intense that Picasso might have spent a lifetime evoking it in such pictures.

V

However, he did not stop there. He did not this time so much evolve a different manner as take his art, break it and

re-assemble the pieces in a revolutionary manner which frightened some of his patrons. What a terrible loss to French art, a
patron of his 'rose' pictures lamented on seeing his new paintings.

These new paintings were not easy to understand. They were
the result of many complex and various pressures: Picasso's
own desire, above all no doubt, to go beyond mere represen-
tation, however charming. Revolutionary ideas had quietly
been occupying a number of other painters in France, back into
the 19th century; of these Cézanne was the chief and the least
known to the public. After his death in 1906 his pictures began
to be seen and to be appreciated. In addition there was interest
in non-European arts, arts which had previously been dismissed
as merely barbarous like Negro sculpture. The desire to smash
old conventions and create a new art had already, before
Picasso, been expressed by the other most talented painter then
in Paris: Matisse. Matisse had expressed his revolt not in
intellectual terms but in such riots of colour and pattern that he
and his disciples had been labelled *les fauves*, the wild beasts.
Picasso and Matisse met, but there was tension rather than
friendship between them. It was only a few years ago that
the two painters, by then old and world-famous, resumed
acquaintance and started a friendship which was broken by
Matisse's death. Before that they exchanged pictures—again;
once as young men they had done so, and each is said to have
chosen, perhaps unconsciously, a poor example of the other's
work.

Certainly, in the first years of the century Matisse must have
appeared, while a very different painter, a rival to Picasso. In
1907 Picasso painted his large challenging canvas, *Les Demoiselles d'Avignon*—a quite irrelevant title which was years later
given to this picture of five nude women by one of the painter's
friends. Although this was not perhaps his first painting in the
new style, it was his first important painting in the new style:
Cubism.

Twenty years after, Picasso remarked that Cubism was still
not properly understood. And later he said that when he and
his friends invented Cubism they had no intention of inventing
it; that is, they began to paint in a certain way and this way was
quite natural to them. They saw their subjects not in the light of

everyday realism but as structures—sometimes geometrical structures—which had to be created out of the ordinary appearance of objects. Cézanne had already hinted that this was a way of seeing, though he had oddly enough not mentioned the cube. "You must see in nature," he had written to a friend, "the cylinder, the sphere, the cone." As well as the outward appearance of objects there is an internal structure—just as behind the façade of a building is the scaffolding of walls and ceilings and floors. The Cubists were tired of painting only the façade; they wanted to show the interior arrangements as well. Since they disliked the limitation of one viewpoint they would draw a head in profile but put in the two eyes or perhaps the nose seen frontally—as if walking round the head while painting it. Two of the ladies in the *Demoiselles d'Avignon* have 'Cubist' faces: one has a profile nose on a full face, and the other has an oval slice of face with no ears at all, like an African mask.

These experiments seemed very daring and revolutionary, and Picasso's remark about not being understood is still true in part today. But the convention of, for example, the eye seen frontally on a face in profile is as old as Egyptian tomb paintings and the idea that shapes just as shapes have a beauty of their own regardless of what they *represent* is as old as Plato. It was because Western painting had been dominated for so long by the conventions of realism—and after all it is only by a convention that three-dimensional things can be represented in the two dimensions of pictures—that the work of Picasso and his group seemed monstrous and revolutionary. People asked, and still ask, what such pictures mean; but pictures are there to please the eye not to have messages like posters. That is the difference between art and advertisements.

It was not for some time that Picasso followed up the experiment of the *Demoiselles*. The following year he met the young painter Braque and the two began to work together on Cubism. The word itself gained currency. Matisse was said to have spoken of Braque's work as consisting of 'little cubes' and the official spokesman of the movement, the poet Apollinaire, adopted for his friends the title 'The Cubist Painters' in 1911. There began to be Cubist portraits, and Picasso painted his friend and dealer, Kahnweiler, in a picture

A great artist, Picasso invented new ways of painting
to express what he felt about the life of our times

that was a complicated mosaic of cubes all broken up like a jumbled cross-word puzzle.

Not every cubist picture was a masterpiece and there are plenty of problems connected with representing reality that Cubism did not solve. Picasso did not stay working exclusively in that style; both he and Braque moved on to the introduction of real objects into their paintings—scraps of newspaper, pieces of wood, a pipe, and so on. Their still-lives became an actual assortment of objects glued to the picture surface, and this certainly saved the business of elaborately painting to imitate newspaper or wood. Both painters, however, returned to painting still-life without such tricks. Braque began to explore a marvellous combination of a few colours, lemon yellow, and terracotta, and black; Picasso, in equally exciting colour schemes, often scarlet and black and orange and white, painted a series of still-lives with the constantly repeated properties of a guitar, tablecloth, a classical bust, that are among the easiest of his paintings to enjoy.

VI

Meanwhile he had grown famous. Before the outbreak of the 1914 war he was not, perhaps, very well known. He had lived very much in a coterie, rather isolated as a painter and exhibiting his pictures only seldom. When the war began Picasso was at Avignon. Not being French, he was not required to fight but many of his friends went off to the war—among them the gallant non-French Apollinaire who was to die of his wounds in 1919. Many things were finished by the outbreak of war, and the first phase of Cubism finished as well. Picasso was to return to it, but in lighter mood—alluding to it, but hardly making his whole composition so earnestly within that convention.

He embarked on a whole series of metamorphoses—and he has preserved that ability to change his style or to return to an earlier manner of his. In the middle of the war, in 1917, he left Paris for Rome to collaborate on designs for the Russian Ballet of Diaghilev. The publicity which attached to so many of the Russian Ballet's activities attached to Picasso. He became famous for his scene designs, and the ballet world awoke in him reminiscences of his rose period: harlequins and pierrots and dancers again appear in his pictures. He himself married one of the dancers in the company. In 1921 his son Paul was born and this event set him painting and drawing on the theme of maternity and childhood. The themes of his son and the theatre mingle in charming pictures like those in which the small boy appears as a pierrot—pictures which present no puzzle and in which Picasso's own sense of happiness is constantly communicated.

The pattern of his life did not settle, however, any more than the pattern of his art. His summers were spent away from Paris, sometimes in Spain, more often on the French Riviera, and even during these quite short periods he might invent and exhaust a new manner. At times he developed classical themes of Grecian women on the sea shore, or brooding among broken columns; at another he experimented with surrealist ideas. This facility was as dangerous as tempting. Picasso seems to have felt the danger and more than once stopped painting for a marked period of time. As a distraction he began writing; his poems have been published—perhaps because they were by a great painter—and a play he wrote later was acted at a club theatre in London.

VII

He had not been concerned very much in world affairs, still less in politics. The outbreak of the Spanish Civil War was, however, too close to his life to be ignored; and in fact it seems to have freed him from an uncreative and barren spell. His hatred of Franco found expression in a rude comic strip and his generosity towards the Republican cause made him sell pictures to raise money and buy paintings by his exiled compatriots. Early in 1937 he was commissioned to paint a mural for the Spanish government's pavilion at the Paris World's Fair. In April of that year the Spanish town of Guernica was reported bombed by German planes intervening for Franco. Two days later Picasso set to work on his accusatory mural, in grey, black, and white, *Guernica*, which is his angry imaginative interpretation of the bombing. Before finishing the picture, he issued a statement in which his detestation of Franco's government, and all it stood for, was made quite plain.

In the Second World War it was postcards of *Guernica* that

Picasso gave away to German officers visiting his studio in Paris. The war, and the years which have followed, marked the height of Picasso's fame. Throughout the war he was a symbol—though of what exactly it is hard to say; at the liberation of Paris his studio was crowded by soldiers and visitors, friends, foreigners, journalists, many of whom wrote down their talks with him. It was a public event when he joined the Communist Party in the same year and the dove which he designed for the World Congress of Peace in 1949 was instantly famous.

VIII

His later years were spent almost entirely on the French Riviera where, in nearly perfect weather, he worked on ceaselessly. Apart from his ceramics, there were whole series of lithographs and drawings, developing new themes. In addition he often practised sculpture, in stone and bronze or simply assembled from objects he had found. In the early 1950s a personal crisis drove him to the frenzied production of a whole series of drawings, 180 in nine weeks, which comment on and illustrate the idea of painter and model: the painter often old, bespectacled, grotesque, the model eternally piquant and lovely. These drawings may stand as Picasso's testament to the ruthless power of beauty, and to its power of enduring when painters, and other men, grow fat and aged and then die.

But, by a paradox, they are also a tribute to the creativity of the mind which produced them. Picasso mirrored his age, interpreted it, perhaps symbolized its restless shifting aspect in his own restless pursuit of new beauty, new ideas to express. Everything suggested something to him: pebbles on the shore, loaves of bread, even a pair of discarded handlebars from an old bicycle.

Although, during his last years, he returned to themes he had previously explored, Picasso never ceased to experiment. When he died in 1973 aged ninety-one he was almost universally recognized as the greatest artist of the twentieth century.

Part of Picasso's genius belongs with genius of all periods. Another part belongs with our own period; the great painter is a kind of historian. To paint well, Cézanne said, is to express one's own epoch.

The Piccard Brothers

TWIN LIVES IN THE SPIRIT OF JULES VERNE

Egon Larsen

I

SOME eighty years ago, a six-foot-tall student, with blue eyes behind a pair of thick glasses, entered a barber's shop in Munich. "I want a really good shave," he said. "My beard grows so fast, and I'm invited for dinner tonight."

"Don't you worry," said the barber. "You'll get the best shave you've ever had, with my personal guarantee—I'll shave you again, free of charge, if your chin isn't still as soft as a baby's by tonight."

The student had his shave, paid, and left. A quarter of an hour later he was back again. His chin and upper lip were bristling with stubbles. "Just look," he said. "That wasn't a good shave. I told you my beard grows very fast !"

The poor barber's eyes nearly popped out of their sockets. Never in all his life had he seen a beard grow at such speed. But he stuck to his promise, and shaved his strange customer free of charge. The young man gave him a generous tip.

In the café at the corner he joined his twin brother. The two laughed until their ribs ached. Their little experiment had been a complete success.

II

Once the Piccard brothers had started their scientific adventures, the public and the Press often found themselves in the same dilemma as that Munich barber—they couldn't keep Auguste apart from Jean. Not only because the twins, even in their seventies, still looked very much alike, with their bird's necks and their shaggy crescents of hair around the bulging domes of their heads; but because they were both what may be

325

termed vertical explorers: research workers high up in the stratosphere and down in the deep blue sea.

It was not chance which made them choose the same careers, and dream the same dreams. The origin of their unusual ambitions can be traced back to the boys' room in their father's house in Basle, at the end of the last century. They were three then—Auguste, Jean, and the spirit of Jules Verne.

That French writer, who was the first to publish what we now call science fiction, kindled the boys' imagination. He wrote about submarine voyages even before man had learnt to travel under the sea; he described trips to the moon long before the first aeroplane had left the ground. All through their lives the Piccards acknowledged that it was Jules Verne with his tales of space flight, balloon travels and deep-sea expeditions who impressed them so much that they decided to become explorers. Rarely has a nursery dream become reality to such an astonishing extent!

With their target firmly before their minds' eyes they made their way through grammar school. When they went to Munich to enroll at the university, Auguste decided for physics and Jean for chemistry.

In those first years of our century, the possibility of flying was very much in the public mind—Otto Lilienthal, the German pioneer of gliding, had been killed during one of his attempts, and Count Zeppelin, a Württemberg cavalry officer, was making his first flights in his cigar-shaped, rigid airships. But no heavier-than-air machine had yet flown successfully, although inventors and sportsmen in many countries were trying out their sometimes quite fantastic contraptions. It was the challenge of that unsolved problem which prompted Jean Piccard to study for a degree in aeronautical engineering.

Before he was ready to go into practical aeronautics, however, the Wright brothers succeeded in making their heavier-than-air machine fly, and Jean lost interest in that field of activity, at least for the time being. At the outbreak of the First World War he was already a lecturer in chemistry at Munich University, but as a Swiss citizen he had to return to his own country. In 1916, however, he accepted a chair at the university of Chicago. In 1919, he married a Swiss girl, Jeannette Ridlon, with whom he had three sons. A few years later, he was appointed research instructor in chemistry at the famous Massachusetts Institute of Technology.

Auguste, too, followed a scientific career on traditional lines. He became a professor at the Zurich Technical College in 1917, and accepted a chair at Brussels University in 1922. Two years earlier, he too had married a Swiss girl, Marianne Denis, with whom he had five children. It was a settled, academic way of life for the Piccard twins. Had their Jules Verne dreams been completely forgotten?

III

They were middle-aged men in their forties when the great break in their lives came. Auguste had become more and more interested in meteorology. He began to wonder if the answers to quite a number of unsolved questions might not be found in the stratosphere—that upper part of the earth's atmosphere, which extends beyond an altitude of eight miles from the ground, and which has some curious natural laws of its own. What intrigued the Professor most of all was the mystery of the so-called cosmic rays, those strange messengers from outer space whose intensity appeared to increase with the altitude.

Auguste Piccard approached the director of the Belgian National Research Foundation with the most unusual request which that distinguished institution had ever received. He wanted to go up in a balloon, higher than any man had done before, and he asked the Foundation to pay for what he admitted was a somewhat crazy venture.

To his own surprise, Piccard got the substantial sum which he needed to build an entirely new type of balloon, a vehicle that could travel up to the stratosphere and keep its occupants alive.

On the morning of May 27, 1931, the balloon was ready to ascend from an airfield near Augsburg in Bavaria. The professor had decided to start from a point in Central Europe so that his balloon would not be blown out over the sea before coming down. It consisted of an elongated envelope filled with hydrogen, attached to which was an aluminium sphere, the gondola, which could be sealed hermetically. Piccard had chosen a young fellow-scientist, Professor Kipfer, as his companion.

"You should take an ice-axe and a rope with you in case you land on a glacier," someone suggested to Piccard.

"Why not a dinner-suit as well, in case we come down in the park of some Grand Hotel?" retorted Piccard.

Just before the hour fixed for the start a gust of wind damaged the valve mechanism. Everybody suggested that the dangerous flight should be postponed, and repairs properly done by experts. Auguste Piccard refused to listen, and carried out some emergency repairs while they were already ascending. His refusal to postpone the flight nearly cost him and Kipfer their lives.

Within two hours, the balloon reached a height of about ten miles—three miles higher than any human being had been before. "That's enough for a start," said Piccard. "Let's descend."

And then they discovered that their valve rope did not work. They were unable to release gas from the balloon!

"We are prisoners in the air," Piccard wrote in his logbook.

For seventeen hours they floated perilously over the Alps, without any means of controlling their flight. Slowly, slowly the balloon descended as the hydrogen gas was seeping through the envelope. Late at night they landed—had they not been warned?—on a Swiss glacier.

There they spent the coldest night of their lives until a search party found them in the morning. They were brought down to the nearest village in a triumphal procession.

Auguste Piccard discovered, to his own surprise, that he had become world-famous within twenty-four hours.

A year later, he undertook his second flight into the stratosphere, starting from Zürich airport. He broke his own record by reaching a height of nearly eleven miles. This time, his companion was a young Belgian scientist, Max Cosyns.

The flight ended in an orchard in Northern Italy. The Italians nearly went mad with excitement. In his own country, Switzerland, Piccard was all the rage; Piccard cigarettes appeared in the shops, *meringues à la Piccard* in the cafés. America invited him to a lecture tour, and there was a great family reunion.

"You've beaten me to it this time," said Jean. "But I'll break your record yet, Auguste. Henry Ford has promised me the money for a stratosphere balloon."

"You should both be ashamed of yourselves," said Auguste's wife, Marianne. "You're just like boys. Can't you start something less dangerous to amuse yourselves?"

"Don't worry," said Auguste. "I shan't go up into the stratosphere again. I'm too old for such acrobatics." The brothers had just turned forty-eight.

"If Jean goes up, I'll go with him," declared his wife, Jeannette. Her husband smiled. What an absurd idea: a woman in a stratosphere balloon!

But there she was one fine day in October, 1934, climbing into the gondola with Jean on Ford Airport, Dearborn, Michigan. The third passenger was Lily, the family turtle; Jean took her along partly as a mascot and partly because he wanted to see how she would behave in the stratosphere.

The balloon had just started on its journey when the loose end of the gasbag got caught in the steel cables from which the gondola was suspended. Jean wanted to descend and postpone the flight. But Jeannette climbed out of the manhole, and holding on to the cables with one hand she freed the gasbag with the other at a height of 1000 feet.

Jean, Jeannette, and Lily beat Auguste by a mile and half, reaching an altitude of nearly 58,000 feet. A new record was established.

IV

Three years later, Jean Piccard was offered a chair as Professor of Aeronautical Engineering at the university of Minnesota. There he built a new type of stratosphere vehicle, consisting of 95 small balloons and a gondola. First he went up alone, but reached an altitude of 'only' 48,000 feet. As the balloon descended it drifted dangerously near the Mississippi. To make it come down before it would reach the river Jean shot with a pistol into his little balloons—with the result that the whole thing caught fire.

Some farmers returning from their fields found the professor sitting in a tree, unscathed but for his singed eyebrows.

Now it was Auguste's turn again. Poor Marianne: he did not keep his promise not to go up again. However, during the series of ascents which he now undertook with Max Cosyns he was less interested in breaking Jean's record of 1934 than in

Jean Piccard's wife climbed out of the manhole and freed
the gasbag at a height of a thousand feet

cosmic ray and meteorological research. The newspapers could not keep his name out of the headlines. Once he needed additional funds for an ascent from Poland, and made it known that he would take a paying passenger up with him— return fare: £20,000. Twenty-two people, at all ages from 14 to 71, applied; among them were two Japanese millionaires and a dozen ladies. One of the latter wrote that she wished to spend 'at least one interesting day in a boring life'; a Swedish composer said she was looking for inspiration for a 'Strato-sphere Symphony', and an American woman stipulated that she must get a fine monument with an appropriate inscription if she failed to return. Piccard was greatly relieved when the money eventually came from a less exacting source, and he took Cosyns with him instead of a paying guest.

V

In the years immediately before the Second World War, little was heard of Auguste Piccard, then well in his fifties. Was he feeling 'too old' at last? Visitors who succeeded in getting inside his quiet, comfortable house near the Bois de la Cambre in Brussels would not have guessed that this unpretentious, somewhat absent-minded savant (who was said once to have hidden from a reporter in the branches of a tree) could be planning anything but lectures at the university and experi-ments in his laboratory. He seemed completely happy in his easy chair, surrounded by bookshelves reaching up to the ceiling and glass cases full of knick-knacks, reading through his specially designed, hinged spectacles, or chatting with Marianne. It was difficult to identify that man with the hero of the strato-sphere.

Only Marianne knew what was going on behind that high forehead. The depths of the ocean had got hold of his imagina-tion.

"What is more natural than that a man should want to see with his own eyes the strange beauty of under-water life?" he said. It was the poetry and romance of such a venture as much as its scientific interest which fascinated him: "I want to see the mysterious denizens of the deep, the giant crustaceans and star-fish and all the other fantastic creatures down there. They've watched many a ship go down for ever—and won't they make big eyes when they see me return to the upper world with my diving-machine!"

Ever since Dr. William Beebe, the New York zoologist, and Otis Barton had reached a depth of 3400 feet in their 'bathy-sphere' in 1934, Auguste Piccard had been working on his own plans for such a machine. It was to be a kind of stratosphere balloon for deep-sea diving, consisting of a large, petrol-filled float and a steel sphere, the 'gondola', suspended from it. Beebe had gone down in a steel ball hanging on a cable; Piccard decided that his 'bathyscaphe', as he called it, should not be tied to a surface vessel, but descend, move, and ascend under its own power. It should have some ballast pieces held to the hull by means of an electro-magnet to make it sink, and an electric motor with a ship's screw so that it could travel along the sea-bed; all the explorer would have to do to ascend was to cut out the electro-magnet so that the ballast would fall off, and the petrol in the float—which is lighter than water—make the bathyscaphe rise.

Auguste Piccard and Max Cosyns began to build models, and test them in an hydraulic cylinder. The bathyscaphe would have to stand up to pressures up to 16,000 lb. per square inch. Their laboratory was already littered with the remains of unsuccessful models wh n work was forcibly interrupted by the outbreak of the war. Piccard returned to Switzerland as Hitler marched into Belgium, but Cosyns stayed on.

Five years later they met again after Cosyns had been released from Dachau concentration camp, where the Gestapo had tried in vain to extract from him under torture some vital secrets of the Belgian resistance movement to which he had belonged.

VI

In the autumn of 1948 the bathyscaphe was ready, and diving tests began near Dakar, in the Gulf of Guinea. Piccard and Cosyns spent 12 hours in their sphere, moving about in shallow water. Then the bathyscaphe was sent down into the deep unmanned, controlled by radio. It reached a depth of more than 4500 feet—Otis Barton had gone down as far as this. During the ascent, however, a storm came up, and for a whole night Piccard, Cosyns, and their helpers were fighting desperately to save their diving-machine. In the morning they examined it: the damage was so extensive that there was no question of going on with the whole venture.

The French naval authorities, which had given the two scientists facilities at Dakar, salvaged the bathyscaphe, and began to repair it for a new attempt; but Piccard was impatient and felt that they were taking too long over the job. The Italian government saw a good opportunity of stealing a march on the French, and offered to build an entirely new bathyscaphe to Piccard's specifications. Piccard accepted, but the construction of the vessel took nearly four years. It was built at Terni, whence it was taken on a cross-country trip to the harbour of Venice; there was another delay when it became snowbound in the mountains.

Piccard's patience was almost exhausted when the new bathyscaphe arrived near the island of Ponza, in the Bay of Naples, the deepest point in the Mediterranean, in the spring of 1953. With him was his son Jacques, who was to be his companion on the record dive he intended to make.

In the meantime, however, French naval engineers had completed the reconstruction of the Dakar bathyscaphe, the FRNS as it was called after its financial backers, the French Scientific Research Foundation. Two naval officers, Lieutenant Houot and First Engineer Willm, had volunteered to dive in it. The French made a special effort to dive before Piccard, and deeper than he. It looked like a deep-sea contest between the two countries; both bathyscaphes were at action stations in June, 1953, Piccard's at Ponza and the French one at a point off Toulon.

Both teams began with preliminary tests. Piccard's vessel, the *Trieste*, started with 30 feet, went down to 150, and then to 200. But before Piccard and son embarked in earnest on their great dive, which was to take them to a depth of 10,000 feet, there came the sensational news that Houot and Willm had already reached a depth of 4900 feet on August 12. The next day, they plunged to over 5000 feet, and on the day after that to nearly 6900.

Piccard took the news in good spirits. "We'll go down much further than that," he said. "But I won't be rushed. I'll play safe." And he went on with his step-by-step tests.

At last on September 30 he was ready for the great dive. At 7 a.m. the professor and his son climbed down through the steel cylinder which served as a kind of conning-tower, leading from the top of the petrol float to the observation sphere underneath it. The Italian corvette *Fenice* stood by for emergencies. The professor had been warned not to dive on that day because he was suffering from a touch of fish poisoning—the lobster he had eaten at a dinner given by the Mayor of Ponza in his honour the night before had not agreed with him, and he looked quite green. "Never mind," he said. "It can't get much worse down there!"

At 8.18 a.m. the bathyscaphe disappeared below the calm surface of the Tyrrhenian Sea, and there came a long period of waiting for the spectators on board the *Fenice*, among them 50 journalists and photographers.

Around 10.30 a.m., just when the *Trieste* was expected to come up, a tanker appeared, steaming happily towards the very spot where the bathyscaphe had submerged. Obviously the master of the tanker had no idea that the area was closed to all shipping by order of the Italian admiralty. The commander of the *Fenice* roared through his megaphone, "Get out of here at once, you confounded idiots! Where is your captain?" The captain was called up from below deck, where he had been sound asleep, and climbed on to the bridge in his pyjamas.

The tanker had hardly turned away when the bathyscaphe emerged from the deep. Piccard and son appeared, grinning all over their faces. "How's your tummy, Professor?" someone shouted from the deck of the *Fenice*. "Couldn't be better!" came the reply. "There's no cure like diving for an upset inside!"

Exhausted, oil-stained, but extremely happy, the two Piccards sat down on the deck of the corvette and told their story. They had achieved more than they had set out to do. They had dived to a depth of 10,335 feet, where the pressure on their spherical cabin had been equal to the weight of a train 25 miles long. They had beaten Houot and Willm; they had become the 'deepest people' in the world. It had cost the Italian navy £40,000, but it had been well worth it—for Italy had beaten France.

In the following year, however, Houot and Willm gained

their laurels back by diving to 13,161 feet. Auguste Piccard—
then seventy years old—left it at that; but in 1960 his son
Jacques established a world record by descending to a depth of
35,800 feet.

VII

In the meantime, Jean had been preparing another stratosphere ascent with a vehicle consisting of 80 small balloons.
He wanted to reach a height of 'at least 90,000 feet' with a good
telescope in order to observe Mars. "Perhaps that mysterious
planet will give up some of its secrets to me," he said. Jeannette,
nearly sixty years old, wanted to go with him. But nothing more
was heard of the plan; perhaps they were persuaded to accept
the fact that such hazardous adventures were just a little too
dangerous for elderly people.

Auguste was designing a successor to the bathyscaphe, the
mesoscaphe, when he died in 1962 (Jean died the following
year), but the project was successfully completed by Jacques,
who continued his father's study of the ocean depths.

Sir Walter Raleigh

THE LAST ELIZABETHAN

Geoffrey Trease

I

"THE Privy Council have some questions to ask you . . ."
Cecil's voice gave nothing away. As always, the
little hunched-up Secretary of State was controlled
and civil. One never knew quite what was going on inside that
crafty brain.

Raleigh was dressed for hunting. He had been waiting there
on the castle terrace for the new king to come out. But today
King James had a quarry more important than any stag in
Windsor Forest. Within a few moments of entering the Council
Chamber, Raleigh knew whose blood James was after—it was
his own.

Calmly he faced the men who had so long been his colleagues
and had now, overnight, turned into his accusers. It was no
surprise that the King disliked him: the dislike was mutual.
James must know, by now, that when old Queen Elizabeth had
died, a few months ago, Raleigh had favoured a republic.
Since coming south to take over his inheritance, the shambling
Scotsman had dismissed him from his official posts and given
him notice to quit his London mansion in the Strand. But what
more could he do? Raleigh's conscience was clear. He had
loyally accepted the Stuart as his king, despite the poor opinion
held of him as a man. Neither in word nor in deed had he
broken any law.

II

It was hard not to laugh when the Council started to question
him. They suspected him—of all fantastic things!—of plotting
treason with the Spaniards. Surely James (who with all his
faults was the most intellectual king in Christendom) could

336

have seen how illogical it was? And if he could not, surely these councillors must? They knew that Spain had no more relentless enemy than Sir Walter Raleigh.

His whole life—almost back to his birth in the Devon farm-house at Hayes Barton, fifty-one years before—was evidence. Spain, and the allies of Spain—he had fought them wherever he had met with them. Standing there at the Council table, he cast his mind back to his first voyage with his half-brother, Humphrey Gilbert. He had commanded a little ship himself, the *Falcon*. They had tried to find the North-west Passage, but they had found trouble with the Spaniards instead. They had come limping back into Plymouth Sound, licking their honour-able wounds.

After that there had been his days as a penniless captain in Ireland, fighting the rebels and the Spaniards who had landed to help them . . . Then he had made an impression at Court, Elizabeth had made him Captain of the Guard—and against whom had he been guarding her, if not the agents of Spain, when he stood at the door of her Privy Chamber in that suit of golden armour which was the talk of the town?

He would have fought the Spaniards oftener, if he had been given the chance. But in those days, when he had been in the Queen's good books, she had not liked him to stray far from her side. Even when the Armada came, he had not been allowed to go out with Drake and his other friends to join in the running fight up the English Channel—but he had managed to be in at the death when they sent in the fire-ships to scatter the galleons near Dunkirk.

Later, when he had blotted his copybook with the Queen, by secretly marrying one of her young Maids of Honour, it had been easier to get away and do some of the adventurous things he had always wanted to do. There had been the expedition to South America—the jungle boat-journey, hundreds of miles up the Orinoco, in quest of the fabled Indian kingdom of El Dorado. That had meant more trouble with the Spaniards. Then there had been the capture and sack of Cadiz—he would limp to the end of his days as a result of his wound in that affair. A year later there had been the Islands Voyage, when they had tried to trap the Spanish treasure convoy near the Azores—and would have done but for the Earl of Essex and his blunderings. There had been some warm skirmishing on the islands. He remembered an opposed landing on the beach, when his loosely cut breeches had been fairly slashed with bullet-holes.

With a record like that it was a little late in the day, surely, to suspect him of high treason in the cause of Spain?

III

Sardonically, Raleigh looked down at the seated councillors from under his heavy eye-lids. He answered their questions with civility but with the cool confidence which, like the Devon burr in his voice, he never lost. That self-confidence was not always an asset. Men had often been jealous of him. They preferred a simple sea-dog like Drake. Raleigh was too clever by half. He knew it, and did not pretend otherwise. But it had never made him popular.

He had faced trouble before, worse than this. The Queen had clapped him into the Tower for marrying Bess. Essex had threatened him with court-martial and immediate execution when they had quarrelled over the Azores expedition. Once he had had to appear before a commission of inquiry in Dorset for holding dangerous religious views. He had come triumphantly out of all these affairs. This latest charge was too ridiculous to stand up for a moment in a court of law.

As the questions went on, he began to feel faintly less confident. So, he was supposed to be involved in this with his old friend Lord Cobham? Well, it would not surprise him to learn that Cobham *had* had some contacts with the Spanish Minister in the Netherlands—but nothing treasonable. After all, did not King James want better relations with Spain? In any case, whatever Cobham had been up to, Raleigh was not mixed up in it. He had seen less and less of Cobham in recent years.

The Council seemed to disbelieve that. The session broke up. Raleigh could go—but he was under house arrest. That did not last long. Soon they came and took him to the Tower. Obviously the King was in earnest about this. But even the King, surely, could not prove black was white?

Days of questioning followed. His old friend and faithful captain, Kemys, was threatened with torture: he refused to invent a scrap of evidence against Raleigh. They told Cobham

338

falsely that Raleigh had betrayed him, and Cobham, breaking down, poured out an invented story to incriminate Raleigh. The prisoners were not allowed to write to each other, but Raleigh managed to transmit a letter hidden inside an apple, and in due course the answer was smuggled back to him: Cobham promised to retract his earlier statement.

There was plague in London that autumn. It postponed the coronation festivities and it caused the trial to be held at Winchester. The King had left nothing to chance. The judges had been carefully picked, the Attorney-General was to prosecute in person, and even the jurymen were changed at the last moment, for fear that the first selection might be men who studied the facts more than the King's wishes.

Raleigh knew now that he was indeed fighting for his life.

He had never known the art of making himself popular and there was no hope of a great national outcry to save him. Men who really knew him loved and respected him—the men who had sailed in his ships, for instance, and the brilliant few who had gathered with him for good talk and good company, poets and historians, scientists and travellers, boyhood friends from Oxford days, new playwrights met at the Mermaid Tavern. But whereas his one-time rival, Essex, had been the darling of the mob, Raleigh had no use for them. His dignity and reserve were mistaken for conceit The mob loathed superiority, loathed anything they could not understand, and therefore loathed Raleigh. His arrest was the most popular order the new king had given. They howled for his head as he was taken through the streets of the plague-stricken city on his way to Winchester. Only the strength of his escort saved him from lynching.

I V

A week later—it was November 17, 1603—Raleigh faced his trial in the hall of Wolvesey Castle. The Lord Chief Justice of England presided. All the great lawyers the King could rely upon were marshalled to secure a verdict of guilty.

Raleigh defended himself. Once, as a youth, he had been admitted to read law in the Middle Temple, but he had never gone far with those studies. He knew enough, though, from a lifetime of public affairs, to see the gaping holes in the prosecution, and he had both the quickness of mind and the eloquence to make rings round the professional lawyers. Even as a boy at Oxford he had been noted as 'proficient in oratory'. Since then, as a poet, as M.P. for Devon, as Lieutenant of Cornwall, as Lord Warden of the tin-mining industry, and in a variety of official positions, he had developed his command of language.

"No man has ever spoken so well before," declared one eye-witness, "and no man ever will in time to come."

Another of his listeners had been sent specially by the King to report what happened. When he returned to James, the man admitted that at first, like most people, he would have gone a hundred miles to see Raleigh hanged—but now, after hearing him, he would go a thousand miles to save his life.

But neither truth nor law nor eloquence could avail against a packed court afraid to deny the King what he demanded. One by one the rules of evidence, the rights of the accused, were brushed aside, and the procedure twisted to suit the prosecution. "English justice has never been so degraded as at the trial of Raleigh." So declared, a year or two afterwards, one of the very judges who conducted it.

The jury took only a few minutes to bring in their verdict. Incredulously Raleigh heard the word, "Guilty," and then the gruesome phrases condemning him to be hanged, drawn and quartered. Even in that moment his dignity did not forsake him. "I hope," he said bitingly, "that the jury may never have to answer for this verdict." As a favour he asked the judges if he might die decently, like a gentleman, by the stroke of the axe. The Secretary of State promised to do what he could.

Raleigh was led away to his cell to prepare for the end. As the account of his defence spread through the kingdom, he came nearer to being a popular hero than ever before in his life.

V

He must think now of his family—of Bess, who had married him for love, braving the old Queen's anger, and who had been so patient and loyal a wife to him ever since, and of his son Wat. They must not starve.

The King had stripped him of his last public offices, even before the court had declared him guilty. He had been turned

340

out of Durham House, which had been his London home since the days of his first dramatic rise to favour. But there was still Sherborne Castle, the country home they loved so much, the place they had chosen and restored and laid out according to their own ideas. Its park and gardens were planted with new trees and shrubs which his sea-captains had brought back from many parts of the world.

A traitor's property was forfeit to the Crown. If James insisted, Sherborne would be lost too. Bess and Wat would be left penniless.

For their sakes, Raleigh forced himself to write humble letters to the King and the Council, pleading for mercy. But the days passed, no reprieve came, and four days before the date fixed for his execution he sat down in his cell at midnight and wrote to his wife:

"You shall receive, dear wife, my last words in these my last lines . . . I would not, with my last Will, present you with sorrows, dear Bess. Let them go to the grave with me, and be buried in the dust . . .

"First, I send you all the thanks my heart can conceive, or my pen express, for your many troubles and cares taken for me. Pay it I never shall in this world . . .

"I trust that my blood will quench their malice that desire my slaughter, and that they will not also seek to kill you and yours with extreme poverty. To what friend to direct you I know not, for all mine have left me in the true time of trial; and I plainly perceive that my death was determined from the first day. If you can live free from want, care for no more: for the rest is but vanity.

"Remember your poor child for his father's sake, that chose you and loved you in his happiest times. Get those letters (if it be possible) which I writ to the Lords, wherein I sued for my life, but God knows it was for you and yours that I desired it, but it is true that I disdain myself for begging it. And know it (dear wife) that your son is the child of a true man, who, in his own respect, despises Death in all his misshapen and ugly forms.

"I cannot write much. God knows how hardly I stole this time, when all sleep. And it is time to separate my thoughts from the world. Beg my dead body, which living was denied you; and either lay it at Sherborne, if the land continue, or in Exeter church, by my father and mother. I can write no more. Time and Death call me away . . ."

341

A day or two later it was announced that none of the prisoners would be executed. They were not pardoned. The sentences stood, but would not be carried out.

Raleigh went back to the Tower, to remain there 'during His Majesty's pleasure'.

VI

James had stopped the execution. Was he frightened by the sudden change Raleigh's heroic defence had produced in public opinion? Had he been influenced by the Queen? Certainly she had shared in the general admiration of Raleigh's behaviour and had pleaded with the King to spare him. But, although James had done so, he had no intention of letting his prisoner go free. He meant Raleigh to end his days in the Tower.

With his usual philosophy, Raleigh made the best of things. His quarters were not too uncomfortable, though the damp rising from the river sometimes brought back the malaria he had picked up on the South American expedition. He was allowed proper meals—indeed, he was charged nearly six pounds a week for his board and lodging. He had his own servants. He took exercise on the terrace. The Lieutenant's Garden contained an unused poultry-shed, and he was given it for his chemical experiments, which had always been one of his many interests. Later he was allowed to build a small room adjoining the shed, so that he could live there.

The King had taken Sherborne and given it to his favourite. Bess took a house on Tower Hill and visited him almost every day. She had a little money of her own, and she used to come in a coach, although it was only a short walk, sweeping grandly through the gates to show her defiance of the power that kept her husband prisoner. Wat came too, and after a year or two there was a baby to bring, for their second son was born and christened Carew.

Raleigh had other visitors, old friends like Captain Kemys and Richard Hakluyt (who wrote the famous *Voyages*), newer friends like Ben Jonson the playwright (whom he made Wat's tutor for a trip to Paris) and even Prince Henry, the King's elder son and as different from James as could be imagined.

A special friendship sprang up between Raleigh and the Prince of Wales, who already, in his 'teens, delighted everyone with his charm and brilliance. For him Raleigh began to write a long *History of the World*. For him he made model ships to demonstrate his new ideas for naval design. They were like two boys as their heads bent together over the work-table—the ageing white-haired prisoner with his sallow cheeks and hooded eyes, and the handsome youth, fresh from tennis or riding or swimming in the Thames.

The years passed. Raleigh had gone to the Tower in 1603. He was still there in 1612, when Prince Henry brought him the news he had given up hope of ever hearing: at Christmas he was to be free. The Prince had begged his release from the King. When he came out, he would have Sherborne Castle again. Henry had got possession of it a few months ago, and he was holding it to restore to its rightful owner.

This was the moment when Raleigh suffered one of his cruellest blows. That autumn Henry caught typhoid fever and died. No more was heard of setting Raleigh free.

VII

Another three years went by. Then the King, short of money as always, was persuaded to let him out to search for a gold-mine in South America, which Raleigh was confident existed from what he had heard on his previous expedition. Now in his middle sixties, the old adventurer—last survivor of all the great Elizabethans—fitted out an expedition to the Spanish Main.

Everything went wrong. The men would not let him lead them up-country, himself—they were afraid they might be deserted by the base-party left on the coast with the ships, so they insisted that Raleigh should stay there. They knew they could trust Raleigh not to sail away and leave them to rot in the jungle.

Without his leadership, they ran into disaster. They not only failed to discover gold, but they got into a fight with the Spaniards (strictly against the orders of the King, who was at peace with Spain), and young Wat Raleigh was killed. Captain Kemys had been in command. When he brought back the tragic news, Raleigh for once lost all his self-control. Kemys listened to his old friend's reproaches, answered only, "Very well, sir, I know what course to take," and went to his cabin. A few minutes later he committed suicide.

"I have a long journey to take," said Raleigh,
"and so must bid the company farewell"

When the violence of his grief was over, Raleigh considered what to do. To return to James empty-handed was to go to almost certain death. He could go to the colony he had founded in Virginia, or he could take service with the King of France who would be delighted to employ him, or he could turn pirate —he had the ships, and men who would follow him. But he had given his word of honour that he would return to England. He went back.

VIII

James was determined now that Raleigh should die, if only to please the Spanish ambassador. There was, of course, a difficulty. He dared not risk a second trial—Raleigh had few enemies left, and many admirers. But if he allowed the original sentence to be carried out after all these years, it would seem more than a little peculiar: *then*, the charge had been plotting with the Spaniards, *now* Raleigh's offence was letting his men fight them. However, James was not going to let a quibble of logic stand in his way. Was he not the King, with a divine right to do as he pleased?

Raleigh was questioned at an inquiry into the expedition. Then he was brought before the King's Bench and the Lord Chief Justice announced that the sentence of fifteen years ago would now take effect. On a cold winter's morning Raleigh went to the scaffold in Old Palace Yard at Westminster. He was courageous and dignified to the last. A quietly-dressed figure in black and grey, he shook hands with his friends, mounted the platform, and made his last speech to the crowd.

"I have been a seafaring man, a soldier, and a courtier—and in the temptations of the least of these there is enough to over-throw a good mind and a good man. I die in the faith professed by the Church of England, and hope for salvation. So I take my leave of you all, making my peace with God. I have a long journey to take, and must bid the company farewell."

He joked to the last, feeling the axe-edge and saying to the executioner: "This is a sharp medicine to cure all my diseases."

The axe fell. There was a groan from the crowd. The executioner did not speak the usual words. No one believed that there was 'the head of a traitor'. Instead, a voice called out from their midst what was in all their minds: "We haven't another such head to be cut off!"

It was true. With Sir Walter Raleigh the last of the Elizabethans—one of the most brilliant and certainly the most versatile—had passed from the scene.

Albert Schweitzer

THE LIFE OF SERVICE

G. F. Lamb

I

"YOU must practise," said the old lady to the small boy as she dragged him to the piano. "You cannot play well unless you practise. And you never know how useful your music may be to you some day."

So the little boy laboriously practised his scales and exercises, while the old lady, who was his great-aunt, listened to make sure that he was doing as he was told.

Her words were true—far truer than she knew. The boy's music was to achieve a quite extraordinary result. Not only did it lead him to become a well-known musician. It also enabled him to build what was to become one of the most famous hospitals in the world.

Let us see how this came about.

The boy, whose name was Albert Schweitzer, was a native of Alsace, a district (situated between France and Germany) that was in turn French, German, and then French again. When Albert was born, in the year 1875, it had recently been taken from France by Germany. His home town was Gunsbach, but at the age of nine he was sent away to stay with his great-aunt and great-uncle in a more important town so that he could attend a larger school than the village school at Gunsbach.

Albert's father was the village pastor, or minister, and as the boy grew older he, too, decided to become a clergyman. He went to the great university at Strasbourg, the chief city of Alsace, where he studied theology and philosophy.

But he had not given up his music. He was particularly interested in church organs, and was taught to play the organ in the local church. One day when he was on holiday in Paris he went with an introduction to Charles Widor, one of the

347

leading organists of the day, and asked to be allowed to play to him.

"What would you like to play?" Widor asked him.

"Bach—of course," said Schweitzer at once. To him J. S. Bach, the famous 18th century composer, was the greatest of all musicians.

Widor was most impressed by the young man's playing. Not only did he give him lessons; he became a close personal friend in spite of the thirty years' difference in age.

II

While he was still a student at Strasbourg, Schweitzer was sitting at his window one day, thinking how fortunate he was to enjoy such a pleasant life. Everything he wanted seemed to come to him. Many of his old school friends had long ago had to start earning their living. As the minister's son he had in many ways enjoyed better opportunities than most of them.

"I must not let myself become selfish," he told himself. "I must do something to help others in return for the happiness I have been so fortunate as to enjoy."

He thought hard, and then came to a bold decision.

"I cannot give p all this at once. I must finish my studies, and then become a minister. I'll give myself another nine years. After that, I shall devote the rest of my life to relieving the sufferings of other people."

It was the kind of thought that is too easily forgotten as time passes. What was notable about Schweitzer's decision was that he kept to it. He obtained his degree, became a minister at a church in Strasbourg, and was invited to lecture at the University where he had formerly studied. He wrote a great book on J. S. Bach, and some important works on religion and philosophy. In the course of nine years he developed into quite a prominent person. He was made Principal of a well-known Theological College in Strasbourg, and was now world-famous as an organist and as a philosopher.

In such circumstances most people would naturally have forgotten or put aside a vow made nine years earlier. But Schweitzer was a very remarkable man, and his vow had not been lightly made. When he reached the age of thirty he was not only ready but determined to give up the distinguished and pleasant life he was enjoying.

His way of carrying out his vow was even more remarkable than the vow itself. He read in a missionary magazine that doctors were badly needed in West Africa to fight the many terrible diseases from which the natives suffered.

"I will become a doctor," Schweitzer decided.

Nearly all his friends and relations strongly disapproved of the intention but Schweitzer's mind was made up. The College Principal, philosopher, and famous organist went back to the university as a learner in order to study medicine.

The medical course was a long and expensive one. Schweitzer kept on with some of his lecturing, preaching, and organ-playing in order to pay for his studies. This double set of activities must have been a tremendous strain on him, especially as he had no natural taste for doctoring. But he kept at it doggedly for six years, and at last emerged as a fully qualified doctor, after which he went to Paris to take a special course in tropical diseases.

Meanwhile he had married a girl almost as courageously unselfish as himself. She was the daughter of one of the lecturers at the University, and while he was learning to be a doctor she trained as a nurse so that she could help him in his work in Africa.

III

The next thing was to decide just where to go. He approached the Paris missionary society whose magazine had inspired him to become a doctor. They had a mission station at Lambaréné in French Equatorial Africa, about 200 miles up the River Ogowe. Schweitzer offered, at his own expense, to set up a surgery there to heal the natives. Some of the missionary officials in Paris were at first unwilling to allow a doctor who was not a member of their mission to practise on their ground; but at length his offer was accepted. Schweitzer collected together all the medical and other supplies that he considered would be necessary. They filled 70 packing-cases.

Much of the money for this equipment came from organ concerts and from a German edition of his book on Bach, so that his music was indeed, as his great-aunt had prophesied, proving useful to him.

After the long sea voyage to West Africa, Schweitzer was taken to the village of Lambaréné by boat. Canoes were waiting to take him to the mission station, an hour's journey up-river.

The mission was set up on three hills between the river and the dense jungle forest, which came to within a few yards of the buildings. The whole clearing was about 650 yards long but only just over 100 yards wide.

Schweitzer's bungalow was wooden, like the other buildings. It was raised a few feet from the ground by iron piles driven into the earth. There were four rooms, and a verandah extended all round the house. A hospital was to be built near the foot of the same hill, but this was not yet ready.

As there was no hospital and no surgery, Schweitzer began by seeing his patients on an open piece of ground near his bungalow. This was not very satisfactory. It was most exhausting working in the hot sun of the tropics. Moreover, almost every evening there was a storm, and all the equipment had to be hurriedly dragged to the shelter of the verandah.

Schweitzer had noticed an old wooden building a little way from his home, and asked what it was.

"It was put up as a fowl-house by the missionary who used to live in your bungalow," he was told.

"Well," said Schweitzer," "now it will have to serve as a hospital."

It was quite small, very dirty, and had no windows—hardly an ideal place for a doctor to work in. But Schweitzer had a genius for making the best of things. He had the building thoroughly cleaned out and whitewashed, put up a few shelves to hold essential medicines, and squeezed in a camp bed for patients to lie on while they were being examined. There were still some holes in the leaf-roof, so he had to wear his sun-helmet to protect himself from the dangerous tropical sun-rays. But the place kept off the worst of the weather, and was better than nothing.

An African named N'Zeng, working on another mission station, had been engaged as an interpreter. But when a message was sent to say that Schweitzer was ready for him, the answer was returned that N'Zeng was busy on a legal dispute. Weeks went by, and still no N'Zeng appeared.

"Your education has begun," one of the missionaries told Schweitzer. "You will soon discover how hard it is to get anything done here, and how unreliable the Africans are."

Schweitzer was not entirely on his own, for his wife, besides keeping house, used to come to help with the patients for several hours a day. But it was not easy to talk with them. Only a few understood French.

One day a patient arrived who spoke French quite fluently. Schweitzer asked him where he had learnt it.

"At Cape Lopez on the coast. I used to be a cook there."

"What is your name?"

"Joseph, Oganga." (The natives all called Schweitzer 'Oganga', which means 'Witch-doctor'.)

He offered Joseph an engagement.

"We cannot pay you very much, I'm afraid. Only 70 francs a month."

"I used to earn 120 francs as a cook."

"We are not as rich as the merchants at Cape Lopez. I do not earn money for the work I am doing. It is to help you and your friends."

Joseph agreed to come as interpreter-assistant. He proved very useful, though he had a rather amusing way of referring to illnesses in terms of his former employment. The Doctor would be solemnly told, "This man's right leg of mutton hurts him," or, "This woman has a pain in her left cutlet." He soon learnt to help with simple work such as bandaging, and was able to give out medicines without getting them mixed.

IV

With Joseph's help the fowl-house hospital flourished. Great numbers of patients arrived as the Doctor's reputation spread. This is not surprising, for he was the only doctor within 300 miles.

Schweitzer found it necessary to draw up a list of rules for patients, and every day these were read out, in the two commonest native dialects, to those waiting near the fowlhouse.

"You must not spit near the house. You must not talk too

loudly while you are waiting. You must bring enough food for one day, as you cannot all be treated early. You must return all bottles and tin boxes which have had medicines in them."

As time went on, the rules became well known. Patients carried the message back to their various villages.

Each patient was given a numbered cardboard disc to hang round his neck. The same number was entered in the medical record book, and beside it were put the patient's name, complaint, and the treatment given to him. The natives rarely lost their discs—largely because they regarded them as charms to ward off disease.

Schweitzer's day would begin at about 8.30 a.m., at which time Joseph would come out and read the list of rules. Consultations continued till about 12.30 p.m., when the doctor went to his bungalow for lunch, and the patients lay in the shade and ate their bananas. This fruit was the main food of the natives in these parts.

After lunch Schweitzer allowed himself a period of recreation. He had been presented by the Paris Bach Society with a special piano fitted with pedals like an organ, so that even in remote Lambaréné he could enjoy the music he played so brilliantly. For an hour after lunch each day the wonderful music of Bach rolled across the clearing and away into the jungle.

Surgery consultations began again at 2 p.m. and continued till about six o'clock. It was a hard life, but the Doctor felt well rewarded by the gratitude of his patients.

v

About six months after Schweitzer's arrival at the mission station the main part of the new hospital was ready. It was a simple building with corrugated-iron walls and a cement floor. There were two rooms, each thirteen feet square; one was a consulting-room, the other an operating theatre. The rooms had very large windows, covered with fine mosquito netting instead of glass. White calico was stretched under the roof to prevent mosquitoes from finding their way in through holes in the leaf-tiles.

The following month the rest of the hospital was put up, Schweitzer himself helping in the work. The new buildings consisted of a waiting-room, and a ward (or sleeping-place) for patients who had to stay at the hospital. In an English hospital this ward would be a long high room with neat white-quilted beds along each side. In Schweitzer's hospital the ward was a simple hut, forty feet long, built of logs, with a roof of raffia leaves—just like the huts they were used to living in.

We might expect that providing enough beds would be a serious difficulty; but this, in fact, was the easiest part of the whole undertaking. The patients (or their friends) literally made their own beds. On the beaten earth beneath the raffia roof Schweitzer marked out sixteen large oblongs. Then he handed an axe to the attendants of each patient.

"Put up a bed just here, on one of these spaces. You know where to find wood for it."

The natives went off in their canoes and arrived back with armfuls of logs. Four upright posts were driven into the ground within each oblong. Side-pieces were firmly fastened to these posts, and then several shorter pieces going across from side to side. Dried grass was piled on top to make a mattress.

Before nightfall on the same day every bed in the hospital was ready for use. Schweitzer now had to make another necessary rule. The bed-makers could share them with the patients if convenient—but they were forbidden to put the patients on the floor and occupy the whole bed themselves!

The fowl-house hospital had been too small to allow Mrs. Schweitzer to work there as well as Joseph, but the new hospital gave her more scope to use her nursing skill. One of her particular tasks was to give anaesthetics when operations were necessary, putting the patients to sleep with ether or chloroform so that her husband could operate without their feeling anything. The natives were particularly impressed by this.

"It is wonderful," they cried. "First Oganga kills the patients. Then he cures them. Then he brings them to life again."

All kinds of illnesses came his way, the most serious being the dreaded sleeping-sickness, carried by mosquitoes and tsetse-flies. This fearful disease is so infectious and deadly that in parts of Africa it has killed off one person in every three. The danger that his sleeping-sickness patients might infect the others worried Schweitzer a good deal for some time, but at length he was able to have a small hut erected specially for them on the other side of the river.

VI

Rather more than a year after Schweitzer's arrival in Lambaréné, a disaster fell upon the world. Germany went to war against Belgium, France, and Britain.

Even in the remote African forest the effect was felt. As Alsace, though really part of France, had belonged to Germany since 1870, Doctor and Mrs. Schweitzer were considered to be German citizens—and they were working in territory held by one of their enemies. It might be expected that since they were doing nothing but good, the French authorities would have been content to let them go on doing it. But war fever affects people in strange ways. A message arrived for the Doctor and his wife, sent by the District Commandant.

"You are prisoners of war. You may stay in your house, but you must not leave it, and you must not speak to anybody in Lambaréné, no matter whether they are white people or black people."

After a time this order was relaxed, thanks to the efforts of M. Widor in France and the protests of the missionaries and other Frenchmen in the Lambaréné district. Once more the inhabitants of the district were able to receive medical attention from the only doctor within hundreds of miles.

But this was not the end of the matter. Nearly three years later the French authorities at home decided that the Doctor and his wife must be brought from Africa and be interned in a prison-camp in France. The great work that he had been doing had to be abandoned after all, and the hospital was left to the mercy of the jungle.

We might suppose that after such treatment the Doctor would never again return to French territory to help anyone. But there is nothing at all small-minded in the character of such men as Schweitzer. When the war was over he was eager to go back to help the natives of French Equatorial Africa again. For a time he travelled about Europe, giving lectures and organ recitals to collect money for his activities. Once more his music was helping him to heal the sick.

354

ALBERT SCHWEITZER

VII

In February 1924 he started out on his second journey to Lambaréné, this time taking with him, as a volunteer helper, a young Oxford undergraduate named Noel Gillespie. The Doctor and his wife now had a little daughter, and Mrs. Schweitzer had to stay at home to look after her.

Schweitzer found the hospital at Lambaréné in a fearful state. In seven years the greedy jungle had almost swallowed it.

"It might be the Sleeping Beauty's place of concealment," Schweitzer commented. The corrugated-iron walls were still standing, but the palm-leaf roofs were badly damaged, and the log-hut wards overgrown with grass and brushwood. Huge trees had sprung up around them, and the paths between the buildings were just a tangled mass of grass and creepers.

It needed a great deal of courage to restore a hospital from such chaos, but Schweitzer was not daunted. With Gillespie's valuable help he brought the buildings and paths back to order, and at the same time tried to find opportunities to see the many patients who were beginning to come again to the mission station. A few of the natives were sometimes drawn into helping in the renewing of the hospital; but Schweitzer found that it was seldom easy to get the Africans to labour for the benefit of future patients whom they did not know, and who perhaps would belong to different tribes. One patient, however, was an exception. He had some knowledge of carpentry, and not only was he willing to help in the rebuilding of the hospital after the First World War but was helping there still, many years later.

Further medical assistance now began to arrive from Europe. Another Alsatian doctor turned up, and was followed by a Swiss doctor. There was also a nurse from Strasbourg. The additional help made it possible for Schweitzer's hospital to do more and more for the natives, but it also made it clear to him how badly he needed more space.

One day he took a canoe out by himself and went upstream. About two miles away he came to a clearing where there had once been a primitive African village. For a long time he explored the uneven ground. Then he returned, and called his fellow doctors and his nurses together.

"We are going to move the hospital," he told them. The

355

In seven years the greedy jungle had almost swallowed
up Schweitzer's hospital

decision was received with shouts of joy that made the natives wonder what was happening.

Permission to occupy the land was given by the District Commissioner, and the heavy work of clearing the ground and erecting the buildings began. There was the usual difficulty of obtaining labour, for the timber trade was flourishing and drew away most of the able-bodied natives. Patients and their friends were again pressed into service, but they had an unfortunate way of slipping into the jungle when there was hard work to be done.

However, the hospital was put up at last, with Schweitzer supervising every detail. It was laid upon a foundation of hardwood piles, into which ants could not bore. Hundreds of these piles were cut from a hardwood forest some 16 miles away. Upon these the rooms and wards were erected, walls and roofs alike being of corrugated iron; the floors were wooden. The wards were made long and narrow so that the air could sweep through, and ran east and west, so that the sun could not beat down upon the side walls and half stifle the patients.

Altogether the erection took about a year, and then came the considerable task of removing patients and equipment by boats. The operation was completed in a single day, thanks to the vigorous efforts of Schweitzer and his helpers.

The patients were as delighted as the doctors and nurses.

"This is a good hut, Oganga," they cried as they peered into the long wards and felt the strong corrugated-iron walls.

The new buildings were able to receive over 250 patients and their attendants. This was a great size for a small settlement in remote West Africa—and a tremendous advance on one little fowl-house.

VIII

Now that Schweitzer had capable European helpers he was able to give himself some leave. For the next ten years he spent a good deal of time in Europe, lecturing and playing the organ in several countries in order to collect more money for his hospital. He was able, too, to spend some of his time enjoying the company of his wife and daughter at home. But during these years he went back several times to Africa to see that all was going well.

In 1939 war again disturbed his activities, with Germany once more fighting against Britain and France. This time, however, there was no question of internment. After the First World War Alsace had been taken back by France, so Schweitzer was now a *French* citizen. He went out to Lambaréné, and was joined by his wife.

In spite of difficulties over supplies, the hospital managed to keep going. The timber trade was unable to flourish in war time, so there was far more labour available. The Doctor took advantage of this by having a great many fruit trees planted in the hospital grounds. By the time peace came, in 1945, Schweitzer was seventy years old, but there was no thought of his giving up the work he had so unselfishly taken on.

In 1952 Schweitzer, who in his later years was much concerned with the question of peace in the modern world, was awarded the Nobel Peace Prize. In the following year he received the medal of the Royal African Society, together with a money prize, 'for dedicated service in Africa'. The money he at once used to provide a separate village for lepers, placed at a little distance from the main hospital buildings. He himself helped to put up the new buildings. In 1955 he celebrated his eightieth birthday; and in the same year he came to England and was awarded the Order of Merit, one of the highest distinctions of Great Britain, and one offered to only a very few people. He received the honour from the Queen at Buckingham Palace. He died at Lambaréné in 1965, and was buried there.

That, briefly, is the story of Albert Schweitzer—the man whose music enabled him to found a hospital, and whose vow to serve other, made when he was still a young student, led him to become, perhaps, the most widely loved and respected man of our time.

William Shakespeare

THE GLORY OF ENGLISH LITERATURE

John Bayley

I

WILLIAM SHAKESPEARE was born in 1564 at Stratford-on-Avon in Warwickshire, a town very close to the geographical centre of England. For six years Queen Elizabeth had been on the throne, and the great age of optimism and development—geographical and colonial, artistic and literary—with which we associate her reign, had just begun. But although the Elizabethan exploits are so familiar to us and although we feel such admiration for the great men of the period, we also feel—as Virginia Woolf has pointed out—a sense of their ultimate mysteriousness, and hence obviously, the mysteriousness of Shakespeare, the greatest Elizabethan of all. What causes this feeling? Chiefly perhaps the very richness and versatility of the age, which produces so many bewildering contradictions. How surprised we should be today, for example, to find a daring and successful admiral composing between battles a long and beautiful epic poem dedicated to the Queen! Or how remarkable we should find a country parson who was simultaneously able to fulfil his clerical duties, to manage an armaments factory, and to engage in learned debates upon the classics with scholars all over Europe. It would be startling, too, to find that the greatest writer of the age had made a large part of his personal fortune not from writing but from shrewd and perhaps unscrupulous speculations in the stock market and in real estate. But neither Sir Walter Raleigh, the admiral, nor Thomas Hanmer the parson, nor Shakespeare the writer, seem to have impressed the men of the time as being specially outstanding and remarkable. The mysterious Elizabethans took such achievements and such a breadth of abilities much more for granted than we do.

359

Like so many of his famous contemporaries, Shakespeare's family background is modest and obscure. His father was a butcher and grazier of Stratford, a solid citizen who took part in the municipal affairs, his mother, Mary Arden, the daughter of a prosperous yeoman farmer.

Shakespeare was educated at the free grammar school in Stratford, where he would have learnt a certain amount of Latin, mathematics and scripture. There is no evidence that he was a particularly bright pupil, but the small Latin and less Greek that was sneeringly attributed to him by his more intellectually minded playwright contemporaries like Ben Jonson, probably means no more than that he took little interest in such studies once he had left school. In *The Merry Wives of Windsor* he gives us a cheerful little sketch of the contemporary method of teaching Latin.

At the age of eighteen, after leaving school, he married Anne Hathaway, the daughter of a local farmer, and he may for a time have been apprenticed to his father's trade, but his father's money troubles had become serious, and in 1585 he left Stratford to seek his fortune in London. There is a tradition that he left in a hurry after being caught poaching the deer of Sir Thomas Lucy, a local baronet whom Shakespeare afterwards satirised in the character of Shallow in Henry IV, but there is as little foundation for this as there is for the other possibility that he may have been a schoolmaster for a time, or even a soldier. What is certain is that round about 1590 he had become a member of the Lord Chamberlain's company of actors in London.

II

In spite of the hostility shown against it by many prominent men of the time, including Elizabeth's chief adviser, Lord Burghley, and the powerful class of puritans ; and in spite of the fact that all actors, on pain of being prosecuted as 'rogues and vagabonds', had to have a special licence, like a car or dog licence, to carry on their trade, the theatres of the time were a flourishing and growing concern. A mixed audience attended them, shopkeepers, apprentices, 'young men about town', and the poorest and most ignorant class, grooms, porters and servants, who paid a penny to stand in the pit, and were known as

'the groundlings'. All these people had somehow to be entertained and amused or they would prefer to patronize the
theatre's rivals, the gardens where cock-fighting and bear-baiting
took place. The plays were therefore a mixture of the crudely
sensational—a sort of acted horror comic—and the richly
poetical, full of flowery descriptions and figures of speech,
which pleased the gentry.

Shakespeare seems to have taken to this world like a duck to
water, and there is no reason to suppose that he was not fully
prepared—when he came to take a hand in writing plays—to
carry on the moneymaking formula. Perhaps the most extraordinary aspect of his genius is his ability to work—as it were—
with the tools available, instead of attempting to impose on the
audience his own kind of play, or any new and original form of
art. Instead he was not only prepared to revise or put fresh
scenes into plays written by others—rather as a script writer
might do for the films today, but also to take all his plots, with
the single exception of his last play, *The Tempest*, from other
men's stories—Italian tales by Boccaccio and Cinthio, and
historical chronicles by Holinshed and Plutarch. Thus it seems
quite implausible to say, as critics used to in the past, that
because *Titus Andronicus* contains horrible and blood-curling
scenes that these could not have been written by the Shakespeare who wrote the tender and compassionate scenes of
King Lear and *The Winter's Tale*—Shakespeare was quite capable of producing horror in cold blood if that was what was
needed, and he seems to have lacked entirely what we should
nowadays call an artistic conscience. That is to say he did not
take literature seriously: he had no abstract sense of the
greatness of his calling, and we cannot imagine him lamenting
the absence of a National Theatre, or solemnly discussing—
as we are so prone to do today—the future of tragedy, or the
possibility of new sorts of poetic drama. One proof of this is his
total indifference to the fate of his own work—he made no
effort to secure the publication of his plays, or even of his
sonnets, and only took pains over the correct appearances of
his two long formal poems, *Venus and Adonis*, (published in
1593), and *The Rape of Lucrece* (1594), probably because
both were dedicated to his friend and patron, Henry Wriothesley, the Earl of Southampton.

III

The part that this young handsome and accomplished noble-man played in Shakespeare's life has always been a source of much dispute and conjecture. Patrons were an important part of the Elizabethan literary scene, particularly as each company of players was nominally under the protection of one of them. Thus Shakespeare's company was first under the patronage of the Lord Chamberlain, Lord Hunsdon, while their rival com-pany, for whom worked Marlowe and the famous actor Alleyn, had the hereditary Lord High Admiral of England as their patron and were known as the Admiral's Men. It has been suggested that many of the sonnets were addressed by Shake-speare to Southampton, and though there is no space here to go into the many complex issues involved we must glance briefly at the two most controversial ones—the dating of the sonnets and the identity of the mysterious 'Mr. W. H.', to whom they are apparently dedicated. Where dating is con-cerned, the crucial sonnet is number 107:

The mortal moon hath her eclipse endured
And the sad augurs mock their own presage;
Incertainties now crown themselves assured
And peace proclaims olives of endless age.

Does this refer, as some critics have held, to the defeat of the Armada in 1588—the death-bearing fleet advancing up the channel in a moon-shaped crescent—or to the death of Queen Elizabeth in 1603, when the peaceful accession of James I confounded the gloomy prophets of disaster and seemed to usher in a new era of prosperity? On this depends whether Shakespeare wrote the sonnets as a young man, or at the height of his maturity, when the period of the great tragedies was just beginning.

The question of the dedication is more complex. There are three main possibilities. First and least plausible, Mr. W. H. is an inverted anagram of Henry Wriothesley, Earl of Southamp-ton. Second, that it refers to a young actor in Shakespeare's company; and third and perhaps most probable, that it has nothing to do with Shakespeare at all, but was the dedication of Thomas Thorpe, the publisher who printed the sonnets without the author's co-operation in 1609, and was addressed simply to another publishing friend of his—William Hall.

IV

With a fair amount of certainty we can date Shakespeare's first dramatic efforts to 1591, the year after his arrival in London. His first play was probably *Love's Labour's Lost*, a lighthearted comedy embodying much keen and witty observation of the fashionable London world of gallants and fantastics, and satirizing good-humouredly their bubbling ideas and their affected modes of speech. It was followed, probably in the same year, by *Two Gentlemen of Verona*, and *The Comedy of Errors*, and soon after came *Romeo and Juliet*, Shakespeare's first tragedy, and the first of the plays to show his true poetic quality. We must imagine all these as being composed in the intervals of an active life in the theatre, taking parts and helping with all the manifold business of production, sometimes in London, but touring in the provinces, too, when the summer outbreaks of plague had closed the London play-houses. On March 3, 1592, a new piece called *Henry VI* was acted in London, and won a great popular triumph. Indeed so successful was it that the management promptly followed it up with two more 'parts'. Shakespeare was almost certainly the chief collaborator in it, but it is unlikely that he wrote it all. We know that its success made at least one of his fellow writers jealous, for we find Greene, in his last death-bed scribble, referring with indignation to one who 'is, in his own conceit, the only Shakescene in a countrie'.

The popularity of *Henry VI* was largely due to the fact that the Elizabethans were much more interested in history than we are. They regarded it as something that was still going on; the revolts and murders of a hundred years before might break out afresh any day, and the portrayal in the plays of a weak king and warring nobles was something that every Elizabethan could appreciate from his own time. They loved to find parallels in the past, moreover, in much the same way that many of us referred to Munich while the Suez crisis was on, except that they took their examples from further back in history. It is significant that when the Earl of Essex attempted his rebellion against Elizabeth in 1601, he and Southampton requested—or perhaps

363

rather commanded—Shakespeare's company to put on *Richard II*, which showed an unsuitable monarch being excusably deposed by a strong and just usurper who would bring back peace to the country. The popularity of the historical plays was exploited by Shakespeare in *Richard III*, in the name part of which Burbage, Shakespeare's friend and co-sharer in the company, first won fame. Then came *Richard II* and *King John*, with the two parts of *Henry IV* bringing Shakespeare's skill in the presentation of history on the stage to a climax with the great comical but also historical figure of Falstaff. Comedy and History here met and mingled, instead of being produced separately, and both are the gainers. *The Taming of the Shrew*, *Midsummer Night's Dream*, and *The Merchant of Venice* may be assigned to the years 1596 and 97, the latter play taking as its popular comic villain the same kind of rich Jew whom Marlowe had popularized in *The Jew of Malta*, and who was perhaps founded on the historical figure of Dr. Lopez, unjustly executed in 1594 on a charge of attempting to poison the Queen. We know that in 1594 Shakespeare was first summoned with the most famous actors of the day to play before the Queen, and from then until the end of the reign his plays were regularly acted at the court of Whitehall or the palace at Greenwich. The Queen is said to 1 ve had a special weakness for Falstaff and to have commissioned *The Merry Wives of Windsor* in order to see the fat knight in love.

About the year 1598 Shakespeare's company began to be threatened by the competition of the troop of boy actors—the choristers of St. Paul's—whose well-trained performances became so popular that they took custom away from the regular playhouses. At this time Shakespeare was writing his first tragedies, *Julius Caesar* and *Hamlet*, and in *Hamlet* he refers to the difficulty, pointing out with characteristic fairness and good humour that the boys would probably grow up to be actors in their turn, so that by 'exclaiming against their own succession' they were destroying their future livelihood. However, with the accession of James I in 1603, who took an even livelier interest in the theatre than Elizabeth had done, the fortunes of the company improved again. To these years belong the greatest of the tragedies: *Othello*, *King Lear*, *Macbeth* and *Antony and Cleopatra*, all of which were written before

Like other dramatists, Shakespeare may sometimes have
had second thoughts when hearing his lines spoken at
rehearsals

1608. To the same years belong the so-called 'dark comedies', *Measure for Measure* and *All's Well that Ends Well*—'dark' because although they end happily much of the material of tragic evil is mixed in with their plots and characters. It used to be the fashion to suppose that Shakespeare at this time must have been going through a period of disillusion and depression, perhaps even culminating in nervous breakdown, but there is no evidence for this view, and it seems contradicted by what we know from contemporary sources of his sane, gentle, and balanced temperament. What is certain is that at this time he was making his fortune, buying house property, speculating cannily in wheat and similar commodities, and acting in a way befitting the man of means who in 1597 had been able to buy New Place, the largest (though probably also the most tumbledown) house in his native Stratford, and who in the same year had persuaded his father to apply to the College of Heralds for a coat of arms.

V

In 1610 Shakespeare's company finally ousted the 'children' and acquired the Blackfriars Theatre, and to this year belongs *Cymbeline*, the first of the three tragi-comedies or Romances. The reason for the popularity of this new type of play was no doubt partly because the Theatre was equipped for candle-light and much more elaborate scenery, favouring a piece full of magical events and transformations; and partly because James and his high-spirited Queen, Anne of Denmark, were very fond themselves of dressing up and acting in the courtly entertainments known as Masques which these last plays much resemble. We know that *The Winter's Tale* was acted before the King at Whitehall on November 5, 1612, and in the summer of the same year *The Tempest* probably Shakespeare's last play, was performed. It was a fitting conclusion to his active career as playwright and actor manager; his 'revels now were ended' and though he perhaps took a hand, with his younger contemporary Fletcher, in plays written from his retirement, he spent the rest of his days at Stratford, dying on April 23, 1616, at the age of fifty-two. He was buried in Stratford church, where his tomb and monument can be seen, together with a doggerel verse, unlikely to have been composed by him, in which a curse was pronounced on anyone venturing to disturb his grave. We have no portrait of him which is certainly authentic, though his Collected Works are usually ornamented with the facsmile engraving of the bust that crowns his tomb. Many critics have protested however that our greatest poet could not possibly have looked like that!

In 1623 his collected plays were published in the so-called *First Folio*, edited by Heminge and Condell, his two chief fellow shareholders in the theatre. His fame continued to grow steadily, and in 1709 the first critical edition of his works appeared, edited by Rowe. In the 18th and 19th centuries, culminating in A. C. Bradley's *Shakespearean Tragedy*, criticism of the plays centred on the characters, but recently there has been a tendency to see them more in the light of dramatic poems, with their themes illuminated and carried forward by means of imagery, an attitude associated principally with Wilson Knight (*The Wheel of Fire*), and D. A. Traversi (*Approaches to Shakespeare*).

George Bernard Shaw

THE IRISH SHAKESPEARE

St. John Ervine

I

MEN and women of genius are, like liquorice, of all sorts. They may write poetry or invent sewing-machines, but they have several characteristics in common. They confer immense benefit on mankind, but are not always well rewarded for their service. Some of them, after a period of poverty and neglect, become, like Bernard Shaw, rich and world-renowned. Others, such as Aristides, who was called 'the Just' so often that the very sound of the words enraged his countrymen, die so poor that their compatriots have to pay the cost of their burial. Beethoven died in poverty. Mozart was thrown into a pauper's grave. Samuel Crompton, who invented the spinning-mule and revolutionized the cotton industry, was cheated of his right reward and depended for support in his old age on an annuity of £63 which was bought for him by some of his friends. Dickens, at the age of ten, earned his living in a blacking factory because his shiftless father was in the Marshalsea Prison for debt, but he made himself rich and eminent by his novels. Our debt to the great is unpayable, so we make little or no effort to pay it. Renown, presumably, is enough. But what would England be if Nelson had lost the Battle of Trafalgar? Even that great victory was not sufficient. It had to be supported by Wellington's victory at Waterloo. Our debt is increased beyond our understanding when we realize that if it had not been for the work and genius in each generation of insufficiently rewarded people, we might all be living like savages, cultivating small patches of land very badly.

Two facts about civilization are plain. One is that Europe, the smallest of the five continents, has enriched the world more than any other. The second is that three small nations, Israel,

Greece and Elizabethan England, did more than all the rest to civilize mankind. Christianity, indeed, began in the most westerly part of Asia, which did not accept it, but it was spread by Europe. The young lightly-clad shepherd, David, stretched the mail-clad giant, Goliath, dead on the ground with a stone in his skull.

Bernard Shaw—he greatly disliked his George—who was born on Saturday, July 26, 1856, and died at his country-house, Shaw's Corner, Ayot St. Lawrence, Hertfordshire, on November 2, 1950, is a remarkable example of the ups and downs sometimes experienced by people of genius. In the first nine years of his career as a writer, he earned £6. When, at the age of ninety-four, he died, his estate was valued at £367,233 13s., the largest fortune left by any writer in the history of literature. It is common when an author of genius dies, for there to be a revival of interest in his work, but this revival seldom lasts long. The great man is put back on the shelf and left to moulder in the dust that falls on eminence no less than on mediocrity. But Bernard Shaw has surprised even his most ardent admirers by escaping the general fate. The interest in his work is not less today than it was during his life. At least one of his plays is being performed somewhere in the world every working night, and the probability is that several are. A musical comedy, *My Fair Lady*, which is based on his comedy, *Pygmalion*, broke all the records for receipts and run in New York. A main factor in its success is that the authors had the wisdom to use as much of Shaw's dialogue as could be fitted into their scheme. It is made remarkable by the dislike he felt for such adaptations, and it is certain that had he been alive when *My Fair Lady* was produced, he would have made great efforts to have its production prevented. His anger was deep when a popular musical comedy, *The Chocolate Soldier*, was made out of his comedy, *Arms and the Man*, and he is said to have refused to accept any share of the royalties from it. There is nothing surprising in these successes, for Shaw's work is largely operatic in character: which may be due to his boyhood in a home full of music.

II

His mother was Lucinda Elizabeth Gurly, the only daughter of the two children born to Walter Bagnal Gurly, a thriftless landowner who lived mainly on mortages and loans which were rarely repaid. Gurly, in one of his financial crises from which he saw no escape except by marriage to a wealthy girl who would not ask any questions when her fortune had been spent, looked around until he met a gentle, pretty and subservient girl, Lucinda Whitcroft, the daughter of a wealthy landowner, John Whitcroft, who not only managed his estate with skill and profit, but derived a substantial income from the possession of several pawnshops in Dublin. Whitcroft was willing to let his submissive daughter marry the spendthrift, but he took care to make his future son-in-law assign his property to trustees as part of the bride's dowry; and at a later date, he arranged a bequest to his grand-daughter, G.B.S.'s mother, so that her father could not dissipate it. Gurly, however, had little respect for law, and he made away with a substantial part of this sum before he was warned by a solicitor that if he did not mend his monetary manners he would land himself in gaol. Ten years after her marriage, the first Mrs. Gurly died, leaving a son and a daughter, Lucinda Elizabeth, a firm-willed girl, who became the mother of Bernard Shaw.

Lucinda Elizabeth had removed herself from her father's dun-infested house before his second marriage, and was living with her Aunt Ellen Whitcroft, a hunchback with a pretty face and a ferocious temper. Aunt Ellen somehow convinced herself that her niece was certain to marry a peer, and she was, therefore, enraged when the girl married an elderly detrimental, George Carr Shaw, who was her senior by seventeen years and was notoriously feckless. Why this girl of twenty-one married him is almost impossible to understand. She had no love for him nor anything that could be called affection. He was a failure in everything he undertook, and his sense of money was so slight that it could scarcely be called a sense. He could not keep a job. Through family influence, he was given a sinecure in the Dublin Law Courts which involved him in no regular attendance at his office nor any knowledge of the law he was supposed to administer. Its unimportance was too much even for the temper of that time, and it was abolished. Shaw was compensated by a pension of £60 a year which he commuted for £500, a bad bargain for him, and this sum was spent on a dilapidated corn mill which, after many dangerous mischances, enabled the well-meaning but insignificant owner of it to live in meagre comfort. Aunt Ellen cut her niece out of her will, and not a penny of the £4000 she left was bequeathed to the luckless Lucinda. Three children were born to the Shaws: Lucinda Frances Carr, commonly called Lucy: Elinor Agnes, known as Yuppy, who died of consumption when she was twenty; and George Bernard. It was a loveless home, ruled by a disillusioned young woman. The meals were erratic, ill-cooked and monotonous. But the house had one grace that almost atoned for its faults: it was full of music. A remarkable musician, George John Vandaleur Lee, was living in Dublin then, and he became the prevailing influence in the life of the Shaws and their friends. Lee trained Mrs. Shaw so that she became a singer of considerable quality, in possession of a pure mezzo-soprano voice. Lee persuaded the Shaws to join him in the tenancy of a larger house than the one in which their children had been born; and there seemed to be a pleasing prospect of modest prosperity before them. But he was a restless man, and he suddenly decided to leave Ireland and settle in England. This was a disaster for Mrs. Shaw, who was beginning to have a vogue as a vocalist; and she decided that since her livelihood as a musician depended on Lee, she and her two daughters would follow him to London, leaving her son, a lad of fourteen, to live in lodgings with his father. The boy had begun to earn his living. Through the influence of a relative he was given a post in a land agents' office, where he was so successful that he was appointed chief cashier when sixteen at a salary of £48 a year, an unusually large salary for a lad of his age. It will be well here to state that G.B.S. was an exceedingly able business man, who felt profound contempt for authors who professed inability to cast a column of figures. Had he remained in the land agency, he would probably have become a partner in the firm.

But his life was displeasing to him, though he was likeable and genial and popular with his associates. His father, who had been sobered by his doctor (who told him that if he did not reform his habits he would drop dead in the street), was no companion for his son, who, remarkably enough showed no particular interest in the drama; nor, indeed, did he display any signs of liking for literature of any sort, though he was fairly well-read. His sudden decision at the age of twenty, made a week after the death of his sister Agnes, to leave Dublin and join his mother in London, was, no doubt, the result of an accumulation of troubles such as are likely to beset a lad who has no real home. He was not welcomed by Mrs. Shaw or her elder daughter, and he seems to have undergone an extraordinary change of character during his passage from Dublin to Holyhead. Lively and sociable in Dublin, he became solitary and silent in London. He decided to be a novelist, and he toiled regularly and industriously at the manufacture of fiction, without, however, persuading any publisher to buy a single script. He completed five novels and began, but did not finish, a sixth, of which only a chapter and a page or two of the second chapter were written. If ever a man had failure stamped on him, G.B.S. was the man at that time.

III

Fortune, however, though it seemed to be frowning on him, was preparing his career. A chance encounter with a Scot in the British Museum was to change the whole conditions of his life. This Scot was William Archer, who became his close friend and benefactor. It would not be easy to find two men more dissimilar than Bernard Shaw and William Archer, but they managed to become intimates. Archer put work in Shaw's way. Offered a job, he declined it on the ground that he was already fully employed, but added that he had a friend, an uncommonly able Irishman, called Bernard Shaw, who was just the man for the post. The friendship of these two men was one of the beautiful aspects of both their lives.

Success now prevailed in G.B.S.'s life, despite the failure of his novels. He is unique in the history of criticism for the fact that he was an exceedingly able writer on *all* the arts, writing as ably on music as he wrote on drama, and illuminating every subject he discussed with wit and knowledge. But he still did not think of himself as a dramatist, and he was almost forty before he began seriously to do so. His success came at a time when the world's mind was making a drastic change of thought that is not yet complete. Writers at the end of the last quarter of the 19th century were still primarily, if not entirely, treated as

entertainers. They were not regarded as sociologists or reformers, though some of them, notably Dickens, were. Dickens,
indeed, despite his world renown, was considered by earnest
people to be less influential and important than Darwin and
Karl Marx. Yet Dickens began his career as a novelist with
works, such as *Nicholas Nickleby* and *Oliver Twist* and *David
Copperfield*, which were as reformatory as any of the works of
Galsworthy and Shaw. The generation to which Shaw belonged,
a generation which included such earnest and ardent reformers
as H. G. Wells and John Galsworthy, was interested chiefly in
changing not only institutions and ways of thought, but the
entire structure of society. Almost the whole of Galsworthy's
plays are about social problems. *Strife* expounds his belief
that strikes are wasteful ways of settling industrial disputes,
since they generally ended with one side half starved and the
other side half ruined. In *Justice*, he reminds us that the law-
breaker's punishment does not end when he has served his
sentence. Wells, who might have become a great comic writer,
second only to Dickens, sacrificed this probability to his
passion for remaking the world. Even the poets, whose minds
more than other men's, should be concerned with essentials,
allowed themselves to be diverted from their function by the
craze for social and political action, and some of his readers
have trouble in deciding whether Mr. T. S. Eliot is a poet or a
sociologist.

Shaw, though his renown has substantially survived his age,
belonged to it unmistakably: a fact which was, perhaps, inevitable in a man born when he was in Ireland. The Famine of the
Forties, known to the Irish as The Great Hunger, ended about
twelve years before his birth, and it had reduced the population
by half. It was not the first, nor was it the last or worst of the
famines from which Ireland had suffered, nor was Ireland the
only country which endured this anguish. The harvest in
England had failed fourteen times in succession during the
French and Napoleonic Wars, and there were bread riots
throughout the nation. Famine, indeed, like plague in the
Middle Ages, was as common as colds are today, and large
numbers of people could have been said to have been hungry
all their lives. The Ireland into which he was born was as deeply
stricken as any battlefield.

His own social and economic position was a peculiar one. He was a Protestant in a city chiefly populated by Roman Catholics, and he belonged to a declining branch of a family which, through his mother, belonged to the upper class and, through his father, to a highly able and successful part of the middle class, though his father was, in almost every respect, a failure. The effect of his relationship was that he spent his youth in some isolation from his relatives.

Ireland was, and still is, inhabited by three unusually dissimilar groups, whose intercourse is far less than that of any groups in Great Britain. They are (a) the Roman Catholics, the largest group, most of whom are poor and agricultural; (b) the Ascendancy, as they were called, or landowners, who are Protestants and comparatively prosperous, though less so than they were and rapidly dwindling in numbers; and (c) the Ulster Protestants, the majority of whom are Presbyterians or other Dissenters. The last group founded and maintain practically the whole of the industrial system of Ireland. Gaels are not expert in establishing large businesses. The three substantial industries in Eire, Guinness's Brewery and Jacob's biscuit factory in Dublin, and Henry Ford's small motor car works in Cork, were all founded by Protestants. Obviously, a country in which industry is conducted almost on a sectarian basis, and in which the population is divided into a large group who were deprived of power and property through conquest and a small group whose members have risen to wealth and authority mainly through the same means, was certain to develop a division of interest and purpose unusual in other nations, especially in north-western Europe. When their division into a small group of expropriators and a very large group of the expropriated, is allied to a deeper vision, that of religious belief, in which the larger group is inflexibly convinced that its religion is the only true faith in the world and that a person belonging to a different persuasion is in such a state of spiritual insecurity that he is almost certain to be damned hereafter, the ground for separation and snobbery is bound to be greatly enlarged. The Shaws were fairly self-sufficient, and G.B.S. was less aware than most people of social cleavages; but even he felt humiliated in his boyhood when he was sent to a school where the pupils were, for the most part, Papists.

IV

Shaw in England did not at first develop any of the eccentricities in food and dress that he was to acquire. He developed a shyness that he had not displayed in Dublin, a disability which increased the difficulty he had in finding his feet in his new environment. His rigid determination to become a writer was not diminished by his failure to make any publisher find merit in his work. People perceived that he was very intelligent, but they perceived, too, that he seemed incapable of using his intelligence effectively. He had wit and good temper and he was almost femininely fastidious. There was no rancour in his nature, and he was always ready to hold out both hands in reconciliation. He accused himself of 'living on' his mother, but the statement is false. He had saved enough money in Dublin to be able to maintain himself for some time in the small style of her house. But even if he had lived on her, who was better off than his father, the 'living' was slight and cost her little. Boys of his class live on their parents until after they leave their university, but are not reproached for doing so. His room was not needed by anybody else, and the wretched meals he was given cannot have cost much. He was costing her far less than his sister Agnes, who had never earned a farthing and had to be maintained in a sanatorium in the Isle of Wight until her death.

Shaw's decision to become a novelist is explicable only because the novel is the most obvious form of writing that occurs to anyone wishing to become a writer. Apart from Shakespeare, Sheridan and Goldsmith, few dramatists were read or even published, and these three were more often seen on the stage than read. But the difference between a dramatist and a novelist is too great to be overcome. The first tells his story in a much shorter form than the novelist, and he tells it in dialogue. The second tells his story in the form of narrative, with dialogue subordinate to description. A long play, such as *Hamlet*, has only about 30,000 words in it, but a short novel rarely has less than 75,000 words, and such books as Tolstoy's *War and Peace* are immensely long. The reader can take as long as he likes over a novel, but the playgoer must see the whole play in less than three hours, even if the play, as most of

A born playwright (though slow to find it out), Shaw was
quick to demonstrate how each part should be played

Shakespeare's are, has to be cut to ribbons to enable him to do so. The suburban playgoer must catch his last train home, and trains do not dally for playgoers. Most people, especially those of the working-class, tell a story as a dramatist tells it, with a great deal of 'he said' and 'then she said'. Shaw took a long time to discover the form in which his talent could work best, but when he discovered it, he seldom worked in any other form. He was a born dramatist, as conversational as Shakespeare.

Yet his works which are not plays are numerous and some of them are very long, as, indeed, sociological works of the sort that he wrote almost must be, since they involve explanations which are deadly in drama. His intimacy with Sidney Webb, a man who had not only a plan for solving all problems, but had several plans for their solution, so that if one were disapproved, another could be put in its place, gave him a slant on human affairs such as a writer of his eminence seldom possesses; and it is arguable that this slant was a disadvantage. It made him think in terms of politics when he should have been thinking in terms of people. Politics are ephemeral: people appear, as a mass, to be imperishable. If ever a race seemed certain to be eliminated from the earth, the Jews were that people, for they have suffered every sort of disaster, including four centuries of servility in Egypt, yet they have survived and increased and are able and powerful. Man is durable. The weakest of the creatures, he has mastered all the others, who exist on his sufferance. It is this fact which impresses Shaw in his work more than any other. There is a will to live and to improve in man which is, Shaw, says, planted in him by what he calls the Life Force. but which the rest of us are content to call God; and it is this Force which enables him to rule the earth. His warning is that Man will perish if ever he relaxes in his devotion to the purpose of the Life Force, which is only his way of saying that if we sin we shall suffer. It is the duty of man, therefore, to exert himself to the full extent of his ability and power. If he fails to do so, he will be violating the law of life, and he will be scrapped as the mammoth beasts were scrapped, because they could not accommodate themselves to changed conditions and ampler opportunities.

This doctrine is implicit in everything he wrote. Poverty, disease, ignorance, war and class divisions are all inimical to good living, and their continuation is a direct breach of the law of the Life Force. He became a Socialist—it is seldom realized that he and Keir Hardie were the founders of the Labour Party— because he believed that only through an organized and directed community could man survive. A world in which each person fights for his own interest only is one in which man will perish exactly as mastodons have perished. We are not all convinced that this is true, and have become acutely distrustful of societies in which men are excessively ruled and directed by self-appointed rulers and dictators, a distrust which is justified by the fact that dictators nearly always die violently. It was his belief in the need for absolute government of the average man by able dictators which made Shaw favour such people as Hitler and Mussolini. *Any* dictator was better than *no* dictator. But man is a wayward creature, and does not long tolerate political bosses. He has an ineradicable conviction that the general will and desire are more important than the manufactured and selfish ambition of a single person. He sees in nature variety so great, that it is said, there are not two leaves on a tree which are exactly alike. Shaw liked regularity, but irregularity is the law of successful life; and the fact about us, which was amply demonstrated in Shaw's own life, is that improvement is a result of discontent and that all the men and women of genius who have inhabited this earth have been people who were dissatisfied with life as they found it and were determined to change it.

V

His marriage, in 1898, to Charlotte Frances Payne-Townshend, a kinswoman of the Townshends who ran the land agency in which G.B.S. was first employed, was entirely felicitous. The bride, who was wealthy, was forty-one, and the bridegroom, who was now earning a handsome income, was forty-two; and their extraordinarily dissimilar natures blended very happily. Charlotte was kind and generous and, although as independent-minded as her husband, deeply devoted to him. Her death was a disaster to him in his old age, and he retired into solitude at Ayot St. Lawrence, visiting London seldom and seeing only those whom he wished to see. The list of his works is long and remarkably diverse, but they all have the same intention, to make the world habitable by civilized people. He was active in many ways until the end and, but for an accident, he would probably have become a centenarian. While pruning a tree in his garden, he slipped and fell and broke a leg. That was the end of him. He lingered for a few weeks, and then quietly died. His large fortune was intended to finance a scheme for the reformation of the English alphabet, but, if this should not turn out to be feasible, the money was to be divided between the National Gallery of Ireland, where he had learnt what he knew about art, the British Museum, which had been his club and his workshop when he was poor, and the Royal Academy of Dramatic Art, where the people who had helped to make his fortune were trained to act. It was one of the most public-spirited wills any person has ever made; and it proved that he never forgot a benefactor.

His personal kindness and benefaction were great and unadvertised. How generous he was may best be illustrated by a story which is told here for the first time in print. He had heard that a man who disliked him had fallen ill and was financially distressed. G.B.S. called on a friend of this man and said, "I should like to help him, but I'm afraid he'd feel embarrassed by help from me, so will you please take this sum and give it to him and pretend it's from you?" That was the sort of man G.B.S. always was.

Socrates

THE MAN OF CHARACTER

L. A. G. Strong

I

SOCRATES, who was born 2500 years ago, can be called the patron saint of all who want to know the truth about life. Besides being one of the clearest thinkers ever born, he was tremendously strong, fearless, a soldier, and most lovable. He was short, squat, bearded, broad, and very ugly, with a snub nose, wide nostrils, and thick lips; yet young people flocked around him, and he enjoyed their company.

When he was forty, Socrates was told that the oracle at Delphi, the accepted voice of religious truth, said that no one at Athens was wiser than he. Staggered by this, he devoted the rest of his life to an attempt to find out what human beings were doing on earth, and why they had been put here. The conclusions he came to were so disturbing to the official beliefs that important folk became very angry, and accused him of misleading the young. Finally, when affairs at Athens had gone wrong and people wanted a scapegoat, Socrates was publicly tried and sentenced to death. He might have got off if he had apologized, but his robust defence was thought to make matters worse, and at the age of seventy he became one of the many martyrs in the cause of truth and justice.

II

Of Socrates's early life we know very little. Our knowledge of him is drawn from two main sources: his friend and pupil, Plato, who kept detailed records of his conversations and doings: and the historian Xenophon. Each presents a different character, and, since Plato's is by far the more vivid and interesting, some people, thinking that he exaggerated through hero-worship, have preferred Xenophon's flatter account. I take the opposite view, for two reasons. Xenophon was much less gifted and intelligent than Plato, and so saw less in Socrates. More important, he thought that Socrates should never have been brought to trial, and is therefore at pains to hide his eccentricities and make him appear as ordinary as possible. If Socrates had been as Xenophon makes out, it is safe to say that he would have died in his bed.

He was born at Athens in 470 or 469 B.C. His father was a stone-cutter, called Sophroniscus, his mother's name was Phaenarete. They were humble folk, but not really poor, or Socrates could not have done his national service in a branch of the infantry which called for a property qualification. As a child he had religious training and seems to have been initiated into certain of the mysteries. In his 'teens he met the philosophers Parmenides and Zeno, and read the works of Anaxagoras.

It is important not to be put off by the word philosopher. Every boy or girl, indeed every child, who is moved by wonder to ask a question about the world has taken the first step towards being a philosopher. Philosophy—which in Socrates' day included many of the questions now asked by science— is a search for first principles. What are we? What is life? Who or what put us here? What are time and space? How far can we rely on what our senses tell us about the world?

III

The Athens into which Socrates was born was not the capital city of all Greece, but one of a number of small separate states. At his birth she had just repulsed the invading Persian armies, and, under the great Pericles, was approaching the short period of supremacy which is one of civilization's highest peaks. In literature, in drama, sculpture, architecture, and philosophy, the Athenians reached a level which has never been surpassed. Their knowledge of science was rudimentary—though they made some brilliant guesses: their political character was untrustworthy: and the foundations of their state were insecure and based on slavery. Women had a very subordinate part to play. Yet this was a golden age of the mind, maybe the greatest of all, and Socrates lived at its height.

In 431 Athens went to war with a confederation of small states led by Sparta. Socrates had already won fame as a philosopher, and had worsted in argument a celebrated professional, Protagoras, who took fees for instructing pupils in philosophy and virtue. In this year a friend of his put his question to the Delphic Oracle and got the reply already recorded. From that point on Socrates abandoned all other business and gave himself up to the service of truth.

Still, his first duty to Athens was as a soldier. In the war against Sparta he showed not only courage but astonishing indifference to hardship. Alcibiades, a young friend who later went to the bad, told how Socrates saved his life and should have had the decoration which he was given.

"No other man," Alcibiades goes on, "showed such endurance or indifference to bodily hardships. One day, when the frost was at its worst, and nobody left his tent, or, if he had to, went all wrapped up and muffled and with sheepskins on his feet, Socrates went out in the cloak he wore every day, and crossed the ice barefoot."

On another occasion, in the summer, he stood meditating from one dawn all through the day and night till the next, then said his prayers to the rising Sun and went away. In the disastrous retreat from Delium, Socrates was "absolutely unperturbed, stalking about . . . stiff as a heron, and coolly eyeing friend and foe. He came through safe, needless to say. Men of his type are hardly ever touched."

The Athenian general, Laches, said there would have been no defeat if all had been as brave as Socrates.

IV

At some time in the ten years after the start of the war in 431, Socrates married Xanthippe. This unfortunate woman's name has gone down to history as the proverbial type of shrew and nagging wife. There is no contemporary evidence for this. The legend was probably created by the sort of people who like to belittle great men by making out that they were henpecked or suffered petty and trivial misfortunes like the rest of us.

In 423 Socrates was ridiculed by the comic dramatist Aristophanes, who had been a friend of his. In *The Clouds* Socrates figures as a public nuisance, hanging in the air in a sort of basket, so that his ideas should not be corrupted by any contact with earth and reality. His disciples are represented as ragged and dotty, busying themselves with spooks—a parody of Socrates's teaching about the soul, which was incomprehensible to most of his countrymen. One thing is clear from this attack. Socrates must have been exceedingly well known in Athens, so that a reference to him would be as well recognized as—for instance—one to a TV personality today. Aristophanes' audience was the whole populace, for the theatre in Athens was free and a part of public life: there would be no point in caricaturing anyone they would not recognize. The caricature probably had no malice. Socrates, when he referred to it later, showed no resentment, merely saying that he didn't identify himself with 'a certain Socrates' pictured on the stage: and Aristophanes had appeared in one of Plato's finest works, *The Symposium*, an account of a wonderful supper party, with the young man who was to be Socrates' evil genius, Alcibiades.

Alcibiades had brilliant gifts, and his affection and admiration for Socrates brought out the best in him. By degrees, however, he succumbed to the temptations which his gifts brought him, and avoided the man who would, he well knew, have spoken his mind about them. It might have been better if Socrates had not saved his life at Potidaea. Alcibiades afterwards acquired great influence over the Athenian military party. He presently led an expedition against Syracuse, only to be recalled on a charge of having taken part in blasphemous parodies of religious ceremonies. Rather than stand his trial, he escaped, and was condemned to death in his absence. His retort was simple. He at once went over to the enemy, and gave the Spartans his knowledge of Athenian military secrets. Athens lost the war, and the Spartan conqueror Lysander appointed thirty men to govern the city. Their misrule earned them their title of the Thirty Tyrants: and two of them were former friends of Socrates. Thus those who disliked him now had something solid to go on. Look at the way his young friends turned out! Enemies, traitors to the state!

As a matter of fact the Thirty did not like Socrates any better. Wishing to get a handle against him, they ordered him and four other men to arrest and accuse an innocent man. Socrates refused, and would probably have lost his life if the city had not risen against the Thirty and driven them out. This was only a respite. As soon as the city had settled down, Socrates was put on trial for 'corrupting the young' (that is, misleading them and teaching them to doubt the traditional beliefs of their elders, with the sort of results seen in the case of Alcibiades and his like), 'disbelieving in the official gods, and teaching the existence of strange new gods'.

Unfortunately for Socrates, the real charge, that he was directly responsible for the traitors, could not be mentioned in court, owing to an amnesty declared after the driving out of the Tyrants. This meant that Socrates could not reply to it, but had to face a huge unspoken prejudice.

V

Before we come to his trial and defence, let us see, very briefly, the sort of thing Socrates had been doing to arouse such enmity. The possessor of a clear, logical mind, he applied it to matters of every kind, religious and practical. His method was to seek out the persons who were thought to be authorities on whatever subject he was interested in, and ask them a series of questions.

For example, a self-righteous and complacent man named Euthyphro claimed to know what was impious and what was holy. Socrates asked him for guidance, as he himself was accused of impiety, so it was vital to him to know. Euthyphro replied that what was pleasing to the gods was holy, and what was not pleasing to them was impious. Socrates at once pointed out that the gods differed among themselves. They couldn't differ on matters of fact, such as whether one thing was heavier than another: that was settled by weighing them. It must be about abstract matters, such as what things are good or bad, just and unjust.

Euthyphro then amended his definition. "That is holy which all the gods love, and that is impious which they all hate." Socrates still seemed puzzled. "Is the holy loved by the gods because it is holy, or is it holy because it is loved?" And, when Euthyphro didn't understand, Socrates explained the difference between active and passive, between what sees and what is seen, what loves and what is loved. We do not see a thing because it is seen: it is seen because we see it. In the same way, if we love a thing, it is loved because we love it. So, if Euthyphro was right in saying that all the gods love holiness, they love it because it is holy. It is not holy because they love it.

Euthyphro was now forced to admit that what was pleasing to the gods because they loved it was pleasing to them from the very fact that they loved it. On one side was the sort of thing that was loved because the gods loved it: on the other, something that was loved because it was the sort of thing the gods ought to love. Pressed to restate his argument, he caught at a suggestion from Socrates that holiness was a part of justice, and added that it was the part which concerned man's care for the gods.

Socrates soon demolished this. What sort of care? Care that made them better, like a groom's for his horse? Not that sort at all, replied Euthyphro: I mean the sort of care which slaves take of their masters.

"I see. A kind of service we pay to the gods."

"Quite."

"What would you say is benefited by the service of a doctor? Health?"

"Of course."

"In the same way, shipwrights do services to ships, and architects to houses?"

"That's right."

"Tell me then, my dear friend, what work will our service to the gods help? What will they gain by using us as servants?"

Stumped by this, Euthyphro said that holiness consisted in saying prayers to the gods and making sacrifices to them. Socrates made him admit that this was perilously like bargaining.

"Is holiness then a kind of commerce between gods and men?"

Euthyphro didn't like this at all. He liked it even less when Socrates showed that men could not benefit the gods, and went back crossly to his original definition: holiness was what was dear to the gods. He then remembered an important appointment somewhere else, and took himself off.

Socrates' discussions were by no means always destructive, like this one. Most of them reach solid and positive conclusions. But we can easily see how this steady and bland questioning

Socrates drank the cup of hemlock, which was
the painless method of execution

must have irritated people, the more so when young disciples imitated it and cross-examined their elders.

VI

The court which tried Socrates was not like a modern court of law. The jury numbered 500, and the verdict depended on a majority. The accusation, prepared by a man called Anytus, nominally claimed the death penalty, but its real purpose was to frighten Socrates and drive him into voluntary exile, ridding the city of its nuisance. To prosecute, Anytus chose a religious fanatic, one Meletus.

Socrates' defence is one of the great documents in the history of the human mind. It goes far beyond the ethics of a pagan civilization, and, in its reference to a single god, anticipates some of the teachings of Christianity. Asking the court to forgive him if he used simple and ordinary speech, he protested first of all against prejudice and lies. He had never spoken of the queer matters ridiculed by Aristophanes, never undertaken to teach anybody, never demanded payment for what he said. Far from being impious, he had set out on his life's work because he took in full seriousness what the Delphic Oracle had said. Accordingly he had sought out all who seemed wise, politicians, poets, craftsmen, yet had found they were even less wise than he; and so had stirred up many enemies.

He then proceeded to cross-question his accuser, soon had him tied up in knots, and demolished every point of the charge. Turning to the general quarrel between himself and the people, he asserted that, far from doing them harm by obeying the inner voice of his conscience, his *daemon*, he had conferred great benefit on them. He had a stronger religious faith than any of his accusers. "I leave the verdict to you and to God."

In spite of this, the jury by a small majority found him guilty. In Athenian law it was then open to Socrates to suggest an alternative punishment. This odd-sounding law generally worked well, because, if the condemned man proposed too light a penalty, the court would enforce the other. Socrates claimed that, having done no wrong, but conferred a great benefit on Athens, he should be supported for the rest of his life at the State's charge.

387

Incensed by what seemed to them sheer effrontery, the court condemned him to death.

The nobility of his final speech has been an inspiration to free men ever since he made it. Death had no terror: it did not run so fast as wickedness. If it were but a dreamless sleep, what sleep was happier? If, as we were told, it joined us to the great men of earlier times, how good to meet and question them.

"Sirs, you ought therefore to be of good cheer with regard to death, and to consider that this one thing is certainly true. Nothing evil befalls a good man, nor are his affairs neglected by the gods. That which has now befallen me has not come by chance, but I can see clearly now that it is better for me to die and to be set free from material things. This is why my accustomed sign" (his *daemon*) "nowhere forbade me. . . . And now the time has come to depart, I to die, you to live; but which of us goes to a better thing is unknown to all save God."

VII

Usually condemned men were put to death within twenty-four hours. Socrates, because the city was in a state of cere-monial purification, had a month's grace. His friends were allowed to visit him freely, and he spent the time in the kind of conversation dearest to his heart. His friends wanted to rescue him: he refused. The law must be obeyed.

His last day he spent in telling his friends about the immor-tality of the soul. He was delighted when two of them argued and would not accept what he said without a rational proof. Then, in the finest flight his mind had ever taken, he gave them the grounds for his belief.

The officer who announced the hour of death thanked Socrates for all his courtesy and submission, and burst into tears on saying farewell. A man brought in the cup of hemlock, which was the painless method of execution. Socrates drank it, walked about for a little until his legs were heavy, then lay down, and, reminding his friend Crito that they owed a sacrifice to the god of medicine, covered his face with his cloak and died.

George Stephenson

BUILDER OF THE LOCOMOTIVE

Arthur Catherall

I

A T ten o'clock one summer morning, more than a century and a half ago, a cannon boomed in Liverpool and for a moment stilled the excited chatter of many thousands. They were people who had gathered in that great city to watch the opening of the miracle of the day — the railway between Liverpool and Manchester. The Prime Minister, the famous Duke of Wellington, conqueror of Napoleon, had come from London with many lords and ladies to see for himself this new wonder of the age.

Bands were playing. There was one outside the station to play *See the conquering hero come*, there was a band inside the station, and one on the first coach of the Prime Minister's train. Lord Wellington's coach was more like an Indian pavilion than a coach, its sides were elaborately decorated and gilt pillars supported a magnificent red canopy.

Eight trains were to make the run to Manchester. Seven trains carrying guests on one track, and the eighth, driven by George Stephenson himself, was to carry the Prime Minister, chosen guests, and railway directors on the other track.

Safety valves hissed and the engineers waited nervously for the signal. Every precaution against accidents had been taken. The whole length of the double track had been patrolled to make sure that no careless worker had left a pick, spade or barrow on the lines. Even the cross-over points had been removed to make the line doubly safe. So many people had opposed the railway, insisting it would bring disaster, blight to crops, ruination to farmers, and death through boiler explosions to drivers, that no chances were to be taken.

A crashing of cannon, a blare of music from the band on the

389

State train, and George Stephenson allowed steam to enter the engine cylinders. To a pompous chuff-chuffing the 'Northumbrian' moved ahead, and for a few moments a silence fell over the great crowd, to be followed by deafening cheers as one after the other the remaining seven trains, carrying over 700 chosen guests, also began to move off.

Through the gas-lit tunnel which Stephenson had cut through the rock on which part of Liverpool stands, the trains sped, slowly gathering speed until, when they were finally out into the open country, they were moving faster than the fastest stage-coach had ever travelled. It was an exhilarating experience for many, though some of the ladies were frightened. They seemed to be hurtling along at a very dangerous speed—though any slow goods train of today would probably have passed them with ease.

To show what his engines could do, George slowed down the 'Northumbrian' until one after the other the seven trains on the other line passed him, the guests cheering the famous Duke of Wellington as he sat in his coach, bowing and acknowledging their salutes. Once the last train was ahead Stephenson, a smile on his face, opened the 'Northumbrian's' regulator little by little and very soon they caught first one and then the next of the trains ahead, until finally they were leading again. Such speed had never been thought possible before, and when the trains halted to take on water and fuel at Parkside station, half-way between Liverpool and Manchester, there were scenes of the wildest enthusiasm. The 17 miles had been covered in 56 minutes, an amazing speed of 18 m.p.h.

II

It was then, in the midst of the rejoicings and congratulations that tragedy, the first real tragedy of the railways, marred the day; but it gave George Stephenson an opportunity of showing just what his new engines and the railways he had fought so hard for, could do.

Many of the guests had got down on to the railway track, while the engineer of the 'Rocket' drove his train up and down to show how easily he could go either backwards or forwards.

The danger of standing between the rails was not apparent to

The train driven by George Stephenson himself
was to carry the Prime Minister

the excited guests, and a number of them were crowding alongside the Duke of Wellington's coach when suddenly there was a rumble and a hissing. At once there was a chorus of warning cries:

"It's another train. Get off the track! Get off the track!"

The men who a moment before had been awaiting their opportunity to shake hands with the Duke of Wellington, turned and to their horror saw the tall white funnel and yellow boiler of the 'Rocket' as that engine bore down on them.

There was an immediate scramble for safety, but Mr. Huskisson, Member of Parliament for Liverpool, either did not realize the danger soon enough or was too petrified to move. Too late he tried to get clear as the 'Rocket' thundered on through the station with a great clatter of wheels and the hiss of steam.

In all that distinguished company there was no doctor. George Stephenson came down to see what was wrong.

"He mun be takken to a doctor at once," he said, his North Country voice stilling the clamour. "Pick him up, gentle-like. I'll tak him to Manchester."

He had to repeat himself, for those standing about were too stunned to understand just what George meant. That the injured man could be rushed to Manchester by train had not occurred to them.

The bandsmen in the front vehicle of the State train were hurriedly ordered out, the injured man was laid gently on a seat, and George climbed on to the 'Northumbrian'. He opened the throttle slowly to spare Mr. Huskisson any jerk, but very quickly the throttle was at its widest, and in the following 25 minutes that little engine established itself as the fastest piece of man-made mechanism the world had ever known. It hauled the unfortunate Huskisson to Eccles, just outside Manchester, at an average speed of 36 miles per hour. The fastest post chaise would have taken more than twice the time the 'Northumbrian' took, and the journey would not have been half so smooth.

That desperate dash to try to save a man's life proved far more than any arguments could, what George Stephenson had been saying for some time, that steam trains could move quickly and in safety. The great engineers of the land had scoffed at the idea of steam trains, other than for pulling waggons of coal at coal mines. Any speed of more than three or four miles per hour, the experts insisted, would result in the boilers of the engines bursting, there would be derailments; cattle in the fields would be so frightened that cows would refuse to give milk; while it was said that the smoke given off by such trains would blight all the crops.

III

That Stephenson had not been too successful in his arguments with the experts was due to his lack of education. Not until he was eighteen years of age did he go to school. Even then it was a very poor kind of school, attended at night after his day's work at the coal mine was done, and he paid a penny per lesson.

The son of a very poor man, George Stephenson was born on June 9, 1781 in a one-roomed cottage in the Tyneside village of Wylam. His father earned 12s. a week, and as there were eight of them in that one-roomed house it is easy to understand why there was no money to pay even the 2d or 3d per week which attendance at a Dame school cost towards the end of the 18th century.

But by the time he was fifteen years of age his interest in engines, and his study of them, resulted in his being appointed chief fireman at a coal mine at a wage of a shilling a day. At seventeen years of age he became an engineman, watching one of the water-pumps the task of which was to keep the coalmines free of the water that drained into the mine galleries.

With no knowledge from books, George learned how his pump worked by taking it to pieces in his spare time, and re-assembling it. His understanding of the engine mechanism finally resulted in his getting his great opportunity.

At a nearby colliery, where at great expense a new shaft had been made, one of the modern pumping-engines was being installed. Built by the great engineer, Smeaton, it was supposed to be the very last word in pumping-engines. George went to watch the men who were assembling the new machinery. He stood and took in the details, then to the amazement and indignation of the engineers he calmly announced that this mighty new pumping-engine was defective and would most certainly not work. It was like a new boy at school explaining that the Headmaster's arithmetic was faulty.

IV

The pump was finally finished and tried. It would not work! The engineers searched for faults, and could find none. In the meantime the water in the new mine shaft rose day after day. The mine manager grew more and more worried. So long as the pumping-engine was idle, so long was it impossible to get coal from the new mine.

The makers of the engine were sent for. They could find no fault with the engine, nor could they make it work. Finally they announced that the engine would have to be dismantled and taken back to the works. It was a bitter blow for the mine manager, and for all the men who were waiting to work at the new colliery.

Somebody remembered that George Stephenson had said *months before* that the engine would not work, and remembered something else: George had said he could make the engine right, and drain the coal pit within a week. He was sent for. George is said to have been on his way to church when Ralph Dodds, manager of the mine, stopped him to ask if he really thought he could make the new pumping-engine work.

In those days a mine manager was a very important man indeed; he could engage a man or discharge him, and there was no one to say a word about it. George was no doubt startled to have a man like Ralph Dodds seek him out in this way, but he recovered his self-possession after a moment and said:

"Yes, sir, I think I could make the pump work."

The manager of High Pit wasted no time. George was to set to work at once, and Dodds concluded with a promise:

"The engineers hereabouts are all beaten, and if you succeed in accomplishing what they cannot do, you may depend on it I will make you a man for life."

George Stephenson must have been cheered and startled by a remark like that. If he made the engine work, he had won a powerful friend. If he failed, then he would be the laughing stock of the engineers and of everyone else. No one would ever believe again that he knew anything about engines.

On the Monday morning George was at the pit early. The engineering experts were there, and far from pleased at the idea that a youngster like Stephenson, a self-taught engineer, with no workshop background, should be given a chance with the engine which had beaten every one of them.

They stood about, sometimes scoffing sometimes frowning as they watched this youngster doing things to the vitals of Smeaton's engine.

George altered the water injector cock, he raised the cistern by ten feet, he insisted on doubling the steam pressure. One of the alterations had been expressly forbidden by the inventor of the engine, the great Newcomen. One writer says there were bits of wire and oddments about the engine which may have given it a Heath Robinson look, but by Wednesday morning George was ready to try out his changes.

Again there was a collection of experts there to watch, and there must have been a rather frightening silence as George moved over to turn on the steam. Some of the men backed away to a safer distance, remembering that there was twice the steam pressure recommended.

The steam was turned on, and for a few moments there was pandemonium as the watchers scattered. The big pumping-engine came to life with a roar and a clatter which shook the very foundations of the engine-room.

Ralph Dodds, the mine manager, gave an anguished yell as the ground continued to tremble and the clattering roar of the pump made the very air vibrate.

"Why, she was better as she was. Now she'll knock the engine-house down," he roared.

There were grins and nods from the experts, but young Stephenson was already busy making an adjustment here, another there, and within a few moments the rattle and roar steadied, died down, and soon the big pump was running smoothly. What was more, water was spurting in a great column from the pump pipe.

All that day, throughout the night, and throughout Thursday the pump continued steadily lifting water from the flooded shaft. By Friday morning the pit which had been flooded for months, was almost dry, and the same afternoon miners went down to the bottom.

George Stephenson had said he would pump the pit dry within a week, and he had made good his prophecy. What it saved the owners of the High Pit no one today knows; it must have been many hundreds of pounds. They rewarded George with a gift of £10, and a holiday. He had never before possessed £10 and probably had never had a holiday. When he came back from his holiday he was put in charge of the engine he had made work, and some years later was appointed chief engine-wright of the group of collieries to which the High Pit belonged. Ralph Dodds had kept his promise, and put George's feet on the first rung of the ladder which was to take him to a pinnacle where he was acknowledged both in this and other counties as the master mind where steam engines and railways were concerned.

V

Two great things, in addition to his skill as an engineer made him so successful: his courage, and his ability to plan carefully ahead. He was a man of peace, but if there was a fight to be fought, George would fight, and the story of the one fist fight in his life is worth telling. For here again courage was not enough, so he planned his campaign.

As a brakesman at the Black Callerton pit his job was to work the big engine which lowered the cages down into the mine and brought them up again, sometimes filled with tubs of coal, sometimes with a human load of miners. It was a highly skilled job if the cages were to be worked smoothly.

One day a man named Ned Nelson accused George of jerking them badly. Ned was a great hulking brute of a man, feared by many. After swearing at the young brakesman he threatened to knock his head off for his lack of skill.

"You'll get kicked in the shins as you deserve if you go on like this," George told him, and there were gasps from the men around. Nelson was startled, then thrusting out his unshaven chin he asked mockingly:

"Kicked did you say? Who by? Who'll do the kicking?"

"I'll do it," George assured him, at which Nelson guffawed scornfully. He was a burly man in the prime of life, and toughened by years at the coal face while George, though big for his age, was still only a youth.

"There's nobbut one way to settle this!" Nelson roared. "Just one way!" and George nodded agreement. Mining was a rough trade, and the men were rough. Arguments were seldom settled by words, and Nelson's words were a challenge to fight.

A day was fixed, and Ned Nelson went into special training, taking some time off work to get fit. George's sympathisers could not believe he could have been fool enough to agree to fight. The burly Ned Nelson had had many fights, and more than one unlucky opponent had finished up with serious injuries.

A huge crowd assembled in the Dolly Pit field to watch the contest which was to be fought out according to the rough and ready prize-fighting rules of the day. A rope ring was made and the fighters stripped to the waist.

There were many who sympathised with George when they advanced to begin the fight. George was slight by the side of Nelson. The latter was a great barrel-chested man, with corded muscles which made George Stephenson look even more puny.

Nelson rushed in when the signal for the first round was given. His great arms swung like pistons; his bunched fists, hard from years of work underground, were aiming to knock this young brakesman out for the count in a matter of seconds.

Somehow the big fists only thrashed at the air. George swayed this way and that, moving lithely for round after round while Ned Nelson wasted his strength in mad bull-rushes. In the middle of the third round George did not sidestep when Nelson rushed in. Instead he planted the first of a barrage of shrewd blows.

At the end of the seventh round a gasping, tottering Nelson, one eye closed, and his ribs pink from the hammering he had taken held up his hands to show he had had enough.

George's friends who had thought to have carried him away, perhaps badly injured, crowded round to congratulate him. He pushed them away as the beaten Nelson came across, thrusting out a huge hand:

"Will ye shake hands with me, Stephenson?" he asked, and George sealed the beginning of a long friendship with a firm and hearty grip.

VI

George won his fight with Nelson as he won many another fight, whether with canal owners who did not want to see a railway robbing them of high rates, or with a patch of quicksand which threatened a tunnel, by sitting down and thinking how his foe had to be dealt with. He knew Nelson was big and strong, therefore he had to keep out of his way until the great strength was worn down. He had planned his campaign and he won.

In much the same way he planned the invention of his safety lamp for miners, and by one of those rare coincidences, he produced a safety lamp practically identical to the one invented by Sir Humphry Davy. George tested a safety lamp at Killingworth, where he was engineer, four days before the distinguished scientist Sir Humphry Davy demonstrated to the Royal Society his miner's safety lamp. The two lamps were almost alike, yet neither man knew of the other.

George Stephenson began work at eight years of ago earning twopence a day for looking after cattle. At the end of his life he had seen a dream come true, a land criss-crossed by railways, with trains running at speeds which the great engineers and scientists had once declared were not only impossible, but far too dangerous even to attempt. A committee of the House of Commons, supported by experts, turned down a bill for a line from Liverpool to Manchester, asserting that such a line could never be built over the notorious Chat Moss, a great swamp. The same men lived to see the Moss conquered. For that line George promised to attempt to run trains steadily at ten miles an hour. To try to save the life of Huskisson he drove his 'Northumbrian' at 36 miles an hour, and made the impossible, possible.

George Stephenson did not invent the steam engine; he did not invent railways, for they were in use for horse-drawn waggons when he was a boy. What he did was to put a steam engine on wheels, put it on an improved railway, and make swift, safe travel possible in this and many countries throughout the world. On August 18, 1848, he died. The young man who had paid threepence a week for lessons when he was in his teens had become famous and rich.

Sir Christopher Wren

AN ENGLISH LEONARDO

Gilbert Harding

I

IN the year 1666 (one of the easiest dates to remember) the cry, 'London's burning!' echoed late one September night through the narrow, evil-smelling, timbered alleys of old London. We still echo that cry, 'London's burning!' in an old song and go on to offer somewhat obvious but no doubt well-intended advice, 'Pour on water! Pour on water!' The anxious citizens, I am quite sure, did pour on water, hastening down to the darkly running Thames with what containers they could muster, but the conflagration was far too fierce to be checked.

The fire, the Great Fire of London, continued for about a week. How it began we shall never know with any certainty for, in the face of such an overwhelming disaster, rumours spread as quickly as the fire. It was easy to say, and many people did, that the fire had been started by England's enemies (then the Dutch), anticipating the sabotage and war against civilians which, it is generally assumed, only our vile century has practised. Certainly atom bombers could hardly have done better. On September 8 some 200,000 refugees were encamped among their few remaining goods and chattels in the open fields 'towards Islington and Highgate'. Below them were the still smouldering ruins of London; 13,000 houses had been destroyed, together with the Guildhall, the Customs House, the Royal Exchange, the halls of 44 City companies, 87 parish churches and the cathedral church of St. Paul's itself.

One man, then thirty-four years of age, must have contemplated the destruction with much the same feelings of compassion mingled with a challenging sense of opportunity as our forefather, Noah, surveyed the old world after the havoc of

399

the Flood. He was Christopher Wren, who at the early age of twenty-one had been appointed Surveyor-General. A new, magnificent London could now arise, phoenix-like, from these smouldering ruins and for this splendid city Wren already had his dreams. Instead of the huddle of houses, the dark alleys, the dens and slums that had, only that year, harboured the most terrible of plagues, he foresaw long, open vistas, radiating from a new, central cathedral church of St. Paul's and, at the end of the vistas, beautiful parish churches with their elegant steeples gleaming in the morning sunshine.

II

London, and the area around St. Paul's, suffered a destruction no less horrible than that of the Great Fire in the year 1940. For many years afterwards it was possible to wander among scenes of desolation and see broken walls crowned with ragwort, ruins full of dumped junk, old cans and bedsteads, and haunted by thin, poor, hungry cats. Happily today Christopher Wren's masterpiece and greatest memorial, St. Paul's, still stands: the sight would gladden his heart but Wren would have been contemptuous of the rubble still around nearly twenty years later. For, within a *week* of the Great Fire, Wren had quite detailed, wide-sweeping plans for restoration ready to lay before the King—King Charles II.

In one respect the City of London was uncommonly fortunate. Charles II may have had few virtues but he had interests other than 'Sweet Nell of Old Drury': legend says he was catching butterflies with Nell when the Dutch ships were sailing up the Medway. I doubt it; over the Great Fire, and the problems of rebuilding his capital city, Charles II showed imagination and a great sense of civic responsibility. The measures he advocated, both for checking the conflagration and for relieving the confusion and distress by which it was followed, were intelligent, far-sighted and extremely courageous. To a taste for architecture he added an interest in town planning.

Christopher Wren, in those September days of 1666, when the stink of charred wood was everywhere, was exceedingly fortunate. Fate had given him the greatest opportunity ever given to any man, and he served a monarch who was likely to be both approachable and receptive to his grandiose proposals.

Had King Charles occupied the position of an absolute monarch (which otherwise it is exceedingly fortunate that he did not) he and Wren might well have rebuilt a London of supreme and lasting splendour. But that was not to be.

Then, as today, the men of vision had their wings clipped by 'the obstinate Averseness of a great Part of the Citizens to alter'; the red-tapers; the little, puffed-up men of brief authority; the downright greedy; the anti-social 'Unwilling to give up their Properties, tho' for a Time only, into the hands of public Trustees,' all these bone-heads made sure that a splendid opportunity was allowed to pass and a duller, less impressive, compromise resulted.

Certainly tremendous improvements to London were effected in detail. '*Si monumentum requiris, circumspice*'—'For his monument, just look around you'—was the epitaph inscribed upon the tomb of Sir Christopher Wren in his own St. Paul's. No other man has left so great an impression upon a nation's capital: from the Monument to the Great Fire, to the pedestal upon which the statue of King Charles I stands at the top of 'his own Whitehall': from the great St. Paul's dominating the City to the (alas!) shells of City Churches, blitzed but now being restored, there are many lasting memorials to this remarkable man, Sir Christopher Wren, their architect, a 'man of heaven-inspired projects'.

Besides the great and noble cathedral, Wren was responsible for 50 new parish churches, 36 City company halls and a Customs House. For all this his fee was £300!

III

What manner of man was this great architect?

The material on the life of Sir Christopher Wren is meagre but, when a story about him has survived, it always gives a consistent and vivid picture of a man who was remarkably gifted in so many ways, an inquisitive man, a man who loved to experiment. Said a contemporary, "I must affirm that since the time of Archimedes there scarce ever met in one man in so great a perfection such a mechanical hand and so philosophical a mind."

After the Great Fire there was the minor but difficult problem of clearing away the ruins quickly and safely. The great shell of old St. Paul's, in particular, presented many difficulties. Wren had been interested in, and experimented with, gunpowder for some time. He had carried out experiments upon the unlikely value of explosives for cleaning sooty and smoky chimneys, experiments I would dearly like to have watched from a safe distance. To the consternation of the City Fathers he proposed to blow up the fire-charred walls by using nicely calculated charges of gunpowder and his first attempt was highly successful.

The walls rose a few feet in the air and then subsided into neat heaps. But one day, when Wren was not on the site, his second-in-command thought he would have a go. There was an almighty roar and the citizens for hundreds of yards around were bombarded with bits and boulders. Wren was much reviled and it was made very clear to him that the use of gunpowder must cease forthwith. And here we see the temper of Wren's ingenious mind. He was not daunted in the slightest. Having enjoyed a classical education at Westminster School under the great Dr. Busby, he remembered that the ancients managed well enough without gunpowder; they used great battering rams upon the walls of besieged cities. So, within a few days, the dangerous walls were again coming down in clouds of dust before the assaults of mighty battering rams.

IV

Like so many of England's great men, Wren was a parson's son and was born in the rectory at East Knoyle, Wiltshire, on October 31, in the year of our Lord, 1632. His mother, Mary, died when he was a little boy and his elder sister, Susan, was as much a mother to him as a young girl could be. Susan married when Christopher was eleven, marrying William Holder, a mathematician, and a man who was to have a great influence upon his little and, probably, desolate, brother-in-law.

Christopher was to live for ninety-one crowded years: few lives have been so fully lived for he was an 'early starter'. (I hate the word 'prodigy'; it suggests some repulsive and priggish, old-before-his-time swot of a schoolboy.) He left school at fourteen and spent some time in the study of anatomy with Dr. Scarburgh, then going on to Wadham College, Oxford.

No other man than Christopher Wren has left so great
an impression upon a nation's capital

He was Professor of Astronomy at Oxford before he was twenty-eight years old.

Wren was no dry-as-dust, absent-minded professor. He would have made the most superb young uncle for any lively schoolboy with an open mind and a thirsting curiosity about most things.

How wide were the man's interests!

Before he was twenty-one he was something of an authority on the anatomy of the brain. At the request of his king, Charles, he produced some remarkable drawings of insects microscopically enlarged, for he possessed great ability with his pencil. Then again he invented a 'planting instrument', the forerunner of the farmer's drill, a machine 'being drawn by a horse over ploughed and harrowed land that shall plant corn equally without waste'. At one time or another he engaged his active mind upon the problem of obtaining fresh water at sea, carried out experiments upon the purifying and fumigating of sick-rooms—at that time something well worth doing, and was among the first men to experiment in the transfusion of blood, succeeding in transferring blood from one animal to another.

Christopher Wren was the English Leonardo da Vinci: the complete man, the specialist in all things. Today our men of science follow the most narrow of lines: they do not even know everything about flowers, or insects, they know everything about *one* flower, *one* insect. For him knowledge was an ever widening funnel; today, unfortunately, the funnel points the other way towards narrowness.

In physics, medicine, anatomy, agriculture, astronomy, Christopher Wren was always experimenting, always asking questions and trying to find the answer. He worked for some time upon a weather-cock that would record, as it answered the winds, the story of the weather.

Wren was one of the moving spirits in the foundation of the Royal Society, a circle of inquiring men who met from time to time in his rooms when he was a teacher at Gresham College, London.

He was, indeed, first and foremost a man of science, his interest in architecture coming quite late in his life. Let a contemporary praise him: "As one of whom it were doubtful whether he was most to be commended for the divine felicity of his genius or for the sweet humanity of his disposition: formerly, as a boy prodigy, now as a man a miracle, nay, even something superhuman!"

Even allowing for the floridity of that florid age, that is praise indeed.

There is no question that Wren began the research or, in fact, made many vital inventions that others later exploited. Again hear the voice of his times, "I know very well that some of them" (his inventions) "he did only start and design, and that they have since been carried to perfection by the industry of others, yet it is reasonable that the original invention should be ascribed to the true author"—Christopher Wren.

By nature Wren was shy and retiring: a delicate boy, he became a man of small stature.

Who, today, would ask the professor of anatomy at Oxford to design a great university building? Yet Wren cheerfully, and confidently—and most successfully—designed the chapel for Pembroke College, Cambridge, and the Sheldonian Theatre at Oxford, before he undertook his life's work upon the new St. Paul's and the restored City of London.

Today. I am sorry to say, that could not possibly happen. Committees, professional associations, planning authorities, trade unions, all would have something to say. Everyone now seems to be in the straight-jacket of his own narrow job. Unless you have 'trained', got a few letters after your name, and learnt the technique of something or other in an organized way and at the right places, you cannot hope (and few people try) to do anything else. We have no amateurs: indeed the word has become almost a word of contempt.

What a pity! Boys and girls who want to write, act, broadcast, produce films or plays, are far too inclined to wait until someone comes along to teach them how to do it and, after some examinations, present them with a piece of paper saying pompously that they now can. It would be so much better if (like Sir Christopher Wren) they got on with it, if they just started to write or act, and took every opportunity they could to *do* what they want to do. Of course teachers and instructors can help but you teach yourself most by practical experience, by getting on with your chosen interest.

Wren could draw; he knew much of mechanics and something of engineering. He had travelled a little and seen the palaces and churches of Paris but I doubt if, before he was thirty, he had ever designed anything much more ambitious than a telescope. What admirable courage, then, what a superb belief in himself, Wren displayed when he suddenly turned his hand to designing great public buildings and the re-planning of a whole capital city!

He was the Great Amateur.

V

The building of Wren's masterpiece, St. Paul's, was not begun until 1675. The labour went on during the 1680s and the 1690s. By 1697 the choir and the lower parts of the dome structure were completed, though the form of the west end and of the high visible part of the dome had not yet been finally determined. No wonder Wren lived to such a great age; it was almost necessary that he should.

As an old man, hobbling around London on a stick, fifty or more years after the Great Fire, he might feel that he had been forced to compromise, to make the best of a bad job. London was not his London, not the London he and King Charles II had hoped to see rising from the ashes of the Fire. But the spires of his many churches now pointed to the sky, dominating the City in a way we cannot now conceive, because our high cliffs of office-buildings dwarf them and hem them in. His great cathedral, pomp in stone, crowned all.

Wren had more than good reason to feel a sense of achievement: his lasting monuments were everywhere: he had only to look about him.

Wilbur and Orville Wright

CONQUERORS OF THE AIR

Arthur Catherall

I

ONE mid-December day in the year 1903 two young men faced one another on the smooth, wind-swept sands of Kitty Hawk, North Carolina. One had a coin balanced on his thumbnail and, when the other called, he flipped the coin into the air. When it came to rest at their feet Orville Wright looked at his brother and said:

"Go ahead, Wilbur. You called right. You get first chance."

If they were excited neither of them showed it; though what they hoped was going to happen in the next few minutes might make them both famous, and probably rich. Without another word they turned towards their dream child.

It was an odd-looking contraption of spars and frame-works covered with fabric. It resembled our ideas of an aeroplane only in that it had wings and an engine, plus two propellers. The engine had been made in the back room of the Wrights' cycle repair shop at Dayton, more than 500 miles away, even as the crow flies. The propellers, too, were home-made.

There were no landing wheels; the aeroplane being perched on a small trolley which, using materials from the shop, ran on two bicycle-wheel hubs. The trolley was designed to run along a launching platform, the total cost of which was four dollars, about £3.60 in English money today.

Comfort for the pilot had not been thought of. He was to lie on the lower of the two wings, and would manipulate not only the engine controls, but also the wing warping gear supposed to keep the plane on an even keel. The 12-horse-power engine would drive the two propellers by means of ordinary bicycle chains running around sprockets on the ends of the propeller shafts.

There had already been lots of trouble with these twin propeller shafts. A backfire when they first tried the engine had resulted in one of the shafts twisting out of true. A second and stronger set of shafts had also proved unequal to the strain, as a result of which Orville had made the long train journey to Dayton for an even sturdier set of propeller shafts. Now, and they must both have been anxious, the great moment had come.

Wilbur, who was the elder of the two, got into position. The engine was started. With the throttle wide open the propellers dissolved into a blur and with bicycle chains rattling and squeaking, the framework creaking and vibrating, it was obvious that something must happen soon. Either the plane would move or drop to pieces.

Orville bent down and slipped the cable which anchored the plane, and at once it began to move forward, its speed increasing quite rapidly. The handful of spectators, some on the nearby Kill Devil Hill, ceased talking and watched. Not one of them really believed this crazy thing would fly, and within seconds their fears were realised. They started off at a run down to the level sands, hoping that Wilbur Wright had escaped serious injury. The plane had seemed as if it was about to lift when nearing the end of the launching platform, and then without warning it had tipped forward and driven its front elevator into the sand. The roar of the engine stopped.

Wilbur got up and shook himself, then looked at Orville. The front elevator was smashed, so there could be no hope of a further try that day. Harry Moore, a cub reporter from the *Virginia Pilot*, desperately keen to get an exciting story, soberly put away his pencil and notebook, then asked:

"What do you do now, Mr. Wright? My editor was kind of expecting me to . . ."

"Get a good story, eh?" Orville said, and made a little clicking sound of annoyance. "Well, mebbe you will. Come back on the 17th. Yeah, I guess we'll have it right for that date. We'll give you a story . . . a scoop of a story."

Wilbur dusted the sand from his trousers, straightened his tie, and turned his cap the right way round. The days of flying kit had not come, and both the Wrights were in everyday clothes Wilbur had done one thing only to make sure he was dressed for such an epoch-making event as the first powered flight into the air—he had turned his cap back to front so that the wind would not get under the peak and blow the cap off.

I

For two more days the sands at Kitty Hawk were left to the gulls and the winds blowing in from the Atlantic; then the Wrights appeared once more with the damaged plane repaired.

They had spread the news about that they were going to fly on December 17, but only a handful of spectators had arrived to see what these 'crazy Wright boys' would do. There was much more excitement at the sea's edge, for one of the United States's first submarines, the *Moccasin*, had broken away from the tug which was towing it, and had gone hard aground, abreast the Currituck Light.

Alpheas Drinkwater, at that time a telegraphist for the United States Weather Bureau, had been invited to come; for if there was any great news, he would be the one to flash it out to the world. Alpheas did not come. He was too busy keeping the U.S. Navy Yard people informed about the efforts of salvage tugs to get the *Moccasin* off the beach.

For the second attempt Orville Wright laid himself on the lower wing. Again the engine was started, and again the whole framework of that first plane rattled and shuddered. This time Wilbur Wright released the anchoring cable. Once more the frail contraption moved along on its trolley, and then the incredible happened. With Orville Wright in command the plane lifted into the air, leaving its tiny trolley to roll off the runway and kick up a little spurt of sand.

Orville felt the sudden smoothness, realized that his front elevator was coaxing him into the air far too quickly, and tried to adjust it to give level flight. He was already ten feet off the ground.

Instead of straightening out into level flight the plane nose-dived and, 12 seconds after taking off, the first flight had ended. In that short time the first powered plane to fly had covered about 100 feet.

There were three more flights that day, and the best of these

And then the incredible happened—with Orville Wright
in command the plane lifted into the air

saw the aeroplane stay aloft for 59 seconds and cover 852 feet. It was the birth of the flying machine.

Alpheas Drinkwater, still keeping the U.S. Navy Yard informed of the work going on about the stranded submarine *Moccasin*, was irritated that evening when, because of the failure of another telegraph wire, he had to send off several telegrams, one of which was to Katherine Wright, and read: "Flight successful. Will be home for Christmas."

That message should have shaken the world, for it meant the dawn of the era of flying; but it passed unnoticed. Young Moore, the cub reporter from the *Virginia Pilot*, let himself go with a report which told how Wilbur Wright had soared into the air with bird-like ease, and flown three miles over the sea. His exaggeration of the accomplishments of the Wright brothers did not bring him renown. Editors simply refused to believe it. One or two papers printed paragraphs, and it is said that the British *Daily Mail* inserted a tiny paragraph at the bottom of a page headed: "Balloonless Airship".

III

How did all this come about?

Perhaps the editors should not be blamed too much for refusing to believe that man had conquered the air. Other attempts to fly had ended in disaster. Otto Lilienthal, a German, had built a bird-like glider with which he made over 2000 flights before crashing to his death. In the year this German pioneer died, an American, Dr. S. P. Langley, secretary of the Smithsonian Institute, built a steam-powered model aeroplane. It flew extremely well, covering more than half a mile at the amazing speed, for those days, of 25 miles per hour.

Given 50,000 dollars by the U.S. Army towards the cost of building a man-carrying aeroplane, Dr. Langley built one with a specially designed petrol engine of 52 horse-power. It was to be launched from a houseboat moored in the Potomac river; but something went wrong with the launching apparatus and the machine simply ran along the runway and toppled from there into the river. Writers in the American newspapers made great fun of this, and for the time being attempts by man to fly were laughed at.

About this time Wilbur Wright was taking a great deal of

411

interest in the efforts of the German, Otto Lilienthal, to conquer the air. Lilienthal had built his wings but had at length crashed to his death. Wilbur had not had an easy life up to then. Just when he was about to enter college he had an accident which disabled him for seven or eight years, during which time he had to stay at home—a period he spent in caring for his invalid mother.

In his spare time he watched the buzzards as they wheeled about in the air, and tried to discover the reason why they could circle so easily with what appeared to be the merest flick of a wing tip.

In 1890 Wilbur joined his younger brother Orville, who was then publishing a small, weekly newspaper, and began to get even more interested in flying. Orville caught his enthusiasm when Wilbur explained that he felt the secret of successful flight lay in having wing tips which could move as the wing pinions of a bird did.

Leaving the publishing business they went into a cycle repair shop. Here, with plenty of tools to hand, they began to construct their first glider. When completed it weighed a mere 50 lb. It had a small wing span, but had something other experimental glider had not possessed—a balancer at the front of the main wings (today we know them as elevators, and they are incorporated in the wings themselves). In addition to the balancer the two brothers fixed wires to the wing tips, so that they could be twisted in the same manner as the buzzard lifts or turns down the tips of his wing pinions.

Their first glider cost £4 and there was no place for the pilot to sit. He lay between the wings and worked the crude controls from that position. Now came their first visit to Kitty Hawk, where the winds were steady, the sands smooth and soft, and perhaps most important of all, there was a small hill off which the glider could be launched.

Not very satisfied with the glider they made many smaller models, and to see how they reacted to winds, fastened them on their cycle handlebars. Riding as fast as possible they would study the effect of the wind on them. Roads, however, were not like the smooth roads of today, and looking out for bumps and studying a model glider on the handlebars was unsatisfactory.

IV

One evening Wilbur startled his younger brother with a suggestion.

"I think we ought to be able to study the effects of wind with the models placed in a sort of tunnel."

"But where is the wind to come from?" Orville asked. "After all, you'd need something like a hurricane blowing through your tunnel to——"

"I've thought of that," Wilbur interrupted. "Suppose we built a small tunnel and put a fan at one end, the model at the other. We could blow wind through, and be able to study the effects much better."

Today's mighty wind-tunnels, where not only model aeroplanes are tested but also giant airliner models, were born when the first crude tunnel was made at Dayton by the Wright brothers. That small tunnel enabled them to build a third glider and solve a difficulty which had up to then seemed insuperable. It gave them the idea of fitting a rudder at the stern of the glider, and when this was tried out, with elevator and rudder linked by wires, they discovered they could manœuvre their glider easily and with great smoothness. They could climb, bank, dive, turn, and keep a fair amount of control all the time. That year, which was 1902, they made nearly 1000 glider flights; one of which was a record.

We think of record-breaking flights today in terms of round-the-world flights, without touching down, and being re-fuelled in mid-air by tanker aircraft; or flying across the Atlantic and back, breakfast at home, dinner in the evening at home, with a double crossing of the 'herring pond' in between. A record flight in 1902 meant the Wright's glider had risen off the ground and not touched it again for a full 200 yards!

V

In the winter of 1902 Orville brought up the idea of fitting an engine to the glider. Wilbur, four years older than his brother, shrugged and looked very thoughtful.

"It's a question of weight, Orville. To carry the weight of an engine, petrol, and a man, the plane will have to be made

413

bigger, and its probable weight will be in the region of five hundred pounds. I've been working it out, too."

"Sure, I know," Orville agreed; "but we can do it. Look at Langley; how big his machine is."

Wilbur nodded and smiled.

"Yes, look at it," he agreed, "but it hasn't flown yet. And in any case, where can we get an engine? Langley has got that brilliant engineer, Manly, to make him a special engine. He won't make one for us, even if we could afford it."

Orville sat staring at the big stove, glowing red; then his thin lips parted in a smile, and there was a twinkle in his eyes as he looked up saying:

"What about making our own engine?"

They sat in silence for several minutes, looked up, and nodded.

Throughout that winter they worked steadily and finally built a 12 horse-power engine. It worked but was not as efficient as Langley's 52 horse-power model. Now they faced the task of getting a propeller. Enquiries from ship builders convinced them that a propeller made like a ship's propeller would not do.

They finally designed a propeller with blades like small curved wings, and this proved amazingly efficient. To make sure they would get enough 'pull' to lift their plane into the air they decided to use two propellers, and drive these from their one small engine by means of ordinary bicycle chains. Later that year, as described earlier, they were the first men to fly in a power-driven aeroplane, going not at the mercy of the wind, but urged on by the *might* of a 12 horse-power engine. Their best flight that year lasted 59 seconds, and they attained what in those days was the astounding speed of nearly 30 miles per hour.

VI

Though they continued with their experiments throughout 1904 few people would believe they had really flown. The renowned American physicist, Simon Newcomb, had stated definitely that it was quite impossible for anything heavier than air to fly. Newcomb was a clever man, and people preferred to believe him rather than a handful of country folk from Kitty

Hawk who continued to swear they had seen the Wright boys flying in the air.

In 1905 the brothers conquered one of their earlier troubles, a tendency to get into a tailspin when doing short turns, and in October of that year Wilbur made the longest sustained flight ever, keeping airborne for 38 minutes, flying round and round over a small circular course.

Efforts to interest the U.S. War Department were, however, without success. The 50,000 dollars the Department had handed over to Langley, only to have him laughed at by every newspaper in America, seemed to have convinced the authorities that, as Newcomb insisted, flying was impossible for heavier-than-air machines.

Still thought of as 'those crazy Wright boys', Wilbur and Orville went back to Kitty Hawk sands in 1908 with a new machine, and this time they got Mr. D. B. Salley, a renowned free-lance journalist, interested. He saw them fly, and was convinced the world was on the verge of a new era, an age when man would fly as easily as a bird, but probably faster, and farther. He wired his story to leading newspapers, and none would use it. The New York *Herald* did send its own star reporter to Kitty Hawk to see what was going on. When he sent in a long story of a man flying through the air on a machine, swooping and diving, turning this way and that, then coming safely to the ground, the editor not only refused to publish the story, but suspended the reporter.

Oddly enough the man who set the seal of truth on these strange stories of men flying like birds, was the one-time telegraphist who had been at Curritucket Inlet for the U.S. Weather Bureau when the Wrights made their first flight five years earlier. Then he had refused to waste his time over such crazy antics as men trying to fly.

Now, however, he went on to Kill Devil Hill and watched what he described later as a 'two-winged contraption of split fir and cloth bear a man and a clattering engine into the blue'. He went home and swore out an affidavit which did two things, it put the *New York Herald*'s star reporter back in his job, and gave the world the story of man's conquest of the air.

In 1909 Wilbur convinced even the U.S. War Department. Taking the machine to Fort Meyer in Virginia the brothers proved beyond doubt that they could fly, that they could make their machine do what they wanted; and the aeroplane was finally accepted as something which might possibly be useful to the United States if ever they went to war.

From that demonstration Wilbur went to Europe, and at Le Mans and Pau gave further demonstrations, for now the French were interested. King Edward of Great Britain went to see Wilbur fly. The barriers had been broken down, and the crazy Wright boys were now hailed for what they were, the men who had first conquered the air with a powered machine.

Today the jet aircraft boom their way through the sound barrier; distances have been almost annihilated. A man can go to sleep in the Old World and wake up in the New.

VII

How strange that in the 1870's, according to a story published by the *New York Times*, Bishop Wright had a slight argument with the head of a college. The bishop had said that in his opinion everything that could be invented had been invented. The principal of the college shook his head slowly before saying:

"In fifty years' time men will learn to fly like birds."

Shocked, the bishop replied:"Flight is reserved for angels," never dreaming that the two small sons he had left at home, Wilbur and Orville, would be the first of the earth-born 'angels'.